CRAFT AND TRADITION

CRAFT AND TRADITION
Essays in Honour of William Blissett

Edited by
H.B. de Groot and Alexander Leggatt

University of Calgary Press

© 1990 H.B. de Groot and A. Leggatt. All rights reserved

ISBN 0-919813-74-7

University of Calgary Press
2500 University Drive N.W.
Calgary, Alberta, Canada T2N 1N4

Canadian Cataloguing in Publication Data

Main entry under title:

Craft and tradition

    Bibliography: p.
    ISBN 0-919813-74-7

    1. Blissett, William. 2. English literature - History
and criticism. I. Blissett, William. II. de Groot, H.
B., 1939- III. Leggatt, Alexander.
PR14.C73 1988   820'.9   C88-091326-6

All rights reserved. No part of this work covered by the copyrights hereon may be reproduced or used in any form or by any means—graphic, electronic or mechanical—without the prior written permission of the publisher. Any request for photocopying, recording, taping or information storage and retrieval systems of any part of this book shall be directed in writing to the Canadian Reprography Collective, 379 Adelaide Street West, Suite M1, Toronto, Ontario M5V 1S5.

Printed in Canada

∞

Wood engraving used on front cover (entitled "Unicorn and Broken Column") by David Jones (1930) with permission of the Trustees of the David Jones Estate.

Cover design by Rhae Ann Bromley

CONTENTS

Preface ix

Acknowledgements xi

George Johnston (Emeritus Professor of English, Carleton University)
    WFB, with love xvii

Northrop Frye (Victoria College, University of Toronto)
    The Bride from the Strange Land 1

Sean Kane (Trent University)
    Spenser's Broken Symmetries 13

A.C. Hamilton (Queen's University)
    Closure in Spenser's *The Faerie Queene* 23

Gordon Teskey (Cornell University)
    Positioning Spenser's "Letter to Raleigh" 35

Germaine Warkentin (Victoria College, University of Toronto)
    Spenser at the Still Point: A Schematic Device in "Epithalamion" 47

René Graziani (University College, University of Toronto)
    Donne's "Anniversaries" and the Beatification of Elizabeth
    Drury by Poetic Licence 59

S.P. Zitner (Trinity College, University of Toronto)
    Zigzag in *Hamlet* I, v 81

Alexander Leggatt (University College, University of Toronto)
    The Hidden Hero: Shakespeare's *Coriolanus* and Eliot's *Coriolan* 89

R.B. Parker (Trinity College, University of Toronto)
    King Lear, Sir Donald Wolfit and *The Dresser* 99

John Margeson (Emeritus Professor of English, University of Toronto)
    Individualism and Order in the *Byron* Plays of Chapman
    and Jonson's *Catiline* 111

Wyman H. Herendeen (University of Windsor)
    Ben Jonson and the Play of Words 123

A.H. de Quehen (University College, University of Toronto)
    The Silent Woman in the Restoration 137

Emmet Robbins (St. Michael's College, University of Toronto)
    To be Redeemed from Fire by Fire: The Deaths of Heracles
    and Siegfried 147

Philip Wults
    Parsifal and the Right Point of View about Everything 157

H.B. de Groot (University College, University of Toronto)
    Mein Leben: Richard Wagner and the Art of Autobiography 169

Charles Leland (St. Michael's College, University of Toronto)
    "Den ubetvingele kallelse": On the Objectivity of
    Brand's Calling as Priest 185

Ann Saddlemyer (Victoria College, University of Toronto)
    Vision and Design in *The Playboy of the Western World* 203

John Tucker (University of Victoria)
    The Waste Land, Order and Myth 217

Thomas Dilworth (University of Windsor)
    In Parenthesis: The Displacement of Chronicle 229

Vincent Sherry (Villanova University)
    David Jones and Literary Modernism: The Use of the
    Dramatic Monologue 241

W.J. Keith (University College, University of Toronto)
    "Intermixed Lingo": Listening to David Jones 251

Guy Davenport (University of Kentucky)
    Stanley Spencer and David Jones 259

Thomas R. Whitaker (Yale University)
    H.D.'s *Trilogy* and the Poetics of Passage 269

Michael Kirkham (New College, University of Toronto)
    The High Modernism of F.T. Prince 281

J.E. Chamberlin (University College, University of Toronto)
    The Languages of Contemporary West Indian Poetry 295

Kenneth Quinn (Emeritus Professor of Classics, University of Toronto)
    The Sound of Verse 311

Douglas Freake (University College, University of Toronto) and H.B. de Groot
    A Checklist of the Principal Writings of William Blissett 325

PREFACE

In this Festschrift we are not only honouring William Blissett's achievements in scholarship and teaching but trying to reflect something of the range of his interests. Those who know him will immediately object that there is little or nothing on the paintings of Tiepolo, or on César Franck's piano quintet—not to mention baseball or the lives of minor American presidents. But Spenser, Shakespeare, Jonson, Wagner and David Jones are all here. There are essays on modern drama, on neglected poets, on the connections between one artistic medium and another, on the craft of poetry, and on the religious dimension of literature.

We hope that the sheer range of the collection will make its own point: at a time when we complain of excessive specialization while digging deeper into our specialties, William Blissett has shown that another kind of academic life, an informed and intelligent investigation of a wide range of our culture, is not only possible but essential. It is significant that the artists who most attract him—notably Spenser, Jonson, Wagner and Jones—all think on a large scale, and create works not just out of a single personal impulse but out of a broad awareness of tradition. Spenser and Wagner address their own times in the language of older mythologies, Jonson and Jones in their different ways are fascinated by Rome, and Jones in particular—to use his own words—moves with ease "from the cultivation of cabbages to Melchizedek, king of Salem." It is appropriate that so many of the essays here presented show how through works of art one period or culture impinges on another.

That accounts for one of the key words in our title. As a critic and teacher, Professor Blissett has always been interested in how things are made, and that accounts for the other. Even the briefest conversation with him will contain some mischievous play on words; this is the sportive side of that serious interest in language that leads him to make his students do memory work. (He notes that while they grumble at first, "they live to thank me.") It follows that his favourite artists are makers, whose craft demands and rewards the closest analysis. And thus it is appropriate that so many essays in the present volume are based on close attention to words.

Two forms, poetry and drama, and two periods, Renaissance and Modern, account for nearly all of these essays. This is no accident, for it is in these forms and these periods that different cultural lines are most likely to cross. In his attention to both craft and tradition, in the careful layering of one culture on another, David Jones is perhaps the first example one would give of a characteristic interest of Professor Blissett's; but to present a collection of essays on a single figure would have been inappropriate to the occasion and the recipient. We have tried instead to balance craft and tradition, close analysis and broad curiosity. It is a tribute to the force of Professor Blissett's example that our way of doing this has been not to issue specific orders to contributors but simply to ask for essays they thought would interest him.

We are grateful to all contributors for the alacrity with which they responded to our invitation. We wish to thank Cyrilene Beckles and Donna Jones for typing the articles; and we are most grateful to the University College Alumni Association for a generous grant towards publication. We also wish to thank our copy-editors at the University of Calgary Press, Sandy Buker and Sharon Boyle.

ACKNOWLEDGEMENTS

For permission to reproduce excerpts from already published manuscripts, the University of Calgary Press wishes to acknowledge the following publishers, estates and authors.

W.W. Norton and Company, Inc. for Donald Jay Grout, *A History of Western Music*, Shorter Edition, 1964.

University of Toronto Press for *Essays in English Literature from the Renaissance to the Victorian Age Presented to A.S.P. Woodhouse*, ed. M. MacLure and F.W. Watt, 1964.

J.M. Dent and Sons Ltd. for A.S.P. Woodhouse, *Milton The Poet*, 1955.

Yale University Press for Geoffrey Hartman, *Criticism in the Wilderness: The Study of Literature Today*, 1980.

The University of Chicago Press for Geoffrey Hartman, *The Fate of Reading and Other Essays*, 1975.

Princeton University Press for Thomas P. Roche, Jr., *The Kindly Flame: A Study of the Third and Fourth Books of Spenser's "Faerie Queene,"* 1964.

Columbia University Press for *Form and Convention in the Poetry of Edmund Spenser*, ed. William Nelson, 1961.

Mouton de Gruyter, a division of Walter de Gruyter and Co., for John Fletcher, *The Woman's Prize, or the Tamer Tamed*, ed. G.B. Ferguson, 1966.

Faber and Faber Limited for T.S. Eliot, *Complete Poems and Plays*, 1969.

Harcourt, Brace Jovanovich, Inc. for T.S. Eliot, *Complete Poems and Plays*, 1969 (U.S. rights).

Methuen and Co. Ltd. for William Shakespeare, *Coriolanus*, Arden Edition, 1976.

Grove Press Inc. for Ronald Harwood, *The Dresser*.

Oxford University Press (Oxford) for C.H. Herford and Percy and Evelyn Simpson edition, *Ben Jonson*, 1925–52.

Insel Verlag for Richard Wagner, "Eine Mitteilung an meine Freunde," *Dichtungen und Schriften*, ed. Dieter Borchmeyer, vol. 6, 1983.

Houghton Mifflin Company for Henry Adams, *The Education of Henry Adams*, ed. Ernest Samuels, 1973.

Robert Kroetsch for "F.P. Grove: The Finding," published in *An Anthology of Canadian Literature in English*, ed. D. Bennett and R. Brown (Toronto: Oxford University Press, 1983).

Cambridge University Press for Richard Wagner, *Mein Leben*, trans. A. Grey: ed. M. Whittal, 1983.

Oxford University Press (Oxford) for *The Oxford Ibsen*, ed. J.W. McFarlane, 1960–77.

Farrar, Straus and Giroux, Inc. for *Ibsen: Letters and Speeches*, ed. Evert Sprinchorn, 1964.

Macmillan Publishing Company (New York), for W.B. Yeats, *Essays and Introductions* (copyright Mrs. W.B. Yeats 1961), *Autobiography* (copyright 1916, 1936 by Macmillan Publishing Company, renewed 1944, 1964 for Bertha Georgie Yeats), and *The Letters of W.B. Yeats*, ed. Allan Wade (copyright 1953, 1954, and renewed 1982 by Anne Butler Yeats).

A.P. Watt Ltd. for W.B. Yeats, *Autobiographies* and "Sailing to Byzantium" on behalf of Michael B. Yeats and Macmillan London Ltd.

Oxford University Press (Oxford) for *The Collected Letters of John Millington Synge* and *Collected Works*, J.M. Synge.

Wilfrid Laurier University Press for *The Practical Vision: Essays in English Literature in Honour of Flora Roy*, ed. Jane Campbell and James Doyle, 1978.

Elek, Paul, Ltd. for D. Pearsall and E. Salter, *Landscapes and Seasons of the Medieval World* (world rights except U.S. and its dependencies), 1973.

Grafton Books for D. Pearsall and E. Salter, *Landscapes and Seasons of the Medieval World* (U.S. and its dependencies).

Harvard University Press for Jerome Buckley, *The Victorian Temper*, 1951.

Faber and Faber Limited for David Jones, *The Anathemata, In Parenthesis* and *The Sleeping Lord* and *Dai Greatcoat: A Self-Portrait of David Jones in His Letters*, ed. René Hague, 1980.

The Trustees of the Estate of David Jones for unpublished letters and drafts.

Agenda Editions for David Jones, *The Roman Quarry and Other Sequences*, ed. H. Grisewood and René Hague, 1981, and *The Kensington Mass* by David Jones, 1975.

Alfred A. Knopf, Inc. for *The Collected Poems of Wallace Stevens*, 1967.

New Directions Publishing Corp. for *H.D. Collected Poems, 1912–1944*, 1983, copyright 1982 by the Estate of Hilda Doolittle.

Anvil Press Poetry for F.T. Prince, *Collected Poems*, 1979.

Cedar Press and the Caribbean Conference of Churches for "Letter to England" in *Bumbatuck 1* by B. St. John, 1982.

Paul Keens-Douglas, Keensdee Productions Ltd. for "When Moon Shine," 1975.

University of Pittsburgh Press for *Uncle Time* by Dennis Scott, 1973.

Farrar, Straus and Giroux, Inc. for *Sea Grapes, The Joker of Seville* and *O! Babylon* by Derek Walcott and H. Ibsen, *Letters and Speeches*, ed. Evert Sprinchorn (reprinted by permission of Hill and Wang, a division of Farrar, Straus and Giroux, Inc.).

Institute of Social and Economic Research, University of the West Indies, for "Report on the Rastafari Movement," 1960.

Edward Kamau Brathwaite for quotations from *Savacou: A Journal of the Caribbean Artist's Movement*, 3/4 (1970–71).

Richard Literary Agency, Auckland, N.Z., for "Walking on my Feet" from *Collected Poems* by A.R.D. Fairburn.

A.P. Watt Ltd., on behalf of the Executors of the Estate of Robert Graves, for "The Making and Marketing of Poetry" from *Food for Centaurs: Stories, Talks, Critical Studies* by Robert Graves, 1960.

Sigmund Freud Copyrights Ltd., The Institute of Psycho-Analysis and The Hogarth Press for *The Standard Edition of The Complete Psychological Works of Sigmund Freud*, trans. and ed. James Strachey, 1955. U.S. rights controlled by Basic Books.

Executors of the Estate of the late Frieda Lawrence Ravagli for "Moonrise," *The Complete Poems of D.H. Lawrence*, coll. and ed. Vivian de Sola Pinto and F. Warren Roberts. Copyright 1964, 1971 by Angelo Ravagli and C.M. Weekley, executors of the Estate of the late Frieda Lawrence Ravagli. Reprinted by permission of Viking Penguin Inc.

Henry Holt and Company, Inc. for Robert Frost, "Spring Pools" in *The Poetry of Robert Frost*, ed. Edward Connery Latham, 1969.

Random House, Inc. for W.H. Auden, "In Memory of Sigmund Freud," *Collected Poems*, ed. E. Mendolson, 1976 for U.S. rights.

Harcourt, Brace Jovanovich, Inc. for "Coriolan," *Collected Poems 1909-1962*, copyright 1964, 1963 by T.S. Eliot.

The Paulist Press for Poem 18 and Poem 21 reprinted from *The Poems of Paulinus of Nola*, copyright 1975 by Rev. Johannes Quasten, Rev. Walter H. Burghardt, S.H., and Thomas Comerford Lawler.

Faber and Faber Limited for W.H. Auden, "In Memory of Sigmund Freud," *Collected Poems*, ed. Edward Mendolson, 1976.

Harcourt Brace Jovanovich, Inc. for *Downhill All the Way*, copyright © 1967 by Leonard Woolf.

The Executors of the Leonard Woolf Estate and The Hogarth Press for *Downhill All the Way*, world rights excluding the United States.

We are grateful for the use of excerpts from the following, but have been unable to successfully contact:

The Estate of René Hague, for *A Commentary on the Anathema of David Jones* (University of Toronto Press, 1977).

Mr. Derek Walcott, for the manuscript draft of *Another Life*, dated 12 October 1965 and in Notebook I of the West Indies Collection, Library of the University of the West Indies, Mona, Kingston, Jamaica.

WFB, with love

Where in the wide world not?
What opera not attended
once, twice, three times?
What book not read?
What wise thought not thought
and wisely written
with keeping and wit?
And that is not all: teaching—
teacher of heart and eye
and ear,
inward of teaching, inward of poetry,
friend of poets;
friend of good fellowship, good talk,
good stories,
and after a blessed fast
joyous feasting.

Laborare est orare:
God's patient scribe
and bedesman,
our Bill, our WFB,
Professor Blissett.

George Johnston

THE BRIDE FROM THE STRANGE LAND

Northrop Frye

The Book of Ruth is one of the five short books called "rolls" (*megilloth*) among the Writings which have acquired a specific liturgical importance. It is a rather striking fact that, of these five "rolls," three are narratives centered on female figures. The story of the book is familiar but needs to be summarized again for clarity.[1]

Naomi is the widow of a Bethlehemite named Elimelech, who had moved into Moab during a famine in Judea, much as the family of Israel had moved into Egypt for a similar reason centuries earlier. He and the two sons Naomi had borne to him all died, leaving her with two Moabite daughters-in-law, both childless. In so patriarchal a society Naomi feels that she is under something of a curse, and she returns forlornly from Moab to Bethlehem to live out the rest of her blighted life. Her Moabite daughters-in-law, Ruth and Orpah, accompany her to the border of Moab, where she tries to persuade them to go back to their own land. She tells them that she is too old to produce more male children herself, and that even if she did it would be twenty years before they were marriageable, by which time their prospective brides would be twenty years older also. Orpah finds this argument conclusive and returns to Moab; Ruth, in the most famous scene of the book, states her resolution to proceed with Naomi to Bethlehem. It has been well observed that for a young foreign widow to identify her fortunes with those of an older woman, also a widow with no prospects, in such a society was an act of almost incredible courage and loyalty.

Back in the Bethlehem country, Ruth finds herself, by one of those accidents which are clearly not quite accidents, gleaning in the field of Boaz, a kinsman of her late father-in-law. It is the harvest season, when the destitute were allowed to glean in the fields after the reapers had passed through. Boaz's attention proves very easy to catch, and, following Naomi's advice, Ruth soon puts him in the position of wanting to marry her. They are married, and a son is born to them named Obed, who was the grandfather of King David.

Stories about women in the Bible fall into a very few well-marked categories, and there are, I think, three narrative themes that converge on the story of Ruth and Naomi. The first of these themes is that of levirate marriage, where a surviving brother-in-law or other near kinsman of a childless widow is obliged to do his best to provide her with children, preferably, of course, male children. Deuteronomy 25:5–6 says:

> When brothers live together and one of them dies without leaving a son, his widow shall not marry outside the family. Her husband's brother shall have intercourse with her; he shall take her in marriage and do his duty by her as her husband's brother. The first son she bears shall perpetuate the dead brother's name...

The best known story of this type in the Bible is the story of Tamar in Genesis 38. Tamar was the wife of Judah's son Er, and therefore Judah's daughter-in-law. Er was a bad man and the Lord took his life: Tamar was, according to the levirate custom, transferred to his younger brother Onan, who greatly resented and resisted the whole procedure. As God approved of it, he lost his life also. There was a third brother, still a boy, and Judah proposed that Tamar remain in the house until he had grown up. But the third brother was not assigned to Tamar, so Tamar disguised herself as a prostitute and put herself in the way of Judah, who got her pregnant. Hearing that Tamar had been acting like a prostitute, Judah said, with the casual ferocity of the age, "let her be burnt." But Tamar produced the tokens he had given her, and he acknowledged that she was right, because the third brother had been denied her. Of the twin sons she had by Judah, one, Perez, was in the direct line of ancestry to David.

Ruth is also a childless widow, but no brothers are involved, and any claim on relatives of her late husband can hardly have been a legal claim, in view of her Moabite nationality. But Boaz is too strongly attracted to her for that to be an obstacle, and he is very willing to take on the levirate obligation, except that he feels that as there is one still nearer kinsman, the latter should have first choice. The other kinsman, who is not named, resigns in favour of Boaz, and the way is cleared for Ruth's marriage. Boaz's motive in approaching this kinsman was perhaps to establish Ruth's status as an Israelite widow instead of leaving her simply a destitute foreigner to whom he had taken a fancy. The relevance of all this to the custom illustrated by the Tamar story is made clear by the elders of Bethlehem, who say when the marriage is decided on: "May your house be like the house of Perez, whom Tamar bore to Judah" (4:12).

The second story-type is that of the son who is born to a woman past the age of child-bearing, so that the birth is a direct manifestation of divine favour. The best known story of this type is the birth of Isaac to Sarah at an impossibly late age. Because

Sarah laughed at the prospect of bearing another child, the infant was given a name suggesting "laughter" by a slightly miffed deity. There are several other women who bear children after a long period of barrenness, including Rachel and Hannah, the mother of Samuel. When Samuel is born, Hannah sings a triumphant song in praise of a God who can bring down the great people and raise up the small ones at pleasure. The same themes recur in the New Testament. John the Baptist is born to his mother Elizabeth at a late age, his father Zechariah being struck with a temporary dumbness because of his disbelief. The conception of Jesus by Mary is equally miraculous, though not for the same reason, and Mary's song of triumph, known as the Magnificat, is modelled on the song of Hannah and makes the same point about God's power to reverse ordinary social standards.

In the Book of Ruth this theme of late birth is associated, not with Ruth, who is still a young woman, but with her mother-in-law Naomi. After the birth of Obed, Naomi becomes the infant's nurse, and the neighbours offer their congratulations in a very abrupt phrase: "Naomi has a son" (4:12). The identities of Ruth and Naomi are curiously confused in the final chapter, perhaps reflecting an earlier version of the story in which Ruth did not appear at all. In any case the story of Ruth is also a story about the filling, emptying and refilling of the life of Naomi, for whom Ruth acts as a proxy.

The theme of late birth is connected with another frequent theme in the Bible: the passing over of the eldest son, who inherits by primogeniture but does something to forfeit his inheritance. A son born late would be either an only or a younger son. Thus Ishmael is passed over in favour of Isaac, Esau for Jacob, Reuben for Judah and Joseph, Manasseh for Ephraim, and, in a very slight extension of the theme, Saul, the first king of Israel, for David, who becomes Saul's son-in-law and also survives Saul's son and heir, Jonathan. The deliberate choice of a younger son symbolizes a divine intervention into the normal pattern of human affairs, and makes appropriate the theme of God creating revolutions in society, bringing down the great and raising the humble, which we find both in Hannah's song and the Magnificat. It was this aspect of the story of Ruth that impressed Josephus, who gives a rather arid summary of it, clearly regarding it as an interruption of his narrative, and then says: "I was therefore obliged to relate the history of Ruth, because I had a mind to demonstrate the power of God, who, without difficulty, can raise those that are of ordinary parentage to dignity and splendor, to which he advanced David, though he were born of such mean parents" (*The Antiquities of the Jews*, 5. 9. 4).[2]

We can also see a more tenuous resemblance between the story of Ruth and many folktales and legends scattered over the world, of the type familiar in the story of Cinderella, in which a young woman who seems to have every kind of social handicap nevertheless attracts the attention of a man much higher in rank, and eventually marries him. Cinderella had a fairy godmother: Ruth has what is usually a more effective ally in this world, a co-operative mother-in-law. For thousands of years we have had stories of the type we frequently get in Shakespeare's comedies, where a clever and imaginative heroine, who knows what she wants but is not really unscrupulous about getting it, brings about a comic resolution that includes a successful marriage for herself. In the New Comedies of the Hellenistic period, some of which were adapted by Plautus and Terence, the heroine is a slave or prostitute, though really of more respectable parentage because stolen by pirates in infancy or the like. Ruth also begins operations on Boaz by saying, at least according to one reading, "treat me as one of your slave-girls" (2:13).

When Boaz lies down to sleep on the harvest field, somewhat drunk, and Ruth comes to him and asks him to spread his cloak over his "handmaid," it is clear that with a very slight change of tone we should have a rather cynical seduction story in which Boaz is, as we say, being set up. Needless to say, that is not the tone of the Book of Ruth, nor what happens in it. But the type of story being told is first cousin to seduction and bed trick tales like that of Jacob's first night with Leah. Keats, whom we shall mention again later, remarks in one of his letters that it is always a pleasure to rediscover the fact that Cleopatra was a gipsy, Helen a rogue, and Ruth a "deep one."[3] A reference to Ruth in Joyce's *Finnegans Wake* makes the same point much more broadly and includes an oblique allusion to Shakespeare: "You're well held now, Missy Cheekspear, and your panto's off! Fie, for shame, Ruth Wheatacre, after all the booz said!"[4]

The third story-type to be linked with Ruth is the most controversial and complex one. This is the story of the bride from the strange land, which is illustrated perhaps most clearly in Psalm 45. This psalm seems to be a wedding song celebrating the marriage of a king of Israel and a bride who apparently comes from Tyre in Phoenicia. The bride is adjured to forget her religion and adopt that of her new home, but there is no suggestion that there is anything wrong with the marriage itself. In history, however, the most notable marriage between an Israelite king and a Canaanite princess was that of Ahab and Jezebel, which led to all kinds of disaster. Similarly, the Song of Songs seems to have connections with King Solomon and a Shulamite bride, and there are certainly affinities between Ruth and the black but comely bride who did not keep her own vineyard but went out to seek her beloved. But in the historical narrative we are told that Solomon's wives prompted him to build temples to foreign gods, including the god of Moab, on mountains facing the temple on Mount Moriah.

The return under Ezra and Nehemiah included stringent regulations preventing any Israelite from having any connection with "foreign" or "strange" women, however innocuous or non-existent their religious views. What connections had already been made were to be immediately dissolved. It has often been suggested that the Book of Ruth, along with the Book of Jonah, supports a more flexible and less racist attitude toward foreign women, in making the point that the great King David had a great grandmother who was a Moabite. Whether the Book of Ruth is specifically aimed against the policy of Ezra and Nehemiah or not would depend on the date we assigned to it, and there is not much of a consensus among scholars about this, though a majority seems to favour a post-exilic date. But however early we may consider the book to be, it can hardly be earlier than the commandment in Deuteronomy 23:3: "No Ammonite or Moabite, even down to the tenth generation, shall become a member of the assembly of the Lord." Again, there is a variant of the levirate-marriage story which takes the form of parody in Genesis 19, where Lot's two daughters, finding a shortage of eligible men in the country in which they had taken refuge, make their father drunk and have intercourse with him. The two acts of incest produced the Moabites and the Ammonites.

As it is only from the Book of Ruth that we learn that David had a Moabite woman in his ancestry, it is difficult to avoid the conclusion that the book is making something of a political and religious point. Ruth has no interest whatever in Moabite religion: she does not even have any "teraphim," like Rachel. She is therefore welcomed by Boaz in the spirit of the law forbidding the oppression of strangers or widows (Exodus 22:21–22). Nothing could be more solidly Israelite than Leah and Rachel, yet they, as well as Tamar, are invoked by the witnesses of Ruth's marriage to Boaz: "May the Lord make this woman, who has come to your home, like Rachel and Leah, the two who built up the house of Israel" (4:11). Elsewhere we are told that David, when fleeing from Saul, took refuge in Moab and left his father and mother there (I Samuel 22:4), and that the mother of Rehoboam, Solomon's son and successor, was an Ammonite. Solomon himself, of course, was the son of Bathsheba, originally the wife of Uriah the Hittite, and therefore no doubt a Hittite herself, whatever that may mean in the way of "foreignness." In any case there was ample precedent for marriage to "foreign" women, even if much of it is later than the period assigned to Ruth.

2

The Book of Ruth is practically ignored in the New Testament, but there is one curious puzzle in the latter which bears not only on the Book of Ruth but on this particular issue of foreign marriage. The New Testament begins with Matthew's genealogy of Jesus, starting with Abraham and going down through David, Solomon, Zerubbabel and the rest. Luke has an even longer genealogy, though it differs from Matthew's, and he speaks only of fathers and sons. Matthew, however, seems to feel that women do somehow get involved with the genealogical process, and so includes five women in his list. The first is Tamar, whose relevance to the Ruth story we have mentioned. The third is Ruth herself, the only explicit reference to her or her book in the New Testament. The fourth is Bathsheba, mother of Solomon, and the fifth Mary, the mother of Jesus. It is the second name that is the puzzle: the mother of Boaz, whose name is given as Rahab.

The name of Boaz's mother does not occur anywhere else in the Bible, and where the compiler of Matthew got it remains a mystery. It is, of course, the same name as that of the celebrated harlot of Jericho, who is twice mentioned approvingly in the New Testament, as a pattern of faith in the Epistle to the Hebrews, and as a pattern of good works in the Epistle of James. That Matthew could ever have believed this Rahab to be Boaz's mother, as many commentators assume, seems most unlikely. If in fact they were the same, Boaz's somewhat adventurous approach to the married state may have been inherited. It is true that the names of women often appear in the Bible by accident: we know the names of David's sisters, for example, but not that of his mother. But it is just barely conceivable that the name "Rahab" in this context means simply "foreign woman," as the same name is also attached in the Bible to Egypt, with overtones of the hostile or chaotic world outside Israel (cf. Psalms 87:4). So many of the women who are mentioned in the Bible, whether by name or not, were "foreign" in one way or another that they may have some kind of symbolic significance, as representing either the permeation of the outside world by Judaism or the corruption of Judaism, depending on the women and depending also on whether one takes the view of the Book of Ruth or the Book of Nehemiah.

In Blake's *Jerusalem*, Plate 62, there is a list of "foreign" women, including Ruth. In Blake's symbolism all human beings, men and women, are symbolically male, just as they are symbolically female in orthodox symbolism. What is female for Blake is Nature, and Nature has two aspects. As an order of existence controlled and regulated by the creative imagination, she is what Blake calls an "Emanation," Isaiah's "Beulah" or married land; as an objective otherness remaining aloof from humanity she is what Blake calls a "Female Will." As the latter, she is still a product of the human imagination, but in a perverted and projected form. The foreign women in Blake's list symbolize this "Female Will": the only allusion to Ruth I have found that distorts her story by exaggerating the purely symbolic and typological side of it. As a character in history or credible fiction, Blake would have the same affection for Ruth that nearly all her readers have, and shows that in the fine painting of Ruth, Naomi and Orpah which he included in his one exhibition.

Other literary references to the Book of Ruth are rare and curiously barren, though for all I know there may be hidden riches in the Bulgarian and Latvian poems mentioned in reference books. A devotional treatise, called *Introduction au livre de Ruth*, was written by a French abbé named Tardif de Moidrey in the nineteenth century, and was reprinted with a long (hundred-page) introduction by the poet Claudel in 1938. But neither the abbé nor Claudel really tells us much about the book. Dante places Ruth at the end of the *Paradiso* among women destined to be redeemed before the coming of Christ, along with Sarah, Rebecca and others. But he does not mention her by name: he merely calls her the great-grandmother (*bissava*) of David—though David is not mentioned by name either, but is merely referred to as the author of the "Miserere" or fifty-first Psalm, the one that is understood to have been written by him after his sin in the matter of Uriah and Bathsheba. Milton adopts a different kind of typological reference, when he assures a "virtuous young lady," in a sonnet addressed to her, that

> The better part with Mary and with Ruth
> Chosen thou hast.[5]

In the house of Lazarus, where Martha was working in the household and her sister Mary was talking with Jesus, Mary was said by Jesus to have chosen "the better part": "one thing is needful: and Mary hath chosen that good part" (Luke 10:42). Later Christian typology identified these two "parts" with the active and the contemplative lives. The traditional Old Testament types of these were Leah and Rachel, who appear in this symbolic frame in Dante's *Purgatorio*. But of course, the more dramatic contrast in choice between Ruth and Orpah would also be available, and so Milton couples Mary with Ruth. I imagine however that Milton's real reason for referring to Ruth was that she provided a rhyme with "truth" and "youth." Again, Bunyan, in the second part of *The Pilgrim's Progress*, telling the story of Christian's wife leaving the City of Destruction to journey to the New Jerusalem, mentions the parallel with Ruth, mainly, one feels, because he could hardly have avoided it.

Ruth is a common name, and many literary uses of it, such as Wordsworth's poem "Ruth," do not relate to the Biblical book. Neither does Mrs. Gaskell's Victorian novel *Ruth*, which is a straightforward honest story about what we should now call an unmarried mother, written by a clergyman's wife. Margaret Laurence, who is often quite specifically Biblical in her allusions, has a Rachel and a Hagar who certainly reflect something of their Biblical namesakes. But there seems to be no Ruth, nor do I think that the Naomi of Joy Kagawa's *Obasan* has Biblical connections. The situation is similar even with works of Biblical scholarship. The other day I picked up a volume of essays on literary aspects of the Bible, and found five references to Ruth in the index. Three of them, however, turned out to be the first names of contemporary women scholars—perhaps an example of the hazards involved in making an index by computer.

The finest literary treatment of the Ruth story I know is a poem by Victor Hugo called "Booz endormi," one of the *Légendes des siècles*. In an earlier autobiographical poem in *Les contemplations*, Hugo speaks of his affection for Biblical stories, and mentions Ruth, Joseph, and the parable of the Good Samaritan in particular. The juxtaposing of Ruth and the Good Samaritan parable is interesting, as both make the same point: that there may be good people even among hostile or hated nations. There is, I understand, a haggadic tradition that Boaz was an old man of eighty when he met Ruth, and Hugo may have picked this up somewhere, as his Boaz is the same age. In Hugo, the dream of Boaz is a wistful, lonely reverie that culminates in a prophetic vision of what is more frequently called the tree of Jesse, the ancestral line stretching from David's father to Jesus, which is the basis of a superb stained-glass window design in Chartres Cathedral.

In English literature the best known allusion to Ruth is in Keats's "Ode to a Nightingale," where the poet says that the nightingale's song may have pierced

Through the sad heart of Ruth, when, sick for home,
She stood in tears amid the alien corn.

It is a beautiful but curious reference: as we saw, Keats certainly knew the Book of Ruth, but there is no hint in it that Ruth was ever homesick for Moab or that she regarded the corn fields around her as in any sense alien: after all, her late father-in-law still owned some of them. The tendency to sentimentalize the story recurs in a sonnet by Christina Rossetti, called "Autumn Violets," which has as its last line "a grateful Ruth tho' gleaning scanty corn."[6] This is not, it is true, a direct reference to the Biblical book, but we may note that actually, thanks to Boaz's patronage, Ruth did fairly well out of her gleaning. I make these somewhat pedantic comments because I suspect that one reason for the comparative neglect of the Book of Ruth by later writers is the irrepressible cheerfulness of the story, which is all about completely normal people fully understanding one another, and leaves the literary imagination with very little to do. That said, we could justify the Keats allusion by observing that Ruth does not give the impression of being merely a mindless puppet of Providence, and may well have had darker and deeper feelings than the narrative presents.

3

The story of Ruth is so brief and unpretentious that many readers, following Goethe, simply mutter something about a "charming pastoral idyl" and pass on. But if we look at it with any attention, its simplicity becomes very deceptive. Naomi is forced into exile by famine, brought to misery and sterility there, and finally makes her way back to her homeland and ends her life as a happy grandmother. Her lament, the only shadow on the general happiness of the story, where she remarks that her name should not be Naomi ("sweet") but Mara ("bitter"), recalls, on a small scale, some of the complaints of Job, and she uses also Job's favourite name for God, El Shaddai. The names of her deceased sons, Mahlon and Chilion ("weak" and "wasting"), seem clearly allegorical. The first chapter, again, emphasizes the changes on the word "return" (*shub*), which is one of the central thematic words of the whole Bible. Obviously Naomi is returning to her original home in Judea; obviously Orpah is returning to her original home in Moab. What is Ruth doing? According to 1:22, "Ruth the Moabitess returned with her Naomi from the Moabite country." Ruth, then, has both a physical and a spiritual home, and she voluntarily chooses the latter. Hence, like the Israelites leaving Egypt for the Promised Land, she is returning to her appropriate place.

The sense of something providential taking charge of Ruth's life appears in Boaz's remark: "May the God of Israel, under whose wings you have come to take refuge, give you all you deserve" (2:12). Later, as we saw, when Boaz lies down to sleep on the harvest field, Ruth comes to him and asks him to spread the "skirts" of his cloak over his handmaid. The word translated to "wings" and "skirt" is the same (*kanaph*). There are also repeated references to a grace or kindness (*chen*, *chesed*) coming to

Ruth from God through Boaz. Boaz also becomes the *go'el* of Ruth, a most versatile word rendered in the 1611 translation of Job 19:25 as "redeemer." Boaz is the *go'el* (2:20) of Ruth in the sense of being the most likely person to become her levirate husband, and the *go'el* of Naomi in a more general sense (4:14). Words closely related to *go'el*, and translated "redeem" in the Authorized Version, keep echoing all through the business arrangements with the nearer kinsman (4:2ff). It is difficult not to see in the story an epitome or microcosm, in small but concentrated compass, of the entire story of exile, return and redemption that the Bible is telling, of how those that sowed their seed in bitterness may return in joy, bringing their sheaves with them (Psalm 126).

The book ends with a list of David's ancestors back to Perez, which tells us nothing new and is generally assumed to be an editorial addition. The real question is rather what, if the addition were removed, would be the last verse of the book: "Obed was the father of Jesse, the father of David" (4:17). Is this part of the original story or not? If it was, it is clearly the climax to which the whole book is leading up: it indicates a motivation on the part of the writer which is not literary. The statement is given as a historical fact, and it is hard to see how the Book of Ruth could ever have got into the Biblical canon if the statement had not been there or had not met with general acceptance. Many commentators are fond of saying that the book is purely literary, by which they generally mean that it is "merely" literary. But it is difficult to imagine the sort of cultural ambience out of which a "purely literary" story could arise in either pre- or post-exilic Judea. Certainly the literary merits of the book are remarkable, but the skill with which the writer has encapsulated the entire narrative movement of the Bible in four brief chapters is something else again.

A late colleague of mine, Professor W.E. Staples, wrote an article on the Book of Ruth back in 1937, in which he suggested that it was a Midrash on a fertility cult centered at Bethlehem.[7] Staples was a student of S.H. Hooke, who in turn was a disciple of Robertson Smith and Frazer. He interprets the names in the book as cultic names: Elimelech, for example ("God is king"), becomes a Frazerian divine king. Naomi is a fertility goddess, and Ruth is related to her as Proserpine is to Demeter, another aspect of the same person. It is really Naomi who is "redeemed" by Boaz and bears the son, whose original name would have been something like "son of Naomi" and not Obed. In this suggestion Staples has been followed by others who also think that an earlier story has been adapted to fit into the genealogy of David. Bethlehem was an ancient cult-centre, as its name ("house of bread") suggests, and we remember that St. Jerome, the Latin or Vulgate translator of the Bible in the fifth century, remarks that in Bethlehem there was a grove dedicated to Adonis even in his day.

Staples's argument is usually mentioned by later scholars only to be dismissed, and it is of course true that such theses do not carry much conviction now. The main reason is that there is so little evidence for them beyond whatever suggestiveness may be inherent in some of the proper names. But I think that this way of reading the story deserves another look, even if we cannot buy the whole Frazer corn-spirit package.

Writers of stories, however literary, do not invent their stories even when they think they do: they inherit them. There are always and invariably earlier versions of the general shape of their plots (*mythoi*), and these earlier versions go back to the most ancient myths we have. The Bible is comparatively a rather late product of Near Eastern culture, and we can often see in it adaptations of earlier mythical themes. Some stories, like those of Jacob's ladder-vision or Jephthah's daughter, give us faint glints of pre-Biblical cults. With others, like the deluge story, we can now compare Sumerian and other more ancient versions that clearly belong on the same genealogical tree, even if they are not in the direct line of ancestry. So I see no improbability of there being earlier versions of the Ruth story, perhaps centered on Bethlehem, that take us back to very primitive customs connected with harvesting and the myths attached to those customs.

It was inevitable that the Book of Ruth should become associated with the Feast of Weeks, because harvest symbolism and imagery saturate the whole story, especially the two middle chapters. There is no reference to the book in the three volumes of Frazer's *Folklore in the Old Testament*, but *The Golden Bough* has an immense collection of harvest customs from all over the world. Among these we find very frequently ritual copulation on the harvest field, to ensure a productive harvest the next year; the treatment of a passing stranger as an incarnation of the spirit of the harvest, and a mythical relationship between an older and a younger goddess or female nature-spirit, representing the seed-corn of the previous year and the harvest of the present one. The author of Ruth has transformed these plot themes into credible and very warm human relationships: Boaz sleeps on the harvest field and Ruth asks him to shelter her; she returns from her gleaning operation carrying a bushel or so of wheat; the barren Naomi gains a son through Ruth. We may compare the way in which ancient fertility themes are transformed in the Song of Songs into a metaphorical identification of the bride of the marriage with the fertile land.

I think that when people speak of the Book of Ruth as "charming," they are really using a denatured synonym for something more like "serene." It is the unclouded serenity of the story that impresses the reader, a serenity that does for an agricultural and harvest setting what, let us say, the twenty-third Psalm does for a pastoral one. Like that Psalm, it expresses the feeling that if human beings give up their murderous and polluting ways, the physical environment will be seen as something identical with the human one, as something to live in rather than to dominate. At that point "serenity" becomes inadequate too, and moves into what is called *agape* in the Septuagint and New Testament and *ahabah* in Hebrew (compare the verbal form *aheb* in Ruth 4:15), and expresses the highest vision of human life within the context of the will of God that words can make.

NOTES

1. On the Book of Ruth see particularly Robert Alter, *The Art of Biblical Narrative* (New York: Basic Books, 1981), esp. 58–60; Jan Wojcik, "Improvising Rules in the Book of Ruth," *PMLA* 100 (1985): 145–53; D.F. Rauber, "The Book of Ruth," in *Literary Interpretations of Biblical Narratives*, ed. Kenneth R.R. Gros Louis *et al.* (Nashville: Abingdon Press, 1974), 163–76; Katharine Doob Sakenfeld, "Loyalty and Love: The Language of Human Interconnections in the Hebrew Bible," *Michigan Quarterly Review* 22 (1983), 190–204.

2. Quoted from *The Works of Flavius Josephus*, translated by William Whiston (Edinburgh, 1828), 150.

3. Letter to Tom Keats, 9 July 1818, *The Letters of John Keats 1814–1821* ed. H.E. Rollins (Cambridge, Mass.: Harvard Univ. Press, 1958), vol. 1, 320.

4. James Joyce, *Finnegans Wake* (New York: Viking Press, 1939; reprinted 1966), 257.

5. John Milton, "Sonnet IX: 'Lady, that in the prime of earliest youth'," *Poems*, ed. John Carey and Alistair Fowler (London: Longmans, 1968), 287–88.

6. Christina Rossetti, *Poetical Works*, ed. W.M. Rossetti (London: Macmillan, 1904), 383.

7. W.E. Staples, "The Book of Ruth," *American Journal of Semitic Languages and Literature* 53 (1937): 145–57.

SPENSER'S BROKEN SYMMETRIES

Sean Kane

"In mirrours more then one," says the narrator of Book Three of *The Faerie Queene*, announcing the way out of a dilemma.[1] The dilemma is age-old. How can an artist dare to capture the essence of a quality in the imperfect medium of art? The virtue of chastity, which is exhibited in his queen, is "heavens fairest light" (III proem 4), but art works by reflections. Another poet had written of the queen as Cynthia, and the narrator of the Legend of Chastity hopes the same paragon will not refuse to see her qualities portrayed variously, as Gloriana and as Belphoebe, "in th'one her rule, in th'other her rare chastitee" (proem 5). By reflecting her facets in a series of mirrors the poet-narrator can suggest in parts the image that he cannot duplicate in a single definitive copy. For, to hope that even his "living art" can represent something exactly is presumptuous. In art, as in nature, true symmetry is local and momentary, which is to say hypothetical. There is always that noisy disturbance of time and change which breaks the bubble. Knowing how mutability interferes with everything, the poet is nervous lest his daedale hand slip "and her perfections with his error taint" (III proem 2). Perfection is approached in art as in nature by trading off error against time: if we want to get it right, we work as if we had all the time in the world—unless things could be formed at some random-free state of zero temperature, in which case nothing would ever happen. Spenser's depiction of such a timeless state of perfect crystal calls itself into question, as in the vacant image of lovers becoming each other's mirrors in the "Hymn of Beauty": "Like as two mirrours by opposd reflexion, / Doe both expresse the faces first impression" (181–2). A gap of unrealization, the presence of error, breaks the image of pure symmetry at writing degree zero.

There is, then, on the one hand (to project a symmetry, a hypothesis), the inviting deadly symmetry of subject and copy; and, on the other hand, the beckoning movement in the direction of error and time, which does not solve the problem, only sets it in motion, celebrating variety, change, and difference in a "continued allegory," imaging phases of the subject in a kind of mirror game. This is most notably the impulse of the asymmetrical middle books of *The Faerie Queene*, but the openness to patterns of change is characteristic of the poem as a whole with its ragged endings and tentative points of resolution. The poem seems immersed in error, right from the first ambiguous battle of its first error-prone champion.[2] Gabriel Harvey said: "Nature herself is changeable, and most of all delighted with vanitye; and art, after a sort her ape, conformeth herself to the like mutabilitye."[3]

As we move with the flow of change, enjoying what Spenser talks of variously as "colours," "shadows," and "shows," we meet another kind of anxiety, however. We meet it when polyphony starts to sound like noise. The Blatant Beast, the poet's nightmare, echoes this anxiety. Full of "tongues of mortall men" (VI.xii.27), bred in "fowle commixture" (i.8), respecting no distinctions (xii.28), making all things "confounded and disordered" (xii.25), it is pure tail-chasing difference, a mass of narrativity. The entropy it causes is pure disorganization, with pieces and values theoretically equal and unsorted, like the brigands of Book VI who when "they words amongst them multiply" make way for death "in thousand dreadful shapes" (xi.16), or like the approach to the Bower of Bliss where "all things one, and one as nothing was" (II.xii.34). We cannot go too far in the direction of difference and keep distinction. An absolutely perfect crystal is just as impossible as an assembly of right atoms with no crystallinity at all. Because of these aesthetic barriers, which are conditions of existence in a world embedded in communication, the narrator matches his anxiety about the perfectly reflected portrait against another anxiety about the profligate use of multiple mirrors. How can he hope to capture, for instance, except in "endlesse worke" (IV.xii.1) the variety of the rivers present at the marriage of the Thames and the Medway?

> All which not if an hundred tongues to tell,
> And hundred mouthes, and voice of brasse I had,
> And endlesse memorie, that mote excell,
> In order as they came, could I recount them well.
> (IV.xi.9)

The impossibility of capturing the panorama of distinctiveness and change is felt in a swelling catalogue of names, in a generative flux which threatens to overpower that naming. The poet could do it if he had all the time in the world—"endlesse worke" indeed. Great crystals grow slowly.

Yet Spenser is haunted by the idea of perfect structure. It is not being merely fanciful to compare his work with the perfect crystal ball whose images compel Britomart on a quest for her beloved. The crystal, which reflects truly—for no secrets can elude it—is "like to the world it selfe, and seem'd a world of glas" (III.ii.19). Even so, its images are misconstrued by another mirror, the mirror of adolescent fantasy. "So tickle be the termes of mortall state...which do play / With double senses" (III.iv.28), the narrator remarks, when Cymoent, creature of the sea surface (another mirror), learns that Marinell, her perfect son, will fall to time and change. Perhaps the perfect vision of perfect structure is anticipated by the spiritual lovers whose "bright radiant eyes shall plainely see – Th'Idee of his pure glorie" ("Hymn of Heavenly Love," 283–84). Until that "Sabaoths sight" when eternity is envisioned as a pillared edifice (*Mutabilitie* viii.2)—presumably a state of true symmetry—we see as through a glass darkly. Otherwise, only in an isolated world, as cold and lifeless as a soap bubble, can there be perfection. Nothing ever happens in the world of Acrasia, with its symmetries of art and nature, activity and passivity, man and woman—and, "with equall crime" (II.xii.75), loving and being loved. As we go on to describe the other main symmetrical situations in *The Faerie Queene*, we will see the word "equal" frequently. Where qualities are perfectly symmetrical, and so indistinct from each other except as opposites, there is the likelihood that the qualities will take on each other's character, as they seem to under Acrasia's spell.

2

Symmetry is a difficult concept. Leibnitz talked about it in the seventeenth century in relation to the indiscernibility of differences. Once inside the hall of a Palladian building, can you remember whether you turned left or right? One wing is the mirror image of the other. The spectator is then in the position of Marinell trying to choose between Florimell and the false Florimell, her replica—a state of affairs as unnatural "as when two sunnes appeare in the azure skye" (V.iii.19). The false Florimell is "so lively and so like" Florimell (III.viii.5); the false Una is "so lively, and so like" Una (I.i.45), Spenser obviously anticipates our apprehensions about cloning. Of course, there is the apparent balance of the human face which, Pascal said, makes us "demand symmetry horizontally and in breadth only" (*Pensées*, 1670, no. 50), and in the apparition of Belphoebe (II.iii.21–31) symmetry is emphasized (with the usual asides about "fraile pen") because she is a classical deity, and statuesque. Her legs are "like two faire marble pillours ... Which doe the temple of the Gods support" (28). But in mortal natures such an equivalence of parts is an illusion, or, at least, bilateral symmetry and metamerism is pronounced but it is not worked through to perfection since a gain in order here is paid for in disorder somewhere down the line. This statement directs us to physics (classical and quantum), the proper context of the term symmetry. One electron is like another; molecular bonds are identical; and, at the grander level, one time is like another time in regard to the conservation of energy in the development of a system, one position in space is like another in regard to its conservation of momentum. In the great conservation laws, time and space are constants, or can be so treated when showing that in the behaviour of a system energy and momentum must be conserved. I allude to physics because Spenser's pictures of conditions of symmetry tend to emphasize material properties such as force and energy and mass. Here I am referring to pure, unmediated states of equivalence where there is an indiscernibility of difference and hence a switching of roles and a mirroring of behaviour. I am disregarding the paired figures of the benign allegorical houses where symmetry is constrained by hierarchical design, as in the case of Love and Hate in the temple of Venus (in fact, an asymmetrical pairing, since Hate is the older brother [IV.x.32]). In depicting the states of unmediated opposition, Spenser suggests that certain mechanistic habits of thinking and behaviour are the extensions of a materialist outlook, whether in regard to a reality seen exclusively as an arena of matter and energy or whether in regard to relationships treated as items of property. In other words, symmetrical thought is an illusion modelled on the behaviour of ideally isolated systems, such as machines—like the set of scales on which Avarice, as on some utilitarian calculus, "right and wrong ylike in equall ballaunce waide" (I.iv.27). A list of these symmetrical conditions will serve to suggest that for Spenser the illusion of symmetry is the hallmark of the classical mind. Though not symmetrophobic, Spenser is alert to the code of power implied by pure symmetrical thinking long before equivalence, identity, and opposition became metaphors for all kinds of relationships during the Age of Reason.

3

Symmetry usually appears in *The Faerie Queene* ironically in images of senseless combat. To take our examples in order, Redcrosse and Sansfoy meet like "two rams stird with ambitious pride," then stand "unmoved as a rocke" (I.ii.16). Later with Sansjoy, the second of the identical triplets and the mirror image of Redcrosse's morose delight, "both stricken strike, and beaten both do beat" (v.7) in the first suggestion of the paradoxical quality of symmetrical encounters. Paradox in this case is a state of affairs in which each term is the other's definition. "All Cretans are liars," said Epimenides the Cretan, making the definitive statement of a closed system of mind. "So th'one for wrong, the other strives for right" (v.8), the narrator says. But then he repeats it: "So th'one for wrong, the other strives for right" (9). There is a circular repetition to such events. They say if you feed the Cretan paradox to a computer, it will answer "yes, no, yes, no, yes, no..." until it destroys itself or runs out of tape.

In Book II, these mutually defining pairings are everywhere, suggesting a fault in the classical conception of temperance as the wilful management of extremes. Symmetry is also a condition qualities and people fall into when hierarchy is lost. Amavia ("her that loves to live") becomes equivalent but opposed to Mortdant ("him that death does give" [i.55]). Perissa and Elissa are each other's complements in the worst sense, and many readers have difficulty distinguishing them, and their mutually defining consorts, from each other in their "straunge sort of fight" (ii.26). The house of the golden mean is a Palladian, not, strictly speaking, an Aristotelian house, for Aristotle remarked that the temperate individual should be like Ulysses steering between Scylla and Charybdis (*Odyssey* 7.219–20): stay closer to the danger you do know, to avoid the one you don't (*Nicomachean Ethics* 2.9, 1109a 30)—like backing a car out of a garage. The Renaissance, in its urge for symmetry, got it wrong.[4] In Medina's house, the opposites are created "by equall shares in equall fee," a tactic that proves insufficient to contain their "diverse qualitee" (ii.13). It is a mechanical arrangement. No wonder love "maketh warre, he maketh peace againe" in the oscillation, another form of repetitive behaviour, that denotes the logic of a machine. Here "peace is but continuall jarre" (ii.26), resembling the relationship between two superpowers. Like Huddibras and Sansloy, Trompart and Braggadocchio use each other as mirrors, onto which they project their own suppressed failings, seeing reflected instead their imagined moral superiority to the other. But then the mirrors switch places. When Belphoebe appears, Trompart is suddenly full of bravado; Braggadocchio hides in a thicket. An occasion of mirth is counterbalanced by Guyon against an occasion of fury, the tutelary powers in these episodes being Cymochles and Pyrochles, enantiomorphs who take on each other's temperaments to the degree that Pyrochles does not know if he is in greater danger of being "drent" or "brent" (vi.49). Mammon and Guyon talk to each other as if they were talking to mirrors, but the pseudo-identity cultivated through opposition here is difficult to explain,[5] touching on some spirit of gamesmanship in Guyon that drives him to "beguile the Guyler of the pray" (vii.64). They are like two eighteenth-century generals, supporting each other's fantasies. There are Impotence and Impatience, clearly extensions of the allopathic brothers, but they make up one of several pairings, like Pilate and Tantalus in the house of Mammon, or Prays-desire and Shamefastnesse in the house of Alma, which illustrate more than they lengthen out a pattern of enantiodromia. Vertdant, senseless in Acrasia's lap with his armour hung upon a tree (xii.79–80), is more generally definitive. He suggests a false symmetry of *eros* and *furor* that demands its victim's regular immersion in the defining opposite of the quality espoused, a failure to discern difference that claimed Aeneas.

Britomart, until the end of Book III, is in a similar dilemma because she has equated the two ideals in a martial quest for love. Consequently, she has to disentangle the conflicting injunctions "Be Bold, Be not too bold" (III.xi.54) from her personality. The double bind arises when love becomes a contest between pursuer and pursued. Belphoebe's answer is to become the bold pursuer of things in her own realm, though like Amoret, her faint-hearted twin, she can be in vogue as a love object as her flirting with Timias shows.

In Book IV, the sons of Agape are not symmetrical because they form a hierarchy, signified by the interwoven terms of a syllogism (ii.42). But their battle with Campbell, which is like that of two tigers (iii.16), takes the saying "bloody yet unbowed" to a new level of mirth:

> Yet victors both them selves alwayes esteemed.
> And all the while the disentrayled blood
> Adowne their sides like little rivers stremed.
>
> (iii.28)

"The case in doubtfull ballance hong" (37), says the narrator, after some thirty stanzas of gore. The image of a set of scales seems appropriate because when aethereal and mundane love come head to head in the next canto in the tournament of the girdle, the outcome sways back and forth. The conflict is focussed, then re-focussed, in the combat between Britomart and Artegall, who "traverst to and fro, / Sometimes pursewing, and sometimes pursewed: (IV.vi.18). In this book of "deare lovers, foes perpetuall" (i.24), Aemylia is captured by the greedy lust she fears in her beloved Amyas; Amyas is captivated by the loose affection he fears in Aemylia—hardly the "sweet countervayle" between rapt lovers in the original ending of Book 3.

In the Legend of Justice, the egalitarian giant, who "strove extremities to way, / Th'one to diminish, th'other for to eeke" (V.ii.49), is all symmetry. The set of scales he holds signifies a method swollen into a philosophy, like that of a general superintendent of the Canadian Methodist Church who declared, "the perfect sociology, perfectly applied, will realize the kingdom of God on earth." The giant becomes what he believes in, a thousand presumably equal and indistinguishable pieces of matter. With Amidas and Bracidas, however, Artegall administers the natural justice that has gone to the giant's head, here adjudicating a dispute originating in a father who "did equally bequeath his lands in fee" (iv.7). Such justice answers easily to what it was developed for by rational law, namely property rights, and Artegall can announce breezily, "equall right in equall things doth stand" (iv.19) between two brothers whose names suggest a symmetry. Britomart and Radigund are like lioness and tiger over prey: "Both challenge it with equall greedinesse" (vii.30) because they are rival queens, one the impostor of the other, a kind of false-Elizabeth.

Symmetries are more latent than this in the "strange waies" of Book VI. The overpolished Briana and the underpolished Crudor make up a unity of opposites that reflects courtesy hardly at all: each needs the other as a foil. The artificially refined Blandina and the brutal Turpine are another set of unnatural complements. So are the self-conscious Mirabella and the innocently spontaneous Serena. Altogether they bracket a conception of courtesy as the integration of primal animal energy and cultural form. Calidore, who embodies this natural grace, expresses in his exchange with Meliboe a rather tired heroic ardour, all Virgilian "travell" and "toyle" and "restlesse paine," seeking comfort in an over-mellow Lucretian *otium*, also dangerously pursued as an end in itself. Opposites attract here because both outlooks are essentially naturalistic, as Charles Cochrane observed. In their common notes of "melancholic resignation" and "resigned melancholy" there is little to distinguish between "the epic of civilized materialism, and that of material civilization."[6]

3

The remark of Cochrane's, from an essay which argues that the Romans gave the world a philosophy of property, points us again to the outlook in which symmetrical thought takes form. This is the view of a world as exclusively finite and material in composition. Such an outlook requires as its companion a philosophy of force levered mechanically against mass to do work. "Classicism," Cochrane said, "resolved the concept of power into a subjective and an objective factor: the former, character (art and industry); the latter, circumstance (fate and fortune or the gods)."[7] Human effort is thus symmetrized with a fickle and recalcitrant *Fortuna*. The "continual jarre" of this adversarial relationship is clear in the first of the passages from Spenser to be quoted in detail—though not from *The Faerie Queene*. It is *The Ruins of Rome*, a poem written early in Spenser's career and probably revised later for publication.

Here Spenser pictures Rome in a state of paradox with itself. The paradox is generated in the attitude of equivalent opposition by which Rome defines, while it is defined by, the world it conquers:

Rome was th'whole world, and al the world was *Rome*,
And if things nam'd their names doo equalize,
When land and sea ye name, then name ye *Rome*:
And naming *Rome* ye land and sea comprize.
(359–62)

Did we turn left or right in the Palladian hall? It becomes impossible to discern the difference between subduer and subdued: each depends on the other for its definition. The consequence is a closed system, a homology that Spenser finds absurd:

This Citie, more than that great *Phrygian* mother
Renowm'd for fruite of famous progenie,
Whose greatnes by the greatnes of none other,
But by her selfe her equall match could see:
Rome onely might to *Rome* compared bee,
And onely *Rome* could make great *Rome* to tremble.
(75–80)

Symmetry is broken by the tiniest error. Wherever there is an error, the memory of that error will force an error somewhere else. In the case of Rome, and indeed of any philosophy that matches effort against opposition and counts on adversity to confirm the will's hypothetical supremacy, that error will be strife—in Spenser's thinking, the error which made the Roman spirit arm its hand against its heart (431) when the pursuit of virtue failed. The tearing to pieces that results, in a civil fury like "equall beasts" (324), resembles a mechanical system which can only express its inherent paradox by oscillating to the point of self-destruction:

she, which with her mightie powre
Tam'd all the world, hath tam'd herselfe at last,
The pray of time, which all things doth devouwre.
(34–36)

The undercutting of symmetry by change is personified in the contest between Artegall and Radigund, our second example. Artegall's training in natural law, his Herculean obsession with mastery, and his corresponding repression of *eros* for *furor*, mark him as the archetypal classical founder-hero. Radigund, with her moon and scimitar symbolism, and her mood swings, is the capricious physical world projected by the classical will as *Fortuna*. She is the shadowy consort on which an ethic of the will depends, as seen ironically in Artegall's promising Terpine, her latest victim, that "Fortune" will restore his ruined name (iv.34) and in Radigund's own resolve to "try her Fortune" in single combat (iv.47), and in the crowd's "Wayting, how Fortune would resolve that daungerous dout" (v.5). Remove the necessary opposing principle in Artegall's outlook, and he is like a workaholic without work. This is what Radigund cleverly does by exhibiting a sudden vulnerability that undermines the challenge to performance Artegall counts on to define his behaviour. The adversaries are symmetrical opposites, held together by a scorn for love conceived as a weakness in the personality, so it is not surprising that they switch roles, with Artegall doing woman's work and Radigund behaving like a virago, resolving to conquer her will by an effort of will. "Till I the conquest of my will recover" (v.51), is the way she puts it, oblivious to the paradoxical futility of the statement. Artegall, "left to her will by his owne wilful blame" (20), realizes that he too has fallen to the inner weakness which is the hidden face of cultivated power: "So was he overcome, not overcome, / But to her yeelded of his owne accord" (17). The mutual victimization of character *versus* circumstance is broken by Britomart, who embodies justice at a supernatural rather than natural level. Her spiritual law overcomes the divisions between a so-called clear intelligence and a fickle sensuality planted in the soul by the classical symmetry of mind and matter.

The realm of nature as it is conceived by classical philosophy is also the setting for the final symmetrical dispute, that between Jove and Mutabilitie over who should rule the world. The world they argue over is, of course, exclusively material, as proved by the evidence they marshall, all of it elaborately physical and taxonomic. Representing as it does Spenser's final parody of the limits of classical vision, the poem depicts subjective self-assertion in Mutabilitie and objective necessity in Jove as the two faces of the classical logos of power. We have come to see in these fantasmal situations how the competing agents rely on the simultaneous presence and exclusion of their opposites, where, according to the mutual paranoia of the opposition each party finds its identity at the expense of a weakness it does not want to face in itself, and instead conveniently projects onto the other party. In terms of this closed logic, Mutabilitie begins to sound like Jove's voice of necessity; Jove, for his part, inadvertently speaks Mutabilitie's language of freedom, specifically the freedom to rule what he has won by force: "For, we by Conquest of our soveraine might, / And by eternall doome of Fates decree, / Have wonne the Empire" (*Mutabilitie* v.33). Freedom and necessity—or, if you prefer, might and right—define each other to the point where no other argument is possible. And Mutabilitie's claim is similar in form. In fact, the two gods are one in their captivation by the spectacle of visible order; both speak the language of *scientia*, the union of knowledge and power based on sensory evidence;

both bend reality around a single explanatory principle, whether constancy or change, which turns out to be the imprint of their own ego; and for both Roman deities, the exterior object world is the projection of their lust to dominate. Jove's lust to dominate is the embodiment not of constancy so much as "a cosmological worldliness that is pleased to regard the outward governance of the universe as ultimate"; Mutabilitie's is a "force of restless innovation."[8] The more the speakers resemble each other in this symmetrical contest, the clearer it becomes that they are not constancy and change as absolute and therefore exclusive principles, but rather what we might think of as form and process. Applying biological terms, we might interpret the gods as articulating the principle of heredity and environment, where Jove represents the rigour of internal selection, the consistency of homology, and Mutabilitie, the vagaries of natural selection and the prospect of new forms. Considered as the two faces of evolution, therefore, Mutabilitie illustrates the necessity for the generation of classes of diversity (the pageant of the months and seasons and hours is her evidence, not Jove's). Jove is the naming or categorization itself, the necessity of rules (vii.40).

The Mutabilitie cantos articulate the dilemma preoccupying the narrator in the proem to Book III. The impulse in nature to the elaboration of variety threatens to overpower the consistency of the tried-and-true. But at the same time, the movement in nature towards symmetry frustrates the law of growth and change. Nature, "ever young yet full of eld, / Still mooving, yet unmoved" (vii.13), announces, in effect, that the two principles co-operate in evolution. They co-operate in art as well, a junior partner in the process, and the great marriage of the rivers passage of Book 4 shows how tight the co-operation must be between the act of depicting variety and the act of naming. Having invoked the principle of hierarchy that allows for the place of change in natural order, Nature suddenly vanishes, as if to announce that the debate is an illusion of the created world. Having described Nature's vanishing, *The Faerie Queene* ends just as abruptly, as if to announce the higher vision that is beyond the power of art to embody.

NOTES

1. Book III proem 5. I refer throughout to the *Variorum*, ed. Edwin Greenlaw et al., 11 volumes (Baltimore: The Johns Hopkins Press, 1932–57). Renaissance spellings have been regularized (u/v, vv/w, i/j).

2. Gordon Teskey, "From Allegory to Dialectic: Imagining Error in Spenser and Milton," *PMLA*, 101 (1986): 9–23.

3. Gabriel Harvey, *Letter Book*, ed. E.J.L. Scott (Camden Society, n.s. 33, 1884), 87.

4. For example, Wylkinson's *Ethics*: "Vertues be found in thynges that have a meane between extremities, which are either to much or to little." John Wylkinson, *The Ethiques of Aristotle, that is to say, preceptes of good behavoure and perfighte*

honestie, now newly translated into English (1547), chap. 8. Holland's Plutarch promotes the same sense of an arithmetical or golden mean: "Even so, morall vertue being a motion and facultie about the unreasonable part of the soule, tempereth the remission and intention; and in one word taketh away the excess and defect of the passions, reducing ech of them to a certain Mediocritie and moderation that falleth not on any one side." *The Philosophie, commonly called, The Morals* (London, 1603), 69.

5. Sean Kane, "The Paradoxes of Idealism: Book Two of *The Faerie Queene*," *John Donne Journal*, 2 (1983): 81–109.

6. "The Latin Spirit in Literature," *University of Toronto Quarterly* 2 (1933): 315–38 [330].

7. *Christianity and Classical Culture: A Study of Thought and Action from Augustus to Augustine* (1940; New York and London: Oxford Univ. Press, 1957), 157.

8. William Blissett, "Spenser's *Mutabilitie*," *Essays in English Literature from the Renaissance to the Victorian Age, presented to A.S.P. Woodhouse*, ed. Millar MacLure and F.W. Watt (Toronto: Univ. of Toronto Press, 1964), 24–42.

CLOSURE IN SPENSER'S *THE FAERIE QUEENE*

A.C. Hamilton

My reason for choosing to discuss closure in Spenser's *Faerie Queene* is that until the mid-1960s, the chief business of criticism was to impose some kind of closure on a literary work, while today closure of any kind is held to be impossible. From Aristotle until that time, criticism was structuralist in the sense that it projected a literary work spatially as an aesthetic object whose meaning could be determined by showing how structure or form unifies its content. As the major uncompleted poem in our language, *The Faerie Queene* may be illuminated by this shift in criticism.

In our century, historical criticism demonstrated a work's unity by detailing its correspondence to some context, either in the age or the writer's life. A.S.P. Woodhouse, for example, argues that Milton's point of departure in his poems is "something problematical in his own extra-aesthetic experience, problematical and productive of emotional tension, and by submitting it to the discipline and direction of an aesthetic pattern, at once structural and progressive, he solves or transcends the problem, and resolves the emotional tension."[1] As Cleanth Brooks has testified, New Criticism displays a literary work as a "well wrought urn" organically unified by certain themes, images, or metaphors; and one of the articles of his faith is "that the primary concern of criticism is with the problem of unity—the kind of whole which the literary work forms or fails to form, and the relation of the various parts to each other in building up this whole."[2] Formalist criticism, as the name suggests, investigated the writer's "primary intuition of form which enabled him to synthesize his materials into an ordered whole."[3] However much the various kinds of criticism disagreed among themselves, all agreed on imposing closure on a literary work by interpreting it as a unified whole in Aristotle's terms, a plot with beginning, middle, and an end.[4] Like a piece of music, a literary work presents a succession of discords resolved in final concord.

In contrast, the main business of deconstructive criticism today is to reject or subvert stable historically verifiable interpretations or transcendent meanings, and to emphasize the gaps, fissures, indeterminacies, and erasures in the consequently fractured literary text. In effect, it effectively denies closure. As Gary F. Waller notes, "for New Criticism, the text is a complex but organic harmony; for deconstruction, a text is a plurality, its contradictions and polysemy disrupting any pretense at organic unity."[5] For the new New Criticism, according to Geoffrey H. Hartman, "writing is a labyrinth, a topological puzzle and textual crossword; the reader, for his part, must lose himself for a while in a hermeneutic 'infinitizing' that makes all rules of closure appear arbitrary." For its context, he refers to modern resistance to closure as a restlessness: "we seem unable to close off a subject, or any inquiry. Closure is death."[6]

The unfinished state of *The Faerie Queene* has always posed a special problem for criticism, and statements about its possible resolution or closure have been an "interpretive endgame" for many years. Earlier critics invoked the Letter to Raleigh to point to a final apocalyptic marriage of King Arthur and Gloriana that would resolve all problems of understanding the poem. For A.S.P. Woodhouse, "the twelfth book was to have completed the pattern of the whole and, like the Epilogue in *Comus*, to have furnished the vantage point from which all that went before might be seen in its true relations and its full significance."[7] Historical critics allowed indeterminacy of meaning but assumed that the poem's *discordia concors* was finally resolved. In his study of Books III and IV, Thomas P. Roche, Jr. sees concord continually emerging from discord according to the traditional metaphysics of creation: "out of the discord of chaos came the concord of creation, out of the discord of the Fall came the concord of the Redemption, out of the discord of man's disordered passions comes the concord of love and propagation."[8] Other critics found that the present six books make any projected ending problematic. Harry Berger, for example, identified the "secret discipline" of Spenser's imagination as "a double burden, discordant and harmonious," and noted in Book VI that "the contrivance of the narrative, the inconclusiveness of the adventures, the gradual flawing of the romance world, the failure of chivalric action...dramatize the claims imposed by actuality on the life of imagination."[9] Only four years after Roche's book, there appeared Berger's very influential article on "the Spenserian dynamics" which he defined as a poetic *discordia concors* in which "no moment of union or reconciliation, of relief or triumph, is to be construed as absolute—absolute either in the sense of being final, or in the sense of being totally one-sided."[10]

Berger's thesis signals a change in the critical response to *The Faerie Queene*. To name only enough to indicate a consensus, Isabel G. MacCaffrey notes that "the open-endedness of Spenser's poem is expressed in a pattern of reiterated inconclusiveness"; Patricia Parker argues that dilation and deferral are persistent elements in any romance but especially in Spenser's romance with its "tension between the forward movement towards an ending and the delightful, and seductive, dilation which is also the poem itself"; Angus Fletcher examines the tendency of allegory "toward infinite extension" which may be overcome only by "arbitrary closure," a device which he finds strongly exhibited in the whole of Spenser's poem; and Marion Campbell concludes that "Spenser's realization that his poem could not be completed becomes part of his theme, and is presented as an insight into the human condition as much as an acknowledgement of the limitations of poetry." But only in Jonathan Goldberg's deconstructive reading is Berger's denial of closure rigorously upheld: for him, "Spenser's poem is not a world, complete, closed, and referential, but a process demanding endless doing and 'endlesse worke', because it relentlessly undoes itself, denying closure."[11]

The problem of closure in *The Faerie Queene* has been freshly raised by Balachandra Rajan's most recent book in which he studies the nature of closure in some major unfinished long poems from Spenser's *Faerie Queene* to Pound's *Cantos*. He argues that Spenser's poem "began as a poem that was incomplete and ended as a poem that was unfinished," by which he means that it "evolved in such a way as to make it improper to finish."[12] He allows with Goldberg that the anti-closural forces in the poem are not to be regarded simply as obstinately resisting the organizing reach of its grand design but have a status not unequal to the design they disrupt. Unlike Goldberg and the other critics I have cited, he refuses to give privilege to one over the other. Since he generously allows in his opening paragraph that he seeks only to initiate a study of the unfinished poem in English, I propose to continue what he has begun by considering Spenser's poem.

In treating closure, I shall exclude the Cantos of Mutabilitie, as Rajan does not, because their place in the poem's design is too uncertain. In the judgement of Matthew Lownes, the publisher of the 1609 edition, the two cantos "appear to be parcell of some following Booke of the *Faerie Queene*, under the legend of Constancie,"[13] but that is all we know about them. Of course, if they are placed at the end of the six books, one may conclude that they provide a final exposition of mutability which has been a major motif of the previous books; or that the appearance of Nature is the inevitable, climactic epiphany in a poem about our life on the order of nature, especially fitting from the disciple of Chaucer; or that they provide a coda or epilogue to the whole poem, its two cantos commenting on the two parcels of the poem published in 1590 and 1596, followed by two stanzas commenting on the cantos themselves, and concluding with a plea or prayer which rounds out the canon of Spenser's poetry, "graunt me that Sabaoths sight," after which there is only silence. We do not know, however, when the Cantos were written, or how they could form part of a book, or within that book how they would relate to whatever number of books would precede them. If we include the Mutabilitie Cantos in any discussion of the whole poem, inevitably we will see them as the poem's coda or epilogue, "a detached retrospective commentary on the poem as a whole" (William Blissett), or "the culmination of the poem as it now stands, both unifying and illuminating it" (Kathleen Williams), or that through them the poem attains "its final inconclusiveness" (Rajan).[14]

I take "closure" in Aristotle's sense of an ending: that part of the story which requires something before it but nothing after it; or in Barbara Herrnstein Smith's sense: "a structure appears 'closed' when it is experienced as integral: coherent, complete, and stable."[15]

The matter of the poem's ending was present from its conception in Spenser's impossibly ambitious plan to write twenty-four books. No doubt his model was his great "original," Chaucer, who had planned some 120 Canterbury tales but managed to complete only one-sixth of that number. Like Chaucer, Spenser was about to enter the civil service but in a country where he could never hope for leisure and the access to learning which would allow him to complete more than a fragment of the whole. How could he publish separate parcels of a poem which he could never expect to complete, and yet would be in some measure self-contained?

Also there was the problem arising from his decision to write a poem in a mixed genre. Since he aspired to become England's Homer and Virgil, he divided his poem into books, each being a brief epic with its traditional closure, a story with beginning, middle, and end. But he also aspired to become the English Ariosto and Tasso, and therefore divided his poem into cantos whose interlacing narratives cut across the book-divisions. In place of epic's demand for closure there was romance's endless deferral. The consequence of his mingling of the two genres, what Rajan terms "generic contestation," has been brilliantly analyzed by Patricia Parker as "the divagations of romance" with its continual repetition and deferral countering "epic's strong 'sense of an ending'," as a consequence of which "each of the Legends of *The Faerie Queene* provides a variation on the tension between premature end and indefinite extension." Rajan finds the poem "poised between the purposiveness of Virgilian epic and the errancy of Ariostan romance with each inheritance coming increasingly to represent an essential component of the poem's self-declaration, its mediation between pattern and flow, between the movement to closure and the resistance to closure."[16]

The poem's divided inheritance is evident from its inception. As the epic hero, the Red Cross Knight overcomes the serpent Error and her brood in a traditional heroic contest, thereby proving himself worthy of the armour of the Christian knight. Now no longer wandering in the labyrinthine Wood of Error, he is initiated into the quest to journey to Eden to slay the apocalyptic dragon of Revelation 20. As the romance hero, he then falls into error in the house of the wicked magician and thereby begins his wandering in sin. As the epic hero firm in his purpose, he flees the false Una only as the romance hero to accept her surrogate in the wicked witch, Duessa. As the epic hero, he flees the house of Pride; as the romance hero, he falls victim to the folklore giant proud Orgoglio. So the narrative proceeds through epic resolution followed by its undoing, in a plan that allows Spenser to spend a lifetime of writing during which he could produce parcels of his one great poem from time to time, yet continue writing until his death.

At some point in the writing, Spenser decided to publish one parcel of the whole work, the first three books that appeared in 1590 with an appended Letter to Raleigh outlining the grand design of which these books served only as the beginning. One may only speculate how he expected it to be received. Even from a cursory reading, though, we recognize that these books are not a fragment, and later we realize that they form a triptych of the private virtues with Book I serving as a paradigm for all the later books.

Book I is the most simply self-contained. Its final canto is introduced as a moment of imminent closure:

> Behold I see the haven nigh at hand,
> To which I meane my wearie course to bend;
> Vere the maine shete, and beare up with the land,
> The which afore is fairely to be kend,
> And seemeth safe from stormes, that may offend;
> There this faire virgin wearie of her way
> Must landed be, now at her journeyes end:
> There eke my feeble barke a while may stay,
> Till merry wind and weather call her thence away.

This opening stanza is answered by the concluding one to Book I:

> Now strike your sailes ye jolly Mariners,
> For we be come unto a quiet rode,
> Where we must land some of our passengers,
> And light this wearie vessell of her lode.
> Here she a while may make her safe abode,
> Till she repaired have her tackles spent,
> And wants supplide. And then againe abroad
> On the long voyage whereto she is bent:
> Well may she speede and fairely finish her intent.

The story of the quest by a clownish young man to win the grace of the Faerie Queene by slaying the dragon, thereby both learning his true identity as St. George and winning the princess in marriage, achieves both epic and romance closure. In religious terms, the story fulfils the pattern of man's fall, redemption through Christ, and regeneration which prepares for final restoration; and in moral terms, it fashions the "virtue" of holiness which is preliminary to life in this world.

Yet the Knight's victory over the dragon is not apocalyptic, as is its type in Revelation: it only qualifies him for the semi-finals. Before his betrothal to Una may be consummated in marriage, he must engage in an apocalyptic battle to defend the Faerie Queene against the forces of Antichrist; and finally he must forsake all the worldly concerns that provide the stories for the whole poem and begin his pilgrimage to the Heavenly Jerusalem. At the end of Book I, only Una has been restored. The concluding moment of delayed closure—the marriage preparations for what is only a betrothal, and with it, the interruption of the marriage banns by Duessa's slanders and the notice that Archimago will escape his binding—proves characteristic of the poem. Its use here is sanctioned by the story of the Apocalypse: "that dragon that old serpent, which is the devil and Satan" is bound a thousand years but "after that he must be loosed for a little season."[17] The Knight's story continues as long as time; or, more correctly, for the "little season," the immanent apocalyptic present; or, more exactly, as Frank Kermode has argued, for the "time-defeating *aevum*" which serves Spenser as "a concord-fiction."[18]

The story of Book II achieves closure only nominally when Guyon completes his quest: he avenges the deaths of Mortdant and Amavia on behalf of Ruddymane by binding Acrasia, destroying her Bower of Bliss, and freeing Verdant and her other captives. As the book fashions the virtue of temperance, there is the imminent closure announced by Spenser after the temperate body has been seen in the house of Alma and the forces which threaten its destruction have been defeated by Arthur:

Now gins this goodly frame of Temperance
Fairely to rise, and her adorned hed
To pricke of highest praise forth to advance.

Yet the book deliberately frustrates the expectations of conventional epic closure by denying Guyon the hero's due praise: instead of the happy throngs which welcome the Red Cross Knight's slaying of the dragon there is only the disgruntlement of all Acrasia's victims once they are released from bestiality. The ending also frustrates romance closure: it is not sufficient for the hero to bind the witch. Some continuation is called for if only because the largely classical virtue of temperance, which succeeds the Christian "virtue" of holiness, needs to be supplemented by some higher state.

The final canto of Book II begins with the lines I have just cited and concludes almost peremptorily with Guyon's recognition that the power of temperance cannot reform Grill from his inner bestial state. The Palmer confirms Guyon's recognition and therefore he, not the poet, is given the concluding line: "But let us hence depart, whilest wether serves and wind." In its suspension of closure, Book II would seem deliberately designed as a middle book of three.

To any contemporary reader, the exposition of chastity in the concluding book of the 1590 poem would have seemed an inevitable closure: a poem written in praise of the Virgin Queen must turn from masculine temperance, for which the feminine is polarized as virgin and whore, to "that fairest vertue, farre above the rest" which the poet finds "shrined in my Soveraines brest" (III Proem 1). But since that virtue cannot be the object of a quest, its story is related through surrogates, in the stories of Florimell and Marinell, Belphoebe and Timias, Amoret and Scudamour. Since these interlaced stories cannot be concluded within the twelve cantos, given romance's digressiveness, of all the books, Book III achieves the least narrative closure.

Yet Book III does fashion the virtue of chastity, as it set out to do, by showing finally the more-than-human power of that virtue to free love (Amoret) from all possible fear. Amoret's story is resolved, so far as we know, when she is restored to her lover in joyous sexual consummation, a hermaphroditic union of the two sexes in "marriage." Accordingly, the book concludes with two lines about the lovers:

> Thus doe those lovers with sweet countervayle,
> Each other of loves bitter fruit despoile.

to which the poet adds:

> But now my teme begins to faint and fayle,
> All woxen weary of their journall toyle:
> Therefore I will their sweatie yokes assoyle
> At this same furrowes end, till a new day:
> And ye faire Swayns, after your long turmoyle,
> Now cease your worke, and at your pleasure play;
> Now cease your worke; to morrow is an holy day.

The poet's confidential pause with the sense of labour completed—"this same furrowes end"—at the end of the week's work suggests a temporary closure at least with the first parcel of the poem. Its triad of the private virtues treated in the first three books may be said to achieve closure in Aristotle's sense that it does not depend on anything else that may be told.

Spenser anticipated that if his reader was to experience his poem as "integral: coherent, complete, and stable" (closure in Barbara Herrnstein Smith's sense), he would need to append some statement "expounding his whole intention in the course of this worke." Accordingly, he appends the Letter to Raleigh at just the point when it is most needed, for now the reader, no longer imaginatively subject to the poem in the temporal process of reading, is required to understand its "continued Allegory, or darke conceit."

At this point, any reader needs to learn about the larger design of which the three books form part, and especially about the virtues which the poem is fashioning. As the history of Spenser criticism shows, however, he should have told us much more, for we still remain largely ignorant of the nature of the virtues, of their relationships, and of the different kinds of structures needed to fashion them. Being ignorant, we treat Spenser's dark conceit as though it were projected as a well-constructed realistic novel which should have a tidy, logically constructed plot. Spenser says that the first three books "contain" three virtues, the first being "the knight of the Redcrosse, in whome I expresse Holynes" but as yet there is no study of the virtue of holiness. Again, we know little about the nature of chastity as distinct from virginity, how it is "pictured" in Britomart, as Spenser says, and how it is fashioned in Book III even though the separate romance narratives, and especially that of Britomart, remain unresolved. It follows that we know very little about the closure (or the lack of it) in that book and in the 1590 poem.

The unresolved romance narratives provide transition to the second parcel of the poem, Books IV to VI, which appeared together with the first parcel with its "revised" ending to Book III in 1596. Of course, we do not know which ending was the revised one; for all we know, it may have been the 1590 ending, changed from the original 1596 version in order to provide at least some narrative closure to the first three books. Presumably the contemporary reader would have noted that the virtues about to be treated are the public virtues, that Book IV ostensibly concludes most of the stories of Book III, and that the two books form a twenty-four canto book in which chastity encompasses the virtue of friendship.

The final canto of Book IV opens with the poet's statement that his work, like the sea's abundance which he is naming, is endless: "O what an endlesse worke have I in hand." The canto and book conclude with the characteristic delaying of closure when Florimell joined to Marinell fears her apparent lack of modesty and provokes the poet to add the conventional concluding-nonconcluding line: "Which to another place I leave to be perfected." But the personal, political, social, and cosmic harmony—and in this sense closure—achieved through the fashioning of friendship in the closing cantos allows Spenser to see if that harmony may be extended to the political sphere.

In Book V, Spenser fashions the "most sacred vertue...of all the rest" because it resembles God "in his imperiall might." Justice is the virtue of closure as it establishes laws to separate right from wrong, with Talus's use of force as its fully effective executive instrument. Being a divine virtue, it may well be, as Judith Anderson has complained, that "taken as an absolute ideal, [it] makes demands which neither human history nor individual human beings can satisfy"[19] any more than Spenser's readers could satisfy the divine injunction, "be ye therefore perfect." For this reason—and I am only guessing—it is designed as the middle book of its triad: it complements Book IV and is complemented in turn by Book VI.

In any discussion of closure, Book VI is the key book. The final canto begins with the poet's confident statement that he is fulfilling his intention:

> Like as a ship, that through the Ocean wyde
> Directs her course unto one certaine cost,
> Is met of many a counter winde and tyde,
> With which her winged speed is let and crost,
> And she her selfe in stormie surges tost;
> Yet making many a borde, and many a bay,
> Still winneth way, ne hath her compasse lost:
> Right so it fares with me in this long way,
> Whose course is often stayd, yet never is astray.

It concludes with a moment of closure when the poet transfers the action from faeryland to the ordinary world. The Blatant Beast of calumny has escaped, and neither Spenser's knight, Calidore, nor Arthur's knights, Sir Pelleas and Sir Lamoracke "and all his brethren borne in Britaine land" may ever capture him. The failure of Arthur and his knights allows the Beast to range freely attacking the innocent, the learned, and even poets:

> Ne may this homely verse, of many meanest,
> Hope to escape his venemous despite,
> More then my former writs, all were they clearest
> From blamefull blot, and free from all that wite,
> With which some wicked tongues did it backebite,
> And bring into a mighty Peres displeasure,
> That never so deserved to endite.
> Therefore do you my rimes keep better measure,
> And seeke to please, that now is counted wisemens threasure.

The 1596 poem ends as it began with the poet's awareness that his work will be attacked by envy. That Spenser's poetry began with his complaint against envy—in the address "to his Booke" that opens *The Shepheardes Calender*—strongly suggests that he is rounding out the canon of his works. As he had planned, so we may assume, Book VI completes the second triad of the virtues; but as he may not have planned, it completes the poem as he published it.

By the end of Book VI, the Letter is not needed because the poem itself "giveth great light to the Reader, for the better understanding" as it constantly redefines itself, commenting upon what has taken place and anticipating what will take place, ceaselessly undoing itself, continually frustrating any sense of fulfilment, transforming any product into a continuing process of reassessment, subjecting any moment of apparent closure into a fresh beginning, simultaneously constructing and deconstructing any meanings it suggests. Thus William Blissett aptly notes that Spenser is "the poet of the second thought"; Isabel G. MacCaffrey shows how "the poem looks at itself"; and Kathleen Williams notes that the poem has "the inclusiveness and apparently infinite expansion of significance that life has."[20] *The Faerie Queene* must be the most thoroughly revisionist poem in any language. Some of Spenser's techniques have been noted by critics—his elaborate paralleling of books, such as Books I and II; the analogies between Books II and V, and Books III and VI; his setting up Books V and VI as a diptych; or centering the double Book, III and IV, between an opening and concluding pair—but at times one wonders if we have only begun to explore the poem's symmetry.[21] Book VI especially comments on all that has gone before. As the most simply imaginative of the books—what Patricia Parker interprets as the "romance of romance"[22]—it invites a relaxed submission to its stories and at the same time demands that the reader be most actively engaged in generating the meanings of the whole poem in fashioning the virtue of courtesy in relation to the other virtues.

For *The Faerie Queene*, a more adequate response than any effort through close reading to impose closure, or through closer reading to reject it, is to allow that the poem avoids closure altogether because its fashioning of the virtues through the heroes is designed to fashion them in the reader, not in knowledge but in action. Barbara Herrnstein Smith's definition of closure as "the sense of finality, stability, and integrity" that depends on "the reader's experience of the structure of the entire poem"[23] is not what Sidney has in mind when he defends poetry on the ground that its images of virtue "strike, pierce, [and] possess the sight of the soul," that they should be "worn in the tablet of the [reader's] memory."[24] Closure is found in readers in the sense that their future actions will illustrate the various virtues.

One first step may be a thorough reader-response reading of the poem. As paradigm for the whole, Book I shows readers that what happens in the Knight's story achieves closure in their virtuous actions through which they imitate their patron saint. In place of Stanley Fish's "guilty reader," one must substitute the "innocent reader" who rejoices in the poem's radical ambiguity, its endless revision, its mutability in its continual dilation, its constantly enlarging perspectives on the place of the virtues in the active life, and the *discordia concors* of its continued allegory. If its potential but never achieved closure is recognized as designed by the poet to provoke the reader's active, imaginative involvement in its creative act, it will not become an end in itself with the resulting frustration of expectations, but a means of awakening a visionary rather than conceptual response, through which the reader sees and therefore understands.

The modern reader's rejection of form, determined by the tyranny of the present which projects upon *The Faerie Queene* various rationalizations—Spenser's loss of faith in the efficacy of the virtues, his disappointment with the court, or his disillusionment with the power of poetry to influence action—brings us closer to the poem than the earlier effort to isolate it as an aesthetic object. When Spenser concludes the Mutabilitie Cantos with the claim that "all that moveth, doth in *Change* delight," he includes himself. For him, change is revealed imaginatively in the climactic vision of the six books, the hundred naked maidens "all raunged in a ring, and dauncing in delight." Here there is closure but no closure, a harmony within a larger harmony that promises eternal rest but while time lasts there is the delight in his "endlesse worke."

NOTES

1. A.S.P. Woodhouse, *Milton the Poet* (Toronto: J.M. Dent & Sons, 1955), 15.

2. Cleanth Brooks, "The Formalist Critic," *Kenyon Review* 13 (1951): 72. "My Credo" series.

3. R.S. Crane, *The Languages of Criticism and the Structure of Poetry* (Toronto: Univ. of Toronto Press, 1953), 146.

4. Aristotle, *Poetics* 7.

5. Gary F. Waller, "Deconstruction and Renaissance Literature," *Assays* 2 (1982): 73.

6. Geoffrey H. Hartman, *Criticism in the Wilderness: The Study of Literature Today* (New Haven: Yale Univ. Press, 1980), 244; *The Fate of Reading and Other Essays* (Chicago: Chicago Univ. Press, 1975), 251.

7. A.S.P. Woodhouse, "Nature and Grace in *The Faerie Queene*," *ELH* 16 (1949): 201.

8. Thomas P. Roche Jr., *The Kindly Flame: A Study of the Third and Fourth books of Spenser's* Faerie Queene (Princeton: Princeton Univ. Press, 1964), 55.

9. Harry Berger, "A Secret Discipline: *The Faerie Queene*, Book VI," in *Form and Convention in the Poetry of Edmund Spenser*, ed. William Nelson (New York: Columbia Univ. Press, 1961), 74, 41.

10. Harry Berger, "The Spenserian Dynamics," *Studies in English Literature* 8 (1968): 10.

11. Isabel G. MacCaffrey, *Spenser's Allegory: The Anatomy of Imagination* (Princeton: Princeton Univ. Press, 1976), 330; Patricia A. Parker, *Inescapable Romance: Studies in the Poetics of a Mode* (Princeton: Princeton Univ. Press, 1979), 63; Angus Fletcher, *Allegory: The Theory of a Symbolic Mode* (Ithaca: Cornell Univ. Press, 1964), 176, 177; Marion Campbell, "Spenser's Mutabilitie Cantos and the End of *The Faerie Queene*," *Southern Review* (Australia) 15 (1982): 58; Jonathan Goldberg, *Endlesse Worke: Spenser and the Structures of Discourse* (Baltimore: Johns Hopkins Univ. Press, 1981), 26.

12. Balachandra, Rajan, *The Form of the Unfinished: English Poetics from Spenser to Pound* (Princeton: Princeton Univ. Press, 1985), 44.

13. Quotations from *The Faerie Queene* are from the edition by A.C. Hamilton, Longmans Annotated English Poets (London: Longmans, 1977).

14. William Blissett, "Spenser's Mutabilitie," in *Essays in English Literature from the Renaissance to the Victorian Age Presented to A.S.P. Woodhouse*, ed. Millar MacLure and F.W. Watt (Toronto: Univ. of Toronto Press, 1964), 26; Kathleen Williams, " 'Eterne in Mutabilitie': The Unified World of *The Faerie Queene*," *ELH* 19 (1952): 128; Rajan, *Form of the Unfinished*, 44.

15. Barbara Herrnstein Smith, *Poetic Closure: A Study of How Poems End* (Chicago: Univ. of Chicago Press, 1968), 2.

16. Parker, *Inescapable Romance*, 49, 88; Rajan, *Form of the Unfinished*, 83.

17. Rev. 20: 1–3.

18. Frank Kermode, *The Sense of an Ending* (New York: Oxford Univ. Press, 1967 edition), 80.

19. Judith Anderson, " 'Nor man it is': the Knight of Justice in Book V of Spenser's *Faerie Queene*," *PMLA* 85 (1970): 65.

20. William Blissett, "Florimell and Marinell," *Studies in English Literature* 5 (1965): 89; Isabel G. MacCaffrey, *Spenser's Allegory*, 9; Kathleen Williams, *Spenser's "Faerie Queene": The World of Glass* (London: Routledge and Kegan Paul, 1966), xiv.

21. See especially James Nohrnberg, *The Analogy of "The Faerie Queene"* (Princeton: Princeton Univ. Press, 1976).

22. Parker, *Inescapable Romance*, 101ff, see esp. 112.

23. B.H. Smith, *Poetic Closure*, viii.

24. *A Defence of Poetry*, in *Miscellaneous Prose of Sir Philip Sidney*, ed. Katherine Duncan-Jones and Jan van Dorsten (Oxford: Clarendon Press, 1973), 85, 98.

POSITIONING SPENSER'S "LETTER TO RALEIGH"

Gordon Teskey

I dreamt that it was night and that I was lying in my bed...Suddenly the window opened of its own accord, and I was terrified to see that some white wolves were sitting on a big walnut tree in front of the window.[1]

This scene, the most famous in the literature of psychoanalysis, turns out in the course of the analysis to have been a neurotic encoding of an event observed by the Wolf-Man while he was awake. As Freud describes it, the breakthrough in the treatment occurs when the Wolf-Man interprets the opening of the window as the opening of his own eyes. What he saw he saw while he was awake; and in the course of further analysis it is discovered that the event he had observed while awake (and later encoded as a vision of wolves) is what Freud terms the *primal scene*.

Everything in Freud's subsequent analysis hangs by this thread: the interpretation by the patient himself of the opening of the window as the opening of his eyes, which means that the patient saw something while waking that actually occurred. Yet it is important to note, as Stanley Fish has remarked, that the Wolf-Man does not recall waking but interprets one element of the dream as such. The Wolf-Man decides by interpreting the dream from within what the opening of the window must mean—that he is no longer dreaming—and he does so without the external corroboration that a clear recollection of waking may be thought to provide. Thus the Wolf-Man's statement is at once an interpretation assisting in the detached work of analysis and a disclosure rendering up to that analysis a secret buried inside his psyche. Why is the self-interpretation of a neurotic, an interpretation coming out of the neurosis itself, given so much authority?

The answer to this question would seem to be that the self-interpretation of a diseased mind is given just so much authority as is necessary to relieve the pressure on psychoanalysis, which is accused of constructing both the disease and the cure. It is therefore essential to Freud's method, if the charge of suggestion is to be avoided, to legitimate interpretation as a function of the original code, something that spontaneously rises out of the text (in this case the psyche of the Wolf-Man, whether it is dreaming or interpreting) without having been placed there by the analyst. For an analyst, as the word etymologically implies, releases something tied up or concealed without affecting the thing that is freed. His role is therefore more detached from and superior to that of a mediator, or *interpres*, whose task is to re-encode the message of a text by seeming to decode it. To get something out, the interpreter must put something in; and only the patient can be allowed to do that. Thus what the analyst releases from the interior is a process of re-encoding that is already nested in the original code and that follows its natural course, he assures us, without interference from him. In this way he fulfils the oldest wish-fantasy of hermeneutics: that the text, ideally, interpret itself—even if it is necessary for the circuit to take in the analyst in its arc. This is the wish Freud intends, in his analysis of the Wolf-Man, to come true.

But how can the stigma of interpretative intervention be taken away from the analyst and inserted back into the text as its self-disclosure? The principle of self-interpretation is vindicated, and made the vindication of psychoanalysis, when Freud considers the merits of psychoanalyzing children as opposed to adults. Anticipating the criticism that the search for traces of infantile neuroses in adults is vitiated by the interference taking place over the intervening years, Freud states that the analysis of a child would introduce an even more serious kind of interference: the necessary lending of words and thoughts to the child by the analyst. As Fish puts it, the accusation of intervention by the analyst is allowed to surface only to be transferred to the analysand: "it is presented as an accusation not against Freud but his patients, including, presumably, this one."[2]

This statement, though incisive, is not I think exactly correct. For in transferring the accusation of intervention from analyst to patient the accusation does not remain an accusation but is changed into something quite different. It is changed from a stigma of inauthenticity in the analyst's method to an authentic symptom of the neurosis: the Wolf-Man's interpretation must be valid, we assume, because it comes out of the same psyche that has witnessed the primal scene. Yet it is just this authenticity—that the interpretation has its *fons et origo* in the interpreted thing—that undermines the authority of the interpretation as knowledge. For by interpreting the opening of the window as the opening of his own eyes and the cessation of dreaming, the dreamer is caught trying to determine the status of the whole from a position inside that whole. By the same principle that a set cannot be a member of itself, or that the contained cannot enclose its container, the one thing the dreamer cannot decide is whether his dream was a dream or a waking event neurotically encoded to look like a dream after the fact.

It is by a similar fondness for originative authenticity in literature that we prefer a text to interpret itself or that we credit with special authority the gesture by which an author interprets his text from a position somewhere inside, alongside, or even outside that text. For even in the last case, where the author seems to have stepped outside himself and then turned back to press his nose to the glass, we feel that his perspective, however detached it may be, is the perspective of one who has nevertheless been at the centre. And if we do not watch him too closely he will have it both ways. He will have it one way when he assumes by his externality a position of a higher logical type, for no one will then accuse him of attempting in one part of his work to determine the status of the whole in which that part is contained. And he will have it the other way when he insinuates, by a magisterial nod, that he enjoys a peculiar intimacy with the interior of the text which no other critic can have: like Milton's Spirit, this critic has been present from the first as a witness of and a participant in the scene of creation. Such a double role—of laying open an original intention now buried at the work's centre and of offering a belated and, thus, a detached commentary on the work from its margins—is frequently observable in the work of those who claim, from a position outside the text, to declare what is hidden inside it. We see this in the Epistle to Can Grande (which most scholars take to be written by Dante), in Tasso's letters and "Prose Allegory" and of course in Spenser's "Letter to Raleigh," which declares, as we are told, his "*whole intention in the course of this worke.*"[3]

We may note that this doubleness can be observed in the text of the "Letter" without any reference, as yet, to its position. For even inside itself the "Letter" seems to be tending in opposite directions so as to have it, as we have seen Freud to have it, both ways. On the one hand it seems to escape from out of the centre of *The Faerie Queene* and to bring with it an account of that primal event occurring at the "wel-head of the History." On the other hand it seems to invade the text of *The Faerie Queene* from its margins with the purpose of analyzing the poem according to the commonplaces and protocols of Renaissance critical theory, of which the "Letter" is hardly more than an elegant catena. Thus the "Letter" is both central to the interior of the text, because it witnesses the originative scene, and it is an interpretation that is written, and dated, as the last thing composed. By this double movement in the "Letter," an oscillation that may be thought of as a circuit, the text of *The Faerie Queene* seems to curve back and interpret itself without interference from us. We seem not to construct but merely to recognize analogies and patterns that are already hidden inside the poem as its meaning. Once the circuit is closed, the analyst's interpretative performance can be offered to us as a function proceeding not out of him but out of the text. Such is the justification of Spenser's most massive commentator: "what began as a *criticism* of the poem, in the sense of an analysis of its ostensible total form, evolved into a *commentary*, a divulging of the form's hidden allegorical content."[4]

Just as Freud presents himself as merely analyzing the Wolf-Man's self-interpretation, so readers of Spenser are enjoined to stand back from the text, not interfering or introducing suggestions as to what *The Faerie Queene* means but simply allowing the text, by a disclosure that rises out of its centre, to curve back and interpret itself. Of course we recognize analogies and their interconnections, just as Spenser recalls his conceit, but we do not construct them. Above all, we do not interfere with the text by putting anything in: we merely assist—in the French sense of that word—at the text's self-disclosure. And it is in large measure the task of the "Letter," in offering an interpretative disclosure (the oxymoron captures its equivocal role), to close the circuit around which the poem can be both itself and a commentary on itself. Commentary thus becomes an objective procedure witnessed by the reader from a position of antiseptic detachment. It is the making of what Spenser calls, with a slightly different intention, "a pleasing Analysis of all."

There is, however, a stubbornly material difficulty with this paradigm for interpreting Spenser, a difficulty that arises not within the field of interpretation but in a place where the boundaries of that field must be drawn. I refer to the position of the "Letter to Raleigh," which is not set at the front of the text published in 1590 but at the back, even though it is intended to be read first so as to show the reader how to "gripe al the discourse." We know, further, that although the "Letter" is presented as a "fore-conceit," to use the Sidneian term, setting forth Spenser's design, or *idea*, it was written after the first three books of the poem had been entered in the Stationers' Register. And in the 1596 edition of *The Faerie Queene*, in which Books Four to Six were added, the "Letter to Raleigh" does not appear. Therefore if editors are to reprint the "Letter" with *The Faerie Queene* they must determine its status with respect to the poem in order to determine where it will stand. And they must do so in the absence of an authoritative re-positioning by Spenser in 1596. Where should a modern editor of *The Faerie Queene* position the "Letter to Raleigh"?

This problem will perhaps seem more complex when it is recognized that there is no question of restoring the "Letter" to its original place. We may see why this is so by plotting its coordinates in 1590: a) at the end of the third book, as an irruption of commentary at that point in the course of the writing and, b) at the end of everything that has been written, as a recollection and a disclosure of the author's intention. Because, as I have said, the "Letter" was not authoritatively re-positioned in 1596, later editors are inclined to position it according to their assumptions about its interiority with respect to *The Faerie Queene*. What they cannot do is take a neutral position by placing it where Spenser did. For if the "Letter" is placed at the end of the seventh book (satisfying coordinate "b" without satisfying "a"), the editor has decided in favour of its interiority as an intention. And if it is placed at the end of the third book (satisfying "a" without satisfying "b"), the editor has decided in favour of its exteriority as commentary. It should not take much reflection to see why, in a tradition of scholarship that is more comfortable with the idea of the author fulfilling a unified, original design than with the idea of the author momentarily standing back from what he has done to improvise a plausible scheme, editors have chosen to position the "Letter" at the end of the poem as the authoritative plan for the whole. And they have very frequently enhanced this effect by moving the "Letter" to the beginning of the poem, notwithstanding the original description of the "Letter" as being "hereunto *annexed*" (my emphasis).[5] The motive for this transposition—as for the habit, still practised by scholars, of referring to Spenser's "Letter" as *prefatory*—is to make the position of the "Letter" in the whole text of *The Faerie Queene* coincide with the positional claim Spenser makes inside the "Letter" itself: that it discloses the "wel-head of the History."

This matter was first attended to in the deluxe Victorian edition of Alexander Grosart. Deprecating the habit of placing the "Letter" before the text of *The Faerie Queene*, Grosart announced his intention of restoring the "Letter" to its correct place. This place he declares to be after the third book; but because of unspecified exigencies—his exigencies, not Spenser's—he places the "Letter" after the seventh.[6] We have seen, however, that even if Grosart had temerariously positioned the "Letter" after the third book, a choice that would reflect more strongly a writer's conception of its status than would placing it after the seventh, he would still not have got it right: for the original position of the "Letter" was effaced when Spenser wrote Books Four to Seven. Thus in bibliographical terms the problem of where now to position the "Letter" is formally undecidable: no conceivable evidence could resolve it. Yet by examining circumstances surrounding the positioning of the "Letter" in the early folios, we can bring into clearer focus the significance for *The Faerie Queene*, and for literary theory in general, of what may be called the *positionality* of Spenser's "Letter" to Raleigh.[7]

2

Let me review some of the facts. The "Letter to Raleigh" was printed once in Spenser's lifetime, when it appeared at the end of the 1590 quarto of *The Faerie Queene* (containing Books I–III) on signatures 2Pr–2P3r. It is followed, on signatures 2P3v–2P8v, by a collection of commendatory and dedicatory sonnets and poems, by a list of "Faults Escaped in the Print," and by four unpaginated leaves (sigs. 2Q1–4) with further dedicatory sonnets. In the 1596 edition of *The Faerie Queene*, which adds Books IV–VI in a separate quarto, the "Letter" does not reappear (though two commendatory sonnets by Raleigh and the poem by Gabriel Harvey are reprinted after Book III, presumably to fill up the eighth leaf of signature Oo). This edition was the last in Spenser's lifetime; and while he introduced some corrections and changes on the copy-text for Books I to III (which was not manuscript but a copy of 1590), it is almost certain that he did so without seeing the work through the press. Hence many of the "Faults Escaped" listed in 1590 are still at large in 1596; and it is not unlikely that the decision to omit the "Letter" was made by the printer rather than by Spenser.[8]

I mention this hypothesis only to show that it is of no use to us here. For even if we were to find out that the suppression of the "Letter" in 1596 had not been authorized, that knowledge would simply reintroduce the question in a new form. Would Spenser have revised and redated the "Letter" before placing it at the conclusion of Book VI?

Or, if he were to leave it in its original form, and under its original date, would he have placed it in what is now the middle of the text, between Books III and IV? Even for Spenser the problem of where to position the "Letter" in 1596 would be far from simple. We cannot know for certain whether Spenser's intentions were carried out by its suppression. Nor can we submit to any reliable test such propositions as have been advanced, on the assumption that this is so, to explain Spenser's motive: that the "Letter" was omitted because it was no longer consistent with the poem in its expanded form (it was already inconsistent enough on first appearance) or that it was omitted because the additional books made it no longer necessary to provide "great light to the Reader." Neither explanation seems plausible.

One elementary point that does bear insisting upon, however, is that the "Letter" is dated the 23 January 1589 (o.s.), some seven weeks after the entry of *The Faerie Queene* in the Stationers' Register (1 Dec. 1589). It is therefore strange that the "Letter" should conform so imperfectly with what had already been written when it was composed: of the three books it follows, only the action of the first book remains uncontradicted by the account given in the "Letter."[9] And here we must remark upon the insistency with which the "Letter" is presented to us not as being a retrospective interpretation of the epic, as Tasso's prose allegory obviously was (and as he once admitted it to be),[10] but as something thought out before the poet began his poem and merely, or belatedly, recorded on that January 23d. Spenser calls it "a Letter of the Authors expounding his *whole intention in the course of this worke*." I cite from the 1590 edition: so far as we know, those italics are Spenser's.

Now if we consider the inconsistencies between the "Letter" and the poem in the light of this claim that the "Letter" discloses Spenser's original and guiding intention, we may suspect that those inconsistencies have been contrived, or at least allowed to stand, for a purpose. For they tend to confirm the authenticity of the plan as Spenser's original intention. An intention does not suggest rigorous adherence to every article of a preordained scheme but a more loosely conceived bending of the narrative around a general form—a practice that would make such inconsistencies as we find in the "Letter" surprising but not incredible. What would scarcely seem credible is the proposition that Spenser, having referred indirectly in the first three books to the scheme that is more fully described in the "Letter," nevertheless did not think out the scheme in detail until after those books were complete, for in that case he would surely have taken care to avoid inconsistency with a narrative that was already complete. Yet this, unlikely as it may seem, is what I suspect Spenser has done. For by deliberately introducing inconsistencies that will jar with a narrative he has already written, Spenser can persuade us that the scheme of the "Letter" must have been devised before the first three books were written. The inconsistencies become tropes of authority.

Because that authority is set forth in a manner that alerts us to the differences between the plan and the actual poem, the differences themselves are transferred from the field of writing to the field of reading, where the play between text and intention allows a certain freedom of movement in the interpretative game. Thus the problem of discovering the true relation of the "Letter" to *The Faerie Queene*—is it a plan of the whole or a part of the process?—is re-positioned for us as its readers. Do we take the "Letter" to be an originative scheme with which all narrative deviancy in the poem must be squared and toward which all interpretation must be directed? Or should we describe the relation of the "Letter" to the three books that precede it in time as William Blissett has described the relation of "Mutabilitie" to the six books Spenser had completed in 1596, as a "detached retrospective commentary" emerging at that point in the process of writing but also serving as a finale?[11] The subtlety of Blissett's analysis lies not in his demonstration of the finality of "Mutabilitie" as a coda, but in his allowing for the possibility of that finality being effaced were Spenser to have carried on with his writing and incorporated "Mutabilitie" in a continuation of the epic. While we cannot, of course, speculate further in this direction, we may recognize the curiously ambiguous positional status of the cantos themselves, a status that might be described as one of final incompleteness. In some respects, the "Letter to Raleigh" offers the reader a parallel case, one in which a "detached retrospective commentary" at the conclusion of everything written so far is incorporated in and changed by what follows. But is it incorporated or is it abandoned? Before turning to this question, we may examine how some of Spenser's editors have confronted the problem.

The 1609 folio of *The Faerie Queene*, in which Matthew Lownes prints for the first time the "Mutabilitie Cantos," does not print the "Letter" (having used 1596 as copy-text). However, in many copies of Spenser's *Works* printed in folio by Lownes between 1611 and 1617, the "Letter" appears (with the poems associated with it in its only previous appearance, that of 1590) on an uncommitted quire signed with the pilcrow (¶-¶8, ¶8 wanting in some copies and blank in others). Of this quire there are two separate printings (with identical signatures) conjecturally dated 1611 and 1617— the dates when Lownes printed title pages for his collected editions. Generally speaking these editions were put together at need throughout this period using separate printings of individual works. Thus, in many copies of the *Works, The Faerie Queene* appears in the 1609 folio, which is bound with later printings of the minor poems. In one copy of the 1611 folio of Spenser's *Works*, for instance, a copy that uses *The Faerie Queene* of 1609 and prints the minor poems on separate signatures ending with the "Visions of Petrarch," there is, at the conclusion of the volume, the uncommitted quire signed with the pilcrow (¶-¶7, ¶8 wanting), in which the "Letter" is separated from *The Faerie Queene* by all of Spenser's minor poems. In other copies this signature migrates from the back of the book to a position immediately following the colophon on the verso of the last page of the epic, that is, where a modern editor would be most likely to place it. But in a copy of a later edition, that of 1617, the "Letter" appears after *The Shepherd's Calendar* and before the remaining minor poems; and in others it remains at the back of the volume. It was signed, in effect, to have no position.

The purpose of printers' marks such as the pilcrow and the asterisk was to signify material that might be bound anywhere in the volume once it was printed, although usually such marks were used for preliminary material bound before signature A. The pilcrow thus indicates a certain freedom of movement possessed by the quire so signed: its signature does not underwrite, like ordinary signatures, a fixed position in the text but mobility within the text or even between texts. Whereas regular, alphabetical signatures lock specific quires into their places inside the folio so that we can instantly tell when one is out of its place, the pilcrow signifies the externality of the leaves with which it is signed. But even this external position is not at all fixed, since the quire signed with the pilcrow may be bound anywhere inside the volume. Because it is signed neither inside nor outside the volume, it is capable of invading the text at any point, of escaping the text to stand far apart, or of oscillating between two positions. And because it has no position whatever, it draws our attention to its positionality, that is, its capacity to make us interfere with the poem in different ways according to where we happen to place the "Letter to Raleigh."

We have seen, however, that there is one position into which the "Letter" cannot be conveyed by the pilcrow because that position no longer exists: the original position in which Spenser placed it. Even when the "Letter" is placed in the Lownes texts in what now seems the normative position, after "Mutabilitie," that placement does not lie perfectly on what I have called the "b" axis of its original position: at the end of everything that has been written as a disclosure of the poem's original "conceit." For in the Lownes editions the "Letter" is placed after the colophon on the verso of the last leaf of the folio containing *The Faerie Queene* (i.e., on the outside) and *before* the first signature of the minor poems. It is quite literally an external segment of text inserted into the space between the two inward-turning folds of Spenser's *oeuvre*.

This as yet unanchored position of the "Letter" may be confirmed if we note in passing the only other edition of the seventeenth century, that of Roger L'Estrange in 1679, in which the "Letter" migrates back into the middle of the minor poems, following the "Visions of Petrarch" and preceding "Brittains Ida" (now known to be by Phineas Fletcher). It is in this peculiarly unclassified position that the "Letter" is for the first time given a signature (4A, misprinted as 3A) that fixes its position in one place.

In the first scholarly edition of *The Faerie Queene*, that of Hughes in 1715, this ambiguity is strikingly resolved in favour of the interiority of the "Letter": it is placed at the front, after a few preliminaries and a glossary, and separated from the opening lines of *The Faerie Queene* only by the commendatory and dedicatory poems associated with it.[12] By this positioning of the "Letter" at the "wel-head" we are no longer inclined to think of it as commentary rising up at one moment in the stream of the poet's act of creation. We think of it instead as an original intention present at the source and active from the centre throughout. Small wonder that eighteenth-century criticism of *The Faerie Queene* was uniformly preoccupied with Spenser's design.

We may note here in passing an interesting adjustment of this arrangement, or, to be more precise, an interesting qualification of the assertion it makes. This occurs in Thomas Birch's edition of 1751 which, like several others of the period, places the "Letter" and its poems at the front but insulates this material from the epic by a lengthy apparatus of collation tables, glossaries, and a memoir of the poet.[13] Thus the assertion made by placing the "Letter" at the start—that it is more than a commentary because it reveals the poet's original intention—is qualified by surrounding it with material the status of which is obviously marginal. It is suggested that the "Letter," though standing at the front as the poet's essential idea, belongs just as much to the external realm of commentary as it does to the internal realm of intention.

In another edition of the period, that of Ralph Church (1758), something more remarkable occurs.[14] The "Letter" is again positioned at the front of the volume but the dedicatory and commendatory poems, which had always followed the "Letter" since its first appearance in 1590, are now placed before it. This is the final adjustment necessary for transposing the "Letter" from the end to the beginning of *The Faerie Queene* and for making it into an unambiguous explication of Spenser's idea. For when Hughes moved the "Letter" with its associate poems to the front of the text he inadvertently permitted those poems to intervene between the "Letter" and the epic. Therefore, by placing the associate poems before the "Letter" in the linear sequence of the text, Church restored them to the position they had always held with respect to the "Letter," that is, on the side opposite *The Faerie Queene*. Once again the "Letter" can lie alongside the text of the poem.

3

I have spoken of Grosart's criticism of this practice and of his movement of the "Letter" back to the position originally given to it by Lownes: after Book VII. And I have said that even if Grosart had placed the "Letter" after the third book he would still not have got it right since Spenser effaced the original position of the "Letter" simply by extending the poem. I have also observed that Spenser's omission of the "Letter" in 1596 has been explained both as an absence—that the "Letter," being no longer relevant to the poem, was no longer a part of it—and as a presence, that the "Letter" had become so completely internalized in the narrative of Books IV–VI that its repetition on the outside of the poem, as something "annexed," would be supererogatory. Is it incorporated or is it abandoned?

I wish to state now why we can approve neither alternative. If we position the "Letter" at the beginning of the epic we imply that it shows us an original idea, or a presence (Faerie court), working from the inside at every moment of the epic's development and realizing its *telos* increasingly with time, such that it is eventually unnecessary to have the "Letter" at all (just as we remove from the garden the picture of the flower we have planted once it has grown). And if we position the "Letter" at the end of the poem, or after the third book—or even if we choose to position it nowhere—we imply that it is a moment of criticism Spenser subsequently pushed outside his margins. But we have seen that the "Letter" is invested neither with the exteriority of commentary nor with the interiority of an informing idea. It is both an act of criticism that arises belatedly in the course of the writing and the record of an original conception that has informed Spenser's epic from the start. And it is neither. In a practical, editorial sense as well as in a metaphysical sense, we can position the "Letter to Raleigh" nowhere. And yet we are not at all justified in positioning it nowhere if by that we mean simply leaving it out.

Like those musical compositions by Stockhausen and Boulez in which the order of the parts may be changed with each performance, the "Letter" must be allowed to move where it will—where we will—and to declare by the indeterminacy of its position the more powerful fact of its positionality, its ability to oscillate between inside and outside according to the vicissitudes of interpretative play. The positionality of the "Letter" forces us to relinquish the notion, a perhaps slightly idolatrous one, of *The Faerie Queene* as an object enclosed in itself and in relation to which all commentary is an explication—literally a folding-out of what is folded in—of analogies we pretend to have discovered inside it. By recognizing that there is no place where the "Letter" can be situated in a fully responsible text, we are free to engage it as a flexible aid in accomplishing what reading the poem is all about: interpretative play. Considered from this point of view, the "Letter to Raleigh" is a kind of moveable template through which the reader—acting within the circuit instead of positioning himself, as an analyst, above it—may insert information into the text at any point.

I suppose there are examples of this sort of bibliographical problem in music. But *The Faerie Queene* is the only instance I know of in literary studies in which a supplementary text requires us, when we try to understand its relation to the principal text, to position it under erasure.

I wish to thank the staff of the Rare Books Department of Olin Library, Cornell University, and the staff of the Thomas Fisher Rare Book Library, University of Toronto.

NOTES

1. Sigmund Freud, *From the History of an Infantile Neurosis*, vol. 17 in *The Standard Edition of the Complete Psychological Works*, ed. and trans. by James Strachey, Anna Freud *et al.* (London: Hogarth Press, 1955), 29. For the following account of interpretation in Freud, I am indebted to Stanley Fish's "Withholding the Missing Portion: Power, Meaning and Persuasion in Freud's 'the Wolf-Man'," *Times Literary Supplement* (29 Aug. 1986), 935–38.

2. "Withholding the Missing Portion," 935.

3. *Spenser's Faerie Queene*, ed. J.C. Smith, 2 vols. (Oxford: Clarendon Press, 1909). The italics, as I point out elsewhere, appear in the only edition of the "Letter" to appear in Spenser's lifetime.

4. James Nohrnberg, *The Analogy of* The Faerie Queene (Princeton: Princeton Univ. Press, 1976), xii.

5. It is a practice of Renaissance authors (witness Chapman) to place certain statements they have made in a position and in a voice that would suggest that those statements had been made by an editor.

6. *The Complete Works in Verse and Prose of Spenser*, ed. Alexander Grosart, 10 vols. (n.p.: 1882–84), vol. 5, 4: "Dr. Morris, though his text is that of 1590, prefixes these appendices, herein following the (bad) example of later editions. I unhesitatingly recur to the original arrangement of appending (though necessarily at the close of the whole)." Despite his pointed reference to Morris's copy-text for Books I–III being 1590, Grosart makes the startling assertion that the "Letter" was reprinted in 1596, an assertion he supports by giving inconsistent page numbers and by referring the reader to a non-existent bibliographical discussion in his first volume (vol. 8, 314). He seems also to have been misled by entries in the Stationers' Register for 1604 (Arber vol. 3, 269 and vol. 3, 274) when the copyright passed from Ponsonby to Waterson to Lownes, into imagining a folio for that year (vol. 5, 3).

7. Jacques Derrida, *Positions* (Paris: Minuit, 1972), 88–89. A passage on pp. 13–14 of this book is curiously reminiscent of Spenser: "Tous ces textes, qui sont sans doute la préface interminable à un autre texte que j'aimerais avoir un jour la force d'écrire, ou encore l'epigraphe à un autre dont je n'aurais jamais eu l'audace, ne font, en effet, que commenter telle phrase sur un labyrinthe de chiffres...." For some points concerning the term *position* I have drawn from the seminar, "Le terme de *position*: emplois, sens, implications," given by Jacques Derrida at the Cornell Society for the Humanities in September, 1986.

8. I am indebted to J.C. Smith's bibliographical discussion prefacing the first volume of his edition of *Spenser's Faerie Queene* and especially to Francis R. Johnson's *Critical Bibliography of the Works of Edmund Spenser Printed before 1700* (Baltimore: Johns Hopkins Press, 1933). I have examined for this project the copies available in the Olin library at Cornell University: one copy of 1590; two copies of 1596; two copies of the 1609 folio, both of which are bound in with later editions of the minor poems and one of which contains a later printing of the "Letter"; three copies of the *Works* bearing the date 1611 on the title-page (one on microfilm: S.T.C. 23084), two of which place the "Letter" after the colophon (dated 16012 [sic]) for the second part of *The Faerie Queene*, one of which places the "Letter" at the end of the *Works*; two copies of the *Works* bearing the date

1617 on the title-page, one (on microfilm S.T.C. 23085) placing the "Letter" between *The Shepherd's Calender* and the remaining minor poems, the other placing the "Letter" between *The Faerie Queene* and the minor poems. As mentioned in my text, Lownes printed twice the pilcrow signature bearing the "Letter" and the poems associated with it, probably, as Johnson argues (37–38), in 1611 and 1617 when he printed the title pages. Examples of both printings are distributed throughout the copies I have seen.

9. Guyon is not assigned the adventure of Acrasia at Faerie court. Scudamour is not the patron of the virtue represented in the third book.

10. *Le Lettere di Torquato Tasso*, ed. Cesare Guasti (Naples: 1857) vol. 1, no. 79. For a comparison of Tasso's "prose allegory" and Spenser's "Letter," see John Hughes's edition of *The Works of Mr. Edmund Spenser* (London: 1715), lii–liv.

11. William Blissett, "Spenser's *Mutabilitie*," *Essays in English Literature from the Renaissance to the Victorian Age*, ed. Millar MacLure and F.W. Watt (Toronto: Univ. of Toronto Press, 1964), 26.

12. *The Works of Mr. Edmund Spenser*, ed. John Hughes (London: 1715).

13. *The Faerie Queene*, ed. Thomas Birch (London: 1751).

14. *The Faerie Queene*, ed. Ralph Church (London: 1758).

SPENSER AT THE STILL POINT: A SCHEMATIC DEVICE IN "EPITHALAMION"

Germaine Warkentin

Spenser's wedding hymn *Epithalamion* shares with his *Cantoes of Mutabilitie* a preoccupation with the way individual moments in time take their deepest meaning from, and at the same time bestow the intensity of human experience upon, the cosmological setting in which they occur. As Russell J. Meyer has shown, the allegorical pageants and philosophical debate of the *Cantoes* are firmly grounded in a specific historical occasion (nonetheless wondrous for that): the lunar eclipse of 14 April 1595.[1] In the *Cantoes*, Spenser is thus providing a lively, highly figured yet closely reasoned explanation of an entirely public phenomenon, the experience of which was shared by everyone who witnessed the eclipse. And in doing so he at the same time explores an issue fraught (in the last decade of Elizabeth's reign) with public concern: the reconciliation of stability with change. It is interesting to consider the *Cantoes* and *Epithalamion* together, not only because Meyer's more precise dating of the *Cantoes* situates them close to Spenser's great wedding hymn in the poet's creative life, but because the two works can be seen as a diptych which frames the problem of change in deliberately juxtaposed modes: the ceremonial element in *Epithalamion* contrasts with the use of mock epic in the *Cantoes*, the classical allegory of the *Cantoes* with the domestic religious spirit of *Epithalamion*, the civic alarm raised by Mutabilitie's defiance with the private sacrament represented in the poet's marriage. In what follows we should keep in mind Spenser's seeming need to work with such juxtapositions, which in their combinatory pairings seek not only likeness, but difference as well.

The contrasts just mapped have their equivalents in the architecture of the works themselves. The fascination of Meyer's discovery notwithstanding, the *Cantoes of Mutabilitie* pose fewer critical problems than *Epithalamion*; both poems demand greatness of understanding from their readers, but few who take up the *Cantoes* will be much mystified by their mock heroic genre or the familiar pantheon of symbolic personages. In fact it is essential to its effect that the poem, however rich in nuance, be generously accessible to the reader, for all of its mystery is calculated to gather at the end about the veiled and unapproachable figure of "Great Nature, ever young and full of eld," in whom (as her epithet reminds us) likeness and difference are both exhibited and reconciled. Spenser is a genius at withholding effects until he has prepared us for them, and sometimes he works by the operation of contraries, as is certainly the experience of those attracted at first by Mutabilitie's eloquence and the seeming justice of her case who eventually meet as she does with that awesome and succinct presence.

Of course for generations of readers it is *Epithalamion* which has seemed the more straightforward poem; its unified narrative of the joys of a provincial wedding day, and the intensity of its sacramental commitment, draw instant assent from many who know few other Renaissance poems, and especially from those who have recognized in it a central experience of their own private lives. But as the accumulating body of scholarship on the poem's formal structure has shown, there is an equal privacy in Spenser's "device" for his wedding hymn. Hidden within it is a calendrical armature which was first revealed by A. Kent Hieatt in 1960.[2] The existence of that remarkable example of "constructive" form (the term is James Winn's[3]) is now debated by few, but the general consent masks a number of controversies about the ways in which the local elements of such a schematic design might be articulated into the whole. The problems raised by these conflicting or unassimilable details are representative of the whole spectrum of doubts raised in the minds of sceptical readers by constructive form in general and numerological schematics in particular, though as John MacQueen has pointed out, the aesthetic and symbolic function of proportional composition—and indeed its scientific rationale—has been well understood in architecture, music, and art history for some time.[4] The case for such methods of composition has been deftly made by R.G. Peterson, who finds that the most persistent feature of constructive form is symmetry, but points out that symmetrical elements have to be "in fruitful relationship (harmony, contrast, conflict, etc.) with obvious narrative, thematic, or symbolic concerns in the work."[5]

A representative crux in the interpretation of *Epithalamion* has in fact been the alleged "pairing" of the poem's stanzas to create symmetry. Hieatt argued that Spenser carefully matched each of the stanzas from one to twelve with those from thirteen to twenty-four by means of internal allusion. His proposal was attacked by Enid Welsford, and Max Wickert eventually proposed that the stanzas are paired, but to achieve symmetry rather than congruity: "the imaginative order of the poem's second half is not a *da capo* repetition but a mirror inversion of the imaginative order of the first half." William V. Davis and J.C. Eade produced details which substantiated Hieatt; Lee T. Pearcy followed Wickert.[6] Both ways of reading produce undeniable parallels and contrasts between certain pairs of stanzas but less convincing ones for other pairs; the attempts to mate stanza four with either sixteen (in Hieatt's case) or twenty-one (in Wickert's) is particularly unsatisfactory. And of course both schemas are completely consistent (and thus completely rigid) in structure.

The intractability of the problem of pairing is symptomatic of other puzzles posed by interpretative details in the apparent schema of the poem which themselves founder on the objection of inconsistency. The wedding day, 11 June, is the 103d day from 1 March, first day of the lunar year in the almanac regularly printed in the *Book of Common Prayer*; why then, in a carefully crafted numerological poem is the poet's plea "let this one day be mine" made at line 105, a conjunction too close not to be noticed and too imperfect not to be debated? Do inconsistencies like these constitute the "one flaw in the weave" which a carpet or quilt maker leaves behind to signify the hand of a human maker, or to give the spirit of the work its necessary exit? Possibly so, but given the comprehensiveness of Spenser's vision and method, we ought to consider as well what role in the achievement of a cosmologically significant compositional schema might be played by the deliberate inclusion of variations, exceptions, and flaws.

If we concede the minimum, that *Epithalamion* has a calendrical structure, what guidance can be drawn from Spenser's choice of this option? The most obvious is that time is of central importance for the poem, but this does not tell us how Spenser envisioned time. Though his poem takes us sequentially through the events of a single day, "this one day" as he fervently calls it when in stanza seven he claims it as his own, the limited plane of sequential time is situated within a frame possessing several dimensions, levels of existence both below and above that occupied by the eager groom which he must, as he passes through the day upon his own plane, come to know and acknowledge. In this multi-dimensional construct Spenser integrates into a single structure several different temporal orders: that of nature with its days and seasons, the individual who is born and dies, the ferial routine of village life and the festal cycle of the church, the heavenly bodies in their dutiful rounds, and finally the eschatological realm which in the fullness of time will absorb and replace all. Mythopoeically, this vision of time is so tightly integrated that a purely sequential reading is hardly adequate to penetrate its complexity. Like the overtones produced by harmonic chant, the intersecting temporal planes of the poem create a multiplex environment for Spenser's chosen day, one which we have to seek out architectural or sculptural terms to describe; *Epithalamion*, Pearcy observes, is like an orrery, a spatial model of the planetary system.[7] But anything which represents time cannot do so without grasping change, not only the serene rhythm of time's regular motions but unexpected variation and blighting transience as well. Everywhere in his work Spenser insists that it is the very nature of being to unleash in its operations the forces which would seek to undermine it. In constructing his "orrery" (the name itself did not come into use until the seventeenth century) Spenser is framing a statement about the inextricable relationship of the changeless and the variable which T.S. Eliot, in *Burnt Norton*, had to handle by verbal sleight-of-hand: "Except for the point, the still point, / There would be no dance, and there is only the dance."

Spenser's use of spatial in addition to verbal organizing devices can be documented widely in his work, but it is peculiarly visible in one minute but very illuminating feature of *Epithalamion*. The limited scale the poet exploits here makes it possible both to examine closely his imposition of a unifying pattern, and to consider specific questions raised by its apparent flaws. As we saw, readers are divided on the question of whether, and if so in what way, Spenser "paired" the stanzas of *Epithalamion*. But if pairing is a constructive feature of the architecture of the poem, perhaps we should ask what is in fact being paired? A good place to begin with Spenser is always "in the middest," and contemplating the central stanzas of *Epithalamion*— central both thematically and numerically—we notice that they are united not only by their subject, the long-awaited wedding ceremony, but by their line-length, which is nineteen lines each. What happens when, prompted by this hint, we lay out in sequence the line-lengths of the stanzas of *Epithalamion*? The answer is, not much; the pattern yielded is as follows: 18, 18, 19, 18, 18, 18, 19, 19, 19, 18, 19, 19, 19, 19, 17, 18, 19, 19, 19, 19, 18, 19, 18, 7. Though there are evident groups of stanzas, and these groups are interrupted by single stanzas or other groups of different length, there seems to be no regular rhythm in the occurrence either of groups or single stanzas. Only in the case stanza fifteen is there that sharp variation which by the very element of surprise would disclose the presence of the rhythm it interrupts.

But if we return to the stanzas "in the middest" we will find that since twelve and thirteen are paired, so may be eleven and fourteen, for each of these has nineteen lines as well. If so, this would suggest that Spenser might have envisioned a concentric arrangement of the stanzas rather than a sequential patterning. Yet this is hard to credit, since even the beginning reader quickly notices Spenser's spatial comedy in stanza fifteen, where the poet produces a seventeen line stanza for the bridegroom to complain of his ill-fortune in wedding on the longest day and bedding on the shortest night of the year. Stanza fifteen thus can have no mate, though it might be the exception that proves some rule. As we shall see, this is not quite the case, but if we proceed by treating stanza fifteen as a functional variation, we find that the concentric pattern resumes, and the line-lengths of Spenser's stanzas can be paired with a degree of consistency which insists on explanation. Ten and sixteen, nine and seventeen, eight and eighteen, seven and nineteen all pair; there is then a hiatus, but the pattern again recurs to mate four with twenty-one, three with twenty-two, and two with twenty-three. In each case, a stanza in the first half of the poem is paired in line-length with one in the second half, and the result is a concentric scheme. (See figure 1.)

If we consider this design as a simple act of construction, what features do we observe? First and most obvious is that the pattern—if such it is—cannot be "read" sequentially; it is strictly spatial, and thus is inaccessible to solely verbal apprehension. Second, besides the device of pairing it has three contrarious features which undermine

Figure 1

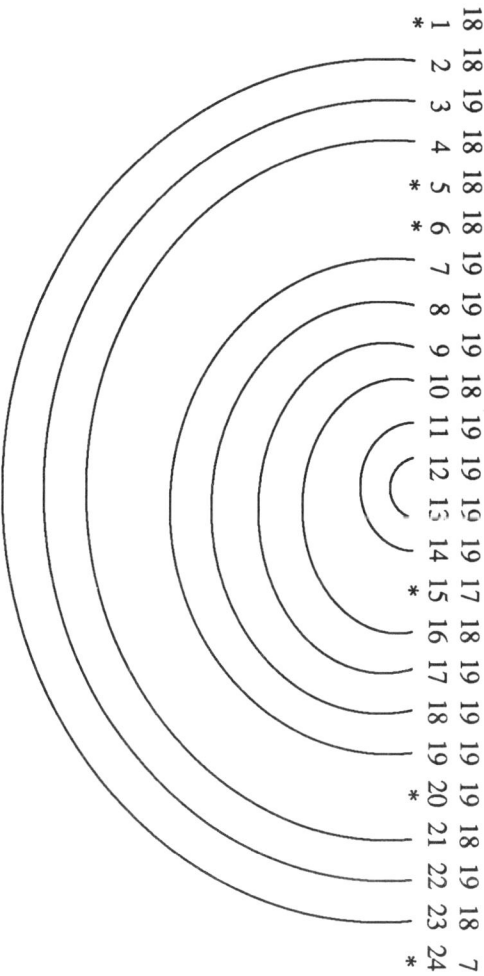

its consistency: the solitude of stanza fifteen, the failure of stanzas one and twenty-four to pair, and the marked variation created by five and six in the first half—each eighteen lines and without a mate in the second half—and stanza twenty in the second half, which is nineteen lines and occurs where the stanza pairing with five or six ought to be. Not only are these three exceptions disruptions of the pattern, but they differ markedly with each other and thus do not constitute, as a group, the elements of a different but internally consistent pattern designed to contrast with the architectural order of the poem as a whole.

The singularity of stanza fifteen, with its seventeen lines, is of course the easiest to interpret, for the numerical joke in the total number of lines produces a releasing element of impudent humour in a poem otherwise joyously dignified. Stanza fifteen is also an important signal of Spenser's architectural purpose, for along with the transparent twenty-four hour / twenty-four stanza schema of the whole, it pointedly alerts us to the role of constructive composition in the making of the poem. Fifteen is not the only stanza with a unique line-length, however; stanza twenty-four has only seven lines, which means that of course it cannot be paired with stanza one. This exception too has its reasons. One and twenty-four have the special function of framing the entire design; this in itself might lead the poet to set them off in some way from the others, though it would not prevent him from matching them in line-length if he wished. But in choosing to make *Epithalamion* resemble, within reason, the Italian *canzone*, Spenser committed himself to the characteristic short terminal "commiato" of that genre. Thus the brevity of stanza twenty-four is not unexpected like that of stanza fifteen, but positively necessary, and this necessity binds it securely to stanza one by a contrastive device which is quite in accordance with generic norms, and which like stanza fifteen exploits the power of contrariousness to make the poem's design both firm and expressive.

There remain the final puzzling anomalies represented by stanzas five, six, and twenty. Surrounded by concentric linkages, these stanzas stand as exceptions to the design; they cannot be made to mate, though one of them should pair with stanza twenty. Stanzas five and six in fact pair with each other, both in their line-length (eighteen) and in their theme, for they deal with the awakening of the bride from her last maiden slumber. If, with this in mind, we turn to stanza twenty, we suddenly see the resourcefulness of Spenser's method, for in stanza twenty the consummation of the marriage takes place, the awakening of the bride into what Elizabethan marriage doctrine insisted was for her the completing life of marriage. Stanzas five and six thus seem to act as handmaidens to stanza twenty: they are two and it is one, their eighteen lines are less, its nineteen lines are more, they prepare and in it is the act. In counterpoising these stanzas at crucial points in his design Spenser has turned away from his constructive scheme towards something more thematic. Yet he escapes his design only to return to it in a spatial paradox: the "pairing" of the two passages on awakening, one in the first half of the poem and one in the second cannot in fact be achieved within the poem's hour-by-hour progression through the events of the spousal day without the interposition of stanza fifteen, with its impertinent flouting of the pattern.

Spenser has thus paired the stanzas of *Epithalamion* in such a way that variations in the overall pattern are made to serve a functional purpose. This is in fact a principle we accept in one of the chief instances of constructive form familiar to us, that of versification. It was Spenser's own generation of poets who confirmed that the metrical patterns evolving in their day required stress-shift, rather than relentless regularity in order to make their rhythmic system expressive. Modulation from key to key in music operates on something of the same principle, as does the musical genre of "theme and variations." In each case a dominant pattern is interrupted by elements which assert their own individuality, yet reveal by contrast the characteristics of the overall scheme of the work. Such an exploitation of variety was made possible, in part, by the extensive debate on the subject of variation, change, and the unpredictable energies of innovation which naturally played a role in the evolution of the cohesive cosmological model prevailing from antique times to Spenser's own day. A considerable literature rose up to explain these transgressive energies, of which one of the best-known texts in Spenser's own generation was Louis Le Roy's *De La Vicissitude ou varieté des choses* (1575), translated into English in 1594; Werner L. Gundersheimer has summarized what is known about Spenser's evident knowledge of this and other works of Le Roy.[8] Le Roy's cyclical historiography is in fact devoted to rationalizing in terms of a secure providential cosmology the more uncomfortable issues raised by innovation in his day. But the influence of his work demonstrates how general was the view that order and change, likeness and difference, were closely linked, thought it is a view we must now labour to recapture. It is not hard to see why a poet of insight adopting a constructive schema would weave variation as well order into his pattern so as to make ever more complex and suggestive statements.

This certainly appears to be the case in *Epithalamion*, for if we pursue yet one more step the pairing of the stanzas in the poem, we find that Spenser has not only imposed a schema and then devised variations which flatter it, but has used the resulting tension between likeness and dissimilarity to extend even further the significance of his poem. There are thus nine pairs in all, and nearly every stanza is linked to its mate by some exquisite detail, several of which have already been noted either by Hieatt or Wickert. Hymen's "Tead" in stanza two reappears in the "thousand torches flaming bright" of stanza twenty-three; the nymphs of stanza three create a pictorial group balanced by Juno and Genius, Hebe and Hymen in twenty-two; the fish of stanza four, emblems of Christ who brings spiritual life, by an awesome juxtaposition are given their human counterpart in the "timely seed" of stanza twenty-one. In stanza seven the poet pleads that "fayrest Phoebus, father of the Muse" will give him "this one day," in its mate stanza nineteen those powers of persuasion stand alone against the spirits unleashed by darkness; in stanza eight maids and men are invited to sing and in stanza eighteen they are instructed to cease; in stanza nine the bride walks forth and in stanza seventeen she is brought into the bridal bower.

Some of these devices are obvious (2/23, 8/18, 9/17); others, particularly the pairing of stanza four (which also proved difficult for Hieatt and Wickert) require contemplation before their connection sheds its mystery. But all of the pairings depend on resemblance or likeness of some sort. And at the pinnacle of the structure there is, of course, the focal similitude of the whole construction, the paired nineteen line stanzas of the wedding ceremony in which the "Anthem" of the human choristers unites with the "Alleluya" of the angelic host.

In a contrastive device almost pictorial in character, however, these climactic stanzas are framed by two pairs which employ dissimilarity, rather than likeness, to create their effect. The first element in this contrastive frame is deceptively simple: stanza ten is a blazon of the bride's beauty, but in its mate, stanza sixteen, the poet simply laments the slow passing of time. Here difference, rather than likeness, arrests our attention. In stanza eleven and sixteen this straightforward instance of dissimilitude is complicated by a pairing which evokes at once both like and unlike, concordant and discordant. In stanza eleven the "inward beauty" of the bride is presented to us in an image, that of "Medusaes mazful hed," the incongruity of which, according to Frank B. Young, is deliberately calculated to shock us out of our admiration of the bride's merely physical beauty and prepare us to understand her law-giving power.[9] The pairing of this stanza with its mate shocks even further, for the integrity of the bride, in whom

> ... dwels sweet Love, and constant Chastity,
> Unspotted Fayth, and comely Womanhood,
> Regard of Honour, and mild Modesty,

where

> ... Vertue raynes as queene in royal throne,
> And giveth lawes alone,
> The which the base affections do obay,
> And yeeld theyr services unto her will

is unrestrainedly juxtaposed to the very image of unrestraint itself, the wine god Bacchus:

> Poure out the wine without restraint or stay,
> Poure not by cups, but by the belly full,
> Poure out to all that wull,
> And sprinkle all the postes and wals with wine,
> That they may sweat, and drunken be withall.
> Crowne ye God Bacchus with a coronall,
> And Hymen also crowne with wreathes of vine.

If Hymen is—however joyously—to be crowned with bacchic "wreathes of vine," the poem's centre of gravity must shift and its programme reorganize itself to accommodate the uncontrolled energy of "base affections" apparently still operating in the pattern. Only when the poet is able to display his own powerful music to restore consonance to the harmonic structure of the work, which he does by exorcising the evil spirits of the night, can the discordant clamour of witches and damned ghosts be stilled and blessed silence descend, as it does in stanza twenty, upon the wedding bed.

In *Burnt Norton* Eliot reverts to strictly verbal paradox in an attempt to express the simultaneity of the stable and the changeful; the very stillness of the "still point" has to be conveyed by identifying that which is "other than" stillness itself, and all the tension of the paradox must be borne by language alone. Spenser is perhaps more fortunate, for the strengths of constructive form make it possible for him to solve on one level of his design a problem which seems intransigent on another. I think it probable, for example, that the three different schemes of pairing discussed in this paper do not contradict each other, but reflect consonances achieved by Spenser on different planes of his design. Stanza ten, for example, viewed within a strictly concentric schema, does in fact pair with stanza fifteen as Wickert suggests, with the beauties of the bride being answered by the erotic response of her groom. This is not a weak and conciliatory attempt to admit the merits of different points of view, but rather the recognition of an objective feature of Spenser's poem. Like a great work of architecture, it offers us many vistas; some of its spaces are intimate, others are functional or designed for pure delight, still others are monumental compositions of sobering grandeur. I would go further, and say that in the case of this or any other example of constructive form, it is likely that the poet began the work of composition (and the reader took up his task as well) by imagining the work as an artifact, rather than by thinking of it in the entirely discursive terms we would employ today.

The counterpoising of Virtue and Bacchus in stanzas eleven and sixteen is the culminating formulation of the problem of restraint and energy which throughout both *Amoretti* and *Epithalamion* is approached at the mounting levels of perception which the architecture of the poem makes possible. In *Amoretti* it appears in Petrarchan guise, as a conflict between female obduracy and male complaint. In *Epithalamion* it is present at every point, even in the terminal *commiato*, where "hasty accidents" and "due time" produce a gentle and domestic diminuendo after the eschatological power of stanza twenty-three. Much thought has rightly been given to the way in which the forces at war in Spenser's poem are made to create "recompense."[10] But of equal importance is the way that need for recompense is *induced* in the poem. Spenser's will to investigate those areas in which our confidence in the order of things breaks down is very great, and he continues to pose the conundrum of the "still point" in ever more interinvolved structures, even to the eighth "unperfite" canto of *The Faerie Queene*. There he meditates first on the overwhelming sway of Mutabilitie in earthly things, and then on Nature's forecast of the coming of "that same time when no more *Change* shall be." Though his concluding prayer is that God will grant him "that Sabaoths sight," his present condition is still earthly, and that blessing has yet to be vouchsafed. It is therefore no surprise that his meditation is expressed not in one summary stanza, but in two separate ones which mirror and balance each other. Unless, of course, in their separateness they are meant to sign the shape of existence as mortals conceive it with yet one more emblem of the mortal plane, that "sodden floor" where, as Eliot puts it in *Burnt Norton*,

> Below, the boarhound and the boar
> Pursue their pattern as before
> Though reconciled among the stars.

NOTES

1. Russell J. Meyer, " 'Fixt in heavens hight': Spenser, Astronomy, and the Date of the *Cantoes of Mutabilitie*," *Spenser Studies* 4 (1984): 115–29.

2. A. Kent Hieatt, *Short Time's Endless Monument: The Symbolism of the Numbers in Edmund Spenser's "Epithalamion"* (New York: Columbia Univ. Press, 1960).

3. Constructive form is discussed by James Winn, *Unsuspected Eloquence: A History of the Relations Between Poetry and Music* (New Haven: Yale Univ. Press, 1981).

4. John MacQueen, *Numerology: Theory and Outline History of a Literary Mode* (Edinburgh: Edinburgh Univ. Press, 1985), 2–3.

5. R.G. Peterson, "Critical Calculations: Measure and Symmetry in Literature," *PMLA* 91 (1976): 367–75.

6. Hieatt, *Short Time's Endless Monument*; see also his "The Daughters of Horus: Order in the Stanzas of *Epithalamion*," in *Form and Convention in the Poetry of Edmund Spenser*, ed. William Nelson (New York: Columbia Univ. Press, 1961), 103–121. In addition see Enid Welsford, *Spenser: Fowre Hymnes and Epithalamion: A Study of Edmund Spenser's Doctrine of Love* (Oxford: Basil Blackwell, 1967), Appendix II *passim*; Max Wickert, "Structure and Ceremony in Spenser's 'Epithalamion'," *ELH* 35 (1968): 135–57; William V. Davis, "Edmund Spenser's 'Epithalamion'," *American Notes & Queries* 7 (1969): 84–85; J.C. Eade, "The Pattern in the Astronomy of Spenser's 'Epithalamion'," *Review of English Studies* n.s. 23 (1972): 173–78; Lee T. Pearcy, "A Case of Allusion: Stanza 18 of Spenser's 'Epithalamion' and Catullus 5," *Classical and Modern Literature* 1 (1981): 243–54.

7. Pearcy, *ibid.*, 248.

8. Werner L. Gundersheimer, *The Life and Works of Louis Le Roy*, Travaux d'humanisme et Renaissance no. 82 (Geneva: Droz, 1966), 133–35.

9. Frank B. Young, "Medusa and the 'Epithalamion': A Problem in Spenserian Imagery," *English Language Notes* 11 (1973): 21–29.

10. Hieatt, *Short Time's Endless Monument*; Welsford, *Spenser: Fowre Hymnes and Epithalamion*; but see also Richard Neuse, "The Triumph Over Hasty Accidents: A Note on the Symbolic Mode of the 'Epithalamion'," *Modern Language Review* 61 (1966): 163–74, and Sherman Hawkins, "Mutabilitie and the Cycle of the Months," in *Form and Convention in the Poetry of Edmund Spenser*, 76–102.

DONNE'S "ANNIVERSARIES" AND THE BEATIFICATION OF ELIZABETH DRURY BY POETIC LICENCE

René Graziani

"'Tis no one thing": Donne's humorous complaint about Thomas Coryat's book of travels is one of those spontaneous remarks coming around to an artist's own mental habits. One would expect poems on the scale of the *Anniversaries*, however, to pursue the "one thing" by more than one means. Especially as Donne was forcing new combinations on traditional kinds. He was appearing simultaneously as elegist, satirist of the times, and visionary poet. The praises of a girl "scarce fifteen"[1] are tuned to a very high pitch indeed to produce intimations of the beatific vision. No simple verdict seems possible on the question of genre. Funeral elegy, satire, poetry of praise, poetry of meditation and philosophical poetry all contribute to this unique work.[2] To keep his different lines together, Donne relied on a number of opposites, body and soul, the world and Elizabeth Drury, and also on a number of unifying conceptions associated with her, notably as the world's soul and as the image of God reflected in man.[3] To be added to these is the unifying force of the image he had in mind when he called both poems the *Anniversaries*. The nature of the occasion intended is my first topic. I do not see it establishing a definitive genre. It should, however, clarify the relation between the two individual poems, *An Anatomy of the World* (1611) and *Of the Progresse of the Soule* (1612) enough to make their being "one thing" more apparent. There is some risk of stating the obvious here, since Donne went a long way towards explaining matters himself. However, commentary to date seems to have missed Donne's idea.

At their simplest, Donne's "anniversaries" undertake an annual commemoration of Elizabeth Drury's death in early December 1610. But beyond this lie some significant alternatives. One is the anniversary as a funereal rite of renewed mourning. This may have been common, and its roots would be in the trentals and anniversaries of the Catholic past, as preserved, for instance, in the records of chantries at St. Paul's.[4] There do not, however, seem to be any extant *poems* of this type before Donne's, though allusions of a sort exist such as the fictional one in *Much Ado* of Claudio's intended performance of sorrowful rites to Hero every year: "Midnight assist our moan: Help us to sigh and groan, Heavily, heavily."[5] George Puttenham reported on lamentation in a similar spirit: "chiefly at the very burialls of the dead, also at monethes mindes and longer times, by custome repeated yearely, when as they used many offices of seruice and loue towardes the dead." Puttenham also mentions "poeticall mournings in verse."[6]

The reader does not find this mood in Donne, however; there is little sorrowful recollection. Donne announces celebratory intentions immediately and the mood of his refrain will prove ambiguous, given the view of death he is to take:

Shee, shee is dead; shee's dead; when thou knowst this,
Thou knowst how poore a trifling thing man is.
(*Anatomy*, 184–85)

Death mostly serves as an occasion to regenerate the reader's spiritual life, and Elizabeth Drury's soul has already made a royal departure for heaven. She unmasks a dead world pretending to be still alive. Not until he reaches his "conclusion" does Donne reveal his key paradox, that for Elizabeth physical death was the real birth, into eternal life. The interesting thing is that Donne also fitted this paradox to its proper, traditional occasion, the annual feast of a saint, where the day the saint died was treated as his "real" birthday:

And, blessed maid...
Accept this tribute, and his first yeares rent,
Who till his darke short tapers end be spent,
As oft as thy feast sees this widowed earth,
Will yearely celebrate thy second birth,
That is, thy death. For though the soule of man
Be got when man is made, 'tis borne but than
When man doth die. Our body's as the wombe,
And as a mid-wife death directs it home.
(*Anatomy*, 443–54)

At this point it finally becomes clear that Donne's model of an anniversary is a saint's feast with its official paradox of death as birth, as much as any ordinary annual rite of mourning.[7] One result of recognizing that Elizabeth Drury's role of saint is more than a local conceit is that it explains such features of the *Anniversaries* as the heavy accent on earthly birth as immersion in corruption and gives extra point to other celebrated images such as the phoenix, the decapitation and the trumpet.

The custom of saints' feast-days derived from the anniversaries the primitive Church had kept of its martyrs; the death-day was treated with joy as a birthday into heaven, and this became the basis of *all* saints' feasts (practically: only the Virgin and St. John the Baptist had feasts for their birthdays proper). Donne's work on *Pseudo-martyr* makes it certain he understood these origins, which were no doubt familiar to everyone. Why Donne delayed conveying that this was the kind of anniversary he particularly had in mind is not clear. One possible explanation is that the idea emerged late in the process of composition: that is, the conceit of performing an anatomy on the corpse of the world after Elizabeth Drury's soul had left it was the main idea originally, and what happened to her soul was developed poetically later. I doubt this, however, in the first place because the images of the sick, diminished world and the freed soul seem mutually reinforcing throughout, and also because the soul's progress homeward seems so integral to the opening of the *Anatomy*. Whatever the explanation, the bold conceit of instituting the feast of a new young "saint" makes an effective bridging passage to the *Progresse*. The reader has no chance of settling on a stock response to the soul's departure from the body either here, with the image of a midwife, or later in the conceits of the *Progresse*, notably the startling one where the soul's birth-in-death is likened to a bullet discharged from an old pistol that falls apart as it is fired:

> But thinke that Death hath now enfranchis'd thee,
> Thou hast thy'expansion now and libertee;
> Thinke that a rusty Peece, discharg'd, is flowne
> In peeces, and the bullet is his owne,
> And freely flies....
> (*Progresse*, 179–83)

For convenience, I shall be examining the birth paradox and the image of Elizabeth Drury as a saint separately. However, one should first look at the current scholarship on the anniversary poem. The notion of a sub-type of the elegiac poem known as the *epitaphium anniversarium* was brought to modern critical attention by O.B. Hardison, who found it mentioned in J.C. Scaliger's *Poetices libri VII* (1561).[8] Scaliger, however, had left the *epitaphium anniversarium* a relatively indistinct entity. He cited no example of a surviving poem of the type, but reported only some references to anniversary tributes to the dead among the ancients (it is not clear that these are poems), the most promising-sounding being those that Artemisia was said to have instituted for her husband Mausolus. More recent scholarship by W.B. Lebans has contributed some more *allusions* to what the writer himself terms this "supposed tradition" of the *anniversarium*: the only new one from antiquity is from Ausonius.[9] Working presumably by deduction, Scaliger ruled that the *epitaphium anniversarium* would be identical in its topics with the *epitaphium recens* except that it would not contain lamentation (*luctus*). Applying this solitary distinction to Donne's poems has produced the conclusion that only the second poem is "strictly an 'anniversary'," which is not very helpful.[10] What the current position implies is that Donne derived his poem from an empty shelf of literary history which he proceeded to fill. For his poem, as he had foretold, did influence others and beget imitations, with John Davies of Hereford (1612) and George Chapman among the first.[11]

But Donne did in fact have an important predecessor. This was the Christian poet Paulinus, Bishop of Nola (353–431), who had composed a series of some thirteen anniversary poems for the feast of St. Felix. Probably the reason they escaped Scaliger's net was that Paulinus did not call them anniversaries but treated them as *natalicia* or birthday poems.[12] Paulinus gave special prominence to the established idea of birth through death:

> So this day which we observe with yearly vows is the day not of his suffering but of his burial. On that day the substances of soul and flesh parted from each other. The soul flew to God, the flesh returned to the earth and rested, hidden in the tomb. It is right that this should be the birthday marked out for saints, for on it they discharge the condition of the flesh and are stripped of the bonds of mortality. They are born for God into the heavenly kingdom, and carry with them the happy hope of resurrection. This is the day I have always so venerated that I considered it my birthday in preference to that on which I was vainly born; the day of my birth indeed is more deserving of grief, for when I was born into this world I came forth a sinner from the womb of a sinner, begotten of black wickedness, so that I was already guilty when my mother bore me.

> So accursed be the day on which I was born out of wickedness into wickedness, and blessed be for me, too, the birthday on which my patron Felix was born amongst the dwellers of heaven and arose to assume that power by which he could cleanse me of my foulness, loose me from my bonds, and redeem and absolve me from the grievous death of my birthday.[13]

His project of an annual poem to the saint is expounded, not for the first or last time, in "Natalis VI":

> I have imposed on myself by a vow of devotion the custom of celebrating this day every year by putting my eloquence to work. This custom demands that I sing of Felix in verses as a yearly tribute from my lips. I must set my joy to music in the song I have promised, and sing of the great merits of my dear patron, for he sought the heights through the narrows and along the hard path where few can make their way, and so he reached the citadel of heaven.[14]

A brief résumé will show how fundamentally different Paulinus is from Donne and how little indebted to him Donne is likely to have been for particulars. Paulinus's series started with a short lyric poem expressing excitement as he is about to realize the dream of returning to St. Felix's shrine at Nola to set up a small religious community. A second short poem celebrates the fulfilment of these hopes a year later. After that, the poems grow lengthier and more public. Paulinus describes the crowds who come to Nola to celebrate the Saint's feast-day (III). Natales IV and V are the biography of the Saint. There follow pious tales of the miracles simple folk have reported, proving Felix's sanctity (VI, VII, VIII). Further yearly poems give descriptions of the buildings and decoration of Felix's shrine, or accounts of members of the community or visitors, or touch on contemporary troubles. The last three complete *natalicia* have as a common thread the idea of Christ's power working through Felix and his relics in the present (XI, XII, XIII).

As a poet, Paulinus was a pupil of Ausonius and is considered one of his best students. There appears to be little in his poetics or rhetoric, however, that Donne was likely to imitate. The fact that Paulinus also wrote an elegy on a child's death which develops some key topics of Christian consolation constitutes some further common ground with Donne, but O.B. Hardison found no specific indebtedness when he examined this elegy, *de Celso puero*, and I cannot find any details in the *Anniversaries* indicating Donne used Paulinus' *natalicia* as a "source."[15] Thus there is no hard evidence Donne had read the poems. On the other hand, it seems unlikely that he read so little early Christian Latin poetry that he had not come across Paulinus, often ranked as only second to Prudentius for Christian interest. Paulinus's poems had been published in two editions and were also accessible in two collections of early Christian poets.[16] There are two references to Paulinus in Donne's *Sermons*, but they are to his famous letters, not to his poetry.[17] Nevertheless, Paulinus is the only poet with an anniversary series at all resembling the one Donne announced in the *Anatomy*, and he had made the birth-in-death of a saint's feast-day very prominent, just as Donne went on to do. Hence I am inclined to believe Donne did know Paulinus's *natalicia* and consciously framed his own project on a model amenable to the mixing of death with celebration.

It is reassuring to be able to confirm the gist of the association independently by pointing to Donne's usage of "anniversary" and *natalicia* in a context of saints' feast-days in *Pseudomartyr*, on which he was working in the year before he wrote the *Anatomy*. At one point Donne discusses what makes martyrdom attractive to contemporaries:

> The externall honours, by which the memories of the Orthodox martyrs in the Primitive Church were celebrated and ennobled (as styling their death *Natalitia*, observing their *Anniversaries*, commemorating them at their altars, and instituting Notaries, to register their actions and passions).[18]

This is not the place to probe Donne's attitude to contemporary martyrdom. His reaction was deeply personal, rooted in family experience and his own need to be independent of its pressures. Nevertheless, his antipathy to the modern zeal for dying for religion could be seen as the other side of the praise of Elizabeth Drury for undemonstrative virtue and painless "religious death," almost as if this was stating a personal preference about sainthood.

When Donne came to anatomizing the world and assessing natural man, he adopted a strategy of making physical birth appear in the worst possible light, making the release of the soul at death appear extremely desirable. Birth images related to the birth-is-death paradox appear several times in the *Anatomy*. Birth has the look of fatality, and delivery becomes an emblem of death (from original sin):

> We are borne ruinous: poore mothers crie,
> That children come not right, nor orderly,
> Except they headlong come, and fall upon
> An ominous precipitation. (95–98)

The notorious last line of the following,

> For that first mariage was our funerall
> One woman at one blow, then kill'd us all,
> And singly, one by one, they kill us now. (105–7)

includes the idea that each physical birth is a death, although of course the play on "death" in orgasm gives another indispensable sense. (A point involved is that original sin is transmitted with physical *life*, and is not in the individual soul at its creation by God.[19]) The world too was "almost created lame"; this "almost" becomes "the world did in her Cradle take a fall" to allow for the brief prelude of innocence. Donne considers the beauty of the first creation:

> When nature was most busie, the first weeke,
> Swadling the new-borne earth, God seemd to like,
> That she should sport herselfe sometimes, and play...
> (347–49)

But it is not long before Donne implies the destined death in infancy (371). "*Travail*, grief [and] perishing" sum up earthly existence (434). The suspension of stellar influence on earth takes the form of aborted birth-processes:

> The father, or the mother barren is.
> The clouds conceive not raine, or doe not powre
> In the due birth-time, downe the balmy showre.
> Th'Ayre doth not motherly sit on the earth,
> To hatch her seasons, and give all things birth.
> Spring-times were common cradles, but are toombes;
> And false-conceptions fill the generall wombs. (380–86)

The image of unhatched seasons is supplemented in a later metaphor of the *Progresse*:

Think thy shell broke, think thy soul hatch'd but now. (184)

The Job-like concentration of *odium vitae* on birth is of course a potent argument against taking death sorrowfully.

Donne's image of the decline of the world and of the birth of man into corruption has its roots in his own earlier work. It seems to be no accident that the title of Donne's second Anniversary, *Of the Progresse of the Soule* (1612) closely resembles that of the earlier *The Progresse of the Soule... Metempsychosis* (1601). In the event, the later poem constitutes an answer to the first in a very important respect, the role assigned to woman. In *Metempsychosis* woman is linked closely with the soul's degeneracy, whereas in the *Progresse* she becomes a symbol of human nature redeemed. The earlier work satirically follows a soul through increasingly corporeal and sensory encounters. From the time of "her first making when she was that apple which Eve eat" ("Epistle"), this corrupt soul is united to a succession of lower forms of life and further projected to pass through a series of historical figures only two of whom are named, Mohamet and Luther, though Queen Elizabeth is also suggested: apparently the movement was to be to a contemporary, satirical climax, although this is not certain as the poem is unfinished. Soul is progressively buried in body. In Donne's second *Anniversary*, however, the direction is from the bodily to the spiritual. Elizabeth Drury figures the soul liberated and pursuing its proper aspirations to unobstructed powers and blisses, and reconstituted as a poetic, spiritual example to a world in process of decomposing without her. This Elizabeth is the opposite of Eve, the mother of mankind who "poisoned the well-head."[20] She reverses sin's penalty of death by receiving it as birth. For the Donne who wrote *Metempsychosis* Elizabeth Drury was distinctly palinodic. "Progress" in *Metempsychosis* was ironic. Its soul's first form was Eve's apple as it broke from the Tree of Knowledge of Good and Evil contaminated by the serpent. In a sense its "progress" is literal and legitimate as it moves through a hierarchy of vegetative and animal powers to reach its rational form in man. But what is shown of this is that, mostly, it catches all the worst features of the forms through which it transmigrates: mandrake, cock-sparrow, several fish forms, whale, mouse, wolf's whelp, bitch and ape:

> Keeping some quality
> Of every past shape, she knew treachery,
> Rapine, deceit, and lust, and ills enow
> To be a woman.
> (*Metempsychosis*, 506–09)

The last episode is the soul's entry into mankind (to produce Cain's offspring) and in process of forming the vital organs of a foetus:

> *Adam* and *Eve* had mingled bloods, and now
> Like Chimiques equall fires, her temperate wombe
> Had stew'd and form'd it: and part did become
> A spungie liver, and did richly allow,
> Like a free conduit, on a high hils brow,
> Life-keeping moisture unto every part,
> Part hardned it selfe to a thicker heart,
> Whose busie furnaces lifes spirits do impart.
>
> Another part became the well of sense,
> The tender well-arm'd feeling braine, from whence,
> Those sinowie strings which do our bodies tie,
> Are raveld out, and fast there by one end,
> Did this Soule limbes, these limbes a soule attend;
> And now they joyn'd...
>
> (*Metempsychosis*, 491–506)

But gestation and birth are overshadowed by sin's disordering of natural appetites and passions, and the whole account is curiously repellent. Donne's powers of evoking distaste for the body have not lessened as he again describes the womb in the second of the *Anniversaries*:

> Thinke that no stubborne sullen Anchorit,
> Which fixt to'a Pillar, or Grave doth sit
> Bedded and Bath'd in all his Ordures, dwels
> So fowly as our soules i' their first-built Cels.
> Thinke in how poore a prison thou didst lie
> After, enabled but to sucke, and crie.
>
> (*Progresse*, 169–74)

When birth conditions are viewed like this, it is no wonder death calls for celebration. Women in the earlier poem "thrust us out, and by them we are led / Astray, from turning to whence we are fled" (96–97); now an exemplary Elizabeth Drury draws mankind towards heaven and redeems the body as well as the soul (*Progresse*, 503-6).

The poem itself, with the impress of Elizabeth Drury on it, becomes a way of repairing the damage. The poem can save her, himself and the world from the "deluge" of "forgetting" in which "thou seest mee strive for life." Donne dramatizes her masterful effect on his muse:

> Immortal Mayd, who though thou wouldst refuse
> The name of Mother, be unto my Muse

> A Father, since her chast Ambition is,
> Yearely to bring forth such a child as this.
> *(Progresse*, 31-36)

Donne's transformation of Elizabeth into a hermaphroditic figure by the addition of a masculine principle makes her more of a power and more of a mystery. She is a form of generation repairing the world's corruption. He likewise thinks of her as giving form to his poem, on the basis of the familiar Aristotelian principle that the soul is the form of the body (72).

One would not want to attribute Donne's birth images solely to the paradox of birth-in-death. Other factors unquestionably contribute: rhetorical training in beginning at the beginning, the fascination of the creation subject, and probably personal anxieties about his wife's pregnancy and about his decision to leave for France with the Drurys against her wishes.[21] Nevertheless, the birth imagery is essential to the anniversary idea. Related images take the theme further: the new world/old world antithesis reflects the birth of the regenerate man from the Old Man of sin (75-77). The image of return to the original chaos to express intellectual disorientation (" 'tis all in pieces; all cohaerence gone" and a world "crumbled out againe t'his Atomis" [211-13]) brilliantly reverses the Ovidian topos of the birth of elemental order. The phoenix is ironically misappropriated to become the symbol of individualism:

> For everyman alone thinkes he hath got
> To be a Phoenix, and that there can bee
> None of that kinde, of which he is, but hee.

Whereas what the Phoenix should be unique for is its symbolism of rebirth in death. The resolution of the irony is that Elizabeth Drury's rebirth typifies the salvation offered to *all* by Christ's phoenix-like death and resurrection. The same theme of the soul's rebirth may also be cryptically enfolded in the beheaded man of the *Progresse* (9-17). The figure seems to spring from some private chamber of horrors in Donne's memory and its immediate effect is to express the tenacity of life. Yet the image is obliquely linked to Donne's iconography of spiritual birth through its rendering of the classic decapitation of martyrdom (though Donne left it open to suggest any kind of execution). Ten years later Donne made the connection of beheading and spiritual birth explicit:

> though we finde the days of the martyrs still called *Natalitia Martyrum*, their birth days, yet that is always intended of the dayes of their death; onely in John Baptist it is intended literally, of his natural birth; for his spirituall birth, his Martyrdome, is remembred by another name *Decollatio Joannis*, John Baptists beheading.[22]

Contrasts of natural birth and spiritual birth thus emerge as an important device in both *Anniversaries*. Turning to the anniversary conceit itself, we find it appearing in Donne's poetry before the *Anatomy*. In the *Songs and Sonets* "The Anniversary" moves from annual commemoration to some of the associations we have been noticing. The "last" day for the lovers' "eyes" or "ears" is the "first" day for their souls to know "a love increased": "When bodies to their graves, souls from their graves remove" (20). More explicitly, on 25 March 1608, two great feasts coincided as Lady Day fell on Good Friday. Donne's imagination was gripped by the strange conjunction of conception and death: "the head / Of life, at once, not yet alive, and dead" ("Upon the Annunciation and Passion falling upon one day, 1608") and he pursued the paradox down many paths. Then in August 1609 a relative of the Countess of Bedford died and Donne composed two elegies for her, in one of which he wittily devised the complementary alternatives of having her either alive as a saint or dead as a feast:

Who if her vertues would have let her stay
Wee'had had a Saint, have now a holiday.
    ("Elegy upon The Death of Mistress Boulstred," 43–44)

In the *Anniversaries* the festal paradox and festal compliment unite. In point of fact Elizabeth Drury generates *two* feasts, the anniversary of her death/birth and the christening of the world.

The conceit that the world needs to be christened with Elizabeth Drury's name may be difficult to follow and for this reason I have attempted to trace what I take to be some of Donne's steps (*Ann.* 31–38). Elizabeth had departed from the world like a queen who has ended a progress through her subjects' estates and her absence produces a sense of let-down and meaninglessness (this Donne subsequently develops through sickness and mourning imagery). Her departure leads to a period of waiting in which the World is compared to "a child kept from the font until / A Prince, expected long, come to fulfil the ceremonies." Not only had the World originally lain nameless, with its spiritual character obscure, until Elizabeth Drury came to dwell in it and so "christened" it, but with her death it has now again lost its name and spiritual identity and these will stay lost unless a name-perpetuating ceremony (equivalent to christening) is instituted—this is what the anniversary poems extolling her fame will constitute. While Elizabeth Drury's name and virtue lie unremembered the world lacks its spiritual character or soul. Donne elaborates the idea further when he attributes three births to the soul: the first at its creation (before physical birth), the second its birth in grace (at baptism), and the third at its release from the body (*Progresse*, 214–15). This puts Donne's conceit of the World awaiting christening (no. 2) into sequence with his conceit of Elizabeth's death as a birth (no. 3). Like birth and, for saints, death, christening has its own special anniversary, the name-day.[23] (Elizabeth Drury's would probably have been the same as Queen Elizabeth's, that is the feast of St. Elizabeth of Hungary, a royal saint, on November 17.) Since Elizabeth Drury is now one of the blessed, Donne proposes that she have her own saint's feast and that the World be christened with her name which it may then celebrate as *its* name-day:

> Her name defin'd thee, gave thee forme and frame,
> And thou forgetst to celebrate thy name.
> *(Anatomy,* 37–38)

Elizabeth Drury as metaphorically a prince, likewise requires a moment's consideration. It owes some of its significance to the complex value structure Donne is building throughout the poem. On the one hand Donne relentlessly applies the belittling technique familiar from "The Sunne Rising" against the worth and the scale of the World and against the stature of man and his pleasures and abilities. On the other hand, liberated soul, identified with the pronoun "shee," is magnified by charismatic powers that include magnetism, perfect *form* (the Ark as the form of salvation), paradise, stellar influence, and alchemical transmutation. Framing the series are royal majesty at the opening and sainthood turning death into birth at the end. These exalted secular and religious identities join forces (*Progresse,* 374–75) as Elizabeth Drury becomes at one and the same time "soveraign State" and "Church" (an epitomization of "all" not unlike that of the lovers in "The Canonization"). Vested in this comprehensive plurality, she stands as high as Donne can follow her in the act of contemplating the One.

Donne's metaphysicality in fact opens up a new level of decorum transcending the old classical high of status and great actions.[24] The principle operates in its simplest form in "Elegy of Prince Henry" where it solves the problem of finding hyperboles for someone who is a prince already by raising the level of difficulty *to the reader* with a conceit making the prince a double centre of two cosmic circumferences. Originally having the effect of raising the seriousness of love poetry, Donne's always concretely founded abstract imagery (nothing, all, centre, change, infiniteness, many, one) becomes in the *Anniversaries* a decorum reinforcing the Christian evaluation of soul, as opposed to world. As in so much of the rest of Donne's poetry, the level of difficulty is raised still further by paradox: birth-in-death. With Elizabeth Drury, Donne seems to be attempting a degree of elevation which one might consider calling Uranian, or alternatively the metaphysical sublime.

It should be noted, incidentally, that Donne's conceit of Elizabeth Drury as a saint may not be unconnected with the fact that the Drury's parish church at Hawstead, where Elizabeth was buried on 17 December 1610, was the church of All Saints. Be that as it may, sainthood had long been a metaphor with love poets and Donne had extended the range with characteristic inventiveness with his sinner-saints. In "The Canonization," on the other hand, saint-making had been analyzed into parts to dramatize a perfect love; Donne's lovers had given up the world, been persecuted, been put on trial, reviled and martyred, performed miracles, and received the full honours of sainthood: symbolic attributes, shrines (modest), invocation and prayer, hymns, and being taken for a pattern of virtue by the faithful. In the *Anniversaries* there is a fundamental difference, however. Sainthood is not a metaphor as it is in the love poem. Yet it is not to be taken quite literally either. Donne works in the space between two senses, one where Elizabeth Drury is in truth one of the blessed, and the other in which the "Shee" of the poem is *not* a saint of the Roman calendar but of the exemplary world invented by the poet. Moreover, Donne's picture of her sainthood is qualified by his Anglican beliefs which entail rejection of certain features.

Canonization had specially caught Donne's interest in the year before he wrote about Elizabeth Drury, but the interest had been that of a satirist. New saints and up-coming beatifications are hot news in *Ignatius his Conclave*, composed in the latter part of 1610 and published in January or February of 1611. First there are scathing remarks about Rome's "last made *Godesse*," St. Frances of Rome, a fifteenth-century mystic who had been canonized in 1608. This brings Donne to Ignatius Loyola and the movement to have him proclaimed a saint. Donne observes some official hesitation:

> Now the Pope would faine have satisfied [their Catholic Majesties] with the title of *Beatus*, which formerly upon the entreaty of the Princes of that Family, he had affoorded to Aloisius Gonzaga of that Order.[25]

On the other hand, the Pope sees reasons for hastening canonization: "as thinking it an unjust thing that...*King killers* should have [no patron saint]."[26] Ignatius was actually beatified on 27 July 1609, to the accompaniment of world-wide Jesuit celebrations (he would be canonized in 1622). Pope Paul V had also canonized Charles Borromeo and beatified Philip Neri and Teresa of Avila at about the same time. In Donne's satirical world canonization would secure Ignatius a special place in hell. However, these scoffs of Donne's at modern papal canonization did not prevent him from revering the Saints of the ancient tradition of the Church, as is perfectly clear in "An Hymn to the Saints, and to Marquis Hamilton" and "A Litany." In the latter poem the Church on Earth joins with the saints in "one, all-partaking fire of love." In the conceit of Elizabeth Drury's sainthood there is thus no reason to search for irony. Nevertheless Donne seems to want to draw distinctions as he calls his subject "Blessed Maid" the first time he addresses her directly in the poem. The title joins together the generic "blessed" and the *Beata* of Catholic nomenclature and it is virtually inconceivable that Donne was unaware of the application of the latter. Besides which, analogy with a *Beata* had the sort of exactitude that would appeal to him. As Donne knew (from close acquaintance with Cardinal Bellarmine's *Disputationes de Controversiis*),[27] not only did beatification mean publication of sainthood for a limited group (for instance a nation, a diocese or a religious order) rather than for the Church as a whole, but the specific honour of a special day of celebration was one of those accorded to "limited" sainthood where many other honours were denied (e.g. the dedication of a church). This possibility notwithstanding, Donne is really more set on differences between Catholic sainthood and his "saint," an attitude confirmed, for instance, by his avoidance of attributing miracles to Elizabeth Drury.

Being at Amiens as he composed the *Progresse* made Donne specially observant of Catholic practice. With humorous courtesy he declines to offend Elizabeth by invoking her as Catholics invoke saints. God alone has the authority to make and proclaim saints—whether Donne intended to object specifically to papal canonization here is impossible to tell. God does, however, call upon his prophets and poets for this purpose. The statement is crucial. Donne is positively claiming that his own right "to say this" is the right of inspiration:

> Here in a place, where mis-devotion frames
> A thousand praiers to saints, whose very names
> The ancient Church knew not, Heaven knowes not yet...
> Immortale Maid, I might invoque thy name.
> Could any Saint provoke that appetite,
> Thou here shouldst make mee a French convertite.
> But thou wouldst not; nor wouldst thou be content,
> To take this, for my second yeeres true Rent,
> Did this Coine beare any'other stampe, then his,
> That gave thee power to doe, me to say this.
> (511–22)

The idea that she should be a pattern for life and death (524) is the basis for treating Elizabeth Drury like a saint.[28] Her exemplariness, rendered in the contemporary language of hyperbole, is one of Donne's most solidly realized effects. It is particularly direct in the picture of her virtues as the perfect "sovereign State" (*Progresse*, 359–74), and (symmetrical with this) in the ironical account of how these virtues still "gilded every state" to make the world appear to have a little goodness left (*Anatomy*, 417–26). To contemplate her through the medium of the poem is to see "God's image" as far as the human eye can see it, that is, obliquely, just as Elizabeth herself had seen "his face" in the book of the creatures ("in any natural stone or tree").[29] "Stamp" (above—applied to a coin) may also suggest an imprimatur, thus combining the matter of authorizing canonization with that of authorizing books (that is, the poem).

The final thoughts in the passage quoted express important ideas about the poetic function. Donne claims the liberty of invoking her specifically in his character of poet. She is like a muse or other being of the kind that poets invoke. Her title in the *Progresse*, "Immortal Maid" (used twice) reflects the claim that poets immortalize their subjects, repeating the idea that "verse the fame enrols" which had concluded the *Anatomy*. As the writer of a divine poem Donne may claim the same metaphor as the preacher or prophet, of being "the trumpet, at whose voice the people came" (528). Donne's own surviving comments on the poem express further thoughts about his role. His explanation to Ben Jonson "that he described the Idea of a Woman, and not as she was"[30] was probably meant to send Jonson to Sir Philip Sidney's *Defence of Poesie*:

> For any understanding knoweth the skill of each artificer
> standeth in that idea or foreconceit of the work....
> And that the poet hath that idea is manifest, by delivering
> them forth in such excellency as he had imagined them.[31]

Sidney had made the perfect exemplar the touchstone of the poetic. Donne's meaning is surely confirmed by his comments on this poem to other friends:

> But for the other part of the imputation of having said too much, my defence is, that my purpose was to say as well as I could.[32]

> ...it became me to say, not what I sawe was just truth, but the best I could conceive; for that had been a new weakness in me, to have praised any body in printed verses, that had not been capable of the best praise I could give.[33]

An echo of a further idea popularized by Sidney appears in a phrase just preceding the last-quoted passage: "no body can imagine *that I who never saw her* could have any other purpose." With this phrase (my italics) Donne is almost certainly alluding to the distinction between poets (strictly speaking, painters) of "the meaner sort...who counterfeit only such faces as are set before them" and is identifying instead with the "right" poet who "painteth not Lucretia *whom he never saw*, but painteth the outward beauty of such a virtue."[34] Such poets range, Sidney goes on,

> only reined with learned discretion, into the divine consideration of what may be and should be. These be they that, as the first and most noble sort, may justly be termed *vates*....For these indeed...move men to take that goodness in hand...and teach, to make them know that goodness whereunto they are moved.[35]

"*Vates*" ("which is as much as a divine foreseer or prophet") seems to be exactly the poetic role Donne claimed in the *Anatomy* (462–74). By comparing his poem and the Song of Moses, he both makes the point about the popular and enduring quality of poetry ("keepe the song still in their memory"), and asserts the sacredness of his office and the poem's highest function. This last is particularly to be found in the equivalence between Moses's sight of the Promised Land and Donne's vision of the beatific fulfilment desired by the soul.[36]

Elizabeth Drury is a poet's pattern of perfection, and Donne expects his one "saint" to generate others. Sidney's notion that the poet produces his exemplary creations so as to beget others—"to bestow a Cyrus upon the world to make many Cyruses"[37]—is echoed in Donne's thoughts about his anniversary scheme:

> These Hymnes may worke on future wits, and so
> May great Grand-children of thy praises grow.
> And so, though not Revive, embalme and spice
> The world, which else would putrify with vice.
> For thus, man may extend thy progeny...
> These Hymnes thy issue, may encrease so long,
> As till Gods great Venite change the song.
> *(Progresse,* 37–44)

Here Donne envisages "imitation" by other poets as well as imitation of virtuous example in the ordinary sense. Both provide an alternative to the author's earlier promise of yearly poems. Having completed a self-sufficient diptych, Donne was leaving it to literary genetics and the morally regenerative force of poetry to fulfil his initial commitment.

His letters show that Donne felt poetically justified in praising Elizabeth Drury to the hilt and far from embarrassed about it. What they do show him anxious about was how his decision to *publish* was being received. The social stigma invited by courtiers or gentlemen who sought to have their verses printed is now well known to the student of literature, thanks to J.W. Saunders.[38] Donne admits his "fault":

> Of my Anniversaries, the fault that I acknowledge in my self is to have descended to print any thing in verse...
>
> I hear from England of many censures of my book of Mris Drury, if any of those censures do but pardon me my descent in Printing any thing in verse, (which if they do, they are more charitable than my self, for I do not pardon my self, but confesse that I did it against my conscience, that is, against my own opinion, that I should not have done so)...[39]

This, it seems to me, does not mean that he regretted having made a bad move, but that he had weighed the pros and cons very seriously. What Donne does not say in these letters, but as good as says in the poems, is that the code of the gentleman had had to yield to the imperative of the *vates* to speak out publicly:

> Since his will is, that to posteritee,
> Thou shouldst for life, and death, a patterne bee,
> And that the world should notice have of this...
> *(Progresse,* 523–28)

He is under the same obligation as Moses whom God commanded "to deliver / Unto all that song." The task of applying his powers to make Elizabeth Drury an enduring public pattern is undertaken with due deliberation:

> Such an opinion (in due measure) made
> Me this great Office boldly to invade.
> *(Anatomy,*467–68)

His conceit of a saint's anniversary feast for Elizabeth Drury thus had the further meaning for Donne of making a statement about publication, canonization being above all an act of publication giving notice of sainthood to the entire Church. Donne's former praises of individuals had been private. This meant that the immediate exemplary good was confined to a small circle of readers. Going into print with the *Anniversaries* was a decisive step, and Donne took the risk of social disapproval, although there may have been a gray area in the protocol governing funeral elegies. In publishing the virtues of Elizabeth Drury he left the familiar milieu of manuscript circulation and writing to please friends, and entered the public sphere in an unequivocally vatic persona. He did not, as we know, continue *publishing* his poetry. The decision was unique to the *Anniversaries,* and the rest of his work as a religious poet remained unaffected by it. But we cannot tell what would have happened if he had not become a priest and found an outlet for his public voice in the prose of the *Devotions* (1624) and the Sermons, published individually and in sets in his own lifetime, some soon after delivery (1622–27).

The decision to publish the *Anniversaries* forms part of the spiritual crisis Donne was going through at this time. We know that one outcome of the trip with the Drurys was a letter to Rochester, Earl of Somerset, in which Donne for the first time spoke of entering the Church:

> Having obeyed at last, after much debatement within me, the inspirations (as I hope) of the Spirit of God, and resolved to make my profession Divinity...[40]

The *Anniversaries* seem to have been a decided step in the same direction. The more usual view of them, of course, is that they reflect Donne playing for time on the question of taking holy orders,[41] in the meantime securing himself some secular patronage. The possibility that there is some truth in this, as well, I hope, as in my opposite assertion, only goes to show how tough Donne's dilemma was. At all events it looks as if some of the poems' essential images lingered in Donne's mind in association with the decision to enter the Church. In the Dedication to the *Devotions* (1624) he alludes to his ordination as "my second birth."[42] The connection extends further. The debate between a "diviner soul" and a "foolish world" is continued in "To Mr. Tilman after he had taken orders" (post-1618). Tilman's priestly role of bringing "man to heaven, and heaven again to man" is reminiscent of Elizabeth Drury's, with one striking difference. The *Anniversaries* keep clear the lines of evaluative antithesis between worthless world and rich soul, marginal new learning and truly satisfying divine knowledge. The poet pushes each to its furthest extreme and maximizes their apartness. The later poem, on the other hand, moves towards reconciliation of opposites. "Gods graces" and "mens offences" meet in strange, sacral symbiosis:

> And so the heavens which beget all things here,
> And the earth our mother, which these things do beare,
> Both these in thee, are in thy Calling knit,
> And make thee now a blest Hermaphrodite. (51–54)

Such unification does not belong to the *Anniversaries*. At the same time one does not find the direct dramatization of inner dividedness of Donne the love poet or divine poet. His roles of satirist and encomiast are antithetical only as to *genre* and remain psychologically consistent: *contemptus mundi* agrees with eulogy of the divine in man. Stress is eternalized in the contrast of worlds, one the corrupt macrocosm with which the writer identifies creatorally, the other a regenerative, poetic image of perfection. The structure indeed, tempts one to see a connection with Thomas More's *Utopia*, and its rendering of the dual vision. First Donne's anatomy exposes what man is. His hymn of Elizabeth Drury then constructs a passionate lyrical model of the ideal, with the figure of a young woman replacing "the best state of a common wealth," and expressing "not what I sawe was just truth, but the best I could conceive."

NOTES

1. Elizabeth Drury died a few weeks before her fifteenth birthday. The phrase is Donne's, but used of the Virgin Mary, not Elizabeth, in "Upon the Annunciation and Passion Falling upon one day, 1608," 1. 14.

2. Discussion of the poems' genre appears in the following: Louis L. Martz, *The Poetry of Meditation*, (New Haven: Yale Univ. Press, 1954); John Peter, *Complaint and Satire in Early Literature* (Oxford: Clarendon Press, 1956); O.B. Hardison, Jr., *The Enduring Monument: A Study of the Idea of Praise in the Renaissance Literary Theory and Practice* (Chapel Hill: Univ. of North Carolina Press, 1962); Frank Manley, *John Donne: The Anniversaries* (Baltimore: The Johns Hopkins Press, 1963); George Williamson, "The Design of Donne's *Anniversaries*" in *Milton and Others* (Chicago: Univ. of Chicago Press, 1965); Rosalie Colie, " 'All in Peeces' ": Problems of Interpretation in Donne's *Anniversary Poems*," in *Just So Much Honour*, ed. Amadeus P. Fiore (University Park, Pa: Pennsylvania State Univ. Press, 1971); Barbara K. Lewalski, *Donne's Anniversaries and Poetry of Praise* (Princeton: Princeton Univ. Press, 1973); Marjorie Hope Nicolson, *The Breaking of the Circle* (New York: Columbia Univ. Press, 1960). Recent commentary includes M. Milgate, ed. *The Epithalamions, Anniversaries and Epicedes* (Oxford: Oxford Univ. Press, 1978), 126–27, and C.A. Patrides, ed., *The Complete English Poems of John Donne* (London: Dent, 1985), 324–25.

3. The last is extensively argued in Lewalski, 108ff.

4. William Dugdale, *The History of St. Paul's Cathedral* (London, 1658), 30–43.

5. William Shakespeare, *Much Ado About Nothing*, V. iii. 16–18.

6. George Puttenham, *The Arte of English Poesie* (London, 1589), 39.

7. Rosalie Colie comments on the general Christian paradox where death is perceived as birth, but without the specific connection with saints' feasts or anniversaries: *Paradoxia Epidemica* (Princeton: Princeton Univ. Press, 1966), 420ff. Louis L. Martz quotes Blount's *Glossographia* (1656): "Those were of old called *Anniversary days*, wheron the martyrdoms or death-days of Saints were celebrated yeerly in the Church; or the days whereon at the yeers end, men were wont yeerly to pray for the souls of their deceased friends according to the continued custom of Roman Catholiques." This misses out the birth analogy. Martz understands 'anniversary' solely as a "a whole year's commemorative tribute, paid in advance," *Poetry of Meditation*, Appendix 2, 354. Also of interest is Dennis Quinn, "Donne's *Anniversaries* as Celebration," *Studies in English Literature* 9 (1969): 97–105.

8. *Poetices*, III. cxxii., and Hardison, *The Enduring Monument*, 170–76.

9. "Donne's *Anniversaries* and the Tradition of the Funeral Elegy," *ELH* 39 (1972): 540.

10. Milgate, 127.

11. Lewalski, *Donne's* Anniversaries, 311–70; Hardison, *The Enduring Monument*, 166ff.

12. They appear as "Natalis I," "II," etc., in the first edition, by Jehan Petit, Paris, 1516. The main influence on Paulinus's series is Latin genethliac poetry, but I can find no trace of further series of *natalitia* developing from Paulinus or otherwise: R.P.H. Green, *The Poetry of Paulinus of Nola: A Study of his Latinity* (Brussels: Latomus, 1971), 29–37.

13. "Natalis 13" (Poem 21), 165–190, in P.G. Walsh ed., *The Poems of St. Paulinus, Bishop of Nola* (New York: Newman Press, 1975), 178–9. This recent English translation and its notes have been invaluable: I am also very grateful to the Library of the Corning Museum of Glass, Corning, N.Y., for the use of their copy of the *editio princeps*, *Pon Paulini Episcopi Nolani...Epistolae & Poemata luculenta* (Paris: Jehan Petit, 1516). Passages from some poems were translated by Henry Vaughan in his biography, *Primitive Holiness. Set forth in the Life of blessed Paulinus* (London, 1654). In this translation at least, Paulinus's verses on the last Judgement lend themselves to speculation about the possibility of influence on Donne's "At the round earths imagined corners";

> These serious thoughts take up my soul, and I
> While yet 'tis day-light, fix my busie eye
> Upon his sacred Rules, lifes precious sum,
> Who in the twilight of the world shall come
> To judge the lofty looks, and shew mankind
> The diff'rence 'twixt the ill and well inclin'd.
> This second coming of the worlds great King
> Makes my heart tremble, and doth timely bring
> A saving care into my watchfull soul,
> Lest in that day all vitiated and foul
> I should be found: That day, times utmost line,
> When all shall perish, but what is divine.
> When the great Trumpets mighty blast shall shake
> The earths foundations, till the hard Rocks quake,
> And melt like piles of snow, when lightnings move
> Like hail, and the white thrones are set above.
> That day, when sent in glory by the Father,
> The Prince of life his blest Elect shall gather;
> Millions of Angels round about him flying,
> While all the kindreds of the earth are crying,
> And he enthron'd upon the clouds shall give
> His last just sentence, who must die, who live.
> This is the fear, this is the saving care,
> That makes me leave false honours, and that share
> Which fell to mee of this fraile world; lest by
> A frequent use of present pleasures I
> Should quite forget the future, and let in
> Foul Atheism, or some presumptuous sin.

From the verse epistle to Ausonius, in *The Works of Henry Vaughan*, ed. L.C. Martin, second edition (Oxford: Clarendon Press, 1957), 349. Cf. Walsh, Poem 10.

14. *The Poems of St. Paulinus*, 114.

15. Hardison, *The Enduring Monument*, 118.

16. Poems: Paris, 1516; Antwerp, 1560; collections: G. Fabricius, *Poetarum veterum ecclesiasticorum opera Christiana* (Basiliae, 1540), and J.J. Grynaeus, *Monumenta S. Patrum orthodoxographa*, 3 vols. (Basiliae, 1569), I: Natalis I–VII.

17. *The Sermons of John Donne*, ed. George R. Potter and Evelyn M. Simpson (Berkeley and Los Angeles: Univ. of California Press, 1959), vol. 4, 153, 402; vol. 5, 242. Paulinus's *Natalicia* are cited a number of times by Cardinal

Bellarmine in writings Donne is known to have been familiar with, both the *Disputationes de Controversiis* (1588–93) mentioned in Walton's *Life*, and the *Apologia Roberti Bellarmini* which he read at the time of *Ignatius His Conclave* (1611): see Izaak Walton, *The Lives of John Donne* (et alia), 1675 (ed. Oxford, 1927, 26), and *Bellarmini...Opera Omnia* (Paris, 1870; repr. Frankfurt, 1965), t. 3, 156, 173, 197; t. 12, 153.

18. *Pseudo-Martyr (1610). A Fascimile...*, ed. F. J. Sypher (Delmer, N.Y.), cap. ii, p. 9.

19. Thomas Aquinas, *Summa Theologica*, II. I. Q. 81, Art. 1, Reply obj. 2.

20. *Metempsychosis*, 93.

21. It seems likely the *Anatomy* was begun while Donne was lodging in London, waiting to set off for France with the Drurys while his wife and children had gone to stay with her sister Frances in the Isle of Wight. To that point Anne seems not to have had any miscarriages, and none of their children had yet died. Both *Anniversaries* had probably been published (in the early months of 1612) before news reached him in April, while he was in Paris, of his wife's delivery of a still-born child: this had been buried 24 January, 1612. The story that Donne, then in Amiens, had had a vision of his wife with a dead child in her arms on the very day of its delivery is told by Walton in the 1675 edition of his *Life*: see R.C. Bald, *John Donne. A Life* (Oxford: Clarendon Press, 1970), 242, and Walton, 40.

22. Sermon 5, "Preached at St. Pauls on midsummer day, 1622," *Sermons* (1959), vol. 4, 146.

23. The name-day aspect of "A Nocturnall upon S. Lucy's Day" remains an open question, since one cannot be certain whether it has any connection with an actual Lucy, such as the Countess of Bedford, or relates to Anne Donne, etc. Regarding Donne himself, it would be interesting to know which St. John he was named after (John was also his father's name), and which name-day he observed. If it was John the Baptist, the beheaded man of the *Progresse* (9–22) could be personally allusive. John's martyrdom, the Decollation, was celebrated on 29 August, but his principal feast is for his natural birth, celebrated on Midsummer day, 24 June. (For Donne's sermon on this day, see p. 67 above.) If on the other hand it was St. John the Evangelist, one might take the eagle in "The Canonization" as a personal allusion.

24. Compare the original Christian revision of decorum discussed by Eric Auerbach, "Sermo Humilis," *Literary Language & Its Public in Late Latin Antiquity and in the Middle Ages*, trans. Ralph Manheim, Bollingen Series vol. 74 (New York: Pantheon Books, 1965), 27–66. The association of the high style with difficulty

was made earlier by Geoffroi de Vinsauf and others who classed some figures as "difficult ornaments" appropriate to the high style (metaphor, antithesis, metonymy, synechdoche, periphrasis, allegory and enigma)—but with no mention of paradox: E. Faral, *Les Arts Poétiques du XIIe et XIIIe Siècles* (Paris, 1924) 89ff and 221ff.

25. *Ignatius His Conclave*, ed. T.S. Healy, S.J. (Oxford: Clarendon Press, 1969), 67, 91.

26. *Ignatius*, 89, 151, 153.

27. *Controversiarum De Ecclesia Triumphante*, Liber Primus, "De beatitudine et canonizati Sanctorum," cap. xi, in *Bellarmini...Opera Omnia* (Paris, 1874, repr. Minerva, Frankfurt-am Main, 1965), Tom. 3, 166; see also Geoffrey Keynes, Kt., *A Bibliography of Dr. John Donne*, fourth edition, (Oxford: Clarendon Press, 1973), 262.

28. It is no detriment to the seriousness of Elizabeth Drury as a pattern of sanctity that Donne undertook to compliment two living ladies with sainthood in a light vein at just about the same time as he was finishing the *Progresse*. In late January 1612 he wrote a verse letter to the two sisters of Sir Robert Rich: Rich was just passing through Amiens and possibly suggested the poem. In "A Letter to the Lady Carey, And Mistress Essex Rich, from Amiens" Donne invokes Lady Carey as a saint, side-stepping charges of heresy and schism, and justifies declaring his devotion openly on the grounds that "pardons" for such offences do not cost much. It reads like a spin-off from the *Progresse* (511 ff.).

29. The idea of *seeing* God's face specially fits Elizabeth Drury because of the beatitude "*Beati mundo core...*": "Blessed are the pure in heart: For they shall see God," Matt. v. i, where the sense of *mundus* as both "clean" and "world" has further relevance.

30. *Conversations with William Drummond of Hawthornden*, in *Ben Jonson*, 11 vols., ed. C.H. Herford and Percy Simpson (Oxford: Clarendon Press, 1925–1952), vol. 1 (1925), 133. C.A. Patrides also makes the connection with Sidney in *The Complete English Poems of John Donne* (London: Dent, 1985), 325.

31. *A Defence of Poetry*, ed. J.A. van Dorsten, (Oxford: Clarendon Press, 1966), 24.

32. "To George Garrard," 14 April 1612, *Letters to Severall Persons of Honour* (1651, repr. Delmas, N.Y.: 1977), 238–39.

33. "To Sir Henry Goodyer," mid-April, 1612, *Letters*, 74–75.

34. *A Defence of Poetry*, Van Dorsten, 26.

35. *A Defence of Poetry*, Van Dorsten, 26–27.

36. Moses sees the Promised Land immediately after the Song, and this may have been in Donne's mind as he compared the Song to his own poem and its account of future joys. The topic of heavenly joys, soon to be taken up by Cardinal Bellarmine, appears to have been in the air. One interesting treatment prior to Donne's was Giles Fletcher's "Christ's Victorie after Death," 27–44, the fourth part of *Christ's Victorie and Triumph* (1610), which blends a sensuous Spenserian idiom with strongly patterned rhetorical surfaces and paradoxical wit.

37. *A Defence of Poetry*, Van Dorsten, 24.

38. *The Profession of English Letters* (London: Routledge and Kegan Paul, 1964), 46–47.

39. *Letters*, 238, 74–75.

40. Edmund Gosse, *Life and Letters of John Donne* (1899), vol. 2, 20–21, cited by Robert S. Jackson, *John Donne's Christian Vocation*, (Evanston Ill.: Northwestern Univ. Press, 1970), 123.

41. For example, R.C. Bald, *Donne and the Drurys* (Cambridge: Cambridge Univ. Press, 1959), 157.

42. Gosse, *Life and Letters of John Donne*, vol. 2, 60.

ZIGZAG IN *HAMLET* I, v

S.P. Zitner

Early in 1611, perhaps, a company as yet unidentified staged a comedy by John Fletcher. Its title, *The Woman's Prize, or The Tamer Tamed*,[1] alludes to Shakespeare's *Taming of the Shrew*. Despite the title, however, *The Woman's Prize* is no forerunner of feminism. Here as elsewhere Fletcher seems unwilling or unable to face, even in jest, the social issues he raises. His Biancas and Livias outsmart his Morosos and Petruchios, but at the end of the play they dwindle precipitously into wives. In the subplot, Livia, one of Petronius's two so-called "masculine daughters," outwits her father and his impossible choice as son-in-law, old Moroso. With the aid of her cousin Bianca, Livia feigns a mortal illness, summons her lover Rowland, her father and Moroso to her bedside where, in the dim light, she persuades them to sign a vaguely described testament of affection. In Act V, Scene iii, Rowland learns that the document is actually a contract of marriage, unwittingly signed by him and witnessed by his father-in-law and his rival. Amazed, Rowland questions Bianca's co-conspirator, Tranio: Am I awake? Am I in health? Was I with Livia? Shall I enjoy her? Swear, Tranio,

ROWLAND	As thou art honest, as thou hast a conscience, As that may wring thee if thou lyest; all these To be no vision, but a truth, and serious.
TRANIO	Then by my honesty, and faith, and conscience; All this is certain.
ROWLAND	Let's remove our places. Sweare it again.

TRANIO   I sweare tis true.

All but the most forgetful theatregoers would have understood the allusion in Rowland's "let's remove our places / Sweare it again." And I guess that whoever understood laughed. The allusion is to Act I, Scene v of *Hamlet* and to the balletic movement in which Hamlet, Marcellus and Horatio cross and recross the stage as the Ghost ominously intones "Swear" from the cellarage beneath them. Fletcher, Beaumont and others often allude to their great precursor, but generally to his words. Here the allusion is to stage movement.

The connection between *A Woman's Prize* and *Hamlet* has been noted. Dover Wilson thought that "the shifting or removing from place to place, as the oaths are taken, is also common form, and occurs again in Fletcher's *Woman's Prize*."[2] Yet, Frances Shirley's encyclopaedic *Swearing and Perjury in Shakespeare's Plays* (1979) is silent on peripatetic oath-taking. The "convention" whereby adjuration requires perambulation is only once honoured—here—in the observance, and then as a joke in the spirit of the play. *The Woman's Prize* has English Maria marrying the famous Kate-tamer Petruchio, now a widower and a fearsome shrew himself. Fletcher's play dodges in and out of Shakespeare's, picking up bits of idea, plot, and dialogue. When Rowland has Tranio move about the stage, no "convention" is being observed. Fletcher is merely playing with the possibility of a ludicrous contrast between Shakespeare's play and his own. That he could do so successfully in this instance suggests how deep an impression had been made by the business in Shakespeare's cellarage scene. Parodies of plot and language are common enough in Elizabethan drama, but Fletcher's is a rare instance in which the business of a particular play is parodied. The stage movement of the cellarage scene is memorable. Yet it is so, I think, not only because it is impressive as spectacle—a ritualized encounter between the earthly and the infernal, the living and the dead—but because it conveys a significant pattern of the play.

2

The title page of the 1603 First Quarto tells us that *Hamlet* was acted divers times by the King's Men in London, Oxford, Cambridge and elsewhere. The Globe Theatre, where the play was first performed in London, had a trap and an understage area to accommodate ghosts, witches, corpses, prisoners pent and other such persons. Despite its supports, the understage was sufficiently clear for an actor to scurry about freely below the platform. He would have been unseen by the audience since cloth hangings were fixed at the stage perimeter between the outermost supports. As the Globe stood on marshy ground the understage seems to have been largely above ground-level. But the dankness, to say nothing of a ghostly or infernal role, would have encouraged a hollow sound from the actor, and the confined acoustics and muffling hangings would have made the sound still more dismal. One can imagine Shakespeare, traditionally credited with the role, ghosting to and fro in the cellarage, delighted with the effect.

The Globe stage was forty-nine-and-a-half feet wide—room enough for an audience to perceive the Ghost's successive cries as coming from quite different locations, and for the answering stage movements to be sweeping.[3]

What happened during performances at the great universities and elsewhere is another matter. If elsewhere were a raised wooden platform, perimeter hangings would have made it possible to stage the scene as at the Globe. At a university or a great hall with no understage it is likely that, as T.J. King suggests, the scene might have been "performed with the Ghost speaking from within." According to Alan Nelson,[4] it is unlikely that *Hamlet* was actually performed at Cambridge, despite Q1's title page, but the construction of the Cambridge playhouse allowed for an understage area, if not for a trap. Lacking a cellarage, however, the graveyard scene, as T.J. King points out, would have required "more drastic textual changes."[5] Yet the consequences of altering a stage direction from *Ghost cries under the stage* to *Ghost cries within* are also drastic. At the very least one loses the shudder of the Ghost's voice coming from "hell." (So the understage was called in contrast to the stage overhang—the "heavens"—projecting from the tiring house.) And at the extreme one loses the symbolism of the several marches across the stage by Hamlet, Marcellus and Horatio. The significance of such losses is the burden of this paper. But before considering questions of meaning, I want to turn to stage history, which furnishes more possibilities than are dreamt of in our hermeneutics.

John Ward's *Hamlet* promptbook (Shattuck 3)[6] of about 1740 cuts the cellarage scene a little and provides few stage directions. Yet the retention of such phrases as Hamlet's "once more remove" suggests movement below stage by the Ghost and onstage by his auditors. A Garrick promptbook of 1773 (Shattuck 5) and another (Shattuck 6), incomplete but probably derived from it, cut about fifteen lines after the Ghost's first understage cry. Shakespeare's text is picked up again at Horatio's, "O day and night, but this is wondrous strange" (line 173). Yet much that is wondrous strange has been omitted: two cries from the Ghost and two marches across the stage. Significantly, the 1773 book retains Hamlet's "O all you host of heaven!" uttered as the Ghost leaves (line 92), but cuts "O earth! what else? / And shall I couple hell?" Richard Daly's promptbook of about 1788 (Shattuck 8) has similar cuts and staging, as does Macready's 1821 promptbook (Shattuck 14). The result in all these versions— in which there is no stage movement in response to the Ghost's commands—is to emphasize with businesslike brevity Hamlet's commitment to the Ghost.

With a Kean promptbook of 1840 (Shattuck 20) a further significant alteration takes place. The word "*beneath*" is lined through and the Ghost now remains onstage. As far as I have been able to determine, the change was not dictated by the absence of an understage. In any case, the Ghost is no longer physically infernal.

J.B. Roberts's promptbook of about 1843 (Shattuck 37) also gives us a radically cut text and a Ghost out in the open. His auditors do not move across the stage. When they are about to swear on Hamlet's sword hilt, they hear the Ghost and shrink away. Their fear is contrasted with Hamlet's steadiness. Despite technical innovations, William Burton (Shattuck 50) in 1852, Edwin Forrest (Shattuck 66) in the 1860s, and Fechter (Shattuck 72) in 1864 employed a similar staging, though Forrest restores the Ghost to the cellarage.

An E.H. Southern and Julia Marlowe promptbook (Shattuck 138), dating from the early 1900s, reflects some surprising developments. Again there is no crossing or recrossing of the stage. At the Ghost's first command, Horatio and Marcellus withdraw their hands from Hamlet's sword. At the second command, Hamlet grasps Marcellus by the wrist, drawing him toward the spectral voice, Horatio following. At the Ghost's final "swear," Horatio and Marcellus attempt once more to remove their hands from Hamlet's sword-hilt, but the Prince holds them fast. He bows reverently over the sword, as then do Horatio and Marcellus. At the end of the scene all are very still, gazing at the ground in front of Hamlet as if the Ghost were still there. Hamlet then moves to centre stage, puts his right arm over his eyes and staggers a trifle to the right as the curtain falls.

If there is a common theme in the characteristic innovations of more recent staging it is psychological determinism. During *Hamlet* try-outs in Toronto, so the story goes, the battery of loudspeakers, through which the now wholly impalpable Ghost was to terrify and command, had not been connected quite to Gielgud's specifications. Instead of being able to follow a coherent sequence of utterances, Richard Burton as Hamlet was forced to swivel now this way now that as the spectral commands came toward him unpredictably. Peter Brook, using a very tall Ghost, had the Prince sprawl on the stage, straining to reach out to a ghostly voice that came from everywhere underneath at once. More recently, the Ghost's "swear" seemed to issue horribly from Jonathan Pryce's midriff as if through demonic possession.

The text of the passages we have been discussing is remarkably consistent in the early quartos and the Folio, evidence of its effectiveness. We can assume that the early stage movement was also consistent, a zigzag about the stage in reaction to the commands from beneath it. This—save at performances in the great halls—seems to have been the staging well into the next century despite some cuts in the text. By the later eighteenth century, notably with Garrick, cuts in the scene eliminate cross- and under-stage movements. One reason for such excisions is suggested in George Joseph Bell's commentary accompanying the Edmund and Charles Kean promptbook of about 1828 (Shattuck 16). "Some things," Bell observes, "make this play almost unfit for the Stage or only for a private Theatre"[7]—notable among them a comic Polonius and a too "palpable," gallery-pleasing Ghost. "Modern" rationalism and decorum were uppermost in Bell's mind. Related to this is another reason suggested by the excision of Hamlet's "O earth! what else?/And shall I couple hell?" after "O all you host of heaven!" There is of course a good deal of merely genteel bowdlerization in the promptbooks. And in the lines themselves Hamlet is evoking all the realms of existence rather than thinking of joining hell—though the phrase centering on the word "couple" is ambiguous enough to suggest an infernal collaboration in the experience Hamlet has just undergone. In any case, I think that the atmosphere of the infernal (hence of the morally problematic, or worse, the superstitious) that the cellarage Ghost brings with him, rather than merely the offending word "hell," prompted the excisions. With the rise of bardolatry and princeolatry we have a cleansing of the Ghost-passages. Hamlet is honest so the Ghost is honest. It is no wonder that he is liberated from the underworld and allowed onstage.

For Shakespeare's cautionary zigzag, stage directions in the promptbooks in the later eighteenth and much of the nineteenth century substitute individual gestures of physical fear or acquiescence. The Southern-Marlowe staging represents a decisive change, with Hamlet forcing Marcellus and Horatio to follow the Ghost's voice. The Ghost is now a fully cleansed spirit, a holy figure bringing no whiff of brimstone. One must swear on or by him, rather than apart from or merely to him. In notable recent productions, earlier versions of stage movement are put aside for business psychologizing the Father-Ghost Son-Hamlet relation.

3

Promptbooks are not performances. Their cuts, stage directions and blocking diagrams are indications, however, of how performance was conceived—far more concrete and detailed than accounts of performance, which are often conventionally phrased, hard to come by, and may reflect unrepresentative occasions. Yet I have hardly given the full record, nor could I, nor can any production history fall into such neat stages as I have suggested. The Barrymore 1922 promptbook (Shattuck 154), for example, seems to return to the earliest staging of the scene, and it was Kemble who first knelt after the Ghost's departure at line 91. But the main outlines of the scene's history are, I think, correct: a change from a palpable, infernal or purgatorial Ghost upon whom Hamlet at first refuses to swear; to a vaguely dread spirit inspiring fear that is conveyed through unconcerted gesture rather than cross-stage movement; to an honoured figure, however frightening, who *ought* to be obeyed; to an overpowering psychic force to whom all *must* capitulate. Implicit in this history is an abandonment of the stage movement of the early texts and its meaning: that despite his declaration that the Ghost is honest, Hamlet does not fully trust it here; doubts it and yet wants to make and to receive commitments to it; needs to swear cooperation with its cause but not literally and hence not figuratively *on* it. The marches over the stage in response to the Ghost's cries crystallize for the eye what the play itself elaborates: a problematic imperative, a prince at once convinced and doubting, and a pattern of action that doubles back on itself before resolving in resignation. But if the stage movement suggests the whole of the play as text, it contradicts Hamlet's immediately prior language of reassurance about the Ghost's honesty. The early stage movement expresses Hamlet's moral fear, rather than the physical fear of others implied by later staging.

It would be pleasant to record agreement to such (rather obvious?) interpretations. But Dover Wilson, as we saw, thought the stage movement governed by a convention. Anne Slater finds it "weird comedy" at the expense of a "stale" device, "literary satire as well as apt psychology and good daemonology."[8] And the late T.J.B. Spencer thought that "Hamlet seems to move his companions around inexplicably," but adds that perhaps Horatio and Marcellus "flee in terror from the spot whence the Ghost's voice comes, and Hamlet follows them to different parts of the stage." Spencer's notes have it yet a third way, since earlier he had commented that "it is not certain they do hear the Ghost any more than the Queen does in III. 4, 103–40."[9] How this last could be conveyed unmistakably to the audience without adding something like Gertrude's pointed dismay in the closet scene, I do not know.

In a long note on the scene the Arden editor[10] warns against the idea that "Hamlet himself at the present moment has doubts of the Ghost's story." "Such a view," he thinks, "would conflict with Hamlet's assertion of the Ghost's honesty, his welcoming its collaboration in the swearing ritual and with 11. 190, 196–97." These lines are "rest, rest perturbed spirit," and the famous couplet on Hamlet's responsibility for setting the times right. One may argue that the lines do not flatly rule out the possibility of Hamlet's doubts. But can one ever assume that there is no conflict between Hamlet's speech and his behaviour? And is his response to the Ghost during the swearing only a welcome of collaboration? Hamlet seems in no need of reinforcements to persuade Horatio and Marcellus to silence; they have agreed to that before the Ghost speaks. The Ghost is a talking point and perhaps excuses the redundancy of repeated oaths whose surface function of reassurance is the occasion for the fine spectacle and its deeper import. Indeed, the sheer fact of the Ghost, of his ambiguity and the ambiguity of his commands—touching as they do Hamlet's primal life-relations—argues Hamlet's need for repeated assurance. Earlier Hamlet had seen his father's death, along with his mother's coarseness and the court's sycophancy to his gross uncle, as merely another, though culminating, fact of defective nature. The feeling-tones for this view were cynicism and depression. But if the Ghost's revelations are imperatives, they are also liberating. The father's death was not "natural"; nor were the mother's coarseness and the uncle's ascendancy. Disillusion and mourning have been turned into a mission. The consequent lifting of depression, if only momentary, is reflected in the half-hysterical levity and in the air of complicit intimacy in Hamlet's jocular nicknames for the Ghost, nicknames which are, in addition, diminutives of propitiation. Thus Hamlet may be said to "welcome" the Ghost's revelations.

But what of his welcoming the Ghost? The Ghost has, of course, told Hamlet that by day he is confined to flames and fasting for "crimes done in [his] days of nature." Yet this confession of criminality does not seem to register with Hamlet, at least not on first hearing. It is the long exposition of betrayal and murder that affects him, leads him to state that the Ghost is honest, in part because such a belief is so liberating. In the cellarage, however, this terminally ambiguous figure reveals, rather than describes, himself as actually in an infernal (or is it purgatorial?) state. Though further oaths suit the Ghost's purposes as well as Hamlet's own, Hamlet now hesitates to swear literally on such a Ghost. Perhaps Hamlet welcomes collaboration, but he has something less than an unqualified welcome for the collaborator. Such is the import of the texts.

When the Ghost first cries from "under the stage"—that unspecific phrase is present in the Q1, Q2 and Folio stage directions—the three hearers are presumably standing apart. They gather to take the oath on Hamlet's sword-hilt. When the Ghost next cries out, the logic of the text is that he is immediately beneath them. Hamlet now orders Marcellus and Horatio away from the voice. The stage spectacle acts out his reservations about the Ghost even as Hamlet is acting out his acceptance of its charge. The cross-stage movements after "*hic et ubique*" (with its ironic religious allusion) and "a worthy pioneer" are certain. How the ritual concluded is perhaps less easily read from the text. But at the Ghost's final "swear," it seems logical to assume that Hamlet's "rest, rest perturbed spirit" represents a concession—an admission that the infernal figure is inescapable, and so must be sworn to as well as upon. To have this final "swear" uttered from anywhere but immediately beneath Hamlet and the others would be to interrupt the series of such utterances and to interrupt it for no apparent reason, thus rendering the series meaningless. To have it repeated from beneath them, but now with a *new* response from Hamlet is to create a meaningful sequence: reservation culminating in resignation. For the Ghost, the oath, despite its nominal object, is now an oath of allegiance.

Hamlet is a play about trying at once to escape and to obey the commands of ambiguous authority, but finally resigning one's self to them. At the end of Hamlet's first encounter with the Ghost, which "winds up" the action of the play, the cellarage episode crystallizes in stage movement the characteristic redoubling of the plot construction, and the complex relation between speaking and acting in the play as a whole. Most immediately, however, the episode mimes the fate of the protagonist. The movement over the cellarage functions as something very like Brecht's "*Grundgestus*"; language and movement tell their own story, demanding that we weigh them against one another and only then together.

NOTES

1. The play has been edited by George B. Ferguson (The Hague: Mouton, 1966), whose text I cite below.

2. J. Dover Wilson, *What Happens in Hamlet* (Cambridge: Cambridge Univ. Press, 1935), 82. For other comments on the relation see *The Works of Beaumont and Fletcher*, ed. Henry Weber (Edinburgh, 1892), vol. 5, 395n, and A.C. Bradley, *Shakespearean Tragedy* (New York: St. Martins Press, 1957), 329.

3. See John Orrell, *The Quest for Shakespeare's Globe* (Cambridge: Cambridge Univ. Press, 1983), 166–67. On the understage see Andrew Gurr, *The*

Shakespearean Stage 1574–1642, second edition (Cambridge: Cambridge Univ. Press, 1980), ch. 4, esp. 125–26.

4. Personal communication.

5. T.J. King, *Shakespearean Staging 1599–1642* (Cambridge, Mass.: Harvard Univ. Press, 1971), 79. Modifications were made to great halls for theatrical purposes: see Orrell, *The Quest for Shakespeare's Globe*, 131–36. But those made in 1605 at Christ Church, Oxford do not seem to have provided for an understage (see Orrell, *The Quest for Shakespeare's Globe*, Appendix B).

6. The numbers refer to the order of listing in Charles H. Shattuck, *The Shakespeare Promptbooks* (Urbana: Univ. of Illinois Press, 1965), 91–127. I wish to record here my thanks to the Folger Shakespeare Library for permission to examine the *Hamlet* promptbooks in their collection.

7. Bell's comments are to be found on the page opposite the list of dramatis personae.

8. Anne Pasternak Slater, *Shakespeare the Director* (Brighton, Sussex: Harvester Press, 1982), 36–37.

9. *Hamlet*, ed. T.J.B. Spencer (Harmondsworth: Penguin, 1980), 241–42.

10. *Hamlet*, ed. Harold Jenkins (London: Methuen, 1982), 457–59. Line numbers cited in this essay are those of the Jenkins edition.

THE HIDDEN HERO: SHAKESPEARE'S *CORIOLANUS* AND ELIOT'S *CORIOLAN*

Alexander Leggatt

"Soon after the publication of 'Marina'," G. Wilson Knight reports, "Eliot asked to see my commentary on *Coriolanus*, then in preparation, because, he said, he was engaged on a poem inspired by Beethoven's *Coriolan*."[1] It is clear that whatever Eliot drew from Beethoven, he was also interested in drawing on Shakespeare's play, which he much admired. He was particularly grateful for Knight's discussion of the play's hard, metallic imagery,[2] and this may have contributed to his opening lines: "Stone, bronze, stone, steel, stone, oakleaves, horses' heels / Over the paving."[3] But the impact of the play on the poem does not stop there, nor with the general situation the poem dramatizes of a military hero at odds with his people. *Coriolan* is a fragment, consisting of only two poems of a projected cycle, and to some extent this has stymied criticism of it. Even essays which trace the figure of Coriolanus in Eliot's work are surprisingly sketchy and tentative about *Coriolan*,[4] and find little to say about the relations between play and poem. But, while I cannot attempt a full exposition, I would like to argue that play and poem are mutually illuminating, and that the poem at one point enters into a significant critical debate about the play. Moreover, the allusions and analogies as they accumulate may help to make Eliot's fragment more coherent than it appears at first encounter.

The title of the first poem, "Triumphal March," calls up Act Two of Shakespeare's play, with the hero's triumphal return from Corioles. The excitement of the crowd, all eager for a glimpse of Eliot's unnamed hero—"will it be he now?... There he is now, look"—recalls Brutus's sour description of the Roman populace "all agreeing / In earnestness to see him" (II.i.210–11).[5] But Eliot makes clear, as does Shakespeare, the separateness of the hero and the crowd. Their lives are quite simply too low for any understanding with (or of) the hero to be possible. Shakespeare's people open the play rioting for corn, and Menenius, putting them off with the fable of the belly, seems to echo their insistence that what matters in the state is the food supply.[6] In war their greatest enthusiasm is for looting, much to Coriolanus's disgust. Eliot's people are equally material: "We can wait with our stools and our sausages"; "Don't throw away that sausage, / It'll come in handy."[7] Along with this materialism goes a lack of spirituality; it is characteristic of both writers that Eliot is much more explicit about this than Shakespeare is; what he shows directly, Shakespeare implies by omission. Shakespeare's characters use the gods for conventional invocations and hyperbole; they occasionally enlist the gods in their political debates, as when Menenius claims the gods, not the patricians, have produced the famine (I.i.71–73) or the plebeians declare "the gods sent not / Corn for rich men only" (I.i.206–7). But the Romans' use, and abuse, of their gods is not a major issue in the play. Eliot, on the other hand, lays great stress on the spiritual emptiness of his people. They watch the religious ceremony from outside, the mystery reported in the flat tones of a public broadcast: "Now they go up to the temple. Then the sacrifice." What follows is worse:

> (And Easter Day, we didn't get to the country,
> So we took young Cyril to church. And they rang a bell
> And he said right out loud, *crumpets*.)

The central feast of the Christian year becomes something to take the children to if a picnic does not work out. The bell is probably the bell rung at the elevation of the Host. The fact that from a distance the Host would look like a very thin crumpet evidently triggers young Cyril's burst of schoolboy impudence, a darkly comic variation on the popular materialism we see elsewhere.

What the people see of the military parade is equally material, beginning with a barrage of statistics: "5,800,000 rifles and carbines, / 102,000 machine guns" and so on—the equipment, in fact, surrendered by Germany after Versailles. This evokes not only the mechanized nature of modern war but its emphasis on the mass rather than the single hero. Battles are fought not by individuals but by armies with heavy equipment. A parade based on this sort of war is more tedious than exciting—"what a time that took"—and Eliot's hero is aloof from it. Shakespeare's hero belongs very much to another kind of warfare, dominated by single combat between great fighters. Cominius reports, "our spoils he kick'd at" (II.ii.124); a list of surrendered equipment would obviously be of no interest to him. In contrast to the impersonality of modern war, he focuses intensely on his relations with Aufidius, to which even the conflict of cities takes second place:

> Were half to half the world by th'ears, and he
> Upon my party, I'd revolt to make
> Only my wars with him. He is a lion
> That I am proud to hunt. (I.i.232–35)

Elsewhere there is sharp emphasis on the single-handedness of the hero's achievements: "he is himself alone, / To answer all the city" (I.iv.51–52); "alone I did it" (V.vi.116). Shakespeare was not to know, of course, how impersonal war would become. But this play embodies the antique heroism of single combat in a very clear way, as two modern productions in particular have demonstrated. Michael Langham at Stratford, Ontario in 1961 and Tyrone Guthrie at the Nottingham Playhouse in 1964 set the play in the early nineteenth century, with revealing results. The political scenes were clear and recognizable; the battles looked strange. Waterloo was not settled by a sabre duel between Wellington and Napoleon. Eliot's poem tells us deliberately what these productions told us inadvertently—that the age of the single hero is past.

Eliot's people, then, see only the externals of war, as of religion, and what they see is unheroic. Their lives are led on the level of sausages and crumpets. They betray their own lack of perception in the words, "we hardly knew ourselves that day, or knew the City," words which echo Menenius's gibe at the tribunes, "you know neither me, yourselves, nor any thing" (II.i.67). When Eliot's hero appears the voice of the people shades into the voice of a more discerning narrator, who sees how guarded, detached and yet intelligent the hero is; then narrative is replaced by lyric, as imagery evokes a spiritual depth behind the hero's public facade:

Look
There he is now, look:
There is no interrogation in his eyes
Or in the hands, quiet over the horse's neck
And the eyes watchful, waiting, perceiving, indifferent.
O hidden under the dove's wing, hidden in the turtle's breast,
Under the palmtree at noon, under the running water
At the still point of the turning world. O hidden.

The people tell themselves to look, but something in the hero remains hidden. That word "hidden," perhaps the key word in *Coriolan*, touches on one of the principal critical debates about Shakespeare's play.

Contrasting Coriolanus with Shakespeare's other tragic heroes, A.C. Bradley observes, "his inward conflicts are veiled from us" and goes on to accuse him of "self-ignorance."[8] Harley Granville-Barker makes much the same observation: "We are never...made free of the inner man," adding that it is appropriate for us *not* to see Coriolanus making up his mind to attack Rome, for he himself probably does not know how the decision took place.[9] More recent critics have echoed this view. For E.A.J. Honigmann, "the hero is not only a mystery in himself, he is also unfathomable in his two most important relationships,"[10] those with Virgilia and Volumnia (to whom we will return). Michael Goldman refers to the hero's "lack of inwardness," adding that there is nothing much to hide: he "still possesses a live human centre, but...it is sadly stunted, nearly mute."[11] It is on this point, what the hero is hiding, that critics divide.

Against Granville-Barker's contention that Coriolanus is not introspective enough to have internal conflicts, Sailendra Kumar Sen has argued that the conflicts, though they appear fitfully, are there.[12] Even in his solitude, William Blissett claims, there is an inner life we can recognize: "That which dies tragically in him is the solitary achiever, whatever is unsocial and not to be educated, alone and raging, in each of us, in every mother's son."[13] In what may be the most striking and suggestive account of Coriolanus's inner life, Una Ellis-Fermor, while admitting that we have to work by "secret impressions" to penetrate the hero's silence—including by the end the silence of "smooth concealing speech"[14]—argues that his inner life can be recovered. What she finds is very different from the solitary rage Blissett sees. Her argument hinges on Coriolanus's greeting to Virgilia, "my gracious silence, hail!" (II.i.174), in which she detects "a longing for the balancing silences, graces, and wisdom banished from the outer world but vital to wholeness of life, and an acknowledgement, albeit inarticulate, that in Virgilia these values were preserved."[15] Blissett's reading is more in tune with the evidence of the play; Ellis-Fermor's by comparison requires an act of faith. But if she were writing about Eliot's poem there would be no problem, for "silence, grace and wisdom" are precisely the inner qualities evoked in the imagery that surrounds his hidden hero.

But what exactly is the relation between the hero and these images? Are these qualities that he has, or qualities he lacks and longs for? "Triumphal March" suggests the first, and "Difficulties of a Statesman" the second. The Christian suggestion of some of the images—the dove's wing, the running water—aid the transition from one poem to the next, as the triumph turns sour. To several critics the palm tree suggests Palm Sunday, and "Triumphal March" is therefore an ironic parody of Christ's entry into Jerusalem. According to Elisabeth Schneider, Eliot's hero "is not the saviour needed but the pseudo-saviour deserved...though still, he is not the still point of the turning world."[16] He is, for Balachandra Rajan, "the substitute the world seeks for the Word."[17] The triumphal entry of Shakespeare's hero is touched by a similar irony: "I have seen the dumb men throng to see him, and / The blind to hear him speak" (II.i.260–61). The dumb can only see, the blind only hear; Coriolanus is not the Saviour. Yet the relationship of Coriolanus and Christ has parallels as well as ironic contrasts. Both go from triumph to betrayal, and from betrayal to death. After the triumphal entry on Palm Sunday comes the arrest in the garden: "Then all the disciples forsook him, and fled" (Matthew 26:56). So Coriolanus complains: "our dastard nobles... / Have all forsook me" (IV.v.76–77). What would have happened in the later poems of the *Coriolan* cycle we do not know; but as Christ dies to save humanity, Shakespeare's Coriolanus, in saving Rome, knowingly delivers himself to death at the hands of Aufidius, "by his own alms empoison'd, / And with his charity slain" (V.vi.11–12). *Coriolanus* is as much concerned with the hard facts of this world as is any play of Shakespeare's; the spiritual vision that touches it does so only glancingly and with ironic effect. But the more overt Christianity of Eliot's poem alerts us to the fact that the spiritual level of Shakespeare's play is also in important respects Christian.

Coriolanus loses his office. The fate of Eliot's hero is worse: he gains office and has to exercise it. As "Triumphal March" is written mostly from the viewpoint of the people, so "Difficulties of a Statesman" is written mostly from the viewpoint of the hero, imitating the movement in Shakespeare's play from public to private drama.[18] The mindless list of military equipment finds its parallel in the equally mindless list of public honours (the sort of honours Shakespeare's hero despises): "The Companions of the Bath, the Knights of the British Empire, the Cavaliers, / O Cavaliers! of the Legion of Honour." The sudden isolation of the word "cavaliers" suggests a longing for the more heroic life it represents. Instead of this life the hero finds himself swamped by the routines of bureaucracy:

> The first thing to do is to form the committees:
> The consultative councils, the standing committees, select committees and
>   sub-committees.
> One Secretary will do for several committees.

Shakespeare could not have anticipated modern bureaucracy any more than he could have anticipated modern war; but he and his contemporaries knew what bureaucracy was, and there may be a hint of it when Sicinius asks an Aedile if he has collected the votes of the people "by tribes" (III.iii.11). We see the way heroism is swallowed up by political routine when a Volscian soldier assures Aufidius that Corioles, which we have just seen Coriolanus capture in such exciting fashion, will be "deliver'd back on good condition" (I.x.2). In politics the ordinary people are made to matter. Eliot's hero is surrounded by demands for "a *representative* committee" (my emphasis) and while Coriolanus has to beg votes from "Hob and Dick" (II.iii.115) his successor must find a job for Arthur Edward Cyril Parker, "with a bonus of thirty shillings at Christmas." (Crumpets at Easter and a bonus at Christmas—that is what Cyril's spiritual life comes to.) Peace has come, but it only produces bureaucratic irritations:

> A commission is appointed
> To confer with a Volscian commission
> About perpetual peace: the fletchers and javelin-makers and smiths
> Have appointed a joint committee to protest against the reduction of orders.

Aufidius's servants would find their preference for war confirmed: peace, they declare, "makes men hate one another...because they then less need one another" (IV.v.236–38). To this Eliot adds a modern gloss: peace is bad for business.

Meanwhile that other peace, the inner peace, eludes the hero. For an aristocrat Shakespeare's Coriolanus takes remarkably little interest in his ancestry; we hear nothing even of his father. It is Virgilia who says that she brought forth young Martius "to keep your name / Living to time" (V.iii.126–27); the hero himself, solitary achiever that he is, has no interest in being part of a line. It is Brutus, not Coriolanus, who gives an account of his enemy's great ancestry (II.iii.235–46). Similarly, Eliot's hero takes no satisfaction in "the row of family portraits, dingy busts, all looking remarkably Roman" and permits himself a sour pun when he describes their "noses strong to break the wind." It is not here that he finds the satisfactions of the inner life. In broken words he recalls the hidden spiritual reality of the earlier poem, as something that was once decisive and real but is now in the past: "O hidden under the...Hidden under the...Where the dove's foot rested and locked for a moment." He turns to what seems to be, as in Shakespeare's play, his strongest relationship:

> Mother
> May we not be some time, almost now, together,
> If the mactations, immolations, oblations, impetrations,
> Are now observed
> May we not be
> O hidden

The hesitation of the second line suggests frustration; the irritable rhythm of the sequence from "mactations" to "impetrations" conveys impatience with the religious routines that are supposed to put us in touch with spiritual reality. The syntactical looseness in the placing of "O hidden" makes us wonder if the words convey the hero's desire to be hidden from the world or his fear that spiritual reality is hidden from him. What is clearest is the longing to be with his mother, sharing with her the spiritual peace he has lost in the routines of life.

There is no indication of her response. Elsewhere we have read back from Eliot to Shakespeare, letting something said in the poem alert us to a significant absence in the play: the overt lack of spirituality in Eliot's people makes us notice that Shakespeare illustrates the same point by omission; the open scorn Eliot's hero feels for the family busts makes us notice that Shakespeare's hero never mentions such things. Now we may reverse the process: the silence of the hero's mother in *Coriolan* acquires extra meaning if we look at the relations of Coriolanus and Volumnia. She has shaped his nature as decisively as any character in Shakespeare shapes another. Their relationship appears correspondingly intense; but at crucial points she lets him down. When she insists he compromise with the people, he is bewildered: "I muse my mother / Does not approve me further" (III.ii.7–8). When he makes it plain that the success of her plea to spare Rome means his death, she says nothing in return. As Eliot's hero cries simply, "Mother...O mother," Shakespeare's shows an uncharacteristic plaintiveness, as though begging her to recognize what she has done:

> O my mother, mother! O!
> You have won a happy victory to Rome;
> But for your son, believe it, O, believe it,
> Most dangerously you have with him prevail'd,
> If not most mortal to him. But let it come. (V.iii.185–89)

The last words suggest a resigned turning away, as he realizes the plea has failed. Shakespeare's hero never seeks with his mother the shared spiritual experience Eliot's would like to have with his.[19] If Ellis-Fermor is correct, that is the relationship he has with Virgilia. Certainly his greeting to his wife, "O, a kiss / Long as my exile, sweet as my revenge!" (V.ii.44–45), conveys an emotional intensity we never hear when he is talking with Volumnia. What he does seek from her is some understanding of the consequences of her influence on him: the integrity that will not let him compromise with the people to gain political office; the unexpected humanity that will bring about his death. In both cases she is unresponsive; and the fact that Eliot reports no response from his hero's mother may be equally ominous.

There is no consolation at home, either in thoughts of noble ancestry or in the understanding of those one loves. That leaves the world outside the city, outside human relations altogether, the world of nature. *Coriolanus* being a city-bound play, this world is much less developed than it frequently is in Shakespeare, but the hints we get of it from the hero himself suggest something dark and inhuman. He goes into exile "like to a lonely dragon that his fen / Makes fear'd and talk'd of more than seen" (IV.i.30–31). Arriving as a stranger in Antium, he claims to dwell "I'th' city of kites and crows" (IV.v.43). His change of allegiance is accompanied, in other words, by a brief sojourn in a subhuman world of monsters, predators and scavengers. He comes out of it inhuman, a nameless thing determined to destroy Rome. The view of nature in "Difficulties of a Statesman" is more enigmatic:

> Meanwhile the guards shake dice on the marches
> And the frogs (O Mantuan) croak in the marshes.
> Fireflies flare against the faint sheet lightning

It seems a low world, in which the cry for "light" at the end of "Triumphal March" is answered only by faint glimmers. Yet it is to the frogs and fireflies, to the world of small creatures, that Eliot's hero seems to turn for comfort in the end:

> O hidden
> Hidden in the stillness of noon, in the silent croaking night.
> Come with the sweep of the little bat's wing, with the small flare of the firefly
>   or lightning bug,
> 'Rising and falling, crowned with dust', the small creatures,
> The small creatures chirp thinly through the dust, through the night.

Shakespeare's hero is broken and remade during his wilderness journey, though he is also dehumanized and needs to be broken again if he is to find himself. Could it be that Eliot's hero also needs some experience with a nonhuman night world, a world of small creatures, as a way of being broken and remade, a necessary reduction and renunciation as part of his spiritual progress? This would be consistent with Eliot's interest in the *via negativa*. Lacking the rest of the cycle, we can only speculate, but we remember that Celia in *The Cocktail Party* is "crucified / Very near an ant-hill."[20]

Whatever spiritual hopes the hero may have are swallowed up in the voices of the political mob. As Shakespeare's citizens break into a group chant of "it shall be so, it shall be so!" that drives Coriolanus to his final blistering denunciation of them (III.iii.119), Eliot's hero is attacked, as on a bad night in the House of Commons, by the group chant of "RESIGN RESIGN RESIGN." Here *Coriolan* breaks off, its hero's response to the popular voice unheard, hidden from us. Shakespeare's hero is also hidden at the end, not behind others' voices but behind his own. He seems to have buried, or lost, his knowledge that Aufidius will kill him, and deals with the Volsces like a man who really expects to spend the rest of his career with them, putting the best face he can on his decision to spare Rome. When Aufifius denounces him he seems amazed and indignant. What has happened to that earlier clear insight? We never know. *Coriolanus* is a finished work, as *Coriolan* is not; but in its final view of the hero it is in its own way a fragment. Both play and poem oppose the hero to a populace whose interests are material and who, though temporarily excited by the heroic, are finally at odds with it. Both show a military hero at a loss in the civilian world of politics and finding no satisfaction in his immediate relationships. Both suggest in this frustrated hero a hidden, inward quality. As Shakespeare allows his people flashes of intelligence Eliot denies to his, so Eliot develops the hero's inner life, particularly its spiritual dimension, more fully than does Shakespeare. But in both cases the hero's full experience finally eludes our grasp.

NOTES

1. G. Wilson Knight, "T.S. Eliot: Some Literary Impressions," *T.S. Eliot: The Man and his Work*, ed. Allen Tate (New York: Delacorte Press, 1966), 247.

2. Knight, "T.S. Eliot," 248.

3. All references to *Coriolan* are to the text in T.S. Eliot, *Complete Poems and Plays* (London: Faber and Faber, 1969).

4. See, for example, Rajeev Taranath, "Coriolanus, The Waste Land and the Coriolan Poems," *Literary Criterion* (Mysore), 6 (1963): 111–20; and E.P. Bollier, "A Broken Coriolanus: A Note on T.S. Eliot's 'Coriolan'," *Southern Review*, 3 (1967): 625–33.

5. All references to *Coriolanus* are to the Arden edition, ed. Philip Brockbank (London: Methuen, 1976).

6. On the importance of this issue in Shakespeare's play, see Paul A. Cantor, *Shakespeare's Rome: Republic and Empire* (Ithaca: Cornell Univ. Press, 1976), 49–50.

7. Balachandra Rajan recalls the sausage-seller who figures in Aristophanes's satire on democracy, *The Knights*. See *The Overwhelming Question* (Toronto: Univ. of Toronto Press, 1976), 142.

8. "Coriolanus" (British Academy Shakespeare Lecture for 1912), *Studies in Shakespeare*, ed. Peter Alexander (London: Oxford Univ. Press, 1964), 222, 229.

9. Harley Granville-Barker, *Prefaces to Shakespeare*, vol. 2 (Princeton: Princeton Univ. Press, 1951), 156.

10. E.A.J. Honigmann, *Shakespeare: Seven Tragedies: The Dramatist's Manipulation of Response* (London: Macmillan, 1976), 172.

11. Michael Goldman, *Shakespeare and the Energies of Drama* (Princeton: Princeton Univ. Press, 1972), 118, 120.

12. Sailendra Kumar Sen, "What Happens in *Coriolanus*," *Shakespeare Quarterly*, 9 (1958): 331–45.

13. William Blissett, "Coriolanus and the Helms of [the] State," *Familiar Colloquy: Essays Presented to Arthur Edward Barker*, ed. Patricia Bruckmann (Ottawa: Oberon Press, 1978), 159.

14. Una Ellis-Fermor, *Shakespeare the Dramatist*, ed. Kenneth Muir (London: Methuen, 1961), 61, 67.

15. Ibid., 74.

16. Elisabeth Schneider, *T.S. Eliot: The Pattern in the Carpet* (Berkeley and Los Angeles: Univ. of California Press, 1975), 145.

17. Rajan, *The Overwhelming Question*, 73.

18. Referring to the poem, Bollier, "Broken Coriolanus," 631, relates this to the movement from public triumph to inner loneliness in Beethoven's *Coriolan* overture as analysed by J.W.N. Sullivan in *Beethoven: His Spiritual Development* (London: Jonathan Cape, 1927).

19. According to Elisabeth Schneider, Eliot was "deeply attached to his strong-willed mother (she had died in 1929, the year before *Coriolan* was begun)" (*Pattern in the Carpet*, 144).

20. T.S. Eliot, *Complete Poems and Plays* (London: Faber and Faber, 1969), 434. The only human figures in the natural world, the guards shaking dice, may suggest the soldiers casting lots for Christ's robe.

KING LEAR, SIR DONALD WOLFIT AND *THE DRESSER*

R.B. Parker

Among recent Shakespearean "offshoots" few have had the success of Ronald Harwood's *The Dresser*, which opened at the Manchester Royal Exchange in March 1980, with Tom Courtenay in the title role of Norman and Freddie Jones as his employer, a failing actor-manager called only "Sir." It transferred to the Queens Theatre in London at the end of September 1980; opened for a successful New York run in 1981, with David Waller replacing Freddie Jones; and in 1983 was made into a film, with Albert Finney's flamboyant reading of Sir winning a nomination for an Oscar.[1]

The Dresser takes place in January 1942, during the German blitz, and is set backstage in a shabby provincial theatre, apparently in the north of England. The action revolves around Norman's determination to protect Sir against the effects of a nervous breakdown, and get him, willy-nilly, back on stage to play his two hundred and twenty-seventh performance of King Lear. The symbiosis of these two characters and the text's alternation between events backstage and the snatches of Shakespearean dialogue heard intermittently "on stage" (which is offstage in *The Dresser*) recall Stoppard's *Rosencrantz and Guildenstern Are Dead*, as does the non-stop, absurdist chatter with which Norman distracts and comforts Sir. The relationship of "Cocky" and "Sir" in *The Roar of the Greasepaint, the Smell of the Crowd* comes to mind too, also the characterization of Archie Rice in *The Entertainer* (a role Wolfit played on radio); and, on a more serious level, the relationship between Clov and Ham (another Wolfit radio part) in *Endgame*, particularly its final tableau of Ham dead with his face covered and Clov unable to leave despite his anger and resentment. Sir's absurdist sense of being goaded onward by a mysterious "him" or "them" also recalls Beckett; and another obvious analogue is Brecht's *Galileo*, where the transformation of an ordinary man to mythic proportions in the scene of the Pope's enrobing is reflected by a sequence in *The Dresser* in which Sir regains control and confidence as he dons his make-up and costume for King Lear: "Once he's assumed the disguise, he's a different man," says Norman (42).² The idea that the characters he impersonates can contaminate an actor's personality may also owe something to two films: *Theatre of Blood* (1971), in which an actor murders critics in the guises of his Shakespearean parts, and more specifically *A Double Life* (1947), in which Ronald Colman plays an actor whose role as Othello fatally swamps his personal identity. "Her Ladyship," Sir's wife, tells of Sir waking her in bed after a performance of "The Black One" in terror lest he do her harm, an incident which also bothers Sir himself (18,24).

The Dresser's main parallels, however, are to *King Lear* itself. Long passages from the tragedy are acted "on stage" in the second act; and, as one would expect from a company of Shakespearean troupers, the dialogue is liberally sprinkled with echoes from it and other Shakespeare plays. Most importantly, there are obvious resemblances between the career of the aged monarch and that of the theatre manager in decline, each trying to maintain tyrannical control over his disintegrating kingdom. Lear's reliance on the love of Cordelia and the Fool is matched by Sir's dependence on the devotion of Norman, who combines aspects of both characters—Sir considers that Shakespeare originally doubled the roles to save money (87)—not to speak of Kent, heartbroken by lack of recognition in the dénouement. Sir's relations to the unsympathetic, sexually and professionally jealous Her Ladyship, to the provocative, conniving Irene (the "company mattress"), and to the faithful Madge, resentful and tongue-tied, reflect Lear's relations to Goneril, Regan, and the bleak side of Cordelia. The storm that provides *King Lear*'s central image gives *The Dresser* one of its key scenes, where adversity also makes men discover their brotherhood ("We're a band of brothers," Norman tells the usually recalcitrant Mr. Oxenby, "and you're one in spite of yourself"); and, as in Shakespeare, this is extrapolated beyond the stage and actual weather—to the German bombing outside and the "storm clouds" of Sir's mental confusion. Sir's exhausted worry towards the end of Act II about what may happen to Norman (86) parallels Lear's concern for the Fool at the height of *his* exhaustion, just as Sir's insistence that only Norman understands the driven nature of Sir's talent ("Norman understands. He knows it is not me but what is given me, bursting out of me, passed on ruthlessly," [69]) reflects Lear's claim that only Poor Tom can tell him what makes "these hard hearts" and is "the cause of thunder"; and at *The Dresser*'s end, Norman sings the Fool's (and Feste's) song about "the rain that raineth every day." Both plays obviously share many of the same themes: service, loyalty, madness, endurance, and the question of who it is who ultimately loves best. As Harwood himself puts it, "*The Dresser*'s compounded impact comes from its being a *Lear* within a *Lear*."³

Critics reacted very differently to this intertextuality, however. At one naive extreme, the play was dismissed as "a contrived story of a shallow man"; its parallels to *Lear* were seen as mere mechanical inflation, "limited, fraudulent, and double-dealing...[because] It's a set up in the most can't lose, sentimental way"[4]; and its depiction of Sir was condemned as a personal "calumny" of Donald Wolfit.[5]

More perceptively, but still negatively, it was seen as a typically modern exercise in anti-heroic irony, scaling down the myth of Lear in order to expose the twentieth-century's impoverishment of spirit.[6] And certainly, compared to "the greatest tragedy in the language" (84), *The Dresser* is radically diminished. Its characters are meaner in their egotism—even Norman ends with the cry "what about me?"—and Sir, in particular, lacks any of Lear's cosmic sense. He is already in midbreakdown when we first see him; and whereas Lear fiercely resists weeping and fights to maintain his rationality and independence, Sir, as we are told in the first line and many times during the play, weeps constantly and is only too ready to surrender to emotionalism and dependency on others. Nor does he share Lear's sense of anagnorisis: despite his momentary care for Norman (which, anyway, he intends partly as a form of harassment), there is no equivalent for Lear's acceptance of responsibility for Cordelia, the Fool, and all "poor naked wretches"; and this lack of anagnorisis reflects the static nature of *The Dresser*'s action, in which there is no real plot but rather a sense of weary existentialist repetition, of crises, jokes, and insults that have been encountered many times before. Thus the dominant mood of the play is one of confession and nostalgia, which cannot rise to spiritual insight or sense of moral victory. Sir wishes to evade the storm, not brave it (with a parallel reversal between the Fool, who tries to dissuade Lear, and Norman, who encourages Sir to re-enter the "storm clouds" of his mind); and what we are left with is a typically modern play about the defeat of everyman, to which the intertextuality of *Lear* gives shape while at the same time emphasizing the difference of scale between the two experiences. In Diane Aquino's striking phrase, Harwood gives us "a Lear that cries."

There is obvious truth in such a reading: *The Dresser* is certainly not *King Lear*. But neither is it so entirely debunking. It makes a positive statement as well as a negative one; and, despite Harwood's disavowal in the Foreword, the key to this double vision is its relation to Sir Donald Wolfit. Harwood has said that the core of *King Lear* for him is its final comment that "the oldest have borne most: we that are young / Shall never see so much, nor live so long";[7] and at one transcendent moment during his performance, Sir says that he seemed to see himself from above, "I saw an old man and the man was me" (70)—echoing Goethe's famous comment that "an old man is always a King Lear." Wolfit's "Lear [was] in truth a very foolish, fond old man," records Caryl Brahms, "his majesty behind him, his human fallibility and the infirmities of wrecked old age upon him; and yet, in everything, a father and a king."[8] My argument will be that the closeness of the role of Sir to Donald Wolfit was no "calumny"; we are not meant to see him merely as a "third rate actor-manager in a tatty tour in the provinces" (as Her Ladyship blisteringly tells him), but also as a very great actor who, despite his egotism and old-fashioned mannerisms, was capable of an emotional response that *did* capture (from time to time) the imaginative grandeur of Lear, and who was moreover a driven man faithful to his sense of mission, of personal "destiny," through breakdown and despair even to death. And it is this courage to go on in the face of despair that links him to Norman, who gives the title to the play, begins it and, even more importantly, ends it, and is equally prominent as Sir—as the Fool is not in *King Lear*.

2

Ronald Harwood certainly knew Wolfit very well. From 1953 to 1959 he was a member of Wolfit's Advance Players, serving as Wolfit's dresser, acting in small parts, and eventually becoming the company's business manager; and Wolfit left him £50 in his will to write his biography.[9] He seems to have tried to avoid a negative response to *The Dresser* from Wolfit's friends by dedicating it to the autobiography of Sir John Martin-Harvey in a programme note to the Manchester try-out (and, indeed, substantial passages are adapted in *The Dresser* from that book); and in his foreword to the published edition he emphasizes that "Sir is not Donald Wolfit," that, in particular, the very antagonizing character of Her Ladyship is not his friend Rosalind Iden, Lady Wolfit, and that he himself is nothing like the homosexual Norman (dedicating the edition to his three children as further proof). However, Lady Wolfit was convinced enough of resemblances to write to *The Sunday Telegraph* complaining that Harwood had taken advantage of her husband's kindness,[10] and to anyone who has read Harwood's biography of Wolfit the parallels are obvious and unavoidable.

To begin with only major facts: during the blitz only Wolfit played Shakespeare in London and toured *Lear* through the provinces; he had just such a miscellaneous company of "old men, cripples, and nancy boys" (to quote Sir [33]), because all able-bodied actors had been conscripted; he had to make do with just such rudimentary sets, props, and hand-me-down costumes; he showed just such apparent meanness about expenses, because he was funding the tours himself and never managed to do more than break even (prompting Hermione Gingold's celebrated *mot*, "Olivier is a *tour de force* while Wolfit is forced to tour"); and just such—in fact, the identical— announcement was made to his audiences when the air raid sirens sounded as Norman delivers to conclude Act I. Sir's autocratic, self-centred production methods, moreover, were the ones that Wolfit was notorious for: all lighting focussed on the character *he* was playing; constant upstaging of other actors, who were warned never to move while he was speaking; and an insistent demand from them for pace—pace— pace so that he could steal attention by speaking his own lines slowly. Sir also has the same concern for special theatrical effects as Wolfit (who told Michael Redgrave he had worked out thirteen special effects for *King Lear* and meant to keep them however Tyrone Guthrie tried to direct him at the Old Vic [*Wolfit*, 214]). Especially, Wolfit had the same Edmund Kean-like reliance on large-scale emotion to make a performance work: "Feel it, my boy," says Sir to Geoffrey, impressed into playing the Fool, "feel it, that's the only way...[but] no crying in the part...*I* have the tears in this play" (45). "To see Wolfit in a play," wrote Caryl Brahms, "is to see a character in a spotlight by reason of his giant acting of it,"[11] and, though he established very thoroughly the "foolish, fond old man" aspect of the role, it was precisely for its emotional size and reckless intensity that Wolfit's King Lear was so famous. He played that role every season from August 1942 (when the first night coincided with a thunderstorm, as Sir says his first Lear did) till October 1953. The premier critic of the day, James Agate, called it, "the greatest piece of Shakespearian acting I have ever seen"; and after one performance the poet Edith Sitwell wrote to Wolfit, "The cosmic grandeur of your *King Lear* left us unable to speak. All imaginable fires of agony and all the light of redemption are there."[13] However, constant repetition of those thirteen special acting effects and the difficulty of sustaining such complete emotional abandonment for performance after performance led to later appearances sometimes being criticized for overacting and for the mechanicalness of which Madge relentlessly reminds him in the middle of Act II (74).

It is not just the overall impression of *The Dresser* that shouts out "Wolfit," moreover; numerous parallels of detail can be found in Harwood's biography. The painting of Sir as Lear to which Norman compares his disrobing in the town square (14) was an actual painting which Wolfit gave to Harwood, then characteristically took back (as Sir reclaims his Kean ring from Madge):

> His first act of friendship came after I witnessed a performance of *King Lear*. Dressed as one of the hundred knights—six in Wolfit's production—I stood in his dressingroom waiting for him to change. I was still hopelessly moved by the last scene and Wolfit...saw my tears and walked solemnly to a portrait of himself as Lear that hung on the wall. He took it down, stuck a piece of paper on the back, and inscribed it. I clutched the gift, turned to leave the room when his voice rang out, "No, my boy, put it back, and take it at the end of the season." (*Wolfit*, xiii)

Similarly, the gesture Norman refers to during the breakdown, "he lifted both hands as he does to convey sterility into Goneril's womb" (15), was one of Wolfit's thirteen special effects and is more explicitly described in the biography:

> And from the air, arms upstretched, Lear clutches the physical parcel, as it were, of his savage imprecation, pulls it down and then, to be rid of it, hurls it at his ingrate daughter. (*Wolfit*, 162)

The fur coat bought on Sir's first Canadian tour which he soils in his breakdown in town is also factual:

> He arrived at the theatre [on the night of a *King Lear* performance] dressed in a voluminous brown teddy-bear coat acquired in Canada while touring with Barry Jackson. Black homburg on head, shoulders stooped, the actor advanced towards the stage door, paused and glanced at nearby bomb damage, appeared to nod gravely as if he understood some symbolic message

contained in the ruins, and marched into the theatre. (This scene was fully represented in the movie. [*Wolfit*, 159])

Rosalind Iden was as completely unused to making decisions for herself as Her Ladyship is in the movie; she also had a ritual of putting on Wolfit's cloak for Lear; because Wolfit's second wife refused to divorce him, for many years Rosalind Iden lived with him without marriage (which gave her at least one breakdown); and her father, like Her Ladyship's, was a famous Shakespeare director, Ben Iden Payne. Like Sir, Wolfit was bitter at not being knighted in 1947 along with Olivier and Gielgud (whom he loathed as much as Sir does "Sir Arthur Palgrove"); and Harwood says he was always called "Sir" till 1957 when he in turn was knighted, and only then did he ask to be addressed as "Donald." For a long time he was passed over for the movies, like Sir, because he played to the cameras too directly. He had little time for the new, socially oriented drama, though, like Mr. Oxenby, the formidable Harold Pinter, not to speak of Harwood himself, was an actor in his company. He considered he had a personal vendetta with Hitler, because they were born on the same day. Like Sir, he was fascinated by but never successful in *The Master Builder*; and like Sir with Kean's ring, Wolfit had a superstitious reverence for props used by previous great actors—and among such memorabilia he willed to the British Theatre Museum two rings, one that had belonged to Henry Irving, the other to Fred Terry.

The props Norman holds for Sir's entrance at the beginning of Act II were precisely those Wolfit always had waiting for him: a whip (that had belonged to another of his heroes, the actor Randall Ayrton) and a silver tray containing a Guiness (he drank eight bottles each performance) and a damp chamois rag (replaced by a powder-puff in the play, to be more easily recognized); and like Sir he economized by powdering his makeup with Brown and Polson's corn flour:

> He undressed and, wrapped in a pink towelling dressing gown, began to make up, painting in the heavy lines on his forehead and about the eyes, whitening his thick bushy eyebrows, high-lighting his nose with a broad line. Next came the white beard, then the wig, stuck down with white-hard varnish. As the make-up took form, as wig and beard were fixed in place, and the joins disappeared under the thick grease-paint, so his hand began to tremble, his eyes to narrow and appear rheumy, his head to shake. At last he powdered—Brown and Polson's corn flour—and brushed it off, once more to reveal the aged face of the King. (*Wolfit*,160)

Like Sir, Wolfit raged that the storm was never loud enough, and had a miscellany of weird equipment to ensure an adequate noise:

> a wind machine, a rain machine, two timpani, a large empty water tank beaten with a padded stick, a sound-effects record, and the inevitable thunder sheet. (*Wolfit*, 248)

And the unsteady, hollow tree with a man inside which was the focus of the storm scene in the movie, was actually an eighteen-foot obelisk which required a stagehand behind to hold it upright. At the 1953 coronation, the stagehand got drunk and on the line "strike flat the thick rotundity o' the world" let the obelisk fall forward onto the back of Wolfit's head:

> When Wolfit came into the wings, he was limping (the bump on his head was concealed by his wig and he did like his injuries to be *seen*). With furtive glances over his shoulder, the madness of Lear still upon him, he cried hoarsely at his stage director, "Pam, Pam, Binkie Beaumont [a fashionable London impresario] has sent men to kill me." (*Wolfit*, 254)

Sir's exultant self-congratulation, "we've done it, Will, we've done it" (84), is based on Wolfit's notorious cry after the first night of his *Tamburlaine* at the Old Vic, "Kit, my boy, we've done it"; and the play closely imitates Wolfit's famous "hanging from the curtain" call and speech to the audience (with the movie adding extra Wolfit details):

> as was his custom, he pounded the curtain with his fist ("let 'em know you're coming" he used to say) and stepped out through the opening, into the light, clutching the curtain for support. The volume of acclaim washed over him; the actor who had not surrendered to the storm, surrendered now to his public. Wearily, he raised a hand for silence—it came at once. In a spent voice he offered his thanks for the way they had received "the greatest tragedy in our language" (*Wolfit*, 164)

Despite certain differences, then, such as Wolfit's younger age in 1942, and despite the Foreword's disclaimer, there can be no doubt that Sir was closely based on Wolfit and his performance of Lear; so Harwood's attitude to Wolfit almost certainly provides a clue as to how he expected audiences to react to Sir. He writes that Wolfit's detractors

> enjoyed thinking of him as a barnstormer, roaring and ranting his way through Shakespeare in Wigan or Southend. Certainly, at his worst, he fitted that description; at his best, he generated passion and power that was magnificent and overwhelming. (*Wolfit*, xvi)

and he quotes with approval Richard Burton's comment after Wolfit's death:

> I considered him to be one of the greatest if not the greatest Lear that I ever saw....I think that he had something that a great many of us are afraid of, which is the ability to have a go and do dangerous things, to take tragedy at its very greatest, almost to the edge of absurdity, and still remain within the line, at its very best. (*Wolfit*, 274)

So if the numerous parallels to Wolfit mean anything, it must surely be that Harwood regards Sir as an erratic but genuinely great actor of what he calls the "unfashionable theatre"—those shabby touring companies that kept the tradition of reckless "emotional" acting alive: "the old way is best," said Wolfit himself (*Wolfit*, 210), "when the heart's blood flows from end to end of the theatre and magic is in the air." And far from seeing him as an ironically diminished everyman, Harwood regarded Wolfit in person as very much larger than life:

> I have never encountered anyone with Wolfit's size of personality, or anyone more unashamedly individual. I am able to remember well the awe in which I first held him, the terror I experienced in his presence both on and off the stage....He was hated and loved, disliked and admired, shunned and welcomed....He was large and yet petty, compassionate and cruel, magnanimous and mean. Above all, he was an actor from the crown of his head to the soles of his feet; and he was intensely human. (*Wolfit*, xiv–xvi)

3

Once alerted to this positive response, it is not hard to see that Sir contains similar contradictions and is meant to seem heroic as well as petty. His claim that playing Shakespeare is a counter-offensive against the Nazi air raids—"each word I speak will be a shield against your savagery, each line I utter protection from your terror" (51)—may seem fatuous in the 1980s, but during the 1940s blitz it was taken very seriously, not only by Wolfit himself but by the people who stayed to listen to Dame Myra Hess playing the piano at the National Gallery while bombs exploded outside. It was in this mood that Olivier shot *Henry V* and made patriotic orations in the Albert Hall, that the Windmill burlesque theatre for years after the war proclaimed "we never closed." For anyone who remembers that time, it conjures up a sense of national solidarity against overwhelming odds—nicely captured in the movie where one can see that most of the weeping audience is in battle dress.

There is also an authentic sense of Sir as a "driven" artist, goaded on by a mysterious power that insists that he give more and more. His anagnorisis should perhaps be seen not in terms of Lear's recognition of responsibility and love, but as recognition of the price that he (and others) must pay for his unrelenting drive for excellence: "You have to keep faith with your aspirations and allow yourself to be enslaved by them, and the bondage is everlasting" (36). This explains his attraction to *The Master Builder*, in which the speech that fascinated Wolfit was Solness's cry,

> Don't you think, Hilde, that there are people singled out by Fate who have been endowed with grace and power to wish for something, desire it so passionately, *will* it so inexorably that, ultimately, they must be granted it? Don't you think so? (*Wolfit*, 205–6)

And closely linked with this is surely our acknowledgement of the courage it takes for Sir to re-enter the "storm clouds" of Lear's madness when he is so close to breakdown himself, to keep "on and on and on" in such dire circumstances: "to go on doing these things year after year, always with the terror increasing, because it's easier to climb than it is to hang on." (37)

The central theme of *The Dresser*, in fact, is this existentialist requirement to *go on*, this human sentence to "struggle and survival" despite despair and age and inevitable defeat. It is this which links Sir to Britain under siege and also, of course, to Norman, who bursts out at one point,

Struggle and survival, you say, that's all that matters, you say, struggle and survival. Well, we all bloody struggle, don't we? I struggle, I struggle, you think it's easy for me, well, I'll tell you something for nothing, it isn't easy, not one little bit, neither the struggle nor the bloody survival. The whole world's struggling for bloody survival, so why can't you? (40)

The limp-wristed, high-camp, bitchy characterization of Norman was thought by some reviewers, especially in the United States, to be as exaggerated as the theatricality of Sir; but as anyone who knew the theatre homosexuals of that generation can vouch, it is actually quite accurate. Camp was their form of defense and self-assertion in a society which totally repudiated homosexuality ("I hold no brief for buggers," growls Sir (47), echoing another famous Wolfit remark); and Norman is, in fact, based on another of Wolfit's dressers, David Dodimead, whose gestures and mincing walk were imitated by Tom Courtenay to the point of straining his spine and having to do a stiff course of Alexander back exercises.

Though at first Norman's speeches may strike one merely as an absurdist maze of *non sequiturs*, irrelevant detail, and foggily elusive reminiscence, a very clear picture of his character emerges from them. The "I had a friend" anecdotes are not just to divert Sir; they reflect Norman's own experience. The "friend" who was rescued from a mental home at Colwyn Bay by the offer of work on *Outward Bound* was pretty clearly Norman himself; and the final aborted "I had a friend once" is both a failure of his usual defense mechanism and an elegy for the departed Sir. The theatre with its camaraderie and creativity is Norman's haven, where "pain is bearable," and he sums up his credo at the end:

Never, never despairing...not once inside the building. Never....And never lonely. Not here...I'm not here for reasons of my own either....I've got what I want and I don't need anyone to know it. Inadequate, yes. But never, never despairing. (91)

And though he is certainly drunk and angry with Sir for not including him in the acknowledgements to Sir's unwritten "My Life" (the book that Wolfit left £50 for

Harwood to write for him), this after all is not what the play ends with. It ends with Norman's very Cordelia-like admission that his hidden solace and motive all along has been nothing less than an "achingly platonic"[13] love for Sir:

> Well, I have only one thing to say about him and I wouldn't say it in front of you [Madge]—or Her Ladyship, or anyone.....Or him. Specially not him. If I said what I have to say he'd find a way to take it out on me. No one will ever know. We all have our little sorrows, ducky, you're not the only one. The littler you are, the larger the sorrow. You think *you* loved him? What about me? (95)

That last phrase echoes Norman's earlier, self-centred "what's to happen to me?" and "what am I going to do?" (93,94), but here in context it also means, "I loved him even more than you"; and appropriately, when even the faithful Madge has left, Norman stays with Sir's dead body, crooning the Fool's sad song of experience, "He that has and a little tiny wit / With hey, ho, the wind and the rain."

The Dresser as a whole demands the same double response of irony and admiration as that final "what about me?" It must be seen not only in the context of Shakespeare's great tragedy but also of Harwood's love-hate relation to Donald Wolfit and Wolfit's own extraordinary performances as King Lear.[14] It celebrates daring and devotion and the courage to keep on, and should not be dismissed as sentimentality nor interpreted solely in terms of intertextual irony.

NOTES

1. There were also three Canadian productions: at the Citadel Theatre in Edmonton in September-October 1982, with John Colicos as Sir and Jeremy Hart as Norman; at the Vancouver Playhouse in October-November 1982, with William Hutt and Robin Phillips; and a Toronto Arts production at the Bayview Playhouse in January- February 1983, with Douglas Campbell and Nicholas Pennell.

2. The text cited will be Ronald Harwood, *The Dresser* (New York: Grove Press, 1981). References to it will be identified by page numbers in brackets.

3. Ronald Harwood, *Time*, 23 November 1981.

4. *Vancouver Sun*, 1 November 1982, C7.

5. Herbert Whittaker, *Globe and Mail*, 5 October 1980, 18.

6. This response was argued cogently by Deborah T. Aquino in a paper entitled "*The Dresser*: A Lear That Cries" at the *Shakespeare Association of America* meeting in Boston, 1984; the rest of the paragraph summarizes her main arguments, with

a few additions. My own point of view developed from being official "respondent" to this paper.

7. As reported by Michiko Kakutani in his review of the New York production, *New York Times*, 1 December 1981, D1.

8. Caryl Brahms, "Sufficient Magic," *Plays and Players* 7 (November 1959): 6.

9. Ronald Harwood, *Sir Donald Wolfit, C.B.E. His Life and Work in the Unfashionable Theatre* (London: Secker and Warburg, 1971), subsequently referred to as *Wolfit*. Wolfit had published his own account of the first half of his career under the title *First Interval* (London: Odhams Press, 1954).

10. "Wolfit and Harwood," *The Sunday Telegraph*, 26 February 1984.

11. Brahms, "Sufficient Magic," 6.

12. Agate and Edith Sitwell are quoted in *Wolfit*, 166–7.

13. Harwood, *Time*, 23 November 1981.

14. Further details about Harwood's relation to Wolfit can be found in an article in *The Sunday Telegraph Magazine* for 19 February 1984, 25ff.

INDIVIDUALISM AND ORDER IN THE *BYRON* PLAYS OF CHAPMAN AND JONSON'S *CATILINE*

John Margeson

It may seem a little perverse to write about two such different plays as *The Conspiracy and Tragedy of Byron* (1608) and *Catiline* (1611) in a single essay; nevertheless, bringing them together may be justified in part by the fact that they have a common basis for plot structure, a conspiracy against the state, and growing out of this structure a serious treatment of ethical and political issues. In their different ways, they exemplify the nature of early seventeenth-century tragedy in the humanist tradition, written for the stage and not for the study, and the practice of two learned playwrights in this form.

Chapman and Jonson did not, perhaps, share Garnier's belief, expressed in the preface to *Cornélie* and other dedications, that tragedy was the form most appropriate to a tragic age: "poème a mon regret trop propre aux malheurs de notre siècle."[1] England had so far been spared the rigours of the religious wars. But certainly the high value placed upon the tragic genre by humanists, its noble eloquence, its power to move and teach readers and auditors, must have had some influence. The recent success of Shakespeare's tragedies in the public theatre may also have had its effect. The Chapman and Jonson tragedies do not seem to have achieved a similar popularity, although *Byron* may have enjoyed a certain notoriety during its first run because of one or two scenes involving Henry IV's queen and his mistress, scenes objected to by the French ambassador and never printed because of the intervention of the censor. Both plays have had their severe critics in later years, *Byron* for its lengthy speeches and lack of action (more epic poem than dramatic tragedy), and *Catiline* for its depiction of positive values in Cicero, who, in George Hibbard's words, "is allowed to commit dramatic suicide by talking himself, the play, and the audience to death."[2]

A small link between the two plays may be found in the reference to Catiline near the beginning of *The Conspiracy of Byron*. Byron as special envoy to the court of the Archduke Albert is being tempted by the Archduke's agent, Picoté, to withdraw his loyalty from his master, the French king. Picoté has a carpet portraying the history of Catiline spread before Byron's feet to exemplify "Roman spirits," and observes "we'll make his feet so tender they shall gall / In all paths but to empire" (I.ii. 19–20).[3] Characteristically, Byron notes the special music and the fact of the carpet but not its message, which is somewhat ironic in its implications. Much later in *The Tragedy*, there is another suggestion of the Catiline story as Byron denounces the degeneracy of his age and declares his plan to destroy society in order to remake it:

We must reform and have a new creation
Of state and government, and on our Chaos
Will I sit brooding up another world.
I...
To the repairing of my country's ruins,
Will ruin it again to re-advance it.
                                    (I.ii. 29–35)

Contemporary writers of learned or historical tragedies were always careful to disclaim any reference in their work to personalities or events of their own times, being wary, on the basis of hard experience, of censorship and prosecution. But considering what we know about Chapman and Jonson, neither was likely to have chosen his particular subject for tragic development if it did not have some relevance to the society of his day. There were obvious connections, as Chapman pointed out and as others had pointed out before him, between the careers of Byron and Essex, Chapman's one time patron, and between the problems faced by Henry IV and Queen Elizabeth when great nobles conspired against them. And Jonson had little need to point to the resemblances between Catiline's conspiracy against the Roman republic and the Gunpowder Plot of recent memory. Beyond these superficial relations with contemporary events, there were issues of wider importance. In the *Byron* plays, the essential conflict lies between the free-wheeling individualism of a military hero at the end of the civil wars and the new order being imposed on a ruptured society by a king strongly aware of the necessity of limiting such individualism. In *Catiline*, the struggle is between the extreme and destructive individualism of a disaffected noble and the fragile order of the republic with its traditions of liberty, represented above all by the "upstart" Cicero.

As pointed out earlier, the two plays have similar plot structures, at least in outline, which depend on conspiracies against ordered government, and the eventual discovery and foiling of the conspiracies. The central characters in each are the rebels or conspirators on one side and the upholders of order on the other. Chapman divided the material he found in his source, Grimestone's *General Inventorie of the History of France*, into a large-scale double play, *The Conspiracy of Byron* and *The Tragedy of*

Byron. The question is often asked why he should have done this when the action of conspiracy, discovery, trial and condemnation was not very extensive without further invention. Chapman could certainly invent, as *Bussy D'Ambois* makes clear. There are no sub-plots and few subsidiary characters of interest. The two plays concentrate remarkably on the main contestants and the great issues at stake. Chapman's development of his material, as he worked out a new form for tragedy, lay in the direction of long, elaborate speeches, rhetorically organized yet dramatic and frequently ironic in their contexts: for the tempters and the tempted, speeches of complaint, boastfulness, anger on the part of Byron, speeches of warning from Henry. The writing is designedly poetic, making use of metaphorical language and extended similes of an epic kind, yet always focussed upon character and motivation, or upon the issues of contention between Byron and the king.

The Conspiracy is based on a series of clever temptations of Byron by the Duke of Savoy and his agent, La Fin, an unscrupulous malcontent at the French court, and the suspense in the action arises from the question of their likely success in bringing about a decisive break between Byron and Henry. Although ambitious and discontented, Byron is a curiously naive would-be rebel, unsure of his goal, easily manipulated through flattery and deception, and so unaware of the duplicity necessary for successful plotting that he cannot recognize it when it is being used against him. Henry, his great antagonist, is portrayed as a wise and just king, aware in general terms of what is happening, but facing a serious dilemma over what he should do with his old comrade-in-arms. The conspirators succeed in arousing Byron to an outburst of furious anger and a desire for revenge, but Henry achieves a reconciliation so that the first play ends on an optimistic note (like *Henry IV Part 1*). *The Tragedy* is a more concentrated play since Savoy plays no part in it, and it has a dramatic urgency growing out of the tragic momentum of the plot. Henry manages to lure Byron back to court, though with much deception and the use of "policy," to face the accusations against him. The latter part of the play is totally concerned with the trial and sentencing, and with Byron's passionate reactions.

With such a plot and the major characters representing divisive and unifying factors within the state, political factors were bound to come to the fore, particularly in a contemporary situation reflecting the religious divisions of northern Europe and the increasing importance of national monarchies like those of France and England. Yet Chapman did not neglect the personal dilemmas and emotions of his characters: the double play moves toward tragedy rather than to a political resolution at the end.

Chapman's development of Byron's character is interesting, not only from the psychological point of view, since he is concerned to show different aspects of Byron's conception of an individual's rights deriving from nature and from personal merit and achievement. When Byron first appears, he seems oblivious of the flattery and deception being practised on him at the Archduke's court in Brussels, and speaks eloquently in Marlovian terms of aspiration as the chief end of man (" 'Tis immortality to die aspiring"). Although later in *The Conspiracy* his contacts with Savoy and La Fin seem to offer goals of a less lofty nature which involve politic stratagems and worldly manoeuvres, he never quite loses this large, yet vague, aspiration of the spirit. At the end of the encounter with the astrologer, La Brosse, for example, he utters a memorable call to "worthy spirits":

> ...be free, all worthy spirits,
> And stretch yourselves for greatness and for height,
> Untruss your slaveries; you have height enough
> Beneath this steep heaven to use all your reaches;
> 'Tis too far off to let you, or respect you.
> (III.iii.130–34)

Another aspect of Byron's individualism that Chapman stresses is Byron's claim to absolute freedom of judgment, quite apart from the rule of law in society, or social norms of conduct. This attitude is presented first as a temptation to Byron by Picoté who speaks in the radical terms of Renaissance scepticism:

> Your Excellency knows that simple loyalty,
> Faith, love, sincerity, are but words, no things,
> Merely devis'd for form;
> (I.ii.116–18)

Although Byron seems to reject Picoté's convoluted argument against "flourishes of form" which have no value except as they work toward "private ends," later in *The Conspiracy* he echoes Picoté in arguing with La Fin, and enlarges the concept into a vision of "all the free-born powers of royal man" (III.i.31), a vision which links him, of course, with Bussy D'Ambois. The most compelling statement of this view occurs at the end of the scene in which Byron declares his freedom from the influence of stars and planets, after La Brosse has told him of the dire prospects of his nativity. To the free spirit

> there's not any law
> Exceeds his knowledge; neither is it lawful
> That he should stoop to any other law.
> He goes before them and commands them all
> That to himself is a law rational
> (III.iii.141–45)

Yet the dramatic irony of the play is already powerful, since it is clear that Byron himself allows passion all too often to overcome reason (as in his beating of the poor astronomer), and that he is scarcely a free spirit if he places his fate in the hands of deceiving flatterers.

It is probably difficult for an audience or a reader to *like* Byron: he is seldom intimate, even with a friend like D'Auvergne, and he brags too much and is inclined to lecture anyone who will listen. His individualism never becomes real individuality; he can be admired for certain qualities but not loved. One such quality is valour, the valour he was able to show in the past. Byron regards himself as a heroic individual set apart from the rest of mankind because of his exploits in the civil wars; he is the soldier who placed Henry securely on his throne; he is the saviour of France. Much of his discontent arises from his sense of injured merit, a lack of appreciation from those he served so well. He can no longer have every honour and prize he asks for, such as the command of the fort at Bourg, which becomes the bone of contention between himself and Henry. In a sense, he is no longer needed in a time of peace, and he therefore denounces "sensual peace" which "confounds valour and cowardice, fame and infamy." (*Tragedy* I.ii. 15–16) His boasting about the past, his linking of himself with the great heroes of antiquity who single-handed saved the state, becomes pathetic during his trial and condemnation as he tells the judges how he saved both them and France, recounts the number of his wounds, and stands a prisoner in the Golden Chamber where once he was honoured in royal fashion. Only one old soldier who is quickly hustled off speaks for him in the execution scene. Yet the proud, aspiring Byron returns briefly in his last speech as he describes the coming flight of his soul to heaven.

In his portrayal of Byron, Chapman is mainly interested in the motivation of the character-type that Byron represents, the heroic soldier unwanted in a time of peace who dreams of glory and is ambitious enough to seek means of action. Byron is never shown as having any awareness that a great and powerful man can scarcely be a law unto himself without disrupting the fabric of society. The dangers of Byron's kind of individualism to the fragile stability of the state are made evident chiefly through the reactions of Henry who is concerned above all with the rule of the kingdom and the security of his throne and his succession.

Chapman pictures Henry as a wise and just king, very nearly the ideal monarch, who fulfils the Erasmian principle that a king should be a good man. Henry is loyal to an old comrade like Byron, not anxious to be suspicious and almost to the last ready to forgive; though not without human failings such as keeping a mistress as well as a queen, he is undoubtedly pious and responsive to the idea of divine law superior to human law. And he endeavours to be a good and just ruler, as when he attempts to remove corrupting influences like La Fin from the court or insists on the rule of law rather than acting peremptorily in punishing Byron, as some of his advisors suggest. His major achievement, however, is in bringing peace to a war-ravaged society and restoring its health. It is the threat of further civil war, aided by such rival powers as Savoy and Spain, that forces him to take decisive action over Byron's dealings with his enemies.

Yet Chapman does not idealize Henry, turning him into some kind of secular saint, any more than Jonson idealizes the good magistrate, Cicero. Henry is vain enough to be rattled and annoyed by Savoy's excessive praise of Byron's exploits in the late wars, so that he falls into the trap of slight denigration of Byron that Savoy has set for him. Like Cicero, he is forced to use trickery and deception to get at the truth of the conspiracy and finds himself praising in a fulsome way the informer, La Fin, whom he had earlier banished from court in contemptuous terms. One begins to see, also, some hint of absolutist tendencies in, for example, his abrupt dismissal of the peers' excuses for not attending Byron's trial:

> I am resolv'd, and will no more endure
> To have my subjects make what I command
> The subject of their oppositions.
> (*Tragedy* V.i.96–98)

Henry's final words in the play—he does not appear in the trial scene nor subsequently—are a dispassionate and unsympathetic comment on what other would-be rebels can learn from Byron's futile rages as a prisoner, and a satisfied view of his present unrivalled state:

> Now I am settled in my sun of height,
> The circular splendour and full sphere of state
> Take all place up from envy
> (V.i.138–40)

Critics have argued that there is a lack of clarity in Chapman's attitude to Henry and to royal absolutism at this point in the play.[4] Is this last statement of Henry's to be read ironically in the light of the other views we have had of him in earlier acts, or is it meant to be taken straight as an admiring portrait of the future security and stability of the French state? Should it be seen against Byron's criticism of the "mizzling policy" of modern kings and tyranny acting upon individual rights and freedoms? If anything is clear, it is that Chapman paints realistically the power of a king in a contemporary state (a factor D'Auvergne has consistently warned Byron to consider), and expresses movingly the tragic downfall of a proud and rebellious noble who adheres to the individual values of an earlier age. The securing of peace and order in the land has its price.

Although also a play about a conspiracy, *Catiline* has a notably different pattern from *Byron* and a more complicated plot. For one thing, there are more characters, quite individually drawn, in *Catiline* and there is also much detailed conspiratorial plotting on both sides, as well as considerable variety of tone. After a taste of supernatural enforcement on the hellish side by the ghost of Sylla, Jonson devotes the first act to Catiline and his bloodthirsty fellow conspirators and the second to the Roman ladies, Fulvia and Sempronia, associated with them, whose life of pleasure and promiscuous love-making provides a demonstration of Jonson's satire as well as a new complication in the plotting. Although Cicero's name has been mentioned in contemptuous terms by the conspirators and the ladies, Cicero himself does not appear until the third act, now newly elected consul and the defender of the republic. It is in this third act that the counteraction against the conspirators begins, as Cicero learns full details from informers and foils an attempt on his life. In the last two acts, the balance of the play swings toward the upholders of order, Cicero and his allies in the Senate; the great rebel, Catiline, is given little of the tragic emphasis that Chapman devotes to Byron in the final act of *Byron's Tragedy*, although the messenger's speech describes Catiline as dying bravely and desperately on the field of battle.

In some ways, Catiline resembles that other self-seeking individual, Sejanus, in that he seems to have no other goal than his own ultimate satisfaction, whether that be power, wealth, or destruction. Yet Catiline's motivation is more complex than Sejanus's, more clearly bound up with a real personality. He clearly wants revenge, not only for being refused the command in the Pontick War but also, as the play develops, for being rejected as consul, and in general terms for being overlooked, forgotten. Like Byron he has a strong sense of injured merit, and like Byron regards himself as capable of sustaining the whole state through his own efforts:

> Was I a man, bred great, as *Rome* her selfe?
> One, form'd for all her honors, all her glories?
> Equall to all her titles? that could stand
> Close up, with ATLAS; and sustaine her name
> As strong, as he doth heav'n?
> (I: 83–87)[5]

Despising his fellow conspirators whose help he must call upon, he declares that he will use them only for his own ends and discard them when he has fulfilled his aims. Although Catiline speaks of ambition and the third chorus enlarges upon this theme, he rarely sounds like an ambitious climber on the model of Richard III or Sejanus. His vision of the destruction of the Rome that has rejected him is a powerful one, and he seems to have no conception of a new order in Rome that would be better than the present one.

Other motives for revolt are brought to the fore whenever Catiline addresses the other conspirators: he appeals to their appetites and desires, whether they be lust or luxury and wealth or the urge for bloodshed and destruction. When they unite in calling for "liberty" (I: 410), the term is highly ironic, suggesting licence, freedom from all restraint, rather than the old Roman ideal. Jonson makes abundantly clear in the first two acts how dangerous this selfish individualism in Catiline and his supporters is for the well-being and safety of society as a whole.

It is Cicero who recognizes this danger and who takes on, with Cato and a few others in the Senate, the role of upholder of order and defender of the republic. As Jonson has also made plain in the opening acts, Roman society at this period is by no means an example of strenuous virtue and traditional values. In addition, Cicero faces the difficulties created by ambiguous figures like Caesar and Crassus who privately give Catiline much support and indulge in constant sarcastic asides during Cicero's speeches of warning and concern in the Senate.

The Senate shows wisdom in selecting the kind of consul prayed for in the second chorus. Yet Cicero is vain about his virtue and conscience; he is undoubtedly a great "talker" (so Sempronia calls him) and suffers from being labeled a "new fellow," "a meere upstart." As Alexander Leggatt observes, he is constantly having to prove himself.[6] And he is forced to use spies and informers in his campaign against the conspirators, people of low moral character, as Henry finds himself doing in *The Tragedy of Byron*. Like Henry also, he is obliged to praise and flatter such informers to ensure their co-operation. Jonson and Chapman point to the compromises and stratagems which even good magistrates or rulers must use in the real world of politics. The problem Jonson raised was an old one, but often seems strikingly new: how does one deal with terrorists; remain passive, isolate them socially and politically, or take punitive action?

Though the play ends in a kind of triumph for Cicero and his "watchfulness," there is an ironic overtone arising from the well-known events that later overtook the republic. Jonson has made very obvious throughout the play the importance of the sinister presence of Caesar, on the sidelines at this point, but waiting his chance. His complete scepticism about absolute values is expressed in the advice he gives Catiline before the crucial meeting of the Senate at which Cicero is to present his evidence (III: 507ff.). He is clearly a more dangerous man than Catiline, and Cicero displays further weakness in refusing Cato's advice that he should also act against Caesar and Crassus. The ending is very different in effect from the ending of *Byron* where Henry's power is completely established as Byron moves toward his tragic despair. With Byron's death, the story is complete and finished. Chapman was not to know that two years after his writing of the play, Henry himself would be assassinated, a fact which may have given a later production a wry irony it did not possess in its first.

The two plays are tragedies which incorporate ideas about the nature of power and individual will, among many other issues, because they are in the humanist tradition of serious commentary on public life. They both fulfil the looser definition of tragedy characteristic of the age in that they possess high seriousness, are properly sententious, written with close attention to matters of style, and end with the death of a major character. Yet only *Byron* has a developing pattern of tragic emotion centered on a character of mixed qualities who can rightly be called a "tragic hero." Anne Barton has written of Jonson's "oddly anti-tragic purpose" in *Catiline*, claiming that he deflects attention away from individual tragic experience toward the social issues which were his main concern: public ruin, civil strife, Rome itself.[7]

One reason for this difference between the two plays lies in the ways they approach their didactic function. *Catiline* has a strongly satiric bias which works through direct condemnation (both Catiline and Cicero take part in this, as well as the Chorus), and through dramatic demonstrations of corruption in action. The second act is such a demonstration. Jonson uses character simplification, a mode of caricature, and exaggeration, as in the portrayal of Cethegus whom he presents as a restless, impatient, and bloodthirsty conspirator, eager to get on with the killing. Such devices, along with the ironic comments made as asides by Caesar and Crassus whenever Cicero is speaking, are often broadly comic in effect. The positive aspect of Jonson's political ideas is revealed in Cicero's character, his decision, and his speeches of justification to the Senate. As George Hibbard has pointed out, however, Jonson's imagination seemed to work at white heat only when he was dealing with the follies, vices, and crimes of mankind.[8] By contrast, Chapman avoids the satiric approach and develops several levels of meaning through the analysis of a heroic character, valiant but self-deluded, unfitted for a time of peace, and a corresponding analysis of the society and its ruler against which he chooses to struggle. The tale that Chapman tells is therefore both a fable with substantial significance and the moving tragedy of an individual.

Yet there is a greater sense of hellishly inspired, deliberately chosen evil in *Catiline* than in the *Byron* plays, from the Ghost of Sylla in the opening scene to the later speech in which Catiline declares his purpose to be known in subsequent ages for his supreme cruelties and his destructive energy directed at Rome (III:714ff.). The atmosphere of evil is intensified in melodramatic ways by the omens of darkness, groans and fire as the conspirators prepare to swear their oath, and by the nature of the black sacrament of drinking wine mixed with the blood of a slaughtered slave. The omens in *Byron* are less horrific, the astrologer's reading of the stars, for example, and the captain's account to Byron of what happened to his wild duck and his favourite horses: they point to a single downfall rather than to a general ruin. There is an uneasy tension expressed in *Catiline* between the demonic force which seems to have taken over the mind and spirit of Catiline and the gods who appear to sleep, though the gods do send a warning at the last moment by the meanest of instruments, a common strumpet, as Cicero puts it. In the *Byron* plays there is an overriding sense of providence, to whom Henry turns for guidance when he must take a final decision about Byron's trial and almost inevitable condemnation (*Tragedy* IV.ii.63ff.). Byron himself is not so much a man possessed by demonic forces as a character distantly related to the central figure of the morality plays: tempted to disloyalty and wrongdoing, brought back to a state of grace by the advice of a wise counsellor (the king), then relapsing into disloyalty once again, and eventually condemned and punished. His portrait is thoroughly contemporary, but indications of the older pattern are apparent in the tragic structure.

Neither Jonson nor Chapman forgot altogether the English tradition of morality play, history play, and popular tragedy in their adaptation and transformation of the content and form of classical and humanist tragedy. Part of Jonson's distinctive achievement depends on a quality which William Blissett has called *Romanitas*, "deep and prolonged familiarity with the history and culture of Eternal Rome."[9] It is this quality which informs the whole of *Catiline* and gives an extra dimension to his portrayal of the state, the magistrates, society itself, and the realities of power in difficult and strenuous times. *Catiline* is Johnson's attempt to relive the Roman experience, and at the same time give it a universal significance, just as *The Conspiracy and Tragedy of Byron* is Chapman's attempt to relive the experience of the last days of Essex.

If I had to distinguish between them, I am tempted, rather wildly, to call Chapman the Wagnerian in his approach and Jonson the Brahmsian. Like Brahms, Jonson built firmly on the classical tradition, but in the process of building, created a highly individual work that took the classical form into a new realm of struggle and triumph for the human spirit. Chapman was no less concerned with the eventual triumph of the human spirit, but he experimented with a new, almost operatic form of tragedy to explore his vision of the heroic character who possesses great valour but little wisdom. Chapman's play is more completely a tragedy, as we have come to understand the term, but both plays remain thought-provoking for the mature mind, for the kind of audience or reader Jonson and Chapman cared about most deeply.

NOTES

1. Quoted by Gillian Jondorf in *Robert Garnier and the Themes of Political Tragedy in the Sixteenth Century* (Cambridge: Cambridge Univ. Press, 1969), 27.

2. George Hibbard, "Ben Jonson and Human Nature," *A Celebration of Ben Jonson*, ed. William Blissett, Julian Patrick, R.W. Van Fossen (Toronto: Univ. of Toronto Press, 1973), 78.

3. I have used *The Plays of George Chapman: The Tragedies*, ed. T.M. Parrott (1910; reissued, New York: Russell and Russell, 1961) for *The Conspiracy and Tragedy of Byron* since my forthcoming edition has not yet been published.

4. Leonard Goldstein, *George Chapman: Aspects of Decadence in Early Seventeenth Century Drama* (Salzburg: Universität, 1975), 361; Robert Ornstein, *The Moral Vision of Jacobean Tragedy* (Madison: Univ. of Wisconsin Press 1960), 68.

5. For Jonson's *Catiline His Conspiracy* I have used the old-spelling edition of Lynn Harold Harris (New Haven: Yale Univ. Press, 1916), not always free from error, but more convenient for me than Herford and Simpson.

6. Alexander Leggatt, *Ben Jonson: His Vision and His Art* (London: Methuen, 1981), 152.

7. Anne Barton, *Ben Jonson, Dramatist* (Cambridge: Cambridge Univ. Press, 1984), 161.

8. George Hibbard, "Ben Jonson and Human Nature," 78. See also Hibbard's "Goodness and Greatness: an Essay on the Tragedies of Ben Jonson and George Chapman," *Renaissance and Modern Studies* 11 (1967): 14, 26.

9. William Blissett, "Roman Ben Jonson," unpublished public lecture given at Scaborough College and University College, University of Toronto, January 1984.

BEN JONSON AND THE PLAY OF WORDS

Wyman H. Herendeen

CENSURE. *Why, this is duller and duller! intolerable! Scurvy! neither* Divel *nor* Foole *in this Play!*

(*The Staple of News*, second intermean)

Jonson knew what he was getting himself into when he created his almost plotless play, *The Staple of News*, with a reversal in it which interrupts the play's inaction (in the fourth intermean) to "analyze" and underscore its arbitrariness. Similar strategies are used in *The Magnetic Lady*; Jonson repeatedly calls attention to the fact that he restrains the "dramatic" element of his last plays, emphasizes the precedence of form over action, and introduces into them various kinds of self-commentary (in the form of the chorus or intermean, for example).[1]

He consistently asks us to stop and listen to (not look at) his play—to follow it with our ears rather than our eyes (an admonition that would not have endeared him to his actors): "For your owne sakes, not his, he bad me say, / Would you were come to heare, not see a Play" (*The Staple of News*, Prologue). He wants us to note the words and language of his plays, and generally uses wordplay to add ambiguities to his characters rather than to give them greater coherence: "But is your name *Love-ill*, Sir, or *Love-well*?" (*The New Inn*, I.vi.95). And for centuries Jonson's critics have dutifully noticed that the characters of his last plays are generated by verbal subtleties rather than feelings. Anne Barton and D.F. MacKenzie see such use of polysemous names as Lovell and Frampul as examples of characters able to escape the fate of personality. Jonson's contemporaries, however, notably Owen Feltham, dismissed them as "jests so nominal" as to be meaningless.[2] Whatever the critical opinion, there is unanimous recognition of the unusually obtrusive presence of self-conscious wordplay in these plays.

Artistically Jonson never made life easy for himself. In the course of his last three plays he admits to their undramatic qualities and insists on the need for our willing suspension of disbelief. Our passive roles are underscored by his repeated use of unexpected reversals in the last acts of these plays.[3] In these and other ways Jonson makes us aware of the processes of reading, writing, and to a lesser extent hearing, these plays. We are told how they work and (lest we not understand) *why* they work. The result is an inordinately self-reflexive quality the full implications of which are described by Alexander Leggatt. They suggest

> what the publication of the Folio had already declared in a more solemn way: that Jonson intended to leave to posterity not a collection of miscellaneous writings but a single body of work to be read as a whole.[4]

More narrowly, they also force us to read the plays as poems, as forms, or imitations of action rather than as "actions"—and we might recall that here also Jonson returns to writing verse drama. As we will see, they do so by making us attend to words, listen, and follow the thread of language in ways that his earlier plays do not.

These are not altogether new ideas in Jonson's drama, but they do mark an emphasis that developed during the period of his absence from the popular stage between 1616 and 1626. Unmistakably Jonsonian, these plays are, nevertheless, quite different from their predecessors, with their prevalent artistic concern for the role of the poet in society. The differences are marked enough to make Jonson's critics question his artistic goals on his return to the stage in 1626, and to wonder what had gone on in his mind in the interim. Many of his contemporaries simply thought that he had lost his mind.[5] But the evidence of the plays encourages us to see the method, not the madness behind the work of a thirty-year veteran of the stage, and the most articulate literary theorist in England prior to Dryden. Recent studies have begun to recognize the originality of these plays, and I would like to go two steps further to suggest that these reflexive concerns for language, words, and texts are the logical development of Jonson's ideas about *ars poetica*, and second, that the logic of that development can be elucidated by tracing some of the dim but discernible steps through the period from 1616 to 1632, from his departure from the stage through the last plays.

Jonson's 1616 Folio is like a triumphal arch in his career. It was, of course, a massive editorial project of extraordinary historical importance as the first collected published "works" by an English playwright. For its preparation, Jonson gathered, organized, edited and revised most of his work. In looking selectively at it as an approach to his later plays, I want to emphasize what it reveals about how the dramatist perceived his art.

The volume consists of prefatory poems, the plays, the "Epigrammes," the "Forrest," "Entertaynments," "Panegyres," "Masques," and "Barriers." Of the plays, only those wholly by Jonson are included. He generally preserved edited or corrected texts: the revised *Every Man in His Humor* and the annotated *Sejanus*, for example. He organized them chronologically, and appended and even rearranged some dedications so that (to offer one example) the first fruits of his art, *Every Man in his Humor*, is dedicated to his mentor, William Camden.[6]

Significantly, the plays appear with Jonson's heretofore unpublished poems, which he describes in the dedication of the "Epigrammes" as "the ripest of my studies," although we must remember that he often stresses that his plays are also "poems." Thus there are links of various sorts from one section to the next which add coherence to the volume. For example, the dedication to Camden opening the volume resonates in epigram fourteen. Characters satirized in the plays appear in street garb in the "Epigrammes"; the vices lust and greed are present in lyric and dramatic poems, as are the Jonsonian virtues of wit, judgment, and chastity. These and numerous other thematic and formal links make the Folio a whole, with its own self-commentary built into it in the form of dedications, annotations, and those poems and plays which are explicitly concerned with aspects of the poet's art. Plays, poems, and entertainments all come from the same world and imagination and have the kind of ordering principle that Jonson describes in *Discoveries* as "the congruent and harmonious fitting of parts in a sentence...[having the] force of knitting and connexion: as in stones well squared, which will rise strong a great way without mortar."[7]

In these few details about the composition of the Folio, we see Jonson striving to "textualize" his work—the word is more appropriate than attractive. On the one hand, by virtue of the revisions, dedications, annotations, and the very act of publication, the plays have here a textual identity different from and more complex than that enjoyed (or not enjoyed) on stage. And in another sense, through their individual and collective identity (as with the sequentiality of the "Epigrammes"), the plays share in the grammar of the Folio, are part of the unfolding meaning of the author's work—or *Works*.[8] In the Folio we enjoy the drama of reading as well as the reading of drama.

Giving printed form to the spoken word was, of course, extremely important for the man who began his ten-year retirement from the public theatre with the massive, history-making Folio, and ended it with *The Staple of News*, where the ritual of printing (as it was for Jonson) is cheapened by the disregard for truth—where "news" and print represent a contradiction having threatening implications:

FIT. O Sir! it is the printing we oppose.
CYM. We not forbid that any *Newes*, be made,
But that 't be printed; for when *Newes* is printed,
It leaves Sir to be *Newes*. While 'tis but written—
(I.v.46–49)

During these years Jonson moved into the world of news, even became news himself: as the creator of court displays (on which his opinions are well known); through the news that came out of Scotland about his infamous journey (which he never recorded, while the "truth" of Drummond's printed gossip continues to be doubted); and through the public recognition of his honorary Oxford degree (1619).

Printed words and events, texts and truth—together they formulated themes of increasing importance for Jonson after 1616—themes which take the place of his other favourite subject, the role of the poet in society.[9] He explores them in the verse that he writes during these years, notably in his long non-dramatic poem, "An Execration Upon Vulcan." Among other things, it is an obsequy to works of his which never reached print, as well as a reminder that even the printed word is not safe from Vulcan's ire. A very personal ode by one for whom words and books meant much, it can be read as an intellectual autobiography in which aspects of Jonson's life and loss are expressed in terms of his library. Much of its rhetorical weight comes from his grudging acceptance of some of Vulcan's judgments on his art and life. He can bear the burning of the Globe (1616) and (more readily) the banqueting house at Whitehall (1619), and can even accept the destruction of some "parcels of a Play, / Fitter to see the fire-light, then the day."[10] But the scope of the poem narrows to the private space of his writing desk and the incomprehensible immolation of innocent incomplete manuscripts worthy of preservation:

> But in my Deske, what was there to accite
> So ravenous, and vast an appetite?
> I dare not say a body, but some parts
> There were of search, and mastry in the Arts.
> (85–88)

The poem is a reassessment of Jonson's intellectual life—a trial by fire—and in the course of it, what he would cling to and bring through the furnace would be his books and writings.

To say that Jonson lost part of himself in the fire is more than mere rhetoric; this poem of his maturity might be compared to another loss recorded in epigram forty-five, on the loss of his son. With his library he lost part of his humanity and his divinity:

>   if it be
> To all as fatall as't hath beene to me,
> And to Pauls-Steeple; which was unto us
> 'Bove all your Fire-workes had at Ephesus,
> Or Alexandria; and though a Divine
> Losse remaines yet, as unrepair'd as mine. (191–96)

Some sense of this loss, and a measure of his valuation of the printed word and perhaps even of his own Folio, can be had from Jonson's lines on the Shakespeare Folio, which must have been penned very near to the time of the fire. His lines on the frontispiece ("To the Reader") could be applied to his own volume, for their concern is the relation between art (two forms of it) and the artist. This emphasis is unusual, completely different from that in his poem on the frontispiece to Ralegh's *History of the World*, for example. Ironically contrasting the verbal and the visual images, he urges that the portrait (like other forms of ocular evidence) cannot offer an effective entry into the genius of the author: "O, could he but have drawne his wit / As well in brasse, as he hath hit / His face; the Print would then surpasse / All, that was ever writ in brasse." This stress on the need to understand the *mind* of the poet is not typical of the form, but it reflects concerns expressed in other of Jonson's works dealing with his own art and its relation to his audience.[11] His lines are not concerned with the beauties of Shakespeare's verse or the spectacle of his plays, but with the way that we can understand him through reading and text: "Reader, looke, / Not on his picture, but his booke." Implicit in the encomium is a theory of art rather unusual for a dramatist, but certainly consistent with other aspects of Jonson's aesthetic. As in Jonson's more ambitious verses "To the Memory of...William Shakespeare" (11:79–80), it begins with the distinction between book and spectacle, and it rests on the integrity of the word, particularly the printed word, as the real emblem of the poet's mind.

During these years Jonson's preoccupation with words, texts, and the writer's craft turned his thoughts to others who had made their way to Parnassus as well as Shakespeare—particulary Edmund Spenser. If this interest was not inspired by the appearance of the 1617 edition of *The Faerie Queene*, or the publication (in 1628) of a "new" poem by Spenser—the falsely attributed *Britannias Ida*, it was certainly fostered by his work on the *English Grammar*, which he wrote between 1619 and 1623 and rewrote in the years after the fire.[12]

The *Grammar* gives us a unique glimpse of Jonson's labours beyond poetry, drama and the court, and of the diversity of material whose loss is lamented in the "Execration." It shows us a man more doggedly dedicated to English letters (in every sense of the word) than his boisterous art reveals. Basically, it is just a different approach to the reform of English art and letters that he began when he undertook to revise *Every Man in His Humor*. Instead of literary form, which he deals with in the *Discoveries*, he is here concerned with etymology and syntax, "the true notation of words...[and] the right ordering of them."[13] Within the context of Jonson's artistic goals, it is as though, in 1616, he had put the literary cart before the horse in his efforts to instruct his countrymen—how could they understand poetry and drama if they could not understand English properly? Although addressed to an audience of "straungers" in a Renaissance version of an English as a Second Language text, his preface echoes with the concerns about communication, understanding, truth, and community that he places before his stage audiences, that other group of "strangers" who must also learn the "art of true, and well speaking." His prefatory remarks addressing the need to redeem the English language read like the introductions and choruses of his last plays: *artes grammaticae* enable us to "communicate all our labours, studies, profits, without an interpreter. We free our language from the opinion of Rudeness and Barbarisme, wherewith it is mistaken to be diseas'd."[14] These skills are the same as those needed by the judicious reader of the "Epigrammes" (see epigrams I, XVII, XVIII), and by the censorious audience who would follow the plays without an "interpreter."[15]

The *Grammar* is an incomplete and derivative work, but in adapting his sources Jonson leaves the indelible mark of his own thoughts and personality during these years. In order to properly elucidate the parts of grammar, he must illustrate them. His preparations for the work sent him back to the early philological and educational works of the English Renaissance. His principal English models and sources are Thomas Smith's *De recta et emendata linguae anglicae scriptione* (1568) and Richard Mulcaster's *The First Part of the Elementary* (1582); these are supplemented by various sixteenth-century continental texts that he is usually careful to acknowledge.[16] From these he draws most of his classical authorities. For the disposition of his own argument he also draws on a contemporary grammar that he does not acknowledge— Alexander Gill's *Logonomia Anglica* (1619 and 1621). Gill is the person who, in 1632 (already a friend of Milton's), perhaps miffed by Jonson's treatment of his treatise, attacked him mercilessly for the inane low humour and dullness of *The Magnetic Lady*. This is the same Gill who almost lost his ears for toasting the assassin of Buckingham in 1628—the year of Jonson's *The New Inn* and probably the time when Jonson was revising the *Grammar*. Innocent as it appears, this work has significant political, personal, and artistic implications.

Gill, obviously completely in agreement with Jonson about the importance of poetry in society, offers pages of passages from Spenser to demonstrate the ornaments of style.[17] In thus setting up Spenser as a model of English language, and effectively canonizing a man not much Jonson's senior, Gill turned Jonson's thoughts once again to the vexed problems not only of language, style, and speech, but also of poetic achievement and posterity. As with his assessment of Shakespeare—honest and admiring as it was—the questions Jonson confronts are not those of the role of the poet in society, but the nature of poetry: stylistic criticism. His idealization of the poet seems to be vindicated, but his own judgment of what poetry is and should be is threatened. To see Spenser, who in Jonson's opinion "writ no language," held up as a model of style in an English grammar must have riled Jonson. That Jonson himself is cited— once (for catalectic verse)—must have only further pained him.[18]

Jonson was a man of strong opinions about art: he saw clearly the distinction between Shakespeare's naturalness and his own art, just as he saw the distinction between Spenser's artificiality and his own colloquial style. In both cases popular opinion seemed to weigh against him and his judgment. At least it did when he was working with Gill's *Logonomia*, where he encountered not only Spenser's spurious medievalism, but other illustrations of aristocratic and Petrarchan verse from Wyatt,

Campion, and others collected in Davison's most flowery of anthologies. In Gill's approach to grammar and style he met with an alien view of poetry and society: with an emotional, amorous, courtly tradition that defied all that Jonson's art stood for.

Jonson's grammar counters that tradition with another one which is radically different in its assumptions about language. In rejecting Gill's illustrations and seeking out his own, Jonson reveals his own poetic concerns and outlines a vernacular tradition which lends weight to the opinions he upholds in his own art and which he will address directly in his last plays. His second book, on syntax, contains few passages from Renaissance love poetry, and offers instead examples going back to the origins of the English vernacular tradition in prose and verse, including Chaucer and Lydgate. Indeed, the three sources for most of Jonson's illustrations, Chaucer, Lydgate, and Gower, form a triumvirate presiding over a tradition of vernacular language reform that Jonson saw himself as part of.[19] Their honest style, Jonson felt, contrasts with the impure Petrarchanism (or Spenserianism) sampled in Gill's work. The hypothetical student reading these two grammars would have met with radically different languages, and would have received two very different kinds of education.

The illustrations from these and many other authors provide an interesting commentary on Jonson's aesthetics. Among the others cited are passages from religious controversialists and from sermons—from various kinds of didactic literature of commitment and polemics, all having typically Jonsonian vigour and immediacy. There are passages from Thomas More, Bishop Jewel, and Thomas Norton, all dealing with rebellion and dissent. Unlike earlier grammars, with their respectful classicism and politically tame poetry, Jonson's prickles with political content and resonates with a strange subtext of controversy. Speaking of the article "A," Jonson offers the following illustrations:

Sir Tho. More. *Such a Serpent is ambition, and desire of vain-glory.*
Chaucer. *Under a Shepheard false, and negligent,*
The Wolfe hath many a Sheepe and Lambe to rent.

Illustrating the idea of "*this*, and *that*, being Demonstratives," he cites John Cheke's *The Hurt of Sedition*; how "before the Participle present, *An*, hath the force of a *Gerund*" is demonstrated by lines from Lydgate:

The King was slaine, and ye did assent
In a Forrest an hunting, when that he went.[20]

His startling final illustration, on the four kinds of sentences, is a passage from John Cheke's warning against sedition:

When common order of the law can take no place in unruly, and disobedient subjects: and all men will of wilfulnesse resist with rage, and thinke their owne violence, to be the best justice: then be wise Magistrates compelled by necessitie, to seeke an extreme remedy, where meane salves helpe not, and bring in the Martiall Law, none other serveth.

Incompleteness is often a cloak for political expression.

It is not enough to say that Jonson's *Grammar* tries to give the reader the true honest English of a better age, and that it is more muscular, involved, and political than that of other grammars. It is also a language of action, incitement, warning, and judgment rather than of ornamentation. It is unmistakably the language of Jonsonian drama, although more explicitly political. Surprisingly frequently, there are warnings about rebellion, allusions to regicide, attacks on disobedience, folly, and vice, even misgovernment. Jonson's text is free of anything like political commentary, and he confines himself to his role of grammarian. How much cunning there is behind these selections is difficult to determine, but we can see that Jonson is offering a more daring view of language than that of Alexander Gill. It is also one whose lesson applies pointedly to the man who, outspoken in his hatred of the King's favourites, illustrates at the best, a naive understanding of the politics of language, and at worst, the dangers of seditiously licentious speech.

In a way quite unusual for a document like this, Jonson's grammar evokes a strong feeling of unrest. Written (and rewritten) at a time of tension, it offers a strange warning that language is volatile. Jonson conceals any design behind this apparently unfinished, posthumously published work. Nevertheless, it reveals his view of the word and language as dangerously explosive, and his illustrations give notice to all parties. The innocent looking parts of grammar are like shrapnel, texts like hand grenades that go off at unexpected times and in unexpected places. Generally, it shows us Jonson's view of words as part of a combative verbal world to which Jonson was reassessing his relation during these years.

Thus, at a time when Jonson *published* only three court masques he was otherwise much occupied, in his verse and prose, with questions which figure prominently in his last plays. These plays are to a large extent about words—about his art too, but about the components of the dramatist's medium rather than about the role of the poet. *The Staple of News* is about words and truth, how printed words pretend to truth and how the news mongers, uncontrolled, threaten to fabricate a simulacrum of reality, a lie which can subvert truth, reason, good sense, and judgment. Almost all anti-masque, it culminates in the restoration of order which is also a return to the past initially undesired by the prodigal Peniboy Junior, and results in the collapse of the house of words (V.i).

In *The New Inn* and *The Magnetic Lady* Jonson uses words and names much as he does in his verse. Names rather than humours shape the identities of many of their characters, and we can see how this is an extension of other of Jonson's interests. As with Compasse, Lovell, and Lady Frampul, names set a parameter of meaning for characters moving from ambiguity to redefinition. Quite literally the thread of meaning for characters is also the thread of style and syntax:

> P.IV. Not that I see through his perplexed plots,
> And hidden ends, nor that my parts depend
> Upon the unwinding this so knotted skeane,
> Doe I beseech your patience.
> (V.ii.41–44)

In *The Staple of News*, *The New Inn* (IV.iv), and *The Magnetic Lady* (IV, Chorus), Jonson describes characters' progress towards recognition in the same terms that he used in *Discoveries* (1623–35?) to define style: "Our style should be like a skein of silk to be carried and found by the right thread, not raveled and perplexed; then all is a knot, a heap."[21]

In this respect, *The New Inn* is largely a drama of definition—most notably of love and valour, and in *The Magnetic Lady* an elaborate pun unravels and comments on the confusion of the plot. As we follow the thread of Jonson's art here (this is a recurrent motif in the play), we disentwine the confused identities of Placentia and Pleasance. The process is one by which we redefine the range of meaning behind them and their names, learn that Pleasance *is* Placentia, that chivalry is fertile love. As in *The New Inn*, with its recollection of Castiglione, Jonson's art here takes us back to Italy, to these two characters' shared meaning in the word *piacenza*, which is first of all a silken weave or fabric (like that which Damplay, Probee, the audience, and Sir Diaphanous Silkworm follow). Lydgate also used the word in its Italian sense.[22] In both plays, dramatic anagnorisis is a process of definition, the play of a drama of words so that Jonson's art is ultimately about itself, its words, and the quest for meaning through form and style.

The links between Jonson's "middle years" and his last plays is also consistent with what some see as symptoms of his growing conservatism.[23] Jonson never introduces into his plays anything as explicitly political as the warning against rebellion that concludes the *Grammar*, but the poet who almost became the Master of Revels writes with what might be regarded as a conservatism that is itself reinforced by the implicit conservatism of the romance mode, with its courtly platonism that appealed to Henrietta Maria.[24] The royalism of his art, if that is what it is, is always that of an outsider and functions more as a warning than a defence. *The Staple of News* is severely critical of the public's inability to judge and interpret the truth of appearances, and by the time of *The Magnetic Lady*, he all but gives up on the ideal of an educated public, resting content to address the King alone. Nevertheless, the institution satirized in *The Staple of News* is, at least in part, one established by the King, the office of the Public Register,[25] so that with popular satire also comes a royal warning which would seem to support suppression of news to avoid the kind of political misjudgment that is instanced in the passages quoted in the *Grammar* and in Gill's behaviour.

In *The New Inn* Jonson defines his setting—the Light Heart Inn—in terms of particular significance for Charles. Again concerned with the range of meaning of his words, Jonson has the Host define his retreat in terms of his personal "inheritance," as his "magna charta"—his right to be lord and master of his own house. The phrase, repeated several times during the play, is one that was in fact part of "every hostlers language" (I.ii.35). It was fresh in the King's memory as well, because of the various objections, in the name of the Magna Charta, to recent "charges" and "impositions" (in the form of a "Benevolence") levied on the people. The resistance culminated in a "Petition of Right" and a bill proferred by Jonson's friend, Edward Coke [26] in the year of *The New Inn's* disastrous performance. Charles granted the petition and thus reconfirmed the authority of the Magna Charta.

With ambiguity typical of Jonson's last plays, its principle in the play is both upheld and redefined, for the Host is both lord of his inn and yet not absolute sole master of it. Like Charles and his subjects, he must recognize the limits of authority. Lovell, for example, defies his host and persists in his melancholy until he submits to Prudence's rule and joins the court of love. Yet, if the Host is not an absolute monarch in his house, he acts a major but not tyrannical role in effecting the final reconciliation. But he too learns things that redefine the terms of his authority, notably that his "guests" are actually his kindred. The Host is finally an enlightened monarch (in both senses) in a house not really his own, one which is presumably soon to be dismantled.

In a similar way Jonson's use of romance both is and is not aristocratic and conservative. The ambiguity is caused, in part, by the adaptation of romance features to domestic city comedy. In this hybrid form we have a characteristically Jonsonian expression of courtly *noblesse* when Lovell defines valour. Although the valiant and wise man "never goes the peoples way" and runs counter to "opinion" (IV.iv.213–15), he is also a man of the people. Echoing Seneca (and the spirit of the Magna Charta), he proposes a definition of valour that is hardly in the mood of *Il Cortegiano* and the other courtly guides which serve here as his model:

> The things true valour is exercis'd about,
> Are poverty, restraint, captivity,
> Banishment, losse of children, long disease.
> (IV.iv.105–108)

With all the other ideals from the Italian handbooks that the scene echoes, Jonson endows his valiant lover with a social conscience and middle-class concerns, not for his prince (as in Castiglione) but for his fellow man and family, those which inspired the resistance to Charles in 1628.

These dramas of redefinition each break down barriers of inclusiveness or exclusiveness of vision. The thread of the plot of *The Magnetic Lady* leads us around and to the centre of family, marriage, and fortune, and it is followed by Compasse. The walls of the New Inn are moveable, impermanent, as the Host and all the other characters must finally acknowledge before their reunion is possible. And in various ways this dramatic effect is achieved by Jonson's redefinition of his characters—by breaking down and revising the meaning of the words and characters that people his art—and we can see here concerns and techniques which are logical advances on his earlier work. Wordplay is even more important in these plays than in earlier of Jonson's plays. The low comedy of *The New Inn*, for example, is almost entirely play on words; *badinage*. Wordplay for its own sake *is* the action of these scenes rather than accompaniment to the action, as was the case in *Bartholomew Fair*, for example.

These characteristics make the plays unusually self-reflexive, even for Jonson, whose plays are all, in one way or another, concerned with art. But as in the *Grammar*, Jonson makes us follow words—characters—as they assume meaning. In grammar this occurs through syntax; in drama, through action, but in these last plays, the actions *are* words, speech, poetry, and text. More often than before, names are verbal (Compasse, Fly, Polish, Practice, Lovell) rather than adjectival. Jonson seems to imagine the play's ideal performance as analogous to reading, as a process of comprehending language through its grammar, again, the kinds of concerns that occupied him from 1616 until his return to the stage. In Jonson's isolation, the ideal drama has an ideal audience—theoretically, the King. As he prepared his *oeuvre* once more for publication, Jonson again imagined his art as unfolding as texts and having the unassailable form of a book, and his plays as plays of the imagination:

A skeine of silke without a knot!
A faire march made without a halt!
A curious forme without a fault!
A printed booke without a blot.
All beauty, and without a spot.
(*The New Inn*. IV.iv.9–13)

NOTES

1. Unless otherwise noted, passages from Jonson's works are from the C.H. Herford and Percy and Evelyn Simpson edition, *Ben Jonson* (Oxford: Clarendon Press, 1925–52), subsequently referred to as *H&S*. Each of the three last plays (I omit *The Sad Shepherd* because of its incompleteness) advances on Jonson's self-referential methods in ways more complicated than can be dealt with here. His techniques include expanded use of choral commentary, textual apparatus such as dedications and notes, and most important here, dialogue and action dealing self-consciously with words, language, and writing. Many of these considerations

enter Alexander Leggatt's chapter "The Poet as Character," in *Ben Jonson: His Vision and Art* (London: Methuen, 1981), 199–233.

2. Anne Barton, *Ben Jonson, Dramatist* (Cambridge: Cambridge Univ. Press, 1984), 170–94, discusses Jonson's use of names and (274–75, 399) emphasizes how particularly in *The New Inn* their ambivalence signals a different kind of Jonsonian character. D.F. McKenzie's full article, *"The Staple of News* and the Late Plays," in W.F. Blissett, Julian Patrick, and R.W. Van Fossen, eds., *A Celebration of Ben Jonson* (Toronto: Univ. of Toronto Press, 1973), 83–129, also addresses changes in Jonson's characterization and use of names after *Bartholomew Fair*. There are significant differences in Jonson's use of names in the early plays and in the "Epigrammes" and the late plays. The fullest discussion of naming in Jonson's verse is Edward Partridge's "Jonson's *Epigrammes*: the Named and the Nameless," *Studies in the Literary Imagination* 6 (1973): 153–98. Owen Feltham's verses on *The New Inn*, where he mocks Jonson's punning names, are printed in *H&S*, vol. 11, 339–40.

3. Katharine Eisaman Maus, *Ben Jonson and the Roman Frame of Mind* (Princeton: Princeton Univ. Press, 1984), 149.

4. Leggatt, "The Poet as Character," 225.

5. There is, of course, Dryden's famous pronouncement on Jonson's "dotages." There was a storm of discussion, for and against these last plays—see *H&S*, vol. 11, 332–55 for the sheaf of responses to them, and 349–50 for verses dealing with the "exhaustion" of Jonson's wit.

6. See W.H. Herendeen, "'Like a circle bounded in itself': Jonson, Camden, and the Strategies of Praise," *Journal of Medieval and Renaissance Studies* 11 (1981): 137–67, for discussion of the Camden dedication, previously intended for *Cynthia's Revels*, and epigram 14.

7. Ben Jonson, *Discoveries*, lines 1976–81.

8. The epigram, the art of writing "on" something, influenced Jonson's view of language and writing, not only in "poetic" but also in dramatic forms; Jonson's theoretical writings increasingly deal with the process of giving meaning through writing (and reading). Until recently, the play of text and context figured more prominently in critical discussions of Jonson's verse than his drama; see Leggatt, "The Poet as Character," 224–6 and 232–74, Partridge, "Jonson's *Epigrammes*," and Herendeen, " 'Like a Circle Bounded in Itself.' "

9. All of Jonson's drama is in some degree concerned with his art, but the Folio plays are more concerned with the social role of the poet, while the last plays have a more particular focus on how to read and understand the poet's work.

10. "An Execration Upon Vulcan," lines 132, 155, 43–44, 85–88.

11. See Margery Corbett and R.W. Lighbown, *The Comely Frontispiece: the Emblematic Title-Page in England, 1550–1660* (London: Routledge and Kegan Paul, 1979), 191–202, for examples of the form.

12. Jonson laments the loss of the *Grammar* in the "Execration"—he obviously thought highly of the work, and he seems to have been rewriting it between 1625 and 1628, although it was published in 1640. The *Grammar*'s concern for language and syntax complements the discussion of form and genre in *Discoveries*, which Jonson also wrote during these years and which also represents part of Jonson's reassessment of his art.

13. Jonson, *Grammar*, 467.

14. The Preface. The emphasis on language and understanding complements that of the critical apparatus accompanying the late plays, and might be contrasted with the different critical concerns in the prologues and dedications of the plays in the Folio.

15. See the Chorus at the end of Act IV of *The Magnetic Lady*.

16. See *H&S* vol. 11, 165, for enumeration of Jonson's sources for the *Grammar*.

17. Alexander Gill, *Logonomia Angelica*, 17. Gill's original and interesting work shows the extent of Spenserian revival at this time; his development of a phonetic spelling is an important contribution to the study of Renaissance prosody.

18. Gill, *Logonomia Angelica*, 143; catalectic verse is a form having lines of diminishing syllabic count. For Jonson's remarks on Spenser's language, see Jonson, *Discoveries*, lines 1806–7.

19. See also Jonson's *Golden Age Restored* (1615). Gower's association with uncorrupted English began as early as Berthelette's edition of his work in 1532 (*H&S*, vol. 10, 558). In 1589, George Puttenham (*The Art of English Poesie*, vol. 1, 31) also links these three poets with the "first age" of English literature and learning, identifies Wyatt, Surrey, and others cited by Gill, with the next generation of Italianate "courtly makers."

20. Jonson, *Grammar*, 535–36.

21. Jonson, *Discoveries*, lines 1997–99.

22. The theme of unravelling the thread of plot and character identity pervades the play and involves more obvious, but less interesting instances of wordplay than that of the shared Latin and Italian stem for these characters. For Lydgate's use of the word (which Jonson probably met with when preparing the *Grammar*), see the Oxford English Dictionary entry for "pleasance."

23. As McKenzie's article points out, Jonson's conservatism is better seen as increasing isolation from his public and from court. Barton, (*Ben Jonson, Dramatist*, 300–320) discusses the retrospective "Elizabethan" elements of Jonson's late work; Annabel Patterson, in *Censorship and Interpretation: The Conditions of Writing and Reading in Early Modern England* (Madison: Univ. of Wisconsin Press, 1984), 121–44, points to the ambiguities behind Jonson's political position.

24. Jonson held the reversion to the office until his death. See Patterson, *Censorship and Interpretation*, 158–85, for an interesting discussion of the political implications of the romance form.

25. See *H&S*, vol.10, 257.

26. For a transcript of the major documents surrounding the petition, see *The Constitutional Documents of the Puritan Revolution, 1625–1660*, selected and edited by Samuel Rawson Gardiner (Oxford, 1906), 65–70.

THE SILENT WOMAN IN THE RESTORATION

A.H. de Quehen

The Silent Woman fared badly in Jonson's own time; but the play enjoyed belated success in the 1660s, during which eleven performances are recorded, as against nine each of *The Alchemist* and *Bartholomew Fair*, and three of *Volpone*.[1] These performances every few months would have justified Dryden's examination of *The Silent Woman* as a work of theatrical as well as theoretical interest. When he drafted his *Essay of Dramatick Poesie*, between June 1665 and the end of 1666, the theatres had been closed by the plague; but Dryden might well recall *The Silent Woman* on stage at Drury Lane in June 1664 or at the Inner Temple the preceding February. When he subsequently revised his "loose papers," Dryden could have in mind the play's production at Court in December 1666 or at Drury Lane in April 1667. The theatrical currency of *The Silent Woman* was fortunate for Dryden, the play being very well suited to his essay's arguments.

Provocative though it proved among the literati, the essay did not save *The Silent Woman* from the recession in Jonson productions through the rest of the seventeenth century. Like *The Alchemist* with single performances in 1674 and 1675, and like *Bartholomew Fair* with a single performance in 1682, *The Silent Woman* was hardly staged in the later part of Charles II's reign and not at all in the years that followed: London players acted it at Oxford in 1673, and it was played in London early in 1685.[2] There was of course an increasing stock of plays written since 1660 from which revivals would be preferred, and after the union of the two Companies in 1682 there was less call for plays new or old; yet the neglect of Jonson was so out of keeping with his great reputation that some redress might be expected. In 1700 a Jonson revival began with *The Silent Woman* and *Volpone* enjoying most productions (roughly two per year), *The Alchemist* and *Bartholomew Fair* rather fewer. *Bartholomew Fair* lost its popularity after 1720 and was not performed at all after 1735; *The Silent Woman* and *Volpone* did well until the 1750s; *The Alchemist* remained a success throughout the century, joined in 1751 by the rediscovered and revised *Every Man in His Humour*. Regular performances of *The Silent Woman*, one or more each year, at Drury Lane came to an end in 1742; then the rival Covent Garden company produced the play between 1745 and 1748; then Drury Lane attempted a last revival in 1752. Last, that is, with Jonson's text, for a version by George Colman was produced at Drury Lane in 1776 and revived for a night in 1784.[3] That was the last performance of *The Silent Woman* until the end of the nineteenth century.

In speaking of "Jonson's text," as opposed to Colman's version, allowance should be made for some cutting and verbal alteration in the earlier eighteenth-century productions. That would seem to have been required when the play was enclosed and punctuated by divertissements of a very different kind: the performance on 13 December 1703 is advertised with "Italian sonatas on the violin by Gasperini. [Dancing] By the Devonshire Girl. *A Comical Entertainment between Scaramouch, Harlequin, and Punchinello*."[4] The entertainment anticipates *Die schweigsame Frau* of Richard Strauss and Stefan Zweig, where the wretched comedians have penetrated the text itself, young Henry (=Dauphine) having gone theatrical and married into a troupe which he brings to his uncle Sir Morosus's home. The last word may be found in the advertisement of the performance on 31 May 1709: "Mr. Wm. Pinkethman will speak an Epilogue riding on an Ass," a hackneyed device pioneered by Joe Haynes, which the polite world continued to find amusing.[5] The early eighteenth- century productions were staged in a distinctly different theatrical milieu from that of the 1660s: the tone and preoccupations of Jonson must have come to seem a little strange, and it is difficult to imagine what direct influence he might have had in the age of Steele.

Many of the allusions to *The Silent Woman* in the Restoration are simply allusions to Morose, showing how the idea of such a character had found a ready place in the literate mind. So, for example, Etherege writes in a letter from Ratisbon that "ceremony is as unsufferable to me as noise was to Morose."[6] Dryden, and after him Dennis and Congreve, worried over Morose's plausibility; but Morose had firmly established himself by filling a gap in his own dramatic context and in that of polite conversation too.[7] None of the critics appears to have had any difficulty in accepting the non-duel between Daw and La Foole, implausible as that sequence of events would be in life; for the non-duel is acceptable, like the marriages or copulations of characters who mistake their partners in the dark, because it is the kind of happening that is expected in a stage comedy, and has occurred in previous ones, in this case *Twelfth Night*. Clerimont's making the women in love with Dauphine is likewise familiar in comedies, where women's sudden shifts of carnal affection typify their supposedly inconstant natures. Morose's function in the drama was familiar enough, but his specific affliction was not. Unaware that it could be found in Libanius, the Restoration critics felt obliged to locate it in nature.[8]

Dryden tries to naturalize the unprecedented Morose by considering him "to be first naturally of a delicate hearing, as many are to whom all sharp sounds are unpleasant" (vol. 17, 59). That consideration would induce the kind of sympathy for Morose in his torment that Strauss and Zweig demand in their opera, where Admiral Sir Morosus has had the powder magazine of his galleon explode and do terrible damage to his ear-drums.[9] Next Dryden would attribute much of Morose's antipathy to "the peevishness of his Age, or the wayward authority of an old man in his own house" (ibid.). No one would feel sorry about that, for it is not accepted that old men have to be peevish or waywardly authoritarian: it is up to them to become sympathetic by having a change of character at the end of Act V. "Ach, meine Guten," sings the again exemplary Sir Morosus, "großartig habt ihr mich kuriert, noch nie hab ich so glücklich mich gefühlt." To provide Morose with that closing line would be in the spirit of Bentley's conclusion to *Paradise Lost*; for Jonson's play is notoriously open-ended, and Truewit in the last line speaks of Morose as yet uncured.

Sympathy for Morose is never considered by Dryden, or by Dennis or Congreve: their question is simply whether he is representative, and (according to Dennis) might therefore instruct noise-haters in the audience. The matter of sympathy does, however, arise in a Restoration character supposedly modelled on Morose: Congreve's Heartwell in *The Old Batchelour* (1693). Jonas A. Barish, who established Heartwell as the prime claimant to descent from Morose, finds "striking verbal parallels"[10] in the following:

Morose. Good sir! have I ever cosen'd any friends of yours of their land? bought their possessions? taken forfeit of their mortgage? begg'd a reversion from 'hem? bastarded their issue? what have I done, that may deserve this?

Truewit. Nothing, sir, that I know, but your itch of marriage.

Morose. Why, if I had made an assassinate upon your father; vitiated your mother; ravished your sisters—(*SW* II.ii.43–50)

Heartwell. Damn your pity. But let me be calm a little.—How have I deserv'd this of you? Any of ye? Sir, have I impair'd the Honour of your House, promis'd your Sister Marriage, and whor'd her? Wherein have I injured you? Did I bring a Physician to your Father when he lay expiring, and endeavour to prolong his life, and you One-and-twenty? Madam, have I had an Opportunity with you and bauk'd it? Did you ever offer me the Favour that I refus'd it? Or—(*OB* V.ii.50–58)

Morose. Would I could redeeme it with the losse of an eye (nephew) a hand, or any other member.

Dauphine. Mary, god forbid, sir, that you should geld your selfe, to anger your wife. (*SW* IV.iv.8–11)

Heartwell. Oh! Any thing, every thing, a Leg or two, or an Arm; nay, I would be divorced from my Virility, to be divorced from my Wife. (*OB* V.ii.75–77)

Congreve concentrates the discussion on sexual and filial relations; the sphere of business—Jonson's land, possessions, mortgage, reversion—has no place. Moreover, Congreve gives the discussion an introverted and ironic turn, both of concept—*prolonging* the father's life, *refusing* the Favour—and of phrase—"a leg or two" (a trivializing formula), "divorced from my Virility, to be divorced from my Wife" (the patterned repetition the Restoration admired). The passages' differences are as striking as their similarities, and even these few lines can suggest Congreve's more level tone and a degree of detachment in Heartwell's framing relatively complex sentences. The general effect of the syntactic contrast in Jonson is of characters isolated in their individual private worlds; Congreve's (Heartwell included) have their identity as part of the same social set with its common patterns of speech.

When the old bachelor Heartwell, a professed woman-hater, has determined to marry Sylvia, whom he cannot help loving, her maid Lucy in search of a parson encounters the hero Bellmour disguised as the fanatic preacher Tribulation Spin-text (a name that could echo *The Alchemist*). Bellmour decides to take advantage of his disguise (already successfully adopted to gain entry to the house and spouse of Alderman Fondlewife) and mock-marry Heartwell to Sylvia; but he makes clear to Lucy that a real marriage would be out of the question. "Look you," he tells her, "*Heartwell* is my Friend" (V.i.60).

A parallel statement "Morose is my friend" could not plausibly be interpolated in the text of *The Silent Woman*; so Bellmour by his assertion dissociates Heartwell from Morose. He also dissociates himself from Dauphine by the emotional commitment, which the text does not require: "Heartwell is not my friend" or no comment at all would be equally consonant with what has gone before. He gathers Heartwell within the boundaries of the social set (where his name already implies his presence) and makes it possible for him to conclude, in the manner of Admiral Sir Morosus, "*Bellmour*, I approve thy mirth, and thank thee." Such sympathetic treatment of Heartwell does, however, exclude from the social set the mock-bride Sylvia, destined instead for an incorrigible fool Sir Joseph Wittol, whose name anticipates her adultery. As Sylvia's only offense has been her seduction by Vainlove and Bellmour himself, her classification as whore raises the familiar question of cast mistresses in Restoration drama (most familiarly Mrs. Fainall in *The Way of the World*). There is in fact a disparity of subject-matter here, which makes it difficult in principle to compare characters from *The Silent Woman* and *The Old Batchelour*: for the characters "exist" as a function of the complete text. Even when characters are uncomplicated by contradictory attributes, for example, the Collegiates and Lady Fidgett and her friends in *The Country Wife*, similarities of feature and function have limited significance if the plays' preoccupations—sexual, ideological, aesthetic—are distinctly different.

The Silent Woman does deal quite extensively with the fashionable life, the use of cosmetics, the inadequacies of marriage, and the inconstancy of women, all favourite (though not exclusively) Restoration topics. *The Silent Woman* just touches on the French (through La Foole), the Church (the parson with a cold), the Law (Morose at Westminster Hall), the Pox (report of Haughty's physicians), and the medical profession (cures of Trusty's mad parents). *The Silent Woman* celebrates drinking in the person of Otter; but that is not upper-class drinking, and there is nothing about whoring and gambling among the principal men. *The Silent Woman* pays more attention to classical and other scholarship than is usual in Restoration plays, and its treatment of homosexuality is at least more explicit. There is some homosexuality in Rochester's shocking lyrics, and plenty of allegations in lampoons—to pick a pertinent example, one associating the Duke of Buckingham with the actor Edward Kynaston, who played female parts and that of Epicoene in 1660–61, and subsequently played Dauphine.[11] In Restoration drama the occasional minor character is unambiguously homosexual (such as the hideous Coupler in *The Relapse*), and there is some room too for actors' interpretations. In this, and in general, however, correspondence of subject-matter is less significant than setting, social distinctions and resultant similarities of tone.

Emrys Jones, in his 1982 Shakespeare Lecture to the British Academy, identifies *The Silent Woman* as "the first West End Comedy," opening as it does on the levee of a fashionable gentleman with nothing in particular to do throughout Act I. Jones notes, "whether consciously or not, Etherege seems to have modelled the opening scene of *The Man of Mode* on Jonson's scene. Etherege's scene in turn furnished a model for Congreve's *Love for Love*."[12] This kind of scene, Jones suggests, would have come naturally to the indoor theatre, for which *The Silent Woman*, as well as the Restoration plays, was written. In fact, levees open a fair number of Restoration comedies, starting as early as Dryden's *Wild Gallant* (1663), though the riser there is not the hero. Shadwell uses the levee opening in half his comedies: *The Humorists* (1671; not the hero), *The Virtuoso* (1676), *A True Widow* (1678), *The Woman-Captain* (1679), *Bury-Fair* (1689), and *The Scowrers* (1690). The idleness of the hero's life may be illustrated too by finding him in his chamber in the *second* scene of the play when the other characters have been out and about in the first, as is the case in Sedley's *The Mulberry Garden* (1668).

Dauphine in *The Silent Woman* is judiciously silent, and can be so because Jonson anticipates a common Restoration practice in giving Dauphine "a gentleman, his friend" (Clerimont) *and* "another friend" (Truewit). So the friends can answer each other and Dauphine avoids self-defining statements—with the result that he talks relatively little when they are all together.

Shadwell, the professed Jonsonian, adopts these threesomes in four of his thirteen comedies: in *Epsom Wells* (1672) Rains, Bevil and Woodly are bracketed in the Dramatis Personae "Men of Wit and Pleasure"; in *A True Widow* Bellamour, Carlos and Stanmore are country gentleman, travelling gentleman and town gentleman; in *The Woman-Captain* Sir Humphrey Scattergood has "His two Friends" Bellamy and Wildman; in *The Scowrers* Sir William Rant, Wildfire and Tope are bracketed "Scowrers."[13] Etherege's first play, *The Comical Revenge*, uses three principal men in a Spanish honourable-rivals scheme: Beaufort and Bruce are rivals, and Lovis is "Friend to *Bruce*."[14] His second play, *She Wou'd If She Cou'd*, has a pair of co-heroes, Courtall and Freeman. *The Man of Mode* (1675) is more complicated: Dorimant, dressing, is joined by Medley the scandaller—a common, useful attribute of co-heroes relegated to supporters' status. Later on in Act I Dorimant observes, "here comes a good third man," and Young Bellair enters, who sustains the role under the patronizing guidance of the two older wits.[15]

Wycherley's use of the threesome is more perplexing. In *Love in a Wood* (1671) Ranger, Vincent and Valentine are bracketed as "Young Gentlemen of the Town" but, typically of threesomes, only two of the men (Ranger and Valentine) marry in Act V. Vincent, despite the use of his lodgings as a setting, drops out of the action. In *The Gentleman Dancing Master* (1672) Gerard and Martin are co-heroes, with Gerard alone gaining a wife and Martin playing supporter. *The Country Wife* (1675) starts with a threesome of Horner, Harcourt and Dorilant, but Dorilant plays no part at all after the end of Act I. In *The Plain Dealer* (1676) there is a threesome on the title-page—Manly, Freeman ("Manly's Lieutenant") and Vernish ("Manly's Bosome, and onely Friend")—but Vernish is as his name requires (and obtuseness or convention prevents Manly seeing) a thoroughly unpleasant villain. Congreve's *Double Dealer* (1693) is quite similar; for its Melfont is another passive hero and, while Careless is more straightforward than the compliant Freeman, Maskwell is almost as false a friend as Vernish. Congreve had used a threesome before in *The Old Batchelour*: Bellmour and Vainlove depend on another, while Sharper, a gambler, stands a little apart; they remain friends throughout. In his last two plays, however, Congreve used pairs of principal men: Valentine and Scandal in *Love for Love* (1695), Mirabell and Fainall, antagonists in *The Way of the World* (1700).

In *An Essay of Dramatick Poesie* Dryden commends "another artifice of the Poet...that is, when he has any Character or humour wherein he would show a *Coup de Maistre*, or his highest skill; he recommends it to your observation by a pleasant description of it before the person first appears" (Vol. 17, 62). In fact, *The Silent Woman* is so remarkable for its looks backwards, forwards, and sideways, that those digressions from the immediate action seem to be what the play is really about. This can be illustrated from Act IV, which opens with Truewit and Clerimont's recapitulation of the great discovery and noise of Act III, and closes with preparations for the legal debate of Act V;[16] If entries and exits are discounted, relatively little physical action is specified: Otter's drinking ritual; Mrs. Otter beating him, and Morose descending; Daw and La Foole kicked and tweaked; Haughty kissing Dauphine. These visually dramatic acts are separated by long conversations, and even if the essentially dramatic parts of those conversations are reckoned to be action too, the total "action" will account for only about forty per cent of Act IV's text. By "essentially dramatic" is meant speaker and addressee discussing themselves here and now—Morose's lament at the beginning of Act IV.iv, for example, or Truewit's discussions with Daw and La Foole preliminary to the kicking and tweaking. The rest of Act IV's text (about sixty per cent) is recapitulation of what has happened,[17] anticipation of what will happen,[18] reflexion on concurrent off-stage events or persons off stage or out of hearing,[19] or, most prevalent, discussion of general topics.[20] Even the "essentially dramatic" exchanges are inclined to be discursive so that Truewit's discussions with Daw and La Foole are largely recapitulation of, and commentary on, imaginary conversations with the other knight. Truewit presents himself as a go-between; although his speeches are indeed indications of a clever talker, they are not self-revelatory as Daw and La Foole's are.

All three principal men talk little about themselves once their credentials have been established in Act I; so infrequently that when they occasionally do so, the lines seem out of context. For example, in Act IV, scene v, Clerimont suddenly asks to be on stage and help to gull La Foole, and Truewit responds, "looke, you'll spoile all: these be ever your tricks" (lines 144–45). It is unclear whether Clerimont is forever meddling in Truewit's business or the complaint is just an outburst of Truewit's self-love. Truewit does impulsively out-talk the other two principal men and in this respect resembles the voluble Witwoud in *The Way of the World*. Truewit is unlike Witwoud, however, because his utterances are not egocentric; like Congreve's hero Mirabell he is what Millamant calls "sententious."[21] Truewit uses the first person singular pronoun a dozen times only in the play's first scene. His use of "we" tends to be impersonal: "See but our common disease! with what justice can wee complaine, that great men will not looke upon us, nor be at leisure to give our affaires such dispatch, as wee expect, when wee will never doe it to our selves: nor heare, nor regard our selves" (I.i.57–61). These sententious reflexions on "us" are a way of not discussing himself or Clerimont. On this same principle Swift assigned the characters in *Polite Conversation* innumerable proverbs, saws, sentences, clichés, stock phrases, etc., so that in a world of empty generalities the characters are never defined.

Truewit does in fact define himself, or at least establish a powerful presence, by the sheer intensity of his discourse, however remote or generalized its objects may be. One need think only of his great oration on marriage that overflows Act II, scene ii. He defines himself in a peculiarly Restoration manner: like Dorimant and Mirabell he does so without revealing himself, except in the exceptional moment of pressure, as when his friends turn on him in Act II, scene iv (his nearest experience to the afflictions of heroes in love). It is up to the actor to provide a producible interpretation of Truewit, or "disambiguate" him. Yet no actor ever needed to disambiguate Morose, ready defined for all, outrageously verbose and always immediate and personal. Whatever the accomplishments of speech in Truewit or in Mirabell, Morose—like Lady Wishfort—is at the very centre of drama, where the dramatic speaker presents himself. Small wonder that the early commentators wrote so much about him.

NOTES

1. *The London Stage*, vol.1, ed. William Van Lennep (Carbondale: Southern Illinois Univ. Press, 1965), 11–160. Plays which did still better—relatively few, such as Fletcher's *Humorous Lieutenant*, Tuke's *Adventures of Five Hours*, Dryden's *Secret Love* and *Sir Martin Mar-all*, the Dryden-Davenant *Tempest*, and Shakespeare's *Henry VIII*—did so because, unlike *The Silent Woman*, they had opening runs of several nights.

2. *The London Stage*, vol. 1, 206, 335. *Volpone* was acted once in 1676, *Everyman in His Humour* in 1670, *Everyman Out of His Humour* in 1675. *Catiline* was acted once in 1675; never in the eighteenth century.

3. Ben Ross Schneider, Jr., *Index to the London Stage* (Carbondale: Southern Illinois Univ. Press, 1979), 469, provides a convenient list of performances detailed in the main work.

4. *The London Stage*, vol. 2, ed. Emmett L. Avery, (Carbondale: Southern Illinois Univ. Press 1960), 50.

5. Ibid. vol. 2, 194.

6. To Henry Guy, 27 March 1687, in *Letters*, ed. Frederick Bracher (Berkeley and Los Angeles: Univ. of California Press, 1974), 106–7.

7. Dryden, *Essay of Dramatick Poesie*, in *Works*, vol. 17, ed. Samuel Holt Monk and A.E. Wallace Maurer (Berkeley and Los Angeles: Univ. of California Press, 1971), 59–61; Dennis, Letter to Congreve, and Congreve, Letter to Dennis, Congreve, *Letters and Documents*, ed. John C. Hodges (London: Macmillan, 1964), 174–75, 180–81.

8. Libanius, Declamation xxvi, 'Morosus qui uxorem loquacem duxerat se ipsum accusans.' On this subsequently recognized source see, among others, R.V. Holdsworth, ed., Jonson, *Epicoene*, (London: Benn, 1979), xxiii–xxv.

9. *Die schweigsame Frau*, Act I, *in med.*; cue nos. 113–14.

10. *Ben Jonson and the Language of Prose Comedy*, (Cambridge, Mass.: Harvard Univ. Press, 1960), n 31. (See also Holdsworth, ed., *Epicoene*, xxi, n 10.) *The Silent Woman* is quoted from *Ben Jonson*, vol. 5, ed. C.H. Herford and Percy

Simpson, (Oxford: Clarendon Press, 1937), and I have modernized u/v usage to accord with that of Congreve. *The Old Batchelour* is quoted from *The Complete Plays of William Congreve*, ed. Herbert Davis (Chicago: Univ. of Chicago Press, 1967).

11. *A Biographical Dictionary of Actors...in London 1660–1800*, vol. 9, comp. Philip H. Highfill, Jr., et al., (Carbondale: Southern Illinois Univ. Press, 1984), 82–83.

12. Etherege was also imitating himself. Act I of *The Comical Revenge* (1664) includes the levée of Sir Frederick Frollick. *She Wou'd If She Cou'd* (1668) opens at the conclusion of the co-hero's levée: "*Enter* Courtall *and* Freeman, *and a* Servant *brushing* Courtall." Courtall says, "So, so, 'tis well: let the coach be made ready"; then asks Freeman, "Well, Frank, what is to be done today?" Visitors delay their departure for two-thirds of the act.

13. In *The Libertine* (1675), another kind of play, Don John has "His Two Friends" Don Antonio and Don Lopez. Alternatively Shadwell uses a pair of co-heroes, such as Bruce and Longvil in *The Virtuoso*.

14. This arrangement is typical of the early Restoration. Shadwell adopts it later, in 1690, for *The Amorous Bigot*, a play set in Spain.

15. *Dramatic Works of Sir George Etherege*, vol. 2, ed. H.F.B. Brett-Smith (Boston and New York: Houghton Mifflin, 1927), 1.i.316.

16. The uproar is presumed to have been continuing during a theatre interval, *The Silent Woman* being a good example of two-part structure, Acts I–3 and IV–V. See Emrys Jones, *Scenic Form in Shakespeare* (Oxford: Clarendon Press, 1971), 87–88.

17. Sc. i. Truewit and Clerimont on Act III; sc. iii. Mrs. Otter on sc. ii; sc. iv. Haughty and then Trusty on Trusty's parents' cure, Haughty and others on Dauphine; sc.iv. Truewit and Clerimont tell what Collegiates said, Truewit reports Daw's fear to Clerimont and Dauphine, they discuss La Foole's fear, they comment on the tweaking; sc. vi. Collegiates reflect on Dauphine; sc. vii. Truewit tells Morose about Daw and la Foole, Morose describes Westminster Hall.

18. Sc. i. Truewit plots to make Collegiates love Dauphine; sc. ii. Otter plans to seclude himself; sc. iv. Collegiates intend to let Morose briefly alone, Truewit's plot to make Collegiates love Dauphine; sc. v. Truewit predicts what he will do with Daw and La Foole, plan for Clerimont to bring Collegiates to watch kicking and tweaking; sc. vi. preparation for Daw and La Foole's meeting as friends; sc. vii. Truewit proposes lawyers' visit, Truewit's preparations to brief Otter and Cutbeard.

19. Sc. i. Dauphine describes the present condition of Morose and the women; sc. iv. Epicoene and Daw on Morose's condition, Truewit and Clerimont on Epicoene, Truewit and others on Daw and La Foole; sc. v. Truewit on Morose at present; sc. vi. Truewit on Collegiates.

20. Sc. i. Truewit on women; sc. ii. Otter and Mrs. Otter on cosmetics; sc. iii. Collegiates on husband-taming, and on promiscuity and mutability; sc. iv. Morose raises question of divorce.

21. *The Way of the World*, II.i.467; the only occurrence of the word in Congreve's plays.

TO BE REDEEMED FROM FIRE BY FIRE: THE DEATHS OF HERACLES AND SIEGFRIED

Emmet Robbins

The only hope, or else despair
Lies in the choice of pyre or pyre—
To be redeemed from fire by fire.
      T.S. Eliot, *Little Gidding*

Wagner openly professed admiration for Aeschylus, and certainly his vast *Ring of the Nibelung* has inevitably invited comparison with the *Oresteia*, the only trilogy to have survived complete from antiquity.[1] Though both the *Ring* and the *Oresteia* end on a note of optimism, Aeschylean optimism is nonetheless the very antithesis of Wagner's. In the Aeschylean trilogies—and the *Oresteia* enables us to form some idea of the design of the others—human action and suffering are directed by the gods to a beneficent end: violence may be the way of divinity, but this violence is grace (*Agamemnon* 182). In Wagner's great tetralogy the cruelty and selfishness of the gods precipitate their fall. One of the dramatist's most strikingly original adaptations of his source material was to combine the Eddic concept of Ragnarök, the doom or twilight of the gods, with the *Volsunga Saga*, in which the trangressions of the gods of Valhalla are expiated not by the gods themselves but solely by their descendants on earth. Wagner established a moral link between the sins of the gods and their downfall. The corrupt pantheon passes away in cataclysm and hope is born for mankind through the elimination of the divine government of the universe.

  Wagner is in reality closer to the Sophoclean than to the Aeschylean vision. It is Nietzsche who implicity reveals this. In *The Birth of Tragedy* Nietzsche attempts to show that Greek tragedy is the supreme art form, one in which the hero manifests his will in the face of a universe that overwhelms him, confirming his stature at the moment of his fall. Tragedy does not purge the emotions of the audience (whatever Aristotle may have meant by this), but strips away our illusions and brings us face to face with the fundamental truths of existence: the apprehension of these truths gives heroism its validation. This insight is arguably the most significant one in the essay. Nietzsche elaborates his intuition in terms of the now famous opposition between Apolline and Dionysiac principles, but recognition of the value of the insight does not require acceptance of Nietzsche's symbols and the names he gives them. The essential point is the conflict between an inexorable individual and an inexorable universe.

It would be hard to deny that the Nietzschean description fits Sophoclean tragedy far better than that of either of the other tragedians.[2] The very idea of "tragic hero," ubiquitous in Nietzsche, is a Sophoclean legacy.[3] In Sophocles' tragic universe self-assertion, suffering, and glory are one. Violence does not bring grace, for there is no insistent theodicy as in Aeschylus. But neither is there mere despair as in Euripides. Nietzsche applies his analysis of Greek tragedy to the work of Wagner too, finding the Hellenic ideal fully realised in *Tristan and Isolde*. But Siegmund and Sieglinde, Siegfried and Brünnhilde of the *Ring* (not completed when Nietzsche published *The Birth of Tragedy*) also meet the Nietzschean criteria. Victims of transhuman powers, they find victory in defeat and the final impression communicated is one of exhilaration. They are tragic heroes of stature, human actors who suffer and in that suffering reveal the measure of their greatness.[4]

We do not have, so far as I know, any statement by Wagner that admits a direct debt to Sophocles. Even if we did, though, it would be of questionable utility. Wagner's own claim that Hans Sachs's speech at the end of *Die Meistersinger* is indebted to the close of the *Eumenides* is not particularly illuminating: one could scarcely have divined the connection, and even with the composer's statement the comparison cannot be pushed very far. The process by which Wagner's energetic mind worked on the material he so omnivorously devoured is not necessarily to be discovered by listening to his own proclamations. In *Opera and Drama* Wagner mentions, in any case, three Sophoclean heroes—Ajax, Philoctetes, and Oedipus—as commendable examples of individuality expressed in a propensity for self-annihilation. They are images of the eternal truth of myth which it is the job of dramatists in every age to expound. In the same work he analyses Sophocles' so-called Theban trilogy (*Oedipus The King, Oedipus at Colonus, Antigone*) and its political significance. There are certainly remarkable points of similarity between the Siegfried legend in the Wagnerian version and the Oedipus legend. Both heroes are exposed at birth. The one kills his father (Laius) and marries his mother (Jocasta), the other overcomes his grandfather (Wotan as the Wanderer) to be united with his aunt (Brünnhilde, whom Siegfried at first sight takes to be his mother). The issue of incest is, of course, paramount in both *Oedipus The King* and in *Die Walküre*.[5] There are, in addition, striking parallels between *Parsifal* and *Philoctetes*. In both we have the drama of a young man,[6] little more than a boy, who grows before our eyes when he learns pity for an older man who, because of an incurable wound, is estranged from a society (the Knights of the Grail, the Greek army before Troy) that needs him desperately. In both cases the wound must be healed and a weapon restored to its crucial place in the life of the imperilled community.

Most impressive of all is the fact that Sophocles and Wagner dramatised the deaths of the supreme heroes of their national mythologies, both sent to their funeral pyres by the women who best loved them. In the *Trachiniae* Heracles, the *pantōn ariston andra tōn epi chthoni* (811) is killed by Deianira in unwitting collaboration with the hero's enemy Nessus. In *Götterdämmerung* (originally entitled *Siegfrieds Tod*) Brünnhilde, openly plotting with Hagen, Siegfried's enemy, compasses the death of *den hehrsten Helden der Welt*.

The dramatists have proceeded in similar fashion. Each has reworked a mass of epic material and focused on the dramatic reaction of a jealous woman confronted with her husband's new bride. Secondary or background material necessary to understanding the situation before us is conveyed in long speeches that recapitulate the action that precedes the confines of the drama. This technique is used throughout the *Ring*; the dialogue of the Norns and Waltraute's long report to Brünnhilde (a sort of messenger speech) are the most notable instances in *Götterdämmerung*. In the *Trachiniae* about one-quarter of the play, an abnormally large proportion even by standards of Greek tragedy, consists of narrative of background material. Further, the density and consistency of the imagery are striking even for Sophocles: there is no finer example of drama with recurring leitmotifs than this play.[7] And it occupies a unique position among the remains of Greek tragedy in another respect: no other play contains a similar amalgam of myth, fairy-tale magic, oracles, battles between beasts and human beings, the quintessentially human element of passion linked with the primordial and the divine—precisely that blend which gives the *Ring* its unique position among the great works that hold the lyric stage.

Sophocles reshaped an epic legacy largely lost to us. There were Heracles epics by Pisander of Rhodes, Panyassis of Halicarnassus, and in particular by Creophylus of Samos. Of the "Capture of Oechalia" by the last named (it was sometimes attributed to Homer himself, attesting both to its antiquity and to the esteem in which it was held) we have only a single line. But this poem was in all probability Sophocles' most important epic source, for it told the story of Heracles' capture and sack of a city in order to win the beautiful Iole. It is reasonable to assume that this maiden played an important role in the poem—the one line we possess appears to be addressed to her. Sophocles' play dramatizes Deianira's reaction to Heracles' bringing home his captured bride, the sexual jealously of the woman who in desperation turns to magic (the Nessus shirt) with disastrous consequences. Uncertain as must be hypotheses that are based on lost sources, it can be said with reasonable certainty that Sophocles' distinctive treatment is to be seen in his presentation of the confrontation of the two women. At the same time, however, he made Iole a silent figure in his play, one with no dramatic personality whatsoever.[8]

Wagner has done much the same. The formidable adversary of Brynhilde in the epic sources, Gudrun of the *Volsunga Saga*, Kriemhilde of the *Nibelungenlied*, becomes the pathetic and almost totally inconsequential Gutrune of *Götterdämmerung*. She is present for little other purpose than to enkindle Brünnhilde's anger by her betrothal to Siegfried. She is there, in other words, as Iole is in the *Trachiniae*. Sexual jealousy is not entirely absent from the Saga. But there Brynhild does not seem to be especially troubled by Sigurd's marriage to Gudrun (which Brynhild in fact prophesied!) and she has herself lived comfortably with Gunnar for some time before the angry exchange between the two queens on a question of honour and precedence precipitates the disaster. Brynhild's wound in the Saga is primarily an affront to her self-esteem. It comes from her realization that her husband Gunnar is not who she boasted he was, since it was Sigurd who rode through the barrier of flame in Gunnar's form. And so her oath to marry none but the very noblest has come to nothing. This it is that makes her take revenge, seek Sigurd's death despite his readiness to renounce Gudrun and return to her. Wagner's Brünnhilde, immediately upon seeing a Siegfried who has forgotten her and become betrothed to another, plots his death. Similarly Deianira meets the Iole who has replaced her in her husband's affections and in seeking to win him back brings about his death. Both Sophocles and Wagner have given a new emphasis in refashioning an epic patrimony and have produced tragedies of eros.

The "world's greatest hero" (for so he is styled in both dramas) is in neither presentation a very attractive figure. Siegfried has always been an embarrassment to lovers of Wagner—there is something coarse and over-robust about the Siegfried of the drama that bears his name, though he is somewhat more attractive in *Götterdämmerung*. It is his music that ultimately gives him stature, a stature which his words and actions do not convey. In like manner the Heracles of the *Trachiniae* has been seen as simply repellent by many readers, as a near tasteless creation in his ferocity and blustering self-absorption. But the greatness of this Sophoclean hero is not something communicated by the words of the tragedy. His special, extra-dramatic importance must be taken into account. The aura of Heracles was, for a Greek audience, part of the air they breathed, a living part of the environment in which the actors' words were heard. All the figures of Attic tragedy come trailing clouds of myth, that of Heracles perhaps more than any other. Apart from the epics one can point to his paramount importance with vase painters and sculptors, his paradigmatic place in Pindar's odes. That he was a favourite figure of the comic stage does not militate against this, for the Greeks from Homer onwards could treat even their gods with good humour. Siegfried and Heracles do not rise from the texts of their dramas as sympathetic.[9] It is the accompanying music that gives the one his appeal, circumambient myth that ennobles the other. Many writers have described for us, none more eloquently than Nietzsche, the kindred capacities of myth and of music to convince us at a level inaccessible to the words of a text.

The women, Deianira and Brünnhilde, are as different as the men are similar, though both, as has been noted, act largely for the same reason—sexual jealousy. It is curious to note that the timid Deianira may have begun life as a sort of Greek Valkyrie. Her name means "slayer of men"—the Amazons themselves are described by the epithet *antianeirai*, "opponents of men." Apollodorus mentions that Deianira rode a chariot and practised martial arts (1.8.1). It was only after her story became linked to that of Heracles that her name was interpreted to mean "destroyer of a husband." Perhaps like the Brynhild of the Saga she originally resisted marriage and preferred to ride into battle. There is nothing of this left in Sophocles' Deianira, who has been seen to embody the quiet virtues admired in fifth-century Athens.[10] Whether this is so or not, she certainly embodies the virtues admired in Victorian England. Sir Richard Jebb, the greatest of modern Sophoclean scholars, writes of her:

> The heroine of the *Trachiniae* has been recognised by general consent as one of the most delicately beautiful creations in literature; and many who feel this charm will also feel that it can no more be described than the perfume of a flower....She, indeed, is a perfect type of gentle womanhood; her whole life has been in her home; a winning influence is felt by all who approach her;...a high and noble courage is the very spring of her gentleness....This Deianeira is a creation of the Hellenic spirit, refined by the sweetness, the restrained strength of Athens at her best.[11]

One hundred years later Deianira does not appear quite the glistening Pentelic marble she seemed to Jebb. Today we find her pathetic, a middle-aged woman overcome by an emotion she cannot control, in her desperation ready to clutch at anything with little or no reflection. It is fascinating to look at the poetry Sophocles puts into her mouth: the entire, rich Greek vocabulary of fear-words settles on her speech. She lives in a world haunted by images of fear and night. Faced with a rival she turns to magic. This problem does not seem to me to be satisfactorily resolved, as it is for many critics, by the simple observation that in fifth-century Athens no stigma attached to the use of love charms. For this is no ordinary love charm. Deianira has kept an ointment of the envenomed blood of her husband's enemy Nessus, taken as he lay dying, and she has chosen to act on that enemy's word. She uses the poisoned blood knowing what it is[12] because she cannot tolerate the presence of Iole. And she acts in secrecy. This pusillanimity and clutching at straws are hardly Jebb's "high and noble courage."

Early in the *Trachiniae* Deianira delivers a lecture on honesty to the herald Lichas, who has deceived her (436–69). We have here, it seems, the key to a curious feature of the play's construction, the duplication of the traditional messenger scene announcing Heracles' return by Lichas's appearance, which does essentially the same thing though it also deceives Deianira on the crucial point, the identity and role of the concubine Iole. Critics like to point to the dramatic excitement generated by having Deianira's hopes raised to a pitch of false joy, only to be dashed when the messenger reveals the full truth. But the duplication is shabby drama if it serves no other purpose than to prolong Deianira's ignorance and intensify a brutal shock.[13] An important effect of this deception scene is to point the contrast between the principles proclaimed by Deianira and her inability to act in accordance with these principles. The famous Sophoclean irony is at work here, for the deceived woman deceives in turn. Deianira gives Lichas, the herald who lied to her, a garment to carry to Heracles without telling him what it is he is carrying. This has fatal consequences for Lichas. Heracles, in his first agony, murders the man who brought him the gift. This is normally seen as an instance of Heracles' brutality, and soon it certainly is. But it must be remembered that it is Deianira's deception that has sent Lichas to his death.

Jebb, who so admired Sophocles' Deianira, makes the further statement in his introduction to the play:

> It was difficult for the Latin races to imagine a woman, supplanted in her husband's love, who did not wish to kill somebody,—her rival, or her husband, or both.[14]

This astonishing statement, which doubtless issues from a conviction of the profound sympathy between Hellenic purity and Northern virtue, was written at approximately the same time that Wagner was creating his Brünnhilde.

Wagner might have been more than a little surprised at the suggestion that he was Latin in his creation of a woman who kills becase she is supplanted in her husband's love.[15] His Brünnhilde is, in any case, one of the great women of any stage, any age. She is fearless, ever a creature of light, from her sleep on the fire-encircled crag to her final immolation. There cannot be two more different exits in all of dramatic literature than those of Deianira and Brünnhilde. The former leaves the stage silently in one of Greek tragedy's most moving exits. Other Sophoclean women (Jocasta in *Oedipus The King*, Eurydice in *Antigone*) leave the stage to commit suicide, but they leave precipitately and comment is made only after their departure, hence their exits are not important in the stage action. Deianira must leave slowly. There is much discussion of her exit but she does not say a word to the questions that are put to her. Brünnhilde holds our attention alone for one of the longest and most thrilling scenes in Wagner. Her exit too is one of drama's great moments. Whereas Deianira never confronts the unfaithful Heracles directly (it is a sobering thought that Deianira and Heracles would have been played by the same actor), Brünnhilde openly and vehemently taxes Siegfried with his infidelity. Frustrated by his apparent inability to recall anything except what suits him at the moment,[16] she openly allies herself with Hagen, who kills him. Deianira's alliance with Heracles' dead enemy is unwitting, but Nessus is, as Dante emphasises, very much the murderer of Heracles.[17] Both women expiate their offences by their own deaths. Neither is allowed to come face to face with her dying husband and so neither can ask for the forgiveness she wants.

Brünnhilde's death is atonement. It is also redemptive, for the fire she ignites brings about the end of the whole corrupt order whose self-centredness has caused the sufferings of these mortals. The piled lumber of Wotan's shattered spear and of the withered World Ash, set ablaze by Brünnhilde's torch, sets Valhalla alight. The fire is also the purifying fire of love:

> Fühl meine Brust auch,
> wie sie entbrennt;
> helles Feuer
> das Herz mir erfasst.
>
> (III.iii)

The final conflagration redeems from the earlier fires of jealousy and anger (cf. "Ratet nun Rache....Zündet mir Zorn," II.iv).

The end of *Götterdämmerung* is an optimistic vision and, as such, has been described as antithetical to tragedy.[18] But is this fair? Aeschylean tragedy is, as we noted, optimistic too. If optimism is basically the belief that something is won through human suffering, optimism is surely consonant with tragic vision. We cannot be willing to award the title tragedy only where we find despair and damnation. Wagner's vision is, however, humanistic. Man is the measure of all things. He arraigns the gods at the bar of his own understanding, burns them for their misdemeanours, and looks with confidence to a brave new world.[19]

It is more difficult to determine the tone of the end of the *Trachiniae*. We may state with confidence that Sophocles would have used, did use, the full force of his genius to combat the Protagorean dictum that man is the measure. It was a contemporary heresy and he met it head on. We must consider the final scene of the *Trachiniae* closely.

Heracles will die offstage on a funeral pyre on Mount Oeta. His cortege assembles and prepares to move away. Hyllus remarks on the great cruelty of the gods. It would be patently absurd, however, to think of toppling these divinities. Olympus will know no twilight. The universe is what it is and there is no hope of a better one, though there is every hope that we may continue in the flawed one we know, especially if we learn the lesson of pity, a lesson to which all gods and most heroes are deaf. The gods are cruel and they abide.

And yet...I have mentioned the mythical baggage that a fifth-century Athenian carried with him into the theatre. The audience that watched the funeral procession carrying the tortured Heracles to his pyre knew full well that Heracles, alone of mortals, came through suffering to a place on Olympus. It is but a slight exaggeration to say that the spectators could look up from their place in the Theatre of Dionysus to the pedimental sculptures of the Parthenon and see Heracles reclining among the

Olympians.[20] The reception of Heracles on Olympus is a standard item in the repertory of the vase painters of the time. Would the audience necessarily have connected apotheosis with funeral pyre?[21] The earliest instances in art of the apotheosis of Heracles from his pyre are perhaps twenty years later than the *Trachiniae*.[22] Is it implicit in the play? If it is, we are present at the birth of a motif that finds its final splendid flowering more than two thousand years later in the art of Tiepolo, the master so beloved of the honorand of this volume. Above the misery of this world, the clouds open to receive a martyr into the courts of heaven. This may be what Hyllus glances at, albeit unknowingly, when he says, immediately following his comment on the cruelty of the gods, that no one foresees the future. Whatever the case, Eliot's lines are applicable to Heracles' death as to Siegfried's, in this sense at least: the fires of the hero's funeral pyre bring redemption from the fires of human passion.

NOTES

I am grateful to Rev. M. Owen Lee, C.S.B. for valuable comments and suggestions.

1. See, for example, Michael Ewans, *Wagner and Aeschylus:* The Ring *and the* Oresteia (London: Faber and Faber, 1982).

2. The two figures discussed at greatest length by Nietzsche are Oedipus and Prometheus. Few contemporary scholars believe in the Aeschylean authorship of the *Prometheus Bound*. One of the (many) reasons for rejecting the traditional attribution is the "Sophoclean" nature of the hero of the play: see, esp. B.M.W. Knox, *The Heroic Temper: Studies in Sophoclean Tragedy* (Berkeley and Los Angeles: Univ. of California Press, 1964), 45–50. H. Lloyd-Jones, *Blood for the Ghosts: Classical Influences in the Nineteenth and Twentieth Centuries* (London: Duckworth, 1982), 132–34, shows the importance of *Prometheus Bound* and the fragmentary *Prometheus Unbound* for the *Ring*.

3. Knox, *The Heroic Temper*, Ch. 1.

4. The fully anthropomorphized Wotan is a Sophoclean figure too—proud, isolated, magnificent, doomed: see Nietzsche's *Richard Wagner in Bayreuth* (1876).

5. See the fascinating analysis by L.J. Rather, *The Dream of Self-Destruction: Wagner's Ring and the Modern World* (Baton Rouge: Louisiana State Univ. Press, 1979), esp. 47–63. Rather finds Siegfried, born of incest and destroyer of an unjust political order (Valhalla), parallel to Antigone, likewise born of incest and overthrower of the state (Creon).

6. The young Neoptolemus was introduced into the story by Sophocles. The epic tradition and the (lost) dramas of Aeschylus and Euripides associated Diomedes

with Odysseus in the bringing of Philoctetes from Lemnos. It was Sophocles who was interested in the young man who learns pity.

7. I list a few: night, Deianira's fear, fire, Zeus, Cypris (Aphrodite), release from toils, the poison, the centaur, learning, hope. Others will wish to extend the list. Many of these poetic motifs cry out for translation into music, for it is through music that their interrelation could most clearly be shown (in the best Wagnerian manner).

8. On Sophocles' adaptation of his source see the sensitive treatment of A. Beck, "Der Empfang Ioles," *Hermes* 81 (1953):10–21.

9. It might be argued that this is beside the point—that we need not be expected to like Heracles and Siegfried: a world of "nice" people is no place for a tragic poet. The fact remains that Heracles and Siegfried are the most unappealing heroes of their respective creators.

10. C. Segal, "Sophocles' *Trachiniae*: Myth, Poetry, and Heroic Values," *Yale Classical Studies* 25 (1977): 99–158.

11. R.C. Jebb, *Sophocles: The Plays and Fragments Part V: The Trachiniae* (Cambridge: Cambridge Univ. Press, 1892), xxxi–ii, xliv.

12. There can be no doubt about this. Deianira herself says (574) that the magic will be effective only if it includes the poison. This startling admission seems to be glossed over by the critics.

13. Sophocles elsewhere portrays the deliberate deception of women—Tecmessa by Ajax, Electra by Orestes. But he does not revel in the psychological torture of his women as, it seems to me, Puccini does.

14. Jebb, *Sophocles* V, xliv.

15. Medea is proof enough (if proof is needed) that the Greeks, like all other races, found it possible to imagine a woman, supplanted in her husband's love, who wished to kill.

16. The magic potion has obliterated Siegfried's memory of what preceded his meeting with Gutrune. But he can forget events subsequent to the drinking of the potion too, as when he tells Brünnhilde that he took the Ring from Fafner, not from her (II.iv). On Siegfried's amnesia, see the interesting essay "Siegfried-Idyll" in Gustav Hillard's *Recht auf Vergangenheit: Essays, Aphorismen, Glossen* (Hamburg: Hoffmann und Campe, 1966).

17.   Quelli è Nesso
che morì per la bella Deianira
e fè di sè la vendetta elli stesso? (*Inf.* XII.67–69)

18. George Steiner, *The Death of Tragedy* (New York: Oxford Univ. Press, 1961), 127–28.

19. Brünnhilde remains to the end the incarnation of Wotan's will. In ending his world as he wants she accomplishes that will. But despite this strain of Schopenhauerian pessimism in the *Ring*, the final impression is one of humanism and optimism: the gods, who are not fit to rule mankind, are overthrown. The new world will have no gods.

20. The reclining figure referred to here is thought by some to be Heracles, by others Dionysus. It usually dated to the decade preceding the outbreak of the Peloponnesian War. The exact date of the *Trachiniae* is unknown, though most critics today would incline to a date in the third quarter of the fifth century.

21. In several plays Sophocles seems to allude in the closing lines to events subsequent to the drama, but in all the other cases the references cast a pall over an apparently "happy" ending: the further sufferings of Orestes are hinted at in the *Electra*, the later transformation of the gentle Neoptolemus in the *Philoctetes*, and the death of Antigone in *Oedipus at Colonus*.

22. Assuming, that is, an early date for the play. The vases in question are from the last quarter of the fifth century. See P.E. Easterling, *Sophocles: Trachiniae* (Cambridge: Cambridge Univ. Press, 1982), 17–18.

PARSIFAL AND THE RIGHT POINT OF VIEW ABOUT EVERYTHING

Philip Wults

The idea for an opera based on the figure of Parsifal first came to Richard Wagner in 1845 at the same time as he began to conceive *Lohengrin* and *Die Meistersinger*. This was part of the fertile period immediately following his poverty-stricken years in Paris (1839–42), the memory of which caused him anguish to the very end of his life. After initial ruminations on the Parsifal subject, Wagner did not return to it in a concentrated way until 1865 when King Ludwig II asked him to write a detailed prose sketch. From 1865 until after the end of the first Bayreuth Festival in 1876 Wagner was prevented by his many other projects from resuming work on *Parsifal*. Nonetheless from 1872 on, he yearned increasingly to begin composing and used every free moment to return to his *Parsifal* universe, reading books about Christianity, Buddhism, the Middle Ages, Arabia, Judaism, animal protection, and evolution, among other things.

Not until he had found a solution for the massive deficit incurred by the Festival of 1876 could Wagner begin to work on *Parsifal* intensively. Even then, it took him almost two years before he could begin the arduous task of putting the *Parsifal* universe into musical notation. As his theoretical works and the story of his life illustrate, he aimed above all else to create integral and organic music dramas. He was, for instance, one of the few composers who always wrote his own texts. With the exception of *Lohengrin*, he composed his works from beginning to end in the consecutive order of the scenes as they appeared in his libretti.

Oddly enough, Wagner strayed from his usual practice in *Parsifal*. The first music which came to him was not, as one might expect, the Prelude to Act I but rather the music for the ballet/chorus of the Flower Maidens in Act II. This starting point contained an irony. Wagner, after all, was the man who had directed so much withering criticism at the abuse of ballet and chorus in the French grand opera. That *Parsifal* should contain a ballet/chorus and that this sort of "divertissement" should be the musical germ of the work is somewhat bizarre; but it was not a mere accident. Throughout the gestation of his last opera, Wagner consciously maintained precisely the scene of the Flowers as one of his first priorities. Almost from the beginning, long before the completion of the composition sketch, he sought the services of Lilli Lehmann not only to sing the lead Flower but also to train the whole Flower ensemble. Lehmann was one of the illustrious sopranos of her day, a diva of the Berlin Opera. The engagement of such a soloist for an ensemble role shows the importance which the composer attached to the scene of the Flowers. When, at relatively short notice, Lehmann had to cancel her long-standing commitment to Wagner, the setback proved such a blow to him that he went into an uncharacteristic depression, doubting even that the opera could be mounted.[1] The preparations continued, however, with extra rehearsal time lavished upon the Flowers. Whatever vexations plagued Wagner during the difficult rehearsals of 1882, he took special joy in his work with the Flowers. During the premiere run of performances in the summer of 1882, he was so enthusiastic about this scene in particular that he habitually called bravos to his Flower Maidens from his *loge*. The Bayreuth audience, already then what it has remained ever since, silenced the sacrilegious interloper with angry hisses.[2]

It would seem, then, that Wagner was less able than his hero Parsifal to resist the visual and aural blandishments of his Flowers. This certainly would have come as a surprise to the Director of the Académie de Musique (the *Opéra*) in Paris, who, in 1861 spent exasperating hours vainly attempting to persuade Wagner to interpolate a ballet into Act II of *Tannhäuser* the better to ravish the eyes of the dandies of the Jockey Club, who never arrived at a performance before the end of Act I and who expected their late arrival to be greeted by lithe and scantily-clad ballerinas. Evidently, such a demand, so vehemently refused by Wagner the idealist in 1861, could be acceded to more readily in 1882 by Wagner the Festival Director.

If the Flower ballet in Act II of *Parsifal* were the opera's only echo of French grand opera we could view it as nothing more than a beautiful aberration. But for some reason, commentators have failed to notice the many other elements of grand opera in *Parsifal* even though these have been staring them in the face for more than a century. Perhaps this point has been overlooked simply because it is so unlikely. Wagner had made a profession of hating things French all his life—French politics, French language, the French press, French fashion, but especially that quintessential French art form, "grand opera," as purveyed by the likes of Giacomo Meyerbeer. After 1842 Wagner even rejected his own grand opera, *Rienzi*, wittily termed "Meyerbeer's best opera" by Hans von Bülow. Writing in 1851, Wagner felt obliged to explain, or rather apologize for, this sin of his youth:

> Before me stood "grand opera" with all its scenic and musical pomp, its multitude of overimpassioned effects of mass and music. Not somehow just

to imitate "grand opera" but to outdo it with unrestrained extravagance in every of its hitherto extant aspects, that was what my ambition as an artist demanded....Only, I saw [the plot] as being exclusively in the form of "five acts" with five glossy "finales," with hymns, processions, and musical sabre rattling.[3]

Although *Parsifal*, like *Rienzi*, has more than its share of effective scene-endings, hymns, processions, and even musical sabre-rattling, it cannot be said that these elements take their place in the opera primarily for the sake of effect. They are not chiefly "effects without causes," Wagner's damningly pithy description of Meyerbeer's works.[4] On the other hand, there are other more significant resemblances between *Parsifal* and notable five-acters like Auber's *La Muette de Portici* (1828), Meyerbeer's *Robert le Diable* (1831), *Les Huguenots* (1836), *Le Prophète* (1849), Halévy's *La Juive* (1835), and Wagner's own *Rienzi* (1842).

Although ostensibly constructed in Wagner's usual three-act format, *Parsifal* clearly has a five-act structure with the *Wandeldekoration* (transformation scenery) in Acts I and III providing transitions between completely integral "acts" or tableaux, as they were called in the grand operas of Meyerbeer and the others. Wagner's five tableaux are not less tableaux than those in the most spectacular of grand operas. Like most grand operas, *Parsifal* begins with an expository outdoor tableau (a forest clearing) which gives ample opportunity for chorus and extras to fill the stage. The major characters, with the exception of Klingsor, are introduced here. The procession of Amfortas, if not the death-throes of the stuffed swan, provides the sort of optical stimulation favoured by grand opera audiences.

Even the renowned librettist Eugène Scribe, who built his fame on making spectacle the central structural component of his libretti, never came up with anything more spectacular than Wagner's *Wandeldekoration*. Using a series of mammoth vertical rollers to spool and unspool painted canvas scenery, the first Bayreuth production of *Parsifal* (1882–1933) created the impression that during the transformation from forest tableau to Temple of the Grail (the second tableau), Gurnemanz and Parsifal walked a distance far greater than the width of the stage.[5] The scene changed around them as Gurnemanz told Parsifal that time had become space. Although the *Wandeldekoration* gave Wagner the pretext for introducing a nice philosophical conceit into his opera, it was close to a Scribean effect without cause. Before the first performances of *Parsifal* in 1882 Wagner even found himself forced to compose extra music (by the metre, as he said) because the scene painters had provided too much painted canvas. Woe to the opera intendant who had requested music by the metre from Wagner earlier in his idealistic career! By and large, history has judged the *Wandeldekoration* an effect without cause; most stage directors, including Wieland Wagner, have replaced the *Wandeldekoration* with a closed curtain.

Wagner's second tableau reaches the height of grand opera, outdoing even the religious processions in *La Juive* and his own *Rienzi*. In the original Bayreuth production, the interior of the Temple of the Grail, meticulously realized on the model of the Cathedral at Siena, provided food for the eye at least as spectacular and awe-inspiring as the detailed architectural wonders presented in the works of Meyerbeer/Scribe by the designers Ciceri and Duponchel. The visual effect was further heightened by the simple device of placing Parsifal downstage as a mute observer of the Grail ceremony.

Preceded by a second *Wandeldekoration*, the Temple returns as the final tableau of the opera. With the opera's ultimate climax, the reunion of Sacred Spear and Holy Grail, the tableau is transformed:

> Climbing the steps of the altar, Parsifal takes the "Grail" out of the tabernacle which has been opened by the boys. Gazing at the Grail, Parsifal sinks to his knees in silent prayer. General soft lighting of the "Grail." Increasing darkness upstage as rays of light from above gain in intensity....Light beam: glow of "Grail" at highest intensity. A white dove floats down from the dome and hovers over Parsifal's head. With her eyes raised to Parsifal, Kundry slowly sinks lifeless before him to the floor. Kneeling, Amfortas and Gurnemanz pay homage to Parsifal, who blesses the worshipping knights by swinging the Grail above them. The stage curtain closes slowly.[6]

Few scenes in all of opera provide so magnificent a vehicle for the lighting technician. In Wagner's own *Festspielhaus*, the theatre which he had in mind while composing *Parsifal*, the play of darkness and light was made even more effective because of the completely darkened theatre. Wagner's *Festspielhaus* audience was left with an especially poignant final impression because of the slow closing curtain, a specially designed curtain, which, because of diagonal draw strings, achieved an effect something like that of a camera aperture. It should be noted that both innovations (house lighting and curtain) had predecessors in the French grand opera. Since at least 1831 the *Opéra* had turned down the house lighting during performances and closed the curtains between acts so that changes of scenery no longer took place in view of the audience.

Parsifal's third tableau (in the realm of Klingsor) provides yet another scenic *tour de force*. The Gothic mystery of Klingsor's tower, transformed a vista into the magic flower garden, the ballet of the Flowers, the miracle of the Spear which hovers over Parsifal's head, the wilting into a wasteland of Klingsor's magic garden—these illusions and *coups de théâtre* would have fitted well into many a grand opera. In fact, the Flower scene is not without French antecedents. Gothic *frissons* abounded in the third tableau of Meyerbeer's *Robert le Diable*, for instance, one of Wagner's special *bêtes noires*. A contemporary account relates how Meyerbeer and Scribe raised nuns from the dead so that they could participate in a cadaverous ballet:

> We are in an abandoned monastery. The walls fall in ruins. The silent tombs are filled with white statues. Mysterious rays of the moon illuminate the melancholy interior with their pale light.....A throng of silent shadows glides through the arches. All the women discard their nun's costumes. They shake off the cold dust of the tombs and immediately return to the delights of their former life. They dance like bacchantes, they gambol like lords, they drink like soldiers.[7]

If Meyerbeer's nuns were too aggressive to inspire Wagner to create his Flowers, a closer analogy may be found in the third tableau of Halévy's *La Juive*, one of the few grand operas which received Wagner's enduring praise. As in *Parsifal* (and most grand operas) the time of the action is the Middle Ages. A banquet is taking place:

> The Emperor Sigismund presides at the banquet, served by four mounted Electors....The interlude...without which there could be no royal banquet, is not forgotten. An enchanted tower appears. Knights besiege it and suddenly each bastion of the tower is changed into a cell housing a nymph who begins to dance as one assuredly did not dance in the Middle Ages.[8]

Although Klingsor's knights remain offstage, the rest of the parallel seems quite close. Perhaps the "interlude" made a strong impression on Wagner when he saw it during his formative years in Paris.

If the fourth tableau of *Parsifal*, the Good Friday meadow, is not titillating in its visual impact, this is neither detrimental to the work nor uncharacteristic of grand opera, which also usually required something of an optical change of pace, a let-up, in the fourth tableau in order to make the final stage picture seem all the more stirring. It is also no accident that precisely this fourth tableau, visually the most subdued, accompanies the most profoundly tranquil and intensely intimate music ever composed by Wagner—the "Good Friday Spell."

The well-made libretti of Eugène Scribe were put together according to carefully thought out conventional patterns. One of the central structural methods of this dramatic technician was to construct each act so that it would be a miniature of the opera as a whole.[9] Wagner was an adherent of this technique, most notably in *Die Meistersinger*, where the plan "Stollen, Stollen, Abgesang" not only provides the structure of the opera, the acts, and Walther's *Preislied*, but also forms the subject of conversation of the characters during much of the opera. That Scribe's organizational technique also applies to *Parsifal* should be evident.

TABLEAU I—WOODS, SHADY AND EARNEST BUT NOT DARK.

1. Exposition: Gurnemanz, Pages, Kundry

2.   Procession Amfortas and Pages

3.   Kundry's character as related by Gurnemanz

4.   Gurnemanz relates story of the Spear

5.   Parsifal — throws aside his weapons

——————————————— *Wandeldekoration* ———————————————

TABLEAU II — TEMPLE OF THE GRAIL, DOMED HALL WITH PILLARS.

1. Voices from above, Titurel, entry procession of Knights

2. Amfortas

3. The grail

4. Exit procession of Knights

5. Parsifal, Gurnemanz

TABLEAU III — KLINGSOR'S MAGIC CASTLE, ON THE SOUTH SIDE OF SAME MOUNTAIN (AS INHABITED BY KNIGHTS OF THE GRAIL), FACING MOORISH SPAIN.

1. Klingsor — in the inner cell of a tower which opens above.

2. Klingsor and Kundry — Klingsor and the whole tower sink quickly at the same time as the

3. Magic Gardens rises, filling the stage completely. Tropical vegetation, richest array of flowers...beautiful maidens...covered with pastel veils quickly thrown over themselves as though they had been suddenly shocked out of their sleep.

4. Kundry, Parsifal — the Kiss

5. Klingsor — the Spear

TABLEAU IV — IN THE DOMAIN OF THE GRAIL. OPEN, INSPIRING SPRING LANDSCAPE...WITH A GENTLY RISING FLOWERY MEADOW.

1. Gurnemanz, Kundry

2. Parsifal, Gurnemanz's recognition of Spear

3. Parsifal narration

4. Kundry baptized. Parsifal anointed

5. Good Friday Spell

——————————————— *Wandeldekoration* ———————————————

TABLEAU V — TEMPLE OF THE GRAIL.

1. Entry Procession of the Knights

2. Amfortas

3. Parsifal. Reunion of Grail and Spear. Dove.

Like the opera as a whole, each of the first four tableaux consists of five parts. As in most grand operas, the last tableau is shorter than the rest. In these works, as in *Parsifal*, the last tableau brings the opera to a fairly rapid close with an impressive visual panorama. In the case of *Parsifal*, the reunion of Sacred Spear and Holy Grail is the target event, the culminating point to which the whole plot builds. It is also the single event depicted in the last tableau. Similarly, each of the four previous tableaux presents only one central event and at most one subsidiary occurrence.

In the first tableau, by throwing aside his bow and arrows after experiencing guilt for killing a swan, Parsifal takes his first step on the long path towards ethical maturation. The sole dramatic event of the second tableau is the uncovering of the Grail. The third tableau presents the Kiss, with which Kundry attempts to secure her seduction of the hero, and a subsidiary event, Parsifal's recovery of the Sacred Spear. Considered both dramatically in its relation to Parsifal's moral development, and structurally in the drama, the Kiss is the work's turning point. Everything which follows is a result and working out of this event. It is the prerequisite for Parsifal's intuition of Amfortas' suffering and therefore his recovery of the Spear. The main joint occurrence of the fourth tableau—Parsifal's baptizing of Kundry and his anointment by Gurnemanz—provides the dramatic resolution of the Kiss as symbol, the attainment by both Parsifal and Kundry of a higher order of Being.

Although the grand operas of Meyerbeer and others often seemed obsessed with religion, they did not present ethical, not to mention spiritual, issues with the sort of seriousness of intent and deeply-felt religiosity which characterizes *Parsifal*. The grand operas were largely vehicles for scenic miracles whereas *Parsifal* is much more than a mere vehicle. This difference leads to the question, why Wagner would base his last and most spiritually ethereal work more closely than any of his previous works (except *Rienzi*) on an operatic form which, for him, embodied everything that was debased and superficial. At least part of the answer to this question lies in Wagnerian artifacts long exposed to light but not yet properly reconstructed and decoded by the army of Wagnerians still too busy sifting through the quasi-archaeological remains of their hero's life.

Right from the beginning of his work on his last opera, Wagner had held two central objectives in mind. The first of these was to prevent it suffering the same fate as had been perpetrated on his other works; namely, being subjected to routine performances in the opera houses of the world. In March of 1877, when he changed the name *Parzifal* to *Parsifal*, he also began using the term "*Bühnenweihfestspiel*," as a label for the work.[10] The term became a sort of Sacred Spear with which to fend off the unholy foe—at once direct, concise, and unanswerable. When any opera house or publisher asked for rights of performance or publication, Wagner and his heirs simply replied that this was no ordinary opera but a *Bühnenweihfestspiel*, a sacred work of consecration meant only for the Bayreuth Festival, a "stage-consecrating festival drama" which would suffer blasphemous desecration were it ever to be performed outside the sacred confines of the Festspielhaus in Bayreuth. "My work is called a *Bühnenweihfestspiel*," Wagner wrote to King Ludwig, "I shall view myself as forced to uphold the solemnity of the stage and intend in this way to find the way to protect my work and its sacred content from being desecrated."[11] For many years, no one was able to invent a defence against this one-word weapon. It proved to be one of the Meister's most inspired strokes of genius—and business acumen. During the first decades of the Bayreuth Festival, when sold-out houses were far less common than half-empty ones, *Parsifal* was the main attraction in enticing opera "pilgrims" to the out-of-the-way Franconian town.

Wagner's second key objective had to do with his son, Siegfried (Fidi). Cosima referred to this in her diary:

> After dinner Richard speaks about Fidi's education and Fidi's future. He would have plenty to do if he became the custodian of his father's spiritual legacy, if he really solidified and created support for the ideas. R. says furthermore that he will write Parsifal for him.[12]

At the moment that he embarked on his last great work, Wagner set out to create not just an opera but a spiritual legacy for his son, who he hoped would follow in his footsteps in heading the Wagnerian movement. Cosima noted this more than once in her diary: "R. working on *Parzifal* which he wants to bequeath to Fidi!"[13] For Wagner, Fidi had always represented a means of immortalizing his message. As he said when Fidi was not yet two, the boy was "my life-insurance company fore and aft," by which he meant overseer of his archival legacy and promoter of his ideology after his death.[14] What this life-insurance was meant to make secure is clear from other remarks in Cosima's diary:

> We go for a walk. On the way I say to him how happy I am that, through him, Fidi will acquire the right point of view about everything—art, philosophy, Jews, religion, politics—so that he will be spared futile meanderings.[15]

It is no accident that *Parsifal* portrays the ethical education of a youngster. The subject had been a part of Wagner's domestic life since Fidi's birth in 1869. Through his "pure fool" Wagner intended to bestow upon his audience as he had bestowed upon his son the "right point of view about everything."

While composing *Parsifal*, Wagner showed special interest in Bach, Haydn, Mozart, Beethoven, and Mendelssohn. One entry in Cosima's diary casts light on the nature of her husband's interest in the latter composer:

> When I came to him in the afternoon, he had just had a look through *Paul* [Mendelssohn's oratorio, *St. Paul*] and he is filled with repugnance for it; the complete Jew is there, facile in form and superficial in content...."And as if Bach can be imitated!" He criticizes my father [Liszt] for writing oratorios.[16]

Wagner had always been filled with repugnance whenever Jewish composers or even Catholic ones like Liszt had used Lutheran music in their compositions. He felt that a proprietary right of his had thereby been violated. Thus Meyerbeer's use in *Les Huguenots* of the hymn "Ein' feste Burg" had always sent Wagner into fits of fury. The same was the case with Mendelssohn's use of the "Dresden Amen" in the opening of his "Reformation" Symphony. In this light, it is interesting to note that, on 8 February 1876 Wagner and his wife attended an amateur performance of this symphony in Bayreuth. On 9 February, the next day, he played for Cosima his first musical notation for *Parsifal*—the theme of the Flowers. A week later, he showed her a more worked-out musical sketch for the Flower music, "Komm holder Knabe...."

Since 1865 Wagner's concentration had turned increasingly to *Parsifal*. But he had not brought himself to write a note of it until a day after hearing Mendelssohn's "Reformation" Symphony. It is probably much more than mere speculation to conclude that Mendelssohn's symphony so irritated Wagner that he reacted by setting down music that was an answer to what he saw as Mendelssohn's "Jewish" desecration of proprietary Christian themes. It is also no coincidence that the openings of *Parsifal* and the "Reformation" Symphony show several close similarities. Both openings centre on the "Dresden Amen." But where the symphony then bustles off in a characteristically sprightly manner, the prelude to *Parsifal* ascends inexorably into a rare region of transcendent religious feeling.[17]

By using the "Dresden Amen" as the first and seminal leitmotif of his *Bühnenweihfestspiel*, Wagner seemed to be attempting to show where Mendelssohn and his ilk had gone wrong. The formal elements of grand opera which pervade *Parsifal* occupy a similar place. Showing a supreme technical mastery of the grand opera form, Wagner refuted the world of Meyerbeer by showing what a grand opera would look and sound like when it had content and style, effects preceded by causes. As thinker, Wagner retained a lifelong need to convey to his fellow man "the right point of view about everything." As dramatist, he never lost his driving youthful ambition to outdo grand opera. As composer, his ability to do so increased to the end of his days.

NOTES

1. See Lilli Lehmann, *Mein Weg* (Leipzig, 1913).

2. The infamous claque of the Paris Opéra, so detested by Wagner, would never have hissed so open-handed a creator as Giacomo Meyerbeer. On the other hand, whereas Meyerbeer paid for the organized approval of his works, Wagner accomplished the amazing feat of persuading his claque—the Wagner Societies—to pay him.

3. Richard Wagner, "Eine Mitteilung an meine Freunde," *Dichtungen und Schriften*, ed. Dieter Borchmeyer, vol. 6 (Frankfurt am Main: Insel Verlag, 1983), 230.

4. Richard Wagner, *Oper und Drama, Dichtungen und Schriften*, vol. 7, 98.

5. The *Wandeldekoration*, like grand opera itself, had its origins in the Boulevard theatres of the 1820s, specifically in Daguerre's Diorama, a device for showing scenery in motion.

6. *Parsifal* libretto, Act III.

7. *La Revue des deux Mondes*, vol. 4 (1831), 539, quoted by William Crosten, *French Grand Opera: An Art and a Business* (New York: King's Crown Press, 1948), 61.

8. *Le Courrier Français*, 27 February, 1835, quoted in Crosten, 65–66.

9. See Patrick J. Smith, *The Tenth Muse* (New York: Knopf, 1970), 219.

10. Cosima Wagner, *Die Tagebücher* (Müchen: Piper, 1976), vol. 1, 14.3.77.

11. *König Ludwig II und Richard Wagner: Briefwechsel* (Karlsruhe, 1936–39), vol. 3, 127–31, 15.7.78.

12. Cosima Wagner, *Die Tagebücher*, vol. 1. 5.1.77.

13. Ibid. vol. 1: 22.2.77; see also vol. 2: 17.6.79.

14. Ibid. vol. 1: 19.3.71.

15. Ibid. vol. 1: 19.6.71.

16. Ibid. vol. 2: 18.1.79

17. One of the best treatments of religion and religiosity in *Parsifal* is William Blissett, "The Liturgy of *Parsifal*," *University of Toronto Quarterly* 49 (1979–80): 117–138.

MEIN LEBEN: RICHARD WAGNER AND THE ART OF AUTOBIOGRAPHY

H.B. de Groot

In the *Education of Henry Adams*, the author relates how in 1850, when he was twelve, he was taken by his father to see his grandmother who, paralysed and bed-ridden, lived in Washington. Adams goes into considerable detail in his description of the journey and the modes of transportation employed: boat across New York Bay, train to Trenton (it was the Camden and Amboy Railroad), steamer to Philadelphia, another boat, another train, yet another boat (to Baltimore this time) and finally by train to Washington. And then Adams comments, with a disarming but also disconcerting candour:

> This was the journey he remembered. The actual journey may have been quite different, but the actual journey has no interest for education. The memory was all that mattered...[1]

Not all writers have found it so easy to subordinate what is factually true to that which is preserved in the memory. Mary McCarthy, for instance, in her *Memoirs of a Catholic Girlhood* subjects each chapter to a running commentary in which the discrepancies between the truth and the semi-fictionalized presentation are ruthlessly pointed out. Yet it would be a mistake to take her comments at face value and to assume that the relationship between narrative and commentary is that between fiction and fact. Logically it would have been perfectly possible for her to add a new commentary in each edition, each new gloss acting as a critical comment on that in an earlier text. Nor should we forget that the earlier version of the *Memoirs* consisted of a series of self-contained *New Yorker* stories, a form of organization which did not make the same demands in terms of coherence and consistency as the book-length version.[2] Consequently, what appears as a determination to tell the exact truth, however belatedly, may be—as much as anything else—a response to the demands of form and genre.

Other tensions between the need to tell the truth and the desire to write fiction exist. The Canadian writer, F.P. Grove, who in his novels tried to record the way of life of a vanished or vanishing pioneer society, also published autobiographies which, as recent research has shown, have little to do with the facts in his life and show an imagination and inventiveness hard to find in his fiction. In *In Search of Myself*, for instance, Grove locates as a turning-point in his life his meeting with a French priest who saw him read Baudelaire in a North Dakota railway station and encouraged him to seek a teaching post in Canada. Did that really happen? As the contemporary Western Canadian writer Robert Kroetsch puts it in a memorable passage:

```
                              did you find
    did you dream the       French priest who hauled you
    out of your fleurs du mal    and headlong
    into a hundred drafts     real

    or imagined     of the sought form
    (there are no models)    and always
    (there are only models)    alone³
```

A good autobiographer will have two aims. The first will be to tell the reader truthfully how things were. This in itself is a complex undertaking since it is difficult, and ultimately impossible, to divorce the truth as it lies at the other end of the years which have passed from the way memory has come to represent that truth.

The need to tell the truth, demanding as it is in itself, needs to be balanced with another, that of presenting the pattern which gives significance to what otherwise would be a mere succession of events, one damn thing after another. Often an autobiographer will attach especial significance to what retrospectively can be seen as turning-points (such as Grove's meeting with the French priest). Of course, such an emphasis could be equally true of a biography and it is indeed in a biographical account that we find a pattern which has served as a paradigm for many autobiographies:

> And as he journeyed, he came near Damascus: and suddenly there shined round about him a light from heaven: And he fell to the earth, and heard a voice saying unto him, Saul, Saul, why persecutest thou me? And he said, Who art thou, Lord? And the Lord said, I am Jesus whom thou persecutest: it is hard for thee to kick against the pricks. And he trembling and astonished said, Lord, what wilt thou have me do? And the Lord said unto him, Arise and go into the city, and it shall be told thee what thou must do. And the men which journeyed with him stood speechless, hearing a voice, but seeing no man. And Saul arose from the earth; and when his eyes were opened, he saw

no man; but they led him by the hand and brought him into Damascus. And
he was three days without sight, and neither did eat nor drink. (Acts 9:3–9)

Paul's conversion is characterized by its suddenness and by violence: the physical
violence of the lightning is paralleled by the inner violence exerted on the whole
personality. The sudden illumination is crucial as it alters (or at least is perceived as
having altered) the course of a whole life. Strindberg recognized the importance of the
presentation of Paul's conversion for the autobiographer when he gave the name *To
Damascus* to his autobiographical trilogy, although there the attainment of illumination is presented not as a sudden and overwhelming event but as the outcome of a
painfully drawn-out process.

The pattern of a sudden conversion leading to a totally altered life is crucial to
other spiritual autobiographies and we find it in St. Augustine, in Bunyan, in Carlyle,
in Newman. We even find a secular parallel in that most unreligious of
autobiographies, that of John Stuart Mill, a parallel of which Mill was acutely aware
as it is explicitly brought out in the chapter which deals with his movement away from
orthodox Benthamism through Marmontel and Wordsworth:

> It was in the autumn of 1826. I was in a dull state of nerves, such as everybody
> is occasionally liable to; unsusceptible to enjoyment or pleasurable excitement; one of those moods when what is pleasure at other times, becomes
> insipid or indifferent; the state, I should think, in which converts to
> Methodism usually are, when smitten by their first 'conviction of sin.'[4]

It is unfortunate that those writing on Wagner's autobiography, *Mein Leben*, have
been largely concerned with trying to determine the truthfulness of his account, have
been interested in catching him out even, while putting little stress on its integrity as
a work of the imagination or on those things which Wagner himself isolates as
especially significant. It is true that the narrator of *Mein Leben* sometimes presents the
reader with an account of his life which appears to be at variance with ascertainable
fact. I am not thinking here of slight errors in dating such as we have in the very first
sentence of the book where Wagner manages to get the date of his baptism wrong.
There are, however, other discrepancies which are rather more disturbing. Wagner tells
us, for instance, that during his first visit to Paris he "hit upon the idea of composing
for Lablache a grand bass aria with a chorus to be introduced into his part as Oroveso
in Belini's *Norma*."[5] Yet is it clear from Ernest Newman's biography that Wagner had
already composed this aria in Riga when he was music director there (the bass was
apparently the best singer in the company and for his own benefit night Wagner wanted
to give him more than what the somewhat uninteresting part of Oroveso provided).[6]
If this is true, then the aria was not composed for Lablache at all but consisted of older
material in which Wagner hoped to interest the French bass.

Equally curious is Wagner's insistence that when he conducted *Rienzi* in Dresden on 15 October 1844 he "made no effort to ascertain the effect of [his] work" on any of the distinguished musicians present (Spontini, Meyerbeer, Lvov), as there is evidence that Wagner spoke at length with Meyerbeer on that occasion (*ML*, 277, 769). Although in the case of the interpolated aria in *Norma* it is quite possible that Wagner misremembered the sequence of events, it seems only too likely that in the other case the older Wagner misrepresented the situation because he wished to assert his lack of respect for Meyerbeer whom he had come to dislike.

More important than such local discrepancies, however, are the overall emphases which often differ from those placed by Wagner's biographers. Minna, Richard's first wife, comes across in *Mein Leben* as a real trooper, someone who showed Wagner loyalty and affection, but also as an essentially middle-class figure, happy to be a *Frau Kapellmeister*, angry with her husband for any signs that he might sacrifice his worldly prospects, and totally unable to understand the spiritual side of her husband's world. It is, of course, true that the marriage foundered and that Wagner came to see Minna and himself as essentially incompatible. What the autobiography suggests, however, is that Wagner recognized this incompatibility from the beginning. Such an awareness simply does not square with the letters which Wagner wrote to her at the time (and which Minna religiously preserved), as these show him to have been very passionately in love.

Another problem relates to Wagner's role in the Dresden uprising of 1849. In *Mein Leben* Wagner suggests that his involvement was the result of a romantic idealism, an exposure to a springtide so violent that it could not easily be resisted and that he was ultimately only interested in the political upheaval in so far as it might lead to an overhaul of the Dresden Opera House and of the conditions in which opera could be performed. It can easily be demonstrated that Wagner was much more actively involved, especially in the running of the radical paper *Das Volksblatt*.[7] It can also be noted that Wagner quite systematically plays down the importance of the women in his life other than Minna and Cosima, so that Mathilde Wesendonk, Jessie Laussot and Friederike Meyer all receive rather short shrift.[8]

It is difficult to resist altogether the suspicion that Wagner had short-term tactical reasons for wishing to represent these events in the way he did. After all, he was dictating the work to Cosima, who would have been less than flattered if due prominence had been given to other women in Richard's life, and the work was being written at the suggestion of King Ludwig of Bavaria, who would be unenthusiastic about Wagner's revolutionary past. Yet it seems reductive to dismiss the question in these terms. An autobiography, after all, is not only an account of events; it is also an interpretation of what happened. If Wagner dismissed his revolutionary activities or his involvement with Jessie Laussot as relatively unimportant, it may be because he came to consider them less than essential in terms of the longer perspective of his life.

Here Wordsworth's autobiography provides a parallel. When Wordsworth came to revise *The Prelude*, he added to the account of his years in London a passage on Edmund Burke which had not been present in the 1805 version of the poem. The addition is thirty-three lines long and comprises an account of Burke's political philosophy in Wordsworth's most rhetorical late manner. The account ends with these lines:

> Could a youth, and one
> In ancient story versed, whose breast had heaved
> Under the weight of classic eloquence,
> Sit, see, and hear, unthankful, uninspired?[9]

The rhetorical question presupposes the answer "no," but all the evidence, including the fact that the lines do not appear in the 1805 text or in any other early manuscript, suggests that, while the young Wordsworth may well have heard Burke speak in Parliament and may, on a rhetorical level, have been impressed, he probably was "unthankful" and "uninspired"—at the time. Yet later Wordsworth must have realized, not only that he ought to have been thankful and inspired but also that, in the longer perspective, he owed much to Burke's vision, to the eloquence with which that vision was expressed and to the integrity of the speaker. If, on one level, Wordsworth is not speaking the truth about his younger self, on another he is replacing an earlier actuality with what he has come to regard as essentially truer to the real self.

If we read Wagner's *Mein Leben*, not with the intention of unmasking him as a liar but in order to understand how he interpreted his life, we might well begin by asking ourselves if there are any turning-points in the narrative which are as crucial to the course of his life and to his own vision of that life as was Paul's experience on the road to Damascus. The answer must be that such turning-points do occur in the narrative and that there are indeed a confusingly large number of them.

The earliest of these turning-points occurred, according to *Mein Leben*, in 1829. In that year the great singer Wilhelmine Schröder-Devrient came to Leipzig as a guest artist in the role of Leonore in Beethoven's *Fidelio*. Wagner was then in his sixteenth year:

> When I look back across my entire life I find no event to place beside this in the impression it produced on me. Whoever can remember this wonderful woman at that period of her life will certainly confirm in some fashion the almost demonic fire irresistibly kindled in them by the profoundly human and ecstatic performance of this incomparable artist. After the opera was over I dashed to the home of one of my friends to write a short letter in which I told her succinctly that my life had henceforth found its meaning, and that if ever she should hear my name favorably mentioned in the world of art, she should

remember that she had on this evening made of me that which I now vowed to become.

Not surprisingly, the young Wagner lacked the technical skills which he would have needed to give shape to his new-found ideals and the effect of this falling short was intensely demoralizing:

> I wanted to write a work that would be worthy of Schröder-Devrient: but as that was by no means within my power I abandoned all artistic efforts in headlong despair, and because academic work could certainly not enlist my attention, I let myself go, living rudderless from day to day in the company of a strange crew of companions, and indulged in all sorts of youthful dissipations. (*ML*, 37)

Paul too, it will be remembered, was initially disoriented by the event which gave his life its meaning.

Mein Leben was by no means Wagner's first essay in autobiography. As early as August 1835 he began to write down, in point form, the most important events in his life. In this early account, now known as "die rote Brieftasche," he stresses the renewed passion for music which he experienced late in 1828 and links this passion with the works of Mozart and Beethoven. He then continues laconically: "Sommer 1829 allein in Leipzig. Lasse Alles liegen, treibe nur Musik ohne Unterricht." The overpowering effect of Schröder-Devrient is not even mentioned.[10]

In 1843 Wagner wrote again about his life, this time in the "Autobiographische Skizze," an account designed to make him and his work better known in Germany after his return from Paris. Again there is no mention of the 1829 experience but Schröder-Devrient does enter the story in his entry for 1833. In that year Wagner was staying in Würzburg, trying to get his first opera *Die Feen* staged, and saw Schröder-Devrient perform the part of Romeo in Bellini's opera *I Capuletti ed i Montecchi*: "I was astounded to recognise such an extraordinary achievement in the performance of such thoroughly insignificant music."[11] The experience led Wagner to compose *Das Liebesverbot*, the most Italianate of his operas.

What was true of the "Autobiographische Skizze" is also true of "Eine Mitteilung an meine Freunde" of 1851. Once again Wagner does not mention the *Fidelio* performances of 1829 and once again he does write about Schröder-Devrient's Romeo of 1833 but this time much more ecstatically than he had done in the earlier account. Now Wagner writes how his pressing desire for women was redirected towards music, and in particular towards French and Italian opera, since the public morality of the day prevented him from giving direct expression to his desire. The joy and the zest with which he approached life would have been debased and have become frivolity, had he not at this time seen the performances of Schröder-Devrient: "Even the most distant contact with this extraordinary woman had on me the effect of an electric shock: for a long time, even until the present moment, have I seen, heard and felt her when I experienced the need for artistic creation."[12]

No doubt Wagner did see Schröder-Devrient in the role of Leonore in 1829 and he probably did write her an ardent fan letter on that occasion, but the accounts of 1843 and 1851 make it clear that it was not that performance but her 1833 Romeo which he then saw as the most powerful experience in his early life. It seems plausible that these special qualities were retrospectively attached to the earlier Leonore. Perhaps the older Wagner came to believe that it was impossible to have seen Schröder-Devrient's Leonore and yet to "sit, see, and hear, unthankful, uninspired."[13]

Another early event to which Wagner accords special significance took place around Easter 1830. The young Wagner had become a gambler and had misappropriated his mother's pension. One night he lost heavily and was down to his last—his mother's last—thaler:

> With this my last t[h]aler I staked my life: for there was no question of returning home; I could see myself in the grey dawn fleeing through fields and woods into the wide blue yonder like a lost prodigal. This despairing mood held me so forcibly that, when my card won, I left my winnings on the board and continued to do so time after time, until I had won a really substantial amount. I now began to win continuously. My luck became so reliable that I dared to gamble against the longest odds: for suddenly it occurred to me vividly that I was gambling for the last time. My luck became so conspicuous that the bank thought it best to close. I had actually regained not only all the money I had previously lost in this one night but also enough to pay all my past debts. The growing elation I felt during this whole process was utterly sacred. With the turn in my luck I clearly sensed God or His angels as if standing beside me and whispering words of warning and consolation. Once again I had to climb over the courtyard gate at daybreak to get into my home: there I fell into a deep and energizing sleep, from which I awakened late, strengthened and as if born again. No sense of shame deterred me from voluntarily telling my mother, to whom I remitted her money, about the events of this decisive night and of my dereliction with her property. She folded her hands and gave thanks to God for this sign of His grace, and expressed her confidence that I had been saved and would never again relapse into similar sins. And temptation really lost its power over me for all time. (*ML*, 50–51)

Nowhere else in *Mein Leben* does Wagner echo so clearly the language of religious conversion. At the same time, if one sets this passage against the corresponding account in a genuine spiritual autobiography such as Augustine's *Confessions* or Bunyan's *Grace Abounding*, the sheer hollowness of Wagner's interpretation of his experience as well as of his mother's endorsement of that interpretation becomes clear. Indeed, Wagner's sense that God is gambling at his side comes close to blasphemy. Ultimately, however, Wagner presents this episode not as a spiritual experience but in terms of its significance in his career as an artist. Shortly after he had been cured from his addiction to gambling, Theodor Weinlich, who had been attempting to teach him music theory, became so discouraged by Wagner's unwillingness to settle down to harmonic exercises that he announced that the lessons would be discontinued. At that point it was the experience in the gambling den which allowed Wagner to beseech his teacher to give him one further chance and to commit himself wholeheartedly to the technical discipline which a composer has to acquire. It is this new commitment which Wagner retrospectively came to see as "the turning-point in [his] life" (*ML*, 55).[14]

There are other events which Wagner presents in a manner reminiscent of Paul's experience on the road to Damascus, events carrying the violent force of a flash of lightning and leading to a sudden illumination which decisively affects the course of his life. One such event is the death of his favourite sister Rosalie in 1837:

During the time when I had vanished from sight, when news of my headstrong marriage and the unfortunate consequences it entailed reached my family, she had been the one, as my mother later told me, who had never lost faith in me, but rather clung to the hope that I should one day come into my own and amount to something. Now, upon the news of her death, along with the memory of our last leave-taking, the whole scope of the immense value of my sister's relationship to me was illuminated as if by lightning, and the influence she exercised on me became clear to me later when, after my first notable successes, my mother tearfully lamented that Rosalie had not lived to see them. (*ML*, 151)

This passage is especially interesting in that Wagner stresses both the immediate impact of the event and the deepening sense of its importance in later years (much in the way that the famous "spots of time" passage in Wordsworth's *Prelude* explores the violent impact of two specific events as well as the long-term significance which only emerged as the events were remembered in the course of the years).

Some of the finest moments in *Mein Leben* are those in which Wagner has been able to write about small events in such a way that they become symbolic; that is to say they capture his own sense of his experience in a more powerful way than purely discursive prose could have done. In 1840 Wagner was in Paris, very much down on his luck, reduced to earning a living of sorts by arranging Donizetti's *La Favorite*, a work which he despised, for various instruments and combinations of instruments, including the *cornet à pistons*. Shortly before accepting this commission he had been walking through Paris burdened with a heavy metronome which had to be returned to its owner:

> A thick fog covered the streets when I stepped outside the house, and the first thing I recognized was my dog Robber, who had been taken from me a year before. At first I thought I was seeing a ghost, but then yelled to him hastily in a shrill and piercing voice; the animal seemed to recognize me and approached rather near; when I strode quickly toward him with outstretched arm, however, the fear of a punishment, such as I had foolishly administered to him once or twice during the latter part of the time he was with us, seemed to dispel every other recollection; he drew back timidly, and when I ran hastily after him, he fled me each time at greater and greater speed. That he had recognized me became clearer and clearer, for I could see him pause at street-corners to look anxiously back at me before setting off again with renewed energy. Thus, I followed him through a labyrinth of streets, hardly distinguishable in the thick mist, until breathless and dripping with sweat, burdened by my metronome, I lost sight of him near the church of St Roch, never to see him again. For a time I stood glued to the spot, staring into the fog. I wondered what the ghostly reappearance of the companion of my adventurous travels on this horrible day could possibly signify. That he had fled his old master with the terror of a wild beast filled my heart with a strange bitterness and seemed to me a terrible omen. (*ML*, 188–89)

Wagner himself was in no doubt about the representative and symbolic significance of this experience for him: "The day on which this happened was one of the most extraordinary of my life, for into it the whole misery of my situation at the time was compressed in the most ghastly way" (*ML*, 188).

Sometimes the flash of lightning serves to illuminate and intensify the darkness of his existence as when he hears that the Parisian theatre which was so promisingly named the *Théâtre de la Renaissance* and which, Wagner hoped, might produce *Das Liebesverbot* had suddenly "gone into bankruptcy and had closed" (*ML*, 181). Wagner can be quite sardonic about such moments of illumination as when he describes the occasion of his meeting with C.F. Meser, his agent and publisher, to discuss the possibility of selling some of his work at the Dresden Easter Trade Fair:

> I tried to buoy [Meser] up and ordered a bottle of the best Haut-Sauternes; a venerable looking flask appeared; I filled our glasses, we raised them to toast success at the fair, and drank—only to shriek suddenly like madmen and try to spit everything out in horror—for by mistake we had been served the strongest tarragon vinegar in the house. 'My God,' cried Meser, 'this really did it!' 'Yes indeed,' I replied, 'I think a lot of things will turn to vinegar for us!' My humor revealed to me in a flash that I would have to look elsewhere for my salvation than to the Easter Trade Fair. (*ML*, 333)

The *Théâtre de la Renaissance* provides no second birth; the Easter Trade Fair brings no salvation even if, like Christ, Wagner has to suffer the bitterness of vinegar.

The moments to which Wagner accords special significance are not all moments of gloom and quite a few scenes (such as the first glimpse of the Swiss mountains) carry a sense of exultation. Sometimes different events, often occurring at widely spaced intervals, are linked so that what emerges is a pattern no longer determined by the single turning-point. One such pattern is established when Wagner describes how, after the Dresden uprising, his departure for Chemnitz had been delayed, so that his friends Heubner and Bakunin, who had gone ahead without him, were arrested but not Wagner himself. His sense of a miraculous escape reminded him of how on an earlier occasion he had almost been killed in a duel: "Like a bolt of lightning it flashed upon my soul how miraculously I had escaped from almost certain calamity in duels with the most experienced swordsmen in my student days" (*ML*, 412).

Sometimes the pattern linking events is much more complex. Among his earliest musical experiences Wagner lists the eerie sustained open fifths with which Beethoven's Ninth Symphony begins.[15] This experience was linked to others: the ghostly fifths on the violins as the orchestra tunes up, the eerie picture in which a skeleton plays the violin to a dying man, and the musical phantoms in E.T.A. Hoffmann's *Phantasiestücken*. The impact of the Ninth Symphony deepened in the course of the years but no performances in Leipzig could ever do justice to Wagner's ideal conception of the work. He did not properly hear it until 1839 when he attended a rehearsal of the Paris Conservatoire orchestra. It was then that he realized how much his attention had been deflected from the things that really mattered to the trivial practicalities of the running of a musical theatre:

> While this inner change of direction had been gradually prepared by the painful experiences of the past few years, it was nevertheless the inexpressible effect of the Ninth Symphony, in a performance I had previously not dreamed possible, which revived my former spirit and gave it new life and strength. I can thus compare this event in my life with the similarly decisive impression which, as a youth of sixteen, I gained from the Fidelio of Schröder-Devrient. (*ML*, 175)

Later in *Mein Leben* Wagner recalls this experience when he describes how on Palm Sunday of the year 1846 he prepared himself for a performance in Dresden of the Ninth Symphony. The orchestral parts had to be borrowed from Leipzig and Wagner now laid eyes on the score for the first time since his boyhood:

> Just as hearing a rehearsal of the first three movements by the incomparable Conservatoire orchestra during my obscure Paris period had suddenly affected me as if by a magic spell, returning me at a stroke, miraculously, to my early youth across all the years of alienation and confusion, and strengthening the new turn taken by my inmost strivings, so now the sounds of that performance, the last I had heard, were reawakened with mysterious

power when I first saw before me with my own eyes that which had remained for me in those earliest days likewise only a mystic vision. (*ML*, 329)

The performance was a triumph and made Wagner feel that he "had the capacity and power to accomplish just about whatever [he] wished if [he] seriously devoted himself to it" (*ML*, 333). The fact that the performance took place on Palm Sunday was fortuitous as for a long time it had been the custom in Dresden to perform an oratorio or a symphony on that occasion, yet the coincidence that the date of his triumph in Dresden was also that of Christ's triumphant entry into Jerusalem has a symbolic appropriateness which cannot have been lost on Wagner.

Palm Sunday is not the only day in the life of Christ to play a role in that of Wagner. Good Friday is still more important. At the end of April 1857 the Wagners moved into *Asyl*, the cottage near Zürich which Otto Wesendonk had provided for them. At first the weather was cold and miserable but then there was a change:

Beautiful spring weather now set in; on Good Friday I awoke to find the sun shining brightly into this house for the first time: the garden was blooming, and the birds singing, and at last I could sit out on the parapeted terrace of the little dwelling and enjoy the longed-for tranquillity that seemed so fraught with promise. Filled with this sentiment, I suddenly said to myself that this was Good Friday and recalled how meaningful this had seemed to me in Wolfram's *Parzival*. Ever since that stay in Marienbad, where I had conceived *Die Meistersinger* and *Lohengrin*, I had not taken another look at that poem; now its ideality came to me in overwhelming form, and from the idea of Good Friday I quickly sketched out an entire drama in three acts. (*ML*, 547)

What Wagner claimed to have sketched out in 1857 was the text of *Parsifal* yet it is possible to see how the ecstatic Good Friday music of the opera grew out of this experience. Once again, however, the overall design of his autobiography is more important to Wagner than factual accuracy, for, as was pointed out long ago, Wagner did not move into *Asyl* until 28 April, whereas Good Friday had occurred on 10 April.[16]

Good Friday recurs later in the narrative for it is on that day, 23 March 1864, that Wagner travelled from Vienna to Munich:

It was Good Friday: the weather was very bad and seemed to reflect the mood of the entire populace, whom I saw proceeding from one church to another in deepest mourning. King Maximilian II, whom the Bavarians had grown to love, had died a few days before, leaving his son to ascend the throne at the youthful but still legitimate age of eighteen and a half. In a display window I saw a portrait of the young king Ludwig II, and felt that special emotion awakened in us by the sight of beauty and youth being placed in what will presumably be a very difficult situation. (*ML*,735)

Good Friday is the most solemn day in the Christian Year but it is not altogether a sad day as the Crucifixion points forward to the Resurrection. For Wagner too (and he would not have considered the parallel blasphemous) the mourning of Good Friday leads to triumph, not on the third day but some five weeks later.

On 3 May Wagner was in Stuttgart and received a *carte de visite* from the Secretary to the King of Bavaria:

> The next day I received Herr Pfistermeister, the Cabinet Secretary of His Majesty the King of Bavaria, in my room....He brought me a note from the young King of Bavaria, together with a portrait and a ring as a present. In words which, though few, penetrated to the core of my being, the young monarch avowed his great admiration for my art and his firm resolve to keep me at his side as a friend for ever, to spare me any malignant strokes of fate. (*ML*, 738)

At lunch that same day it is learnt that Meyerbeer had just died. "Weissheimer," a young friend, "burst out into boorish laughter at the strange coincidence that this operatic master, who had done me so much harm, should not have lived to see this day." But Wagner can now afford to be magnanimous and has no need to be as boorish as his young friend. The same day he leaves for Munich, with Pfitstermeister:

> On the same day I had received the most urgent warnings from Vienna not to return there. But my life was to have no more of such alarms. The dangerous path on which destiny now beckoned me to the highest goals would not be free of worries and troubles of a kind hitherto unknown to me; but under the protection of my exalted friend the meanest cares of subsistence were never to touch me again. (*ML*, 739)

It is with this triumphant blaze that *Mein Leben* ends.

The qualifications in the final sentence of the book make clear that Wagner is anxious to avoid the impression that his life will have a fairy tale ending. Even so, it would be easy to demonstrate that Wagner glosses over those "worries and troubles" which are carefully left unspecified. We know, for instance, that Pfistermeister, who comes across in *Mein Leben* as a Mercury figure, a messenger from the gods, had become a bitter opponent long before Wagner, in 1880, dictated the final section of *Mein Leben*.[17]

Wagner's artistic problem in reaching the end of *Mein Leben* is that which faces any autobiographer. A dramatist or a novelist can end a play or novel on a note of achieved happiness (as in *As You Like It* or *Pride and Prejudice*) or with a tragic emphasis which finds victory in defeat (as in *Hamlet* or *Clarissa*) or in a way which includes elements of both (as when in *The Playboy of the Western World* the achieved freedom of Christy Mahon is set against Pegeen Mike's acute sense of loss). Autobiography, however, resists closure since only death can round off the life lived.[18] Yet a writer also feels the need to conclude the narrative and that need may be difficult to resist. When John Henry Newman wrote the *Apologia pro Vita Sua*, his problem was very similar to Wagner's. Newman writes in great detail about the years in which he was slowly and painfully led towards Catholicism but he presents the later years as the safe port reached after the storm, although we know from other evidence how bitter his fights with the Ultramontane forces within the Church were.

Wagner, then, ends the autobiography as one would expect an autobiographer to end the account of his life, but the artifice with which the ending is reached is rather crude. What one finally remembers about the book is not how lucky Wagner was to meet King Ludwig at the right time but how, earlier, he gradually came in touch with the main springs of his creativity and how his recognition of his artistic vision allowed him to turn his back on everything (and everybody) that was trivial and ephemeral. Nowhere is that growing sense of direction clearer than in his account of how the opening of *Das Rheingold* came to him and it is fitting that an essay on *Mein Leben* should end by quoting that magnificent passage:

> After a sleepless and feverish night, I forced myself to undertake a long walk the following day among the pine-covered hills of the surroundings. Everything seemed to me bleak and bare, and I asked myself why I had come. Returning that afternoon, I stretched out dead-tired on a hard couch, awaiting the long-desired onset of sleep. It did not come; instead, I sank into a kind of somnambulistic state, in which I suddenly had the feeling of being immersed in rapidly flowing water. Its rushing soon resolved itself for me into the musical sound of the chord of E flat major, resounding in persistent broken chords; these in turn transformed themselves into melodic figurations of increasing motion, yet the E flat major triad never changed, and seemed by its continuance to impart infinite significance to the element in which I was sinking. I awoke in sudden terror from this trance, feeling as though the waves were crashing high above my head. I recognized at once that the orchestral prelude to *Das Rheingold*, long dormant within me but up to that moment inchoate, had at last been revealed; and I also saw immediately precisely how it was with me: the vital flood would come from within me, and not from without. (*ML*, 499)

NOTES

1. Henry Adams, *The Education of Henry Adams*, ed. Ernest Samuels (Boston: Houghton Mifflin, 1973), 43.

2. I wrote this essay before the publication of McCarthy's *How I Grew*, which, it would seem, represents a rather different way of rewriting her autobiography: by starting again from scratch.

3. Robert Kroetsch, "F.P. Grove: The Finding," lines 15–21. The poem is printed in *An Anthology of Canadian Literature in English*, ed. Donna Bennett and Russell Brown (Toronto: Oxford Univ. Press, 1983), 244–45. On Grove's life see Douglas O. Spettigue, *F.P.G.: The European Years* (Ottawa: Oberon Press, 1973).

4. John Stuart Mill, *Autobiography*, World's Classics Edition (London: Oxford Univ. Press, 1924; 1963 ed.), 113.

5. Richard Wagner, *My Life*, trans. Andrew Gray, ed. Mary Whittall (Cambridge: Cambridge Univ. Press, 1983), 173; subsequent references to this edition will be given parenthetically in the text as *ML*. In this first quotation I have corrected the translator's "Oroviso"; Wagner himself had used the German form "Orovist," see *Mein Leben*, ed. Martin Gregor-Dellin (München: List Verlag, 1969), vol. 1, 183.

6. Ernest Newman, *The Life of Richard Wagner* (1933; Cambridge: Cambridge Univ. Press, 1976), vol. 1, 229. Newman himself appears to assume that this is a different aria from the one shown to Lablache (vol. 1, 279) but was it?

7. On this question see Newman, *The Life of Richard Wagner*, vol. 2, chapters 4 and 5.

8. This whole question is judiciously dealt with by Martin Gregor-Dellin in his "Afterword" (*ML*, 741–56).

9. Wordsworth, *The Prelude* (1850 version; book 7, lines 540–43); quoted from the edition by J.C. Maxwell (Harmondsworth: Penguin, 1971), 283.

10. Richard Wagner, *Sämtliche Briefe*, ed. Gertrud Strobel and Werner Wolf (Leipzig: VEB Deutscher Verlag für Musik, 1967), vol. 1, 81–92; quotation from 81. Schröder-Devrient is mentioned later in the "rote Brieftasche" (*op. cit.*, 82) but only to record that Wagner was able to bring her to Magdeburg for a concert when he was Music Director there.

11. Translated from *Sämtliche Briefe*, ed. Strobel and Wolf, vol. 1, 101. I like to imagine that something of Schröder-Devrient's quality can be heard on the Angel recording of *I Capuletti ed i Montecchi* in the performance by Janet Baker, surely the finest singer of our time.

12. Translated from Richard Wagner, *Dichtungen und Schriften*, ed. Dieter Borchmeyer (Frankfurt am Main: Insel, 1983), vol. 6, 225.

13. I find I have been anticipated by John Deathridge in his recent biographical introduction in *The New Grove Wagner* (London: Macmillan, 1984), 7. Deathridge, however, goes too far when he asserts that Wagner did not hear Schröder-Devrient in 1829. There is no evidence that Wagner heard her in that year, but it does not follow that he did not. On two other occasions he wrote in some detail about her portrayal of the role. Are these accounts fabrications? Or should we assume that Wagner heard her in a later performance such as the one she gave in Magdeburg in 1835, when he was music director there? Deathridge is in error in referring to "the Red Pocket-Book" as a diary, at least in relation to the earlier entries which constitute a retrospective account begun in the summer of 1835.

14. Wagner writes: "In diese Zeit fiel der Wendepunkt meiner Lebensrichtung, welche die Katastrophe jenes erschütterden Abends im Spielhause herbeiführte" (*Mein Leben*, vol. 1, 63). Andrew Gray translates: "It was then that the turning point of my life occurred, caused by the catastrophe of that terrible night in the gambling den" (*ML*, 55). "Caused by" is an inexact and misleading translation for "herbeiführte" ("brought along with it"). In other words, it is not the experience in the gambling den but the decision to take his craft as a musician seriously which constituted the turning-point in Wagner's life.

15. Wagner writes about "die lang andauernden reinen Quintenklänge" (*Mein Leben*, vol. 1, 43). Gray translates this as "the long sustained perfect fifths" (*ML*, 35) but that misses the point. These are open fifths, that is to say chords without a third. It is the missing third which would have told the listener whether the chord is major or minor and it is the absence of that indication which produces (or at least adds to) the eeriness which Wagner writes about.

16. See Ernest Newman, *Life of Wagner*, vol. 2, 510.

17. See Martin Gregor-Dellin's note, *ML*, 786. On Pfistermeister and his relations to Wagner see also Newman, *Life of Richard Wagner*, vol. 3, esp. 342 ff. (which deal with events as early as 1865) and 484.

18. The problem is equally acute in what early nineteenth-century critics called "fictional autobiographies" and it affects the ending of *Moll Flanders* as well as both endings of *Great Expectations*.

"DEN UBETVINGELE KALLELSE": ON THE OBJECTIVITY OF BRAND'S CALLING AS PRIEST

Charles Leland

Near the beginning of the third act of Ibsen's penultimate play, John Gabriel Borkman tries to justify himself to his wife, Gunhild. He had sacrificed his life and love in order to follow an "irrestible calling" (*"ubetvingelige kallelse"*),[1] a calling which gave him power to release all the buried mineral wealth of the world. It was an inner voice, heard by John Gabriel alone, calling one especially "chosen" (*"utvalgt"*) for a mission—the economic liberation of mankind. Borkman's calling, although referred to in biblical language, is often dismissed as the purely subjective delusion of a dangerous madman.[2]

Long before *John Gabriel Borkman*, indeed forty-six years before, in the very first words of Ibsen's very first play, *Catiline* (1850), the hero also hears an insistent call; it is a call this time to a higher mode of life, not precisely to an absolute, since, as it turns out, there are temporal and political dimensions to the call, but to something approaching an absolute. This calling is certainly less fantastic, less dangerous, less subjective than Borkman's, although Catiline's, like the "soft pipes" on the Grecian Urn, is not heard by "the sensual ear" but "in the depths of the soul":

> I must! I must! Deep down within my soul
> a voice commands, and I will do its bidding;...
> I feel I have the courage and the strength
> to lead a better, nobler life than this...[3]

For many critics Brand is, if possible, even more dangerous than Borkman, certainly more dangerous than Catiline. After all Catiline only seeks to lead a revolution, although this revolution will have spiritual dimensions. Borkman will only reign supreme over material goods, goods of this world, although the new economic community envisioned will bring life and light to many thousands of homes. Brand, on the other hand, seeks supremacy through an absolute, total commitment to the life of the spirit. We all know Shaw's famous judgement: Brand is a villain "by virtue of his determination to do nothing wrong."[4] Pavel Fraenkl in an important article on "*Brand* and European Titanism" maintains that "the hero's original life's call" is nothing more than "the exaltation of the will." Fraenkl speaks of "Brand's subjective conception of God" ("*Brands subjective Gudsforestilling*"). Brand believes, of course, that the call comes from God, but in reality it is only an echo of Brand's own subjective experience. The calling is "the central focus of his conception of himself" ("*Det sentrale i Brands livsbilde er hans Kallstanke*").[5]

We are convinced—almost! But then we look again at Brand's images or conceptions of God. We find very quickly that the images he summons up are not subjective at all. Brand is not a Blake or a Yeats creating his own symbolic or mythological universe. Theologians insist that no image, no picture, can adequately represent the ineffable being of God. On the other hand, we know that the Biblical authors continually use images in order to say *something* according to human modes of perception about the nature of God and his actions. *Nihil in intellectu quod non prius in sensu.* Not one of Brand's images of God is subjective; all are scriptural, with the exception of the one classical image of the young Hercules. And, as has been so beautifully demonstrated through the picture in Daniel Haakonsen's *Ibsen: Mennesket og Kunstneren*, Ibsen doubtless got this image from Michelangelo's "Creation of Adam" in the Sistine Chapel.[6] Furthermore the classical image is not isolated but folded in among easily recognizable scriptural images:

> He is young like Hercules—not
> Some old greybeard in his dotage!
> O, but that voice of his did strike
> With lightning and with terror when
> Like a blazing fire in the bush of thorns
> He stood before Moses on Mount Horeb,
> A giant before the dwarf of dwarfs.
> He did stay the sun in the Vale of Gideon,
> And did perform unnumbered miracles....
> But out of these dismembered wrecks of soul,
> From these truncated torsos of the spirit,
> From these heads, these hands, there shall arise
> A hero, so that the Lord
> May recognize his creature Man once more,
> His greatest masterpiece, his heir,
> His Adam, young and strong.
>
> (3:92–93)

The text draws God, Moses, Joshua (through the allusion to the sun standing still), and Adam together. The "Adam, young and strong," is not, of course, the First Adam, the first member and type of fallen man, but the Second Adam, Christ, the new head of redeemed humanity. Hercules and the Second Adam are linked even more closely through the common adjective "young" ("*ung*"). And this young and powerful Hercules-Adam is Christ, the perfect man formed so exactly in the image of God that he *is* the image of God. Man shares in the image of that young and strong Adam to the extent that he is conformed to it. So the important theme of the recreation of man in the image and likeness of God is sounded. We recall Ibsen's original epigraph to the play taken from Genesis: "And he created man in his own image and likeness" ("*Og han skapte mennesket i sit billede*"). That image of God had been blurred or smudged by sin; the restoration of the image is possible through Christ. This restoration or re-creation is precisely what salvation means, a salvation already achieved through "bridges" between flesh and spirit:

All things created have their measured end...
                                            But there is
One thing that does prevail and endure—
That is the uncreated spirit, once redeemed
From Chaos in the first fresh Spring of time, and still
Extending bridges of unalterable faith
From banks of flesh to banks of spirit.
                     (3:92)

This union of flesh and spirit, definitively achieved through the Incarnation, will be mediated through the instrumentality of Brand as priest. To Einar's question: "You want all men to be created anew?" Brand's reply is

That I do, sure as I know
I was born into this world of course
To heal its sickness and its wrongs.
                     (3:92)

The theological conception of "priest" as *alter Christus*, mediating the healing of Christ through the sacraments and thus affecting the restoration and recreation of man, lies behind Brand's words here and in several other places in the text where he seems to identify himself with Christ. The concept of instrumentality, the theology of the priesthood, and sacramental theology surely would not have been introduced to Ibsen when he was preparing for Confirmation in the Lutheran Church. Perhaps the source of Ibsen's ideas were priests whom he met in Rome. A more likely source, however, would be Ibsen's good friend and hiking companion Christopher Holfeldt-Houen, the Norwegian-born Catholic pastor of Bergen from 1857 to 1881.

In the moral-theological order Brand will also set the example; he will be the first whole man, the first hero, albeit a tragic hero: one who suffers much and dies for his ideals. In this respect Christ is also a tragic hero. But the "comedy" of the Resurrection follows, and the salvation of mankind is achieved thereby. And in what does salvation consist? It is repairing "the ruins of our first parents," as Milton puts it. It is restoring man to the image of God. It is reintegrating man, making him whole again. We find all these ideas in *Brand*, and also the notion of the true hero, the *helt*, who is heroic precisely because he is whole (*hel*) and thus holy (*hellig*). Surely Ibsen, the Master Word-builder, would have sensed not only the puns here but also the reality behind them. Wholeness, health, holiness, integrity, unity are all marks of salvation; these form the image of God to which man is restored through his conformation to Christ. But there will be more of this later!

So then, the conception of God in the play is not a solely personal one, unique to Brand; it is the way God is "figured forth" in the Bible. Nor is the theology Brand's alone; for the most part it is simply orthodox Christian theology. Brand has been accused often enough of being a heretic, most recently in Pater Finn Thorn's interesting study of the play, *Lov og Evangelium*. Indeed, Brand's apparent exaltation of the will seems to smack more of Sartre than of Christ, more of Scotus and Occam than of Thomas Aquinas. But we may, perhaps, see more clearly into the nature of Brand's orthodoxy if we reflect on the nature of his call, on the absolute demands of discipleship, on the *imitatio Christi*, and on the instrumental function of the priest in mediating salvation to individual Christians.

Brand's call is subjective only to the extent that all vocations are, so to speak, personal. God's call to Abraham was to Abraham, as God's call to Paul on the road to Damascus was to Paul. If the vocation is to goodness, that is to good actions, it can be assumed that it comes from God. If we can believe his letter to King Charles XV of Sweden, Ibsen himself heard such a call:

> I am not fighting for an existence free from care but for that lifework which I firmly believe God has given me to do—the work that seems to me to be the most necessary and imperative to Norway, the work of arousing the people of our nation and urging them to think great thoughts.[7]

There is not much difference between what Ibsen sees as his calling ("*at vække Folket og bringe det til at tænke stort*")[8] and what Brand sees as his: to recreate man in the image of the new Adam, "young and strong." And Ibsen knew that the second, the new Adam, according to St. Paul, is Christ:

> For as in Adam all die, even so in Christ shall all be made alive....The first man [Adam] is of earth, earthy; the second man [Christ] is the Lord from heaven. (1 Corinthians 15:22,47)

It is not at all surprising that Ibsen used heavily loaded scriptural language at the time he wrote *Brand*. We have his own testimony that at the time he read "only the Bible. It is powerful and strong."[9] References to Brand's "call" are too numerous to count, and in every reference a biblical tone is heard, a tone which is associated with an objective call from God and not a voice rising subjectively from the hero's own psyche. (Of course the objective call must be interiorized, accepted, and chosen freely.) Especially do we hear resonances from the letters of St. Paul, the most dramatically "called" of all the followers of Christ. Often God's call is associated with his choice of a particular person, or particular persons, or even (as in the case with Israel) a particular people. And Ibsen used "the chosen one" ("*den utvalgt*") or "the chosen ones" ("*de utvalgte*") to good effect in plays as far apart as *Brand* and *John Gabriel Borkman*. Here are just a few of many texts Ibsen might have had in mind as he laboured over *Brand*:

> For ye see your calling, brethren, how that not many wise men after the flesh, not many mighty, not many noble, are called: but God hath chosen the foolish things of the world to confound the wise; and God hath chosen the weak things of the world to confound the things which are mighty; and base things of the world, and things which are despised, hath God chosen...(1 Corinthians 1:26–28)

> I therefore...beseech you that ye walk worthy of the vocation wherewith ye are called...endeavouring to keep the unity of the Spirit in the bond of peace. There is one body, and one Spirit, even as ye are called in one hope of your calling; one Lord, one faith, one baptism, one God and Father of all, who is above all, and through all, and in you all. (Ephesians 4:1,3–6)

Note here the relationship between "call" and "unity" or "oneness"—an idea which must have penetrated deeply into Ibsen's mind, conscious or unconscious, at the time he wrote the play.

> Wherefore also we pray always for you, that our God would count you worthy of this calling, and fulfil all the good pleasure of his goodness, and the work of faith with power: that the name of our Lord Jesus Christ may be glorified in you, and ye in him, according to the grace of God and the Lord Jesus Christ. (2 Thessalonians 1:11–12)

Note here the relationship between the disciple, the one called, and Christ. It is a relationship verging on identity, another Pauline notion which must have influenced Ibsen, at least subconsciously.

> Wherefore the rather, brethren, give diligence to make your calling and election sure...(2 Peter 1:10)

Note here, again, the relationship between "call" and divine "election" or "choice."

> And for this cause he is the mediator of the new testament, that by means of death, for the redemption of the transgressions that were under the first testament, they which are called might receive the promise of eternal inheritance. (Hebrews 9:15)

Note here the relationship between "mediator" and "they which are called," certainly not one of identity, but the relationship is close nevertheless. Not much of a "leap of faith" would be required to see the "mediator" as an *alter Christus*, a priest called to mediate to the elect the new testament, that is, the new saving covenant with God through the sacrifice of Christ. Quotations could easily be multiplied, but I hope that the point has been made: the author, who was reading "nothing but the Bible" while writing his *Brand*, quite naturally absorbed key biblical ideas and the language by which these ideas are expressed. If the language of *Brand* is often biblical, so too are the ideas.

As we have seen, Paul often associates a vocation with God's election or choice. Those "called" are precisely those "chosen" by God. The saints are spoken of in the Apocalypse as "the called and chosen and faithful" (*"kalte og utvalgte og trofaste"* [17:14]). Christ himself is called "God's Messiah, his chosen one" (*"Guds Messias, den utvalgte"*) in Luke 23:35. In identifying Brand with Christ near the end of the play, Gerd sees him as "chosen" (*"utvalgt"*). Gerd even sees Brand as bearing the stigmata and the crown of thorns; his very blood is redemptive:

> In your hair I can see drops of blood...
> The thorn's sharp spikes have slashed savagely
> Across your brow....You shed the blood
> That has power to save us all....
> In your hands are the holes of the nails...
> You are the Chosen One.
> (3:248)

Brand is obviously not Christ himself but an *alter Christus*, a priest who shares in the sacrifice of Christ and who mediates the redemptive fruits of that sacrifice.

It is important to note that Brand's call is explicitly associated with both the notion of sacrifice (*offer*) and with baptism (*dåp*), a sacrament which imprints an indelible "character" on the recipient. Agnes reminds Brand at the end of Act IV:

> Are you forgetting that the baptism
> Of your calling binds you here...
> And of your sacrifice as well?
> (3:193)

Brand had already, a little earlier in the act, reminded Agnes of her vocation, a call which involves sacrifice:

> Do you imagine I would take you
> From your dancing and your play
> Quite thoughtlessly....That I would impose
> Upon your youth the role of willing sacrifice
> In some half-thought-out plan?
> If so, I grieve for both of us
> For then the sacrifice you are to make
> Would be too great, too dearly bought.
> You are my wife. I can demand
> That you give your life entirely
> To this calling. It is my right.
> $(3:183)^{10}$

And, even more interesting, linked with the call and the sacrifice is the notion of grace; the way of grace is paved with sacrificial stones:

BRAND   It is the way of the Will. There is no other.

AGNES   But the way of *grace*...?

BRAND   That way is paved with sacrifical altars. $(3:182)^{11}$

Answering the call involves choice, a definitive and free choice, a decision, often an anguished decision, involving sacrifice. The noun "choice" ("*valg*") and the verb "to choose" ("*å velge*") occur in the text even more often than the noun "call" ("*kall*") and the verb "to call" ("*å kalle*"). Willingly and wholeheartedly to follow the call is the choice of an undivided, integral human being. Thus we note at the end of Act IV Brand's insistence that Agnes's sacrifice be, precisely, a holocaust, a total and willing offering of herself and even of her memories. (One is reminded here of a central doctrine in the writings of St. John of the Cross: the deepest union with God can be achieved only through complete dispossession, not only of material goods but of spiritual consolations as well.) Only when Agnes can surrender little Alf's cap willingly is her sacrifice ratified: it becomes a holocaust. Then in following her calling wholeheartedly, absolutely, and freely she is released into a new life of freedom. The scene is unforgettable in its intense conflation of agony and ecstasy:

AGNES   Stop.

BRAND   What is it now?

AGNES   Oh, you know! [She holds the cap out to him.]

BRAND	[approaching but not taking the cap] Willingly?
AGNES	Willingly?
BRAND	Give it to me. The woman is sitting outside on the steps. [He goes.]
AGNES	Robbed...stripped of everything... The last tie that bound me to the dust! [She stands motionless for a moment; little by little the expression on her face changes to radiant joy. Brand comes back; she rushes joyfully to meet him, throws her arms around his neck and cries:] I am free, Brand! I am free!
BRAND	Agnes!
AGNES	The darkness has gone. All the terrors That weighed like a nightmare on my mind Have now been cast out into the abyss! I have won the battle of the Will! All the mists have cleared away, All the clouds are swept away; Beyond the night, beyond the dark of death, I see the radiance of a rosy dawn!

(3:191)

(One is again reminded of St. John of the Cross's experience of passing through "the dark night of the soul" to the ultimate light, joy, and union with the Beloved.) Agnes's transfiguration is surely one of the greatest theatrical moments in all of Ibsen's work—a challenge to the actress and, no doubt, to the lighting-engineer as well!

The distance between "call" and "martyrdom" is not great, as we see from the darkly ironic words with which Brand addresses Agnes near the beginning of Act III:

I followed my call as to a martyrdom. But now, all that has changed
Look how success has attended me along our way....(3:129)

We know that there will be yet another turning! The ultimate sacrificial offering is the life of the offerer, the life of the priest. So the offerer is both priest and sacrificial victim, as Christ is both priest and victim offering himself in sacrifice. Here again the priest must be an *alter Christus*, conformed to that which is unique in Christ's priesthood—that the priest and victim are one and the same. Brand, as a good Lutheran, seems to believe that all are called to share in Christ's priesthood but that few are willing to respond to this ultimate call, a call to witness Christ's priesthood in the most radical way—by offering one's life in sacrifice. This is the ultimate witness, the witness which is martyrdom. But most, Brand says, are not ready for his kind of witnessing:

> Ah, life, life! To people like these,
> How very dear life seems! Every little runt
> Sets so much store by life, you might think
> The salvation of the world, the spiritual welfare
> Of all mankind lay on his puny shoulders.
> Any sacrifice they'll make...as heaven is my witness!
> Except life! Life must be saved at all costs!
> (3:81)

Calling, decision, choice, willing sacrifice, martyrdom—all are woven together into the marvellously unified texture of the play. Perhaps the unifying factor is, precisely, the undividedness of the hero, the *helhet* of the *hel helt*, the wholeness of the whole hero. An important aspect of this is a call to *be*, that is, a call to oneself, a call to unity in being. We must remember that "being" and "unity" are interchangeable transcendental concepts in scholastic philosophy. The call to *be* is, then, the call to the authentic self, the call to be one and undivided.

> But this is my sacred Call: a man must be himself....
> (3:144)

> O, for room in the worlds's wide arch, a place
> Where I may be myself entirely! That is the lawful right
> Of every man!
> (3:115)

> Be what you have to be
> Wholly and completely, not
> A little bit here and a little bit there.
> (3:89)

The whole person, the hero, becomes the new Adam, "newly created and ripe for God's life" ("*nyskapt og for Gudsliv moden*").

Here also is where the will, the willingness, the choice come in. For the radical decision to follow the call defines the very being of the human person. "We *are* our choices," as Sartre wrote long after Ibsen. "Wir sind nichts; was wir wollen ist alles," Hölderlin wrote. We must even "will to believe," as William James pointed out. But Paul Tillich says it all most clearly: "Man becomes truly human only at the moment of decision."[12] And this decision to follow the call, to make the commitment, the *engagement* (the expression used by both Marcel and Sartre) can only be painful, anguished, precisely because the decision for one course of action is a decision against other courses of action. We accept one course of action only to renounce others. "Decision is never merely self-fulfilment. It is also self-renunciation."[13] Yes, I am making Brand into a kind of Christian existentialist, but others before me (Brian Downs, Bjørn Hemmer) have already pointed in this direction.

So then, Brand's ultimate calling is to choose to *be*, to choose to be *one*, whole and undivided and uncompromising. Brand becomes a character very much like Alyosha in *The Brothers Karamazov*:

> The moment he thought seriously about it he was overcome by the conviction of the existence of immortality and he quite naturally said to himself: "I want to live for immortality, and I won't accept any compromise."...It seemed strange and impossible for Alyosha to go on living as before. It is written: "If thou wilt be perfect, go sell all that thou hast...and come and follow me." So Alyosha said to himself: "I cannot give up two roubles instead of 'all that thou hast' or just go to morning mass instead of 'come and follow me'."[14]

Brand, like Alyosha, must be seen as a particular kind of religious hero. That Dostoevsky and Ibsen should share the vision of a special kind of sanctity does not surprise me in the least. Close contemporaries and deeply serious artists, they both heard "the melancholy, long, withdrawing roar" of the "Sea of Faith" and saw that the unheroic world left behind offered no real hope for human progress and salvation. That Ibsen was interested in the Russian writers we know from the memoirs of John Paulsen (*Samliv med Ibsen*, vol. 2, 93–94).

That Ibsen was thinking in terms of a kind of transcendent unity is already seen in *The Pretenders*, the play immediately preceding *Brand*. It is a unity to which the Norwegians, under their leader Haakon Haakonsen, are called. On the surface the unity is merely political. But the political reality is only to give form or shape to a deeper cultural, or even spiritual, unity to which the people are called.

The scriptural language in this earlier play is surprisingly like that of *Brand*. Duke Skule, in soliloquy, discloses the revelation he has as to the nature of "the kingly thought":

> Ha! Now I have it! No!....Yes, yes! Now I have it! 'Norway was a kingdom: it shall become a nation. All shall be one, and all shall know that they are one!' Ever since Haakon spoke these madman's words, he has always stood before me as the rightful king. Suppose there were a glimmer of a call from God in those strange words. Suppose it was God's thought that He had kept till now to spread abroad—and had chosen Haakon as his sower! (2:294)

Here we have not only the familiar Pauline references to "a call from God" ("*et Gudskald*") and being especially "chosen" ("kåret") for it, but we have also language strangely reminiscent of St. John's Gospel when the unity to which man is called is described:

> Neither pray I for these alone, but for them also which shall believe in me through their word; that they all may be one; as thou, Father, art in me, and I in thee, that they also may be one in us....And the glory which thou gavest me I have given them; that they may be one, even as we are one: I in them and thou in me, that they may be made perfect in one....(John 17:20–23)

The unity hinted at in *The Pretenders* exceeds that of a merely national, earthly unity, but this hint is conveyed only through the resonances of the scriptural language Ibsen used. A final word on the absoluteness of Brand's call. It is this absoluteness which Daniel Haakonsen thinks authenticates the call as specifically religious.[15] It is the absoluteness Alyosha sensed once he came to believe. Most critics cannot excuse Brand for his seeming ruthlessness, his lack of charity in following his vocation. That which demands such sacrifices, not only from oneself but from others, cannot be from God. Berdyagev speaks of "the demonic quality of his moral rigor."[16] Shaw saw Brand as an idealist (that is, fanatic) of the most inhumanly dangerous sort. What keeps Brand from being a genuine fanatic, I think, are his very real and persistent anxiety, his doubts, and his genuine love for Alf and Agnes. Brand, in making his choices, is very sensitive that others will be involved, others for whom he is responsible. This indeed is the source of the anguish he reveals time and time again throughout the play. One is tempted to quote Sartre:

> The existentialist frankly states that man is in anguish. His meaning is as follows: when a man commits himself to anything, fully realizing that he is not only choosing what he will be, but is thereby at the same time a legislator deciding for the whole of mankind—in such a moment a man cannot escape from the sense of complete and profound responsibility.[17]

Also Brand knows that in the gospels the commitment to discipleship and the cost of discipleship are put in incredibly strong words:

> If any man come to me, and hate not his father, and mother, and wife, and children, and brethren, and sisters, yea, and his own life also, he cannot be my disciple. And whosoever doth not bear his cross, and come after me, cannot be my disciple. (Luke 14:26–27)

The words sound inhuman in the extreme. After all, Christ said clearly enough elsewhere that we are to love one another, even our enemies. But the hard words quoted above are, I think, meant to indicate priorities. We are to love him above all else: this is what the words mean. But loving him above all else is not easy. Brand knows it, and

Agnes knows it. And we are meant, I believe, to contrast the end of Brand in Act V and the end of Agnes in Act IV in the light of these priorities. Brand remains torn and doubtful much longer than Agnes, as the invisible choir and the Agnes phantom testify (if I am right in believing that these are projections of Brand's divided mind). Agnes herself, the Pure One as her name suggests, is granted freedom and release and ecstatic joy at the end of her sacrifice, a transcendent joy which is realized in the inspired language quoted above. Brand concludes: "Yes! Now you have truly conquered." Her reply indicates that she realizes that the absoluteness of her victory flows from the absoluteness of her sacrifice, the wholeness of her offering:

BRAND   Yes! Now you have truly conquered.

AGNES   I have conquered...conquered
Terror and the grave! Look up!
Look there, on high!
Do you see him, standing
in the radiance of the throne,
Carefree as he was in life, and
Holding out his arms to us?
If I had a thousand voices,
If I dared to, if I could
I should not raise one whisper
To beg him back again.
Oh, how great, how rich is God
In all his ways and wonders!
My child's own sacrifice,
A sacrifice for guilt,
Has freed my soul from death.
He was born that I might lose him;
I had to be led on thus to victory.

(3:191–92)

Agnes has followed her commitment absolutely, to its ultimate demand of complete self-sacrifice. And thus she has gained the victory. The biblical paradox is realized: she loses her life in order to gain it. Brand articulates the idea at the very end of the act:

The victory of victories is to lose all.
The loss of *All* brought everything to you...
Only what is lost can be possessed for ever!
(3:194)

Now it will be Brand's turn to apply the doctrine to himself. His work as a priest has been effective after all; he has saved one soul at least, the soul of Agnes. She acknowledges this twice in her final words:

> Thank you for your guiding hand:
> How faithfully you strove for me...
> How faithfully you guided me, weary as I was!

He has saved Agnes, but can he save himself? It is interesting that once the victory of Agnes is complete, she, as it were, becomes the priest, indicating the way Brand must go, what he must choose, in order to gain eternal life:

> Now *you* stand in the valley of the Choice.
> On you now falls the burden
> Of this 'All or nothing'!

Brand, in yet another indication of the human tensions within him, hesitates. He cannot sacrifice his beloved Agnes:

> No!
> It shall never, never be!
> In my hands a giant's strength.
> You must not, shall not leave me!
> Let all else on earth be swept away.
> I can do without it all...
> But never, never without you!

But Agnes is strong and knows just the right taunting words to strengthen Brand. She frames her speech with the strong imperative, "choose, at this crossroads in your life!" (*"Velg; du står på veiens skille!"*).

> Choose, at this crossroads in your life!
> Quench the light that burns within me.
> Dam the fresh spring of my Christmas joy.
> Give me back those garments of idolatry—
> The woman still is sitting there outside—
> Let me once again return
> To those fair, heaven-blinded days,
> Lower me again into the mire
> Of my sloth and my sinfulness...
> You may do everything, are free to choose.
> Compared with you, I have no strength.
> So clip my wings, lock up my soul,
> Impose the leaden burden of the daily round!

> Bind me in chains! Drag me down again
> To that mire from which you raised me!
> Let me live as I lived when I writhed in darkness!
> If you dare do this, and will,
> I am your wife as I was before.
> Choose, at this crossroads in your life!

Agnes is a good priest. As Brand had formed her in the image of the strong new Adam who could follow the call even to the point of complete self-sacrifice, so now that her sacrifice and her victory are complete, she begins to form Brand with strong but saving words calculated to speak directly to his mind and heart. The words have their intended effect. A third time Agnes commands: "Choose, at this crossroads in your life!" At this point Brand capitulates: "I have no choice." Agnes responds with human and heart-rending words:

> [throws her arms around his neck]
>   Thank you
> For all you have given me.
> And thank you especially for this!
> How faithfully you guided me, weary as I was!

This scene ends perfectly with quiet "good nights" before the sleep of death and Brand's final interpretation of the whole ("only what is lost can be possessed forever") as he forces his clenched hands against his breast ("*knuger hendene mot brystet*").

AGNES   Brand, good night!

BRAND   Good night!

AGNES   And again good night!
                   Thank you for *all*. Now I can sleep. (3:192–93)

But the visual picture we have of Brand at the end of Act IV runs counter to his words. Agnes has taught him the way of salvation and has exemplified it. Her victory and the saving words flowing from it move him. His final words in the Act give the authoritative biblical interpretation of it all. But we do see him wavering at the absoluteness of the call to sacrifice, and even the final authoritative words are undercut somehow by the twisted clenched hands at his breast. Brand's way "beyond the night, beyond the dark of death" ("*gjennem natten, over døden*") will not be as easy as Agnes's. Whether he, in the end, receives even "a glimpse of a rosy dawn" ("*et skimt av morgenrøden*") remains doubtful. His final words are not the simple calm affirmatives of Agnes's "thank you for all. Now I can sleep" ("*takk for alt. Nu vil jeg sove*") but a tortured, almost defiant question:

> [crushed beneath the onrushing avalanche, but still shouting to the heights]
> Answer me, God, in the jaws of death:
> Is there no salvation for the Will of Man?
> No small measure of salvation...? (3:250)

> [krymper seg under det styrtende skred og sier oppad]
> Svar meg, Gud, i dødens slug;—
> gjelder ei et frelsens fnug
> manneviljens qvantum satis—?!
>> (*Samlede Verker*, vol. 2, 186)

(The sound of the words themselves are ugly, for example "*slug*," "*fnug*".) Already, as early as *Brand*, Ibsen is giving us ambiguous endings. But the death and victory of Agnes are not at all ambiguous. In the end, without hesitation or question, she gives "alt." In the end she alone can say: "*Takk for alt.*"

Realistically and tragically, Brand remains in anguished doubt as to whether the new creation has taken place, whether the new Adam has been born, or indeed, *can* be born. He asks at the end of his great monologue in Act V:

> Is the image in which man's soul is made
> Now utterly forgotten and forlorn?
>> (3:241)

Brand's own tortured thoughts are objectified through the Invisible Choir:

> Never, never will you be like him,
> For of flesh are you created....
> Worm! You can never be like Him
>> (3: 241–42)

But surely Brand as priest had the answer, if he would only accept it. In Christ one is restored in the image of God. Christ, fleshly in his human nature, thus redeems human nature. In Christ man can become like God. Brand also had the example of Agnes, whom he, as a priest, had helped form in the image of God. But the simple Christian faith is not easily won by Brand. In this he remains very much a modern man, divided, questioning, fixed in the tension between faith and doubt. Only after the avalanche has buried him is the voice of God heard—by us. Does Brand hear it also? We cannot be sure.

NOTES

1. "Jeg hadde makten! Og så den ubetvingelige kallelse inneni meg da! Det bunde millioner lå der utover landet, dypt i fjellene, og ropte på meg! Shrek til meg om

befrielse! Men ingen av alle de andre hørte det. Bare jeg alene." Henrik Ibsen, *Samlede Verker*, (Oslo: Gyldendal Norsk Forlag, 1978), vol. 6, 226.

2. For a more sympathetic treatment of Borkman's calling see Charles Leland, "Anagnorisis in *John Gabriel Borkman*," *Contemporary Approaches to Ibsen*, vol. 4 (Oslo: Universitetsforlaget, 1978), 138–54.

3. James Walter McFarlane, ed., *The Oxford Ibsen* (London: Oxford Univ. Press, 1960–77), vol. 1, 39. In this paper the translated quotations from Ibsen's plays are from this edition and will be noted in the text with volume and page number.

4. G.B. Shaw, *Quintessence of Ibsenism* (New York: Hill and Wang, 1966), 59.

5. *Edda* 56 (1956): 88–89.

6. I have slightly modified the translation in three places in order that it conform more closely with the original; the italics are Ibsen's:

> og han [gud] er ung som herkules,—
> ei noen Gudfar på de treds!
> Hans stemme slo med lyn og skrekk
> da han som ild i tornehekk
> for Moses sto på Horebs berg,
> som kjempen står for dverges dverg.
> Han stanset sol i Gibeons dal
> og gjorde undre uten tal....
> men frem av disse sjelestumper,
> av disse åndens torsoklumper,
> av disse hoder, disse hender,
> et *helt* skal gå, så Herren kjenner
> sin *mann* igjen, sitt største verk
> sin ætling, Adam, ung og sterk!
> (*Samlede Verker*, vol. 2, 21–22)

7. Evert Sprinchorn, *Ibsen: Letters and Speeches* (New York: Hill and Wang, 1964), 56–57.

8. *Samlede Verker*, Centenary edition, 1928 (Oslo: Gyldendal Norsk Forlag; Reprinted 1940), vol. 6, 137. The original is much more simple, angular, and strong than the rather languid translation. The Norwegian means literally "to wake up the folk and bring it to think big." One aspect of the genius of the Norwegian language (and landscape) is its rugged simplicity.

Incidentally, Ibsen, said much the same thing in a letter to his publisher Frederik Hegel, dated "Rome, March 15, 1866": "I feel that it is my task in life to use the gifts God has given me to awaken my countrymen from their torpor and to force them to see where the great questions are leading us." Sprinchorn, *Ibsen: Letters and Speeches*, 54–55.

9. "Jeg leser ikke andet end Bibelen,—den er kraftig og stærk!" This is from a letter to Bjørnson dated "Ariccia den 12th September 1865," *Samlede Verker, Centenary edition* vol. 6, 111.

10. The Norwegian original of the last three lines is: "Du er min hustru; jeg tør kreve deg *helt*, for kallets liv å leve" (*Samlede Verker*, vol. 2, 117). Ibsen italicized *helt*, the Norwegian word for both the adverb "wholly" and the noun "hero." Surely he would be sensitive to the significant relationship between the two here.

11. I have altered McFarlane's "mercy" to "grace" which I consider to be closer to the Norwegian "nåde."

12. The quotations from Sartre and Tillich are from Rollo May, "The Emergence of Existential Psychology," *Existential Psychology*, ed. Rollo May (New York: Random House, 1968), 17, 42.

13. John Macquarrie, *Existentialism* (Harmondsworth: Penguin, 1973), 182.

14. Book 1, Ch. 5, quoted in the translation by David Magarshack (Harmondsworth: Penguin, 1958), vol. 1, 26–27.

15. "Henrik Ibsen's *Brand*," *Edda* 41 (1941): 351.

16. James Gail Sheldon, "Berdyayev and Ibsen," *Slavonic and East European Review*, 38 (1959):45.

17. Macquarrie, *Existentialism*, 28.

VISION AND DESIGN IN *THE PLAYBOY OF THE WESTERN WORLD*

Ann Saddlemyer

> We will have a hard fight in Ireland before we get the right for every man to see the world in his own way admitted. Synge is invaluable to us because he has that kind of intense narrow personality which necessarily raises the whole issue. It will be very curious to notice the effect of his new play. He will start next time with many enemies but with many admirers. It will be a fight like that over the first realistic plays of Ibsen.[1]

So wrote William Butler Yeats to the American patron John Quinn after *The Well of the Saints* was performed at the Abbey Theatre in February 1905. Synge would not have found flattering either Yeats's evaluation of his personality or the fighting parallel with Ibsen. But certainly he was not popular in Dublin in 1905, any more than he had been over his first production, *The Shadow of the Glen*, in 1903, and there were some who had found *Riders to the Sea* the following year too morbid.[2] Yeats described *The Well of the Saints*, Synge's first three-act play as, "full with temperament and of a true and yet bizarre beauty";[3] George Moore applauded the "rare literary achievement" as fit libretto for an opera.[4] But the play emptied the theatre, and the players themselves disliked it intensely—Frank Fay went so far as to complain that Synge "had the black drop in him,"[5] while Willie Fay worried because all the characters were bad-tempered.[6] Even Synge's best friend Stephen MacKenna could only console him with the suggestion that the play "will be better understood in France than in these dull lands."[7]

Seemingly unperturbed, Synge replied to Fay that he *wanted* to write "like a monochrome painting, all in shades of the one colour,"[8] and must have been secretly pleased that a translation into German made him the first playwright of the movement to achieve some European stature. But the picture in *The Well of the Saints* of two blind beggars groping their way through a gray and empty landscape, compounding complacent illusion with ironic vindictiveness, has little of the joy we have come to associate with Synge. When Mary and Martin Doul are granted the miracle of sight they are betrayed into an acceptance of the realities of an ugly, cold and jeering world; when they deliberately create new illusions they enter a deeper darkness still, beyond loneliness and blindness. There comic irony—the fool's aspiration for beauty and the dream—mingles with tragic irony—an awareness that the richness of life leads to dissolution and death. As the curtain falls on *The Well of the Saints* we are left with the painful memory of a grotesque old blind couple fumbling their way offstage to the flooded rivers of the south, while the villagers linger to cast a few stones before joining a wedding party in the chapel above. We are uncomfortably caught between feeling and reason: the Douls have chosen to reject the traditional boundaries of church and state, vision and revision, good and evil, saint and devil, blessing and curse—but we are all too aware that such lyrical heroics in this case lead if not to certain death, at least to uncomfortable exile. If this is the vision of the artist, rejection of the ugliness and harshness of our world in a daring embrace of the dangerous world of the imagination, there is little health and no promise of happiness in it.

Meanwhile Synge had begun work on *The Playboy of the Western World*. Whether we are to believe Willie Fay or not, that after the reception of *The Well of the Saints* and *The Shadow of the Glen* Synge vowed, "very well then, the next play I write I will make sure will annoy them,"[9] the riotous response to *The Playboy* has been well documented. Again, some of the players heartily disliked the play. Even George Moore was shocked by the brutality of Pegeen Mike's action in burning Christy's leg ("quite intolerable and wouldn't be acceptable to any audience—French, German or Russian"[10]); while the gentle AE (George Russell) in his turn reported to John Quinn, "the Playboy's father came in with his head bandaged and he looked so realistic and so like a poor battered old man that the audience got a chill and felt that they were really making a jest of parricide and father-beating."[11] Lady Gregory, despite her gallant defence of author and production both then and later in America, pleaded with Synge to soften dialogue and action; she never cared for the play. Agnes Tobin, an American poet and great admirer of Synge's poetry and translations, wrote to Yeats, "it seems a pity to lavish all that on a thing that has about as much connection with real life as a Chinese mask. There are one or two speeches with lovely lyric effects in them—but it seems to me he deliberately perverts his imagination."[12] James Joyce wrote exultantly to his brother from Paris, "Synge will probably be condemned from the pulpit, as a heretic,"[13] and was later to complain that the last act was lifted from Ibsen's *The Master Builder*.[14] Even Yeats, under judicial cross-examination, took refuge in the assertion that the play was "an example of the exaggeration of art."[15] In the considerable newspaper controversy which followed the first production, Synge's admirers such as Stephen Gwynn were embarrassed by treatment of subject matter, while his more intelligent detractors such as D.J. O'Donoghue deplored "the cult of the tramp and beggar, especially the dirty and disreputable tramp and beggar."[16]

That Synge deliberately insisted on extravagance in speech and gesture during that first performance (which he himself directed), I have no doubt; "the Rabelasian [sic] note, the 'gross' note if you will," he replied to an American critic, "must have its climax no matter who may be shocked."[17] And although he later qualified his snappy dismissal to a first-night reporter, "I don't care a rap how the people take it. ...It is a comedy, an extravaganza, made to amuse,"[18] he was serious in both aim and intention. Perhaps even more than Yeats, he tended to treat his actors as puppets: rehearsals of *The Playboy* were intense and concentrated, Synge worrying over every action and the delivery of each individual line. The printed text indicates the care he took over minute details of staging; not only does Christy count all the cups and glasses, but the actress playing Pegeen Mike is told when to stamp an envelope, where to raise a broom, on which words to alter the inflection of her voice.

The careful choreography of the first act is a delight to analyse, as we watch the circuitous game of "question and answer" being played out by Christy's interlocutors. The litany of sins proceeds from larceny through sexual assault and reasonable homicide (bailiffs, agents and landlords) to coining, bigamy, and treason; while the circle draws more and more closely around the hapless Christy, springing back in delighted horror at the admission of parricide to coil even more tightly over an examination of ways and means. This movement is repeated again and again throughout the play, each time more extravagantly mannered, accompanied by changes of costume and accumulation of properties. The piling up of imagery is reflected in the juggling acts Christy must make with pullet, cake and eggs at the beginning of Act Two, bagpipes, fiddle and blackthorn in Act Three. Similarly with the emphasis on costume. Christy appropriates Shawn Keogh's one-way ticket to the Western States, his new hat, coat and breeches with the double seat in Act Two; again in the third act there is a costume change, which Synge described with delight to his fiancée Molly Allgood (who played Pegeen), "I am going to make Christy Mahon come in dressed as a jockey from the mule race...wont Fay look funny!"[19]

Synge was nervous about *The Playboy* throughout rehearsal as he had not been over his earlier work. The play was extremely difficult, he warned Yeats, and he took little comfort in Lady Gregory's encouraging notes from Coole.[20] When she finally saw a rehearsal (and then only of the last act), Lady Gregory wrote rather sadly to Yeats, "You have never looked like a tiger with its cub as Synge did last night with Playboy."[21] Jealous for Yeats's reputation, she refused to have their weak farce *The Pot of Broth* as curtain-raiser.[22] After opening night Synge wrote to Molly, his letter parodying *Riders to the Sea* (which replaced *The Pot of Broth*), "I feel like old Maura today 'Its four fine plays I have though it was a hard birth I had with everyone of them and they coming to the world.' It is better any day to have the row we had last night, than to have your play fizzling out in half-hearted applause."[23] He criticized the actors, including Willie Fay, for fluffing their lines and wished for a better actor to play old Mahon, but concluded complacently that the play was "thoroughly sound," although he was happier with Act I than with Act III. On the whole, then, he had achieved the artistic effect he wished for. But his fellow directors and the company immediately demanded further cuts in both language and action, unwittingly toning down the deliberate extravagance of the overall effect and making the production as naturalistic as the most vehement protestors claimed it was originally intended to be.

That Synge had deliberately infused the play with extravagant brilliance and exaggerated mannerisms is clear from his own comments and worksheets. "It seems so impossible to get our Dublin people to see, obvious as it is," he wrote to a young critic, "that the wildness and, if you will, vices of the Irish peasantry are due, like their extraordinary good points of all kinds, to the *richness* of their nature—a thing that is priceless beyond words."[24] To another correspondent he defended the "want of contrast in the moral attitude" of his characters, insisting that he worked always towards keeping them bound together "as far as possible in one mood."[25] And he publicly stated that there were "several sides" to *The Playboy*, pointing to Shakespeare's Shylock and Molière's Alceste as possible models for his hero[26]— neither of them prototypes of rational, calm, civilized behaviour. He had devoted over two years and more than a thousand pages of painstaking rewriting to the intricate and richly-textured design of the play, making every possible effort to retain clarity and strength of line while elaborating character and action through parallels and contrasts, crescendos and climaxes, "currents" of emotion and atmosphere.[27] The extravagance he depicts in his characters is carefully modulated by a conscious balancing of moods and action until we are subtly drawn into a deliberately amoral world which banishes both priest and "polis."

In both cases it is Shawn Keogh, chosen inheritor of public house and territory, who is made a scapegoat for Synge's purposes. As soon as all are gathered for the evening's entertainment, the men unanimously react with contempt to Shawn's horrified confusion at the suggestion that he remain, unchaperoned, overnight with Pegeen who fears "the harvest boys with their tongues red for drink, and the ten tinkers is camped in the east glen, and the thousand militia...walking idle through the land":

MICHAEL JAMES   It's the will of God, I'm thinking, himself should be seeing to you now.

SHAWN   I would and welcome, Michael James; but I'm afeared of Father Reilly, and what at all would the Holy Father and the Cardinals of Rome be saying if they heard I did the like of that?

With all the force of screaming farce, the hapless Christian flees into the dark, leaving only his coat behind, away from temptation and beyond the concern of those of us who choose to remain on the scene. And with him go not only Father Reilly and the saints of God, but the jurisdiction of the scarlet-coated bishops of the courts of Rome.

As with church, so too with state. When Shawn returns, it is to make way for the "queer dying fellow" from the ditch beyond. It is not long before everyone else on stage agrees, despite Shawn's uneasy objections, that this "bloody-handed murderer" would be the ideal guardian—overnight, alone—of the entranced Pegeen. For "bravery's a treasure in a lonesome place, and a lad would kill his father...would face a foxy divil with a pitchpike on the flags of hell." Law and the instruments of order themselves are beyond the pale in the shebeen (for this public house also trafficks in illicit spirits); drawn in by the vigour of the language, the outrageously rollicking imagery, the sheer force rather than logic of argument, we are wound into the role of participating Chorus, laughing Shawn Keogh's objections to scorn.

Thus freed of legal and moral ties, we can only nod in agreement when Christy explains in the most reasonable of tones why he had to kill his father: "he was a dirty man, God forgive him, and he getting old and crusty, the way I couldn't put up with him at all." Of course he would not use weapons; he had "no licence," and is scandalized at being taken for "a slaughter-boy" when it is suggested that he might have used the "bloody knives" of "the big world." Even Shawn's reappearance can no longer be on Father Reilly's terms, and by Act Two he himself laments the hard case of orphans, "not to have your father that you're used to, and you'd easy kill and make yourself a hero in the sight of all."

There is a seductive pre-lapsarian innocence to all this which, as in the best melodrama, allows us to participate without responsibility. And how skilfully Synge tightens the noose! Every phrase and action has been refined and polished, honed with painstaking craftsmanship, brought to the utmost refraction of light and colour. "In a good play," he wrote in his preface to the published play, "every speech should be as fully flavoured as a nut or apple"; sound and senses, light and action, meaning and colour are drawn together. One bite, and the taste is at once so tangy and flavoursome that we viscerally respond to the experience directly also. When the characters react, so at once do we; we participate in their eloquence and feel with their intensity. This is in fact the simplicity and complicity of the child's world, and notice again how direct Synge's stage instructions are: facial response and tone of voice must reflect immediately the characters' thoughts and reactions. The only pauses and hesitations are those surrounding the play itself, where silence and darkness combine to distance the magical world of the Mayoites from the common weekday life of "the big world" outside. Within that circle, we can jeer with impunity, attack without malice, indulge in horseplay without recompense, suffer fools not at all, and wear our hearts on our sleeves.

Out of this spirit are battles won and heroes made, myths created and dreams come true, for this is the "popular imagination that is fiery and magnificent, and tender" which Synge describes in his preface. The power of the imagination liberates not only Christy's spirit but ours; the richer and more tender that imagination, the more fiery and extravagant the accompanying deed. Thus the more Pegeen Mike believes in the hero she has helped to create, the greater her loss when she dare not follow him "romancing through a romping lifetime from this hour to the dawning of the judgment day." And the greater the need for her to show the pain of that loss by inflicting physical pain in turn as she burns Christy with the hot coal. It is not accidental that the play ends with her wild lamentations, accompanied by a resounding box on Shawn's ear. As the play begins with the costume for her romantic dream—fine-toothed comb, yellow gown, boots, and hat "is suited for a wedding-day," so it ends with her bitter, violent, and noisy grief. In each case the action suits and coincides exactly with feeling and mood.

Accompanying that release into physicality of feeling and desire is the aggrandizement of self, the shift from "mightn't I also" to "I will," from the hesitancy of "is it me?" to the glorious assurance of "it *is* me!" Once again, all must be to scale: Jack must have giants to kill, and giants in turn must breathe recognizable fire. Christy must believe that he can slay his da, and, like Don Quixote, affirm while believing. His triumph is achieved when in Act III he no longer needs to hide behind woman's skirts (quite literally when he rejects the feminine costume offered as disguise by the Widow Quin), and later realizes that he is now independent of Pegeen's approval. When we first hear of Old Mahon it is in the hyperbolic terms of his son, and the fate Christy narrowly escapes is described in appropriately gruesome and horrific images—to kill a king and marry with a mother. As the son grows, so must the father, and so too must the audience. The drunken antics and earthbound tales of the Mayoites are elevated to Dionysiac and truly grotesque proportions. "You'd never see the match," for example, of Kate Cassidy's wake, "the way when we sunk her bones at noonday in her narrow grave, there were five men, aye, and six men, stretched out retching speechless on the holy stones." Even drunken musing ranges from kitchen to charnel house:

JIMMY ...Did you ever hear tell of the skulls they have in the city of Dublin, ranged out like blue jugs in a cabin of Connaught?...Didn't a lad see them and he after coming from harvesting in the Liverpool boat? "They have them there," says he, "making a show of the great people there was one time walking the world. White skulls and black skulls and yellow skulls, and some with full teeth and some haven't only but one."

PHILLY It was no lie, maybe, for when I was a young lad, there was a graveyard beyond the house with the remnants of a man who had thighs as long as your arm. He was a horrid man, I'm telling you, and there was many a fine Sunday I'd put him together for fun, and he with shiny bones you wouldn't meet the like of these days in the cities of the world.

After such an introduction bridging childhood and history, mythology and geography, Old Mahon's skull must be visibly, astonishingly, bloodily gruesome. Rooted, as

Synge believed all poetry should be, "in the clay and worms,"[28] these people, like Old Mahon himself, are constantly "shying clods again the visage of the stars." (There is a fittingly heroic analogue in Mahon's recognition of his son the mule-racer: "I'd know his way of spitting and he astride the moon.")

As cleverly as Synge encourages us to enter this world of harmless though brutal make-believe and sweet though bitter romance, he just as effectively prevents us from resting comfortably within that golden cosmos. The key to our discomfort is, of course, his irony. For once our linguistic, emotional and mimetic skills are developed sufficiently to participate in the miracle of myth-making, we are provided the tools of irony with which to check ourselves. Again, they range from the outrageously simple to the sly and subtle:

PEGEEN   (*with blank amazement*) Is it killed your father?

CHRISTY   (*subsiding*) With the help of God I did surely...

A further check is a favourite device of many Irish dramatists from Sheridan to Beckett; direct mockery of the audience. For Christy's admonishment, in the full glory of established manhood at the end of the play, is directed as much at us as at his on-stage attackers: "Shut your yelling, for if you're after making a mighty man of me this day by the power of a lie, you're after setting me now to think if it's a poor thing to be lonesome it's worse, maybe, go mixing with the fools of earth." The fool of the family (one of the first titles for the play) has indeed achieved the isolation of elevation. One might even question how deliberate was Synge's use of the words "bloody" (before Shaw's *Pygmalion* and claimed by Willie Fay to be the greatest offender)[29] and "shift." During Parnell's last election campaign his opponents waved such items of clothing in mockery over his relationship with Kitty O'Shea. And did the scholar Synge ever read in Leigh Hunt's *Autobiography* of the substitution, insisted upon by his publisher, of the title "The Gentle Armour" for Hunt's original title of his poem, "Battle of the Shift"?[30]

But in the creation of the Widow Quin we have the most effective hindrance to complete audience abandonment. For she too is carved of heroic stuff, though the deed itself, too close to home, won "small glory with the boys itself." And therein lies the key to Pegeen's denunciation, "a strange man is a marvel with his mighty talk; but what's a squabble in your back-yard and the blow of a loy, have taught me that there's a great gap between a gallous story and a dirty deed." Marcus Quin, hit with a rusty pick so that "he never overed it," was "a great warrant to tell stories of holy Ireland till he'd have the old women shedding down tears about their feet." If Marcus Quin is both in mythology and outside of it, what of the fearsome deed of Daneen Sullivan "knocked the eye from a peeler," or those other daring lads recalled by Pegeen to shame Shawn Keogh? The Widow, too, is set apart, "looking on the schooners, hookers, trawlers is sailing the sea." Like Christy yet unlike, isolation has created in her a breadth of sympathy and realistic appraisal not granted her fellow villagers. Serving as an arch in the balance of tension between the "Rabelaisian" and the "romantic," Synge's own critical terminology for the play's pattern, she acts as foil to both Christy and Old Mahon in her lusty humour and materialism, as counterbalance too to Pegeen and the village girls in her experience and longings. It is she who tags Christy "the walking playboy of the western world" with all the ironies that complex title—hoaxer, humbug, mystifier, role-player, strolling performer, storyteller—implies. Through her eyes the west of Ireland dissolves and expands by way of foxy skippers from France and one-way tickets to the western states to the wonderful world of make-believe and the other side of the moon, "when it's the likes of you and me you'd hear the penny poets singing in an August Fair." While the Widow Quin stands apart, observing now with affectionate scorn, again with objective sympathy, we are reminded of the transitory nature of what is being played out before us. Let us not forget that she is summoned out of the dark by Father Reilly himself, to serve as chaperon and guardian over us all.

Thus Synge ensures our enjoyment of the feast while at the same time making us consciously savour each individual dish. We should go to the theatre, he reminds us in the same year of *The Playboy*, "as we go to a dinner, where the food is taken with pleasure and excitement." In that same preface to *The Tinker's Wedding* he further defines the responsibility of drama—and hence the dramatist—to give "the nourishment...on which our imaginations live," the most needful nourishment being humour. Further, he warns us that it is dangerous to limit or destroy that humour, illustrating his thesis with a rollicking farce underscored by wistful sadness at the loss of a different kind of innocence. *The Tinker's Wedding* was begun at the same time as *Riders to the Sea* and *The Shadow of the Glen* but revised after the *Playboy* riots. In this play too there are bold strokes bordering on the grotesque, balanced by sweet songs to nature and earthy good sense. Dying, he urged Yeats to introduce more harshness into *Deirdre of the Sorrows*, though his fellow playwrights were relieved that, even in its unfinished state, the play was all beauty with nothing grotesque.

"On stage one must have reality, and one must have joy." What *was* the reality for Synge? The pain of disillusionment, the ugliness of back-yard squabbles as opposed to artificiality in action, manner and poetry? Can we find a spectrum extensive enough to encompass *The Well of the Saints*, *The Playboy of the Western World*, *The Tinker's Wedding*, and even the uncompleted *Deirdre of the Sorrows*? I believe we can, and that Synge was remarkably consistent in his views on life and art.

Synge, the man, delighted in violence—he resigned from Maud Gonne's l'Association Irlandaise because of her incendiary aims and he thought the anarchist Sebastien Faure, whom he heard in Paris, "très interessant mais fou."[31] But natural violence—the great storms sweeping Aran, the thunderous autumnal days in Wicklow, the harsh bleakness of Kerry and Mayo—these, like the *poítin* of Inishmaan, bring "a shock of joy to the blood." At these moments one lives more keenly, senses more sharply. So too with the potential for violence in the inhabitants of these worlds: his travel essays comment on the wild laughter of a ragged beggar of Aran (possible model for mad Owen of *Deirdre of the Sorrows*), women on their knees plucking live ducks, squealing pigs at the quayside.[32] He described and excused the impulse, universal in the west, to protect the criminal, as due "to the primitive feeling of these people, who are never criminals yet always capable of crime, that a man will do no wrong unless he is under the influence of a passion which is as irresponsible as a storm on the sea."[33] The words "influence" and "irresponsible" are significant. He celebrates this passion not only in his plays but in his poems: the ballads of "Danny" and "The 'Mergency Man" for example, so shocking that Elizabeth Yeats refused to print them; the rejection of AE's "plumed yet skinny Shee" in favour of lovers' ditches, drunken roisterers and poaching bitches; the curse on the woman (his fiancée's sister) who disapproved of *The Playboy* ("Lord, confound this surly sister, / Blight her brow with blotch and blister..."). Even his love poetry has a twist of ruthlessness in it, echoing the drunken reminiscences of *The Playboy* and foreshadowing some of Owen's wild speeches to Deirdre:

And there I asked beneath a lonely cloud
Of strange delight, with one bird singing loud,
What change you'd wrought in graveyard, rock and sea.
This new wild paradise to wake for me....
Yet know no more than knew those merry sins
Had built this stack of thigh-bones, jaws and shins.
                      (from "In Kerry")

"He loves all that has edge, all that is salt in the mouth, all that is rough to the hand, all that heightens the emotions by contest, all that stings into life the sense of tragedy," Yeats wrote of *The Aran Islands*.[34] John Masefield recalls that "his talk was all about men and women and what they did and what they said when life excited them."[35] Jack Yeats remembers Synge's huge enjoyment in the melodramas of Dublin's Queen's Theatre, especially the vehemence of voice and movement and the villain "roar[ing] his contrition with the voice of a bull."[36]

W.B. Yeats refers to his "mischievous wisdom"[37] and, of the plays, "where nearness to his audience moves him to mischief."[38] Synge's letters to Stephen MacKenna were so violent that to protect his friend's memory MacKenna cut out great patches; Synge ruefully reported to Molly his mother's concern about his bad temper. With the same passion, Synge hated the lie, the half-truth, the hypocritical, insisting upon uncompromising honesty and reality. When the players criticized passages of *The Well of the Saints* he replied, "what I write of Irish country life I know to be true and I most emphatically will not change a syllable of it because A. B. or C. may think they know better than I do."[39] Of the early rows over *The Shadow of the Glen* he wrote matter-of-factly to MacKenna, "on the French stage the sex-element of life is given without the other balancing elements, on the Irish stage the people you agree with want the other elements without sex. I restored the sex-element to its natural place, and the people were so surprised they saw the sex only."[40] In the words of his famous preface to *Poems and Translations*:

> It is the timber of poetry that wears most surely, and there is no timber that has not strong roots among the clay and worms....The strong things of life are needed in poetry also, to show that what is exalted, or tender, is not made by feeble blood. It may almost be said that before verse can be human again it must learn to be brutal.

And to be human, life must be seen both steadily and whole, no smoothing away of the rough edges, no softening of harsh contrasts; Pegeen dismisses Shawn as "a middling kind of scarecrow with no savagery or fine words in him at all."

But human passions and desires are, in their turn, only part of the cosmos. The plot of *The Playboy*, Synge explained to MacKenna, is probable in its essence ("essence" underlined four times), "given the psychic state of the locality."[41] In all the plays his people are singularly alive to the natural and supranatural around them. *The Tinker's Wedding* was first entitled "the Movements of May," and young Sarah Casey has had queer thoughts "since the moon did change." The old beggars of *The Well of the Saints* cease their quarrelling long enough to enjoy "them twittering yellow birds do be coming in the spring time from beyond the sea," and "smelling the furze a while back sprouting on the hill." Christy's famous love speeches concentrate on the joys of poaching salmon in the Owen or the Carrowmore and he recalls being lonesome "as the moon of dawn"; Old Mahon jeers at the sexual inadequacy of his loony son in animal imagery, "shooting out his sheep's eyes between the little twigs and leaves, and his two ears rising like a hare looking out through a gap." On a grander scale, Deirdre and Naisi follow the seasons of the year, and Synge writes of the Aran islanders, "their minds have been coloured by endless suggestions from the sea and sky, and seem to form a unity in which all kinds of emotion match one another like the leaves or petals of a flower."[42] His own life as vagabond and naturalist is summed up in the Tramp's speeches in *The Shadow of the Glen* (he signed his love letters to Molly, "Your old Tramp"), and the nature mysticism implicit in his autobiographical writings and travel essays. Inevitably, given his musical training, he sought this harmony of nature, myth and passion in his plays, seeking to present a background of cosmic rhythm against which his characters experience with eager awareness the incidents of everyday life, while longing equally vividly for the excitement and fulfillment of the unusual or the ideal. The two poles of art are tragedy and humour, he wrote in his notebook, and these are given substance and power by the catastrophes of life—moments at which we feel with the greatest intensity and see most clearly our unity with the universe.[43] Thus, the action of *The Playboy* is framed by death—a wake and a parricide—and we are invited to laugh at both; the conclusion celebrates the death of the old Christy in the new man who has passed through the intensity of awakening—a resurrection—and is now *him*self.

All this smacks vaguely of Walter Pater, and it is not surprising to discover that while he was a student in Paris, Synge read *The Renaissance* with care. But Pater wrote of cities and hence, like that of the decadent poets, his art feeds on itself. More useful for Synge was a study of Taine's *Philosophie de l'Art*, which combines intense feeling and insight with a sympathetic awareness of the artist's surroundings. But if I were to identify a more profound influence still, I would turn first to Lafcadio Hearn, in whose *Exotics and Retrospectives* (first published in 1898) we may read the following:

> those old savage sympathies with savage Nature that spring from the deepest sources of our being—always growing with our growth, strengthening with our strength, more and more unfolding with the evolution of our higher sensibilities—would seem destined to sublime at last into forms of cosmical emotion expanding and responding to infinitude.[44]

This passage comes from an essay entitled "Of Moon- Desire." We know that Synge was familiar with the writings of Hearn who was cousin to his brother-in-law. In Hearn's exotic evocation of the evolution of feeling, indeed in the extraordinary life story of this world-wanderer, linguist and story-teller who became a revered teacher in and about Japan, perhaps we find one of the keys to the development of Christy Mahon, poet. But for parallels to Christopher Mahon, playboy, we might look also to the visual arts.

As we have seen, there is a strong sense of line, delineation of facial expressions, choreography of movement, spatial design, and stage detail in *The Playboy of the Western World*, a boldness of outline that reveals Synge's training and interest in engravings, coins, and paintings. Many of his friends during his Paris days were artists, and his diary regularly records long sessions in galleries and museums; for Synge was interested not only in the finished work of art but how the artist achieves his effects.[45] But there is also a deliberately shocking contrast between the "Rabelaisian" (an early scenario speaks of "St. Rabelais the Jester"), and the "romantic," an elaboration of the mischievous into the grotesque, stopping just short of distortion, and a commentary on sexual frustration and threat of evil pushed almost to the bizarre. "I think squeamishness is a disease," Synge expounded to MacKenna, "and that Ireland will gain if Irish writers deal manfully, directly and *decently* with the entire reality of life."[46] What Yeats said of Synge might, indeed, have been said of the artist Aubrey Beardsley and the whole of the "tragic generation":

> I was preparing the way without knowing it for a great satirist and master of irony for master-works stir vaguely in many before they grow definite in one man's mind, jostling other ideas and so not yet established there, a conviction that we should satirize rather than praise, that original virtue arises from the discovery of evil.[47]

Was Synge that master satirist? Certainly his audience is made uncomfortable and self-conscious. If his art had stopped at *The Well of the Saints*, we might be tempted to agree. But Synge went on to write *The Playboy*, which, although just as uncompromising in vision, shares the mystery of the grotesque with an intensity of beauty, and mingles an awareness of the darkness of evil with affirmation in the cleansing powers of joy and laughter. While forcing the audience to truths it might not always wish or be prepared to acknowledge, he decried, as Beardsley did, a limiting moral stance to art and to humour. "The Law-Maker and the Law-Breaker are both needful in society—as the lively and volcanic forces are needed to make earth's crust habitable."[48] In achieving this cosmic and artistic synthesis of opposites in *The Playboy of the Western World*, and in allowing us to participate while remaining keenly aware of what is happening to us *and* to the myth-making Mayoites, Synge passes beyond the narrow uses of comedy to a celebration of the art itself.

NOTES

1. Letter of 15 February 1905, in *The Letters of W. B. Yeats*, ed. Allan Wade (New York: Macmillan, 1955), 447–48.

2. Robert Hogan and James Kilroy, *Laying the Foundations 1902–1904*, vol. 2 of The Modern Irish Drama series (Dublin: Dolmen, 1976), 116–17.

3. William Butler Yeats, *Samhain*, December 1904.

4. George Moore, Letter to the *Irish Times*, 13 February 1905.

5. Quoted by Joseph Holloway, Diaries, National Library of Ireland.

6. W.G. Fay and Catharine Carswell, *The Fays of the Abbey Theatre* (New York: Harcourt Brace, 1935), 168.

7. Quoted by David H. Greene and E.M. Stephens, *J.M. Synge 1871–1909* (New York: Macmillan, 1959), 163.

8. Fay and Carswell, *The Fays of the Abbey Theatre*, 168.

9. Ibid., 211–12.

10. Quoted by Greene and Stephens, *J.M. Synge 1871–1909*, 255–56.

11. George W. Russell, *Letters from AE*, ed. Alan Denson (New York: Abelard-Schuman, 1961), 67.

12. *Letters to William Butler Yeats*, ed. Richard J. Finneran, George Mills Harper and William M. Murphy, vol. 1 (London: Macmillan, 1977), 179.

13. Richard Ellmann, *James Joyce* (New York: Oxford Univ. Press, 1959), 248.

14. Ibid., 129n.

15. James Kilroy, *The "Playboy" Riots* (Dublin: Dolmen Press, 1971), 49, quoting from the *Evening Herald*.

16. Kilroy, *Laying the Foundation 1902–1904*, 72–77.

17. *The Collected Letters of John Millington Synge*, ed. Ann Saddlemyer, vol. 2 (Oxford: Clarendon Press, 1984), 47.

18. Quoted by Kilroy, *Laying the Foundation 1902–1904*, 24.

19. Synge, *Letters*, vol. 1, 213.

20. *Theatre Business: The Correspondence of the First Abbey Theatre Directors*, ed. Ann Saddlemyer (Gerrards Cross: Colin Smythe, 1982), 204–9.

21. *Theatre Business*, 205n.

22. Ibid., 205–6.

23. Synge, *Letters*, vol. 1, 285.

24. Ibid., 297.

25. Ibid., 312.

26. To the *Irish Times*, *Letters*, vol. 1, 286.

27. J.M. Synge, *Collected Works: Plays Book II*, ed. Ann Saddlemyer (London: Oxford Univ. Press, 1968), Appendix B, 296–97. All quotations from the plays are from this edition.

28. J.M. Synge, *Collected Works: Poems*, ed. Robin Skelton (London: Oxford Univ. Press, 1962), xxxvi. All quotations from the poems are from this edition.

29. Fay and Carswell, *The Fays of the Abbey Theatre*, 214.

30. *The Autobiography of Leigh Hunt*, ed. J.E. Morpurgo (London: Cresset Press, 1949), 422.

31. Synge's diaries, Trinity College Dublin Library.

32. *The Aran Islands*, J.M. Synge, *Collected Works: Prose*, ed. Alan Price (London: Oxford Univ. Press, 1966) 79 *et passim*. All quotations from the prose are from this edition.

33. Synge, *The Aran Islands*, 95.

34. "J.M. Synge and the Ireland of his Time," *Essays and Introductions* (London: Macmillan, 1961), 326–27.

35. John Masefield, *John M. Synge* (Letchworth: Garden City Press, 1916), 41.

36. Jack B. Yeats, article in the New York *Evening Sun*, 20 July 1909.

37. *Essays and Introductions*, 320.

38. Ibid., 327.

39. Synge, *Letters*, vol. 1, 91.

40. Ibid., 74.

41. Ibid., 333.

42. Synge, *The Aran Islands*, 102n1.

43. Synge, Notebooks, Trinity College Dublin Library.

44. Lafcadio Hearn, *Exotics and Retrospectives* (Tokyo: Charles E. Tuttle, 1971), 180.

45. "Memories of Synge: A Memoir by Stephen MacKenna," ed. Nicholas Grene and Ann Saddlemyer, *Irish University Review*, Autumn 1982, 141–51.

46. Synge, *Letters*, vol. 1, 76n.

47. W.B. Yeats, *Autobiographies* (London: Macmillan, 1955), 207.

48. Synge, *Letters*, vol. 1, 76n.

THE WASTE LAND, ORDER AND MYTH

John Tucker

In a characteristically learned yet graceful essay entitled "Wagner in *The Waste Land*," William Blissett refers briefly to Poe's dismissal of the long poem as a contradiction in terms. As he observes, the proscription of all but the purely poetic has unavoidable consequences:

> the sort of poem resultant upon this self-denying ordinance is presentational not discursive, a gem-poem not a tree-poem, timeless and spaceless and, if the poet is not careful, vague and formless.[1]

Professor Blissett argues, cogently to my mind, that Eliot was indeed careful in his Wagner-like use of leitmotifs and mythic structures, and that *The Waste Land* is, in consequence, neither vague nor formless. This view may seem too sensible to require defending, but it does run counter to the current wisdom, for the poetic wreck that has begun to emerge with the ebbing of critical passions looks increasingly unstructured: "it is totally, radically nonintegrative and antidiscursive, its parts connected by neither causes, effects, parallelism, nor antithesis."[2] And those who take this position have the master's own support for it. Asked whether Pound's "excisions" had changed "the intellectual structure of the poem," he responded: "No. I think it was just as structureless, only in a more futile way, in the longer version."[3]

I like to think there is a marsupial equivocation here, since in an ungrounded comparison "just as structureless" can legitimately be read "just as structured." Which is not to deny, of course, that Eliot intends to discourage the pursuit of patterns in the poem. And he is abetted in this by Pound's excisions: these may not have changed the intellectual structure of the poem, but they certainly rendered it more obscure.

Nevertheless, the belief that *The Waste Land* is essentially structureless seems to me untenable. Formlessness cannot be divided into five parts and remain formless—even if the divisions are themselves accidental and the parts thus created without integrity.

But are the divisions accidental? Must we accept that "one could reallocate the parts at any point with no noticeable consequence to the overall effect"?[4] The compositional evidence suggests otherwise. One notes the absence of rearrangements among the manuscript fragments and, though Eliot allowed Pound to cut from some parts, he himself removed the entire opening section. And when Pound deleted most of Part IV, Eliot himself suggested cutting the rest. Evidently he conceived of the parts as units, and he understood their order to be governed by some kind of syntax. A protostructuralist, he surely saw the poem as an organic whole, a system "in relation to which, and only in relation to which" individual parts have their significance.[5]

Thus the first step in discerning the total complex structure of the poem must be to discover the logic of its primary divisions. Yet critics have shown themselves remarkably reluctant to address this issue, presumably because the logic in question appears by turns too obvious to need comment or too confused to be articulated. It takes a certain foolhardiness for a critic to argue, even tentatively, that "*perhaps* there was a stage at which Eliot considered the possibility of organizing" the first four sections of the poem around the four elements,[6] or that "each section is seen to represent or, *perhaps* more accurately, to intimate one of the seasons or stages in the cycle of generation."[7] Though the structures proposed are a familiar part of the critical stock-in-trade, the *perhapses* (which bear my emphasis) signal a reluctance to hazard even a literary commonplace.

The patterns that I would propose are, like those just mentioned, analogical and sequential. Very simply, the poem recreates the succession of literary periods and simultaneously, though less clearly, recalls some parts of the Mass. That no one has, to my knowledge, described these patterns may seem to require explanation, for which I would return to that maddening combination of obviousness and obscurity remarked above. The poem allows itself only gestures towards meaningful structure; the word *intimate* is well chosen. *The Waste Land* intimates unities but they are not exclusive, and it intimates patterns but only for a moment. One cannot precisely quantify the period tonality of a given section, nor can one ignore the seemingly anomalous features that each includes. Yet each section has what might be called—to risk a musical analogy—a period signature, albeit a signature whose tonal irresolution appropriately recalls Wagner's writing, particularly in a work like *Tristan*, since

> the complex chromatic alterations of chords in *Tristan*, together with the constant shifting of key, the telescoping of resolutions, and the blurring of progressions by means of suspensions and other nonharmonic tones, produces a novel, ambiguous kind of tonality.[8]

For all this it is possible to break the poem down into the conventional textbook sequence of periods: medieval, Renaissance, Augustan, nineteenth century, and twentieth century. So baldly stated this analysis may seem too reductive, not only of the poem but of the critical-poetic sensibility that informs it, especially since we have been forcefully reminded in recent times of the dangers of too facile periodization.[9] But we may allow our theoretical guard to drop slightly because we are dealing here with period imitations rather than periods. Eliot himself seems never to have doubted the periodic nature of literary evolution. His use of periodizing formulae is both habitual and unembarrassed. On occasion, it is true, one notes a flash of self-consciousness, as when he remarks that "to find the reason for the sanguinary character of much Elizabethan drama...we should have to allow ourselves some daring generalizations concerning the temper of the epoch."[10] But as a rule he does not scruple over such generalizations when he talks of "the Elizabethan mind," "the Victorian mind," "the medieval sensibility," "Dante's age," "the mood of a generation," and so on. And his vision of the periods and their characteristics should not seem unfamiliar. After all, as Hugh Kenner reminds us, he could like the rest of us be "damnably at the mercy of *idées reçues*" and those *idées* that we do not receive with him we frequently receive from him.[11]

The notion that a given section of the poem should have a period quality, should intimate a literary period, is hardly new. The Augustan features of "The Fire Sermon" became unmistakable with the publication of *The Waste Land* manuscripts containing the suppressed Fresca passage and the extended series of heroic stanzas recalling *Annus Mirabilis*. Kenner developed this point some years ago in an essay attentive to the city images and stressing Dryden's invisible presence.[12] But instead of stimulating similar investigations of other sections, Kenner's proposition has been dismissed.[13] No one seems to have tried arguing that "The Fire Sermon" belongs to a sequence, at one time more clearly articulated, and that the other parts of the poem employ methods of period identification which are similar: a pattern of allusions, stylistic pastiche, and imagistic recollections of the age being resurrected.

"The Burial of the Dead," for example, notoriously recalls Chaucer's opening to the *Canterbury Tales*—of which, as Eliot once casually remarked, "everybody can quote the first line."[14] It proceeds through the nineteenth-century medievalism of Wagner's *Tristan* to Dante and a Dantesque vision of infernal London. The tarot descends to us from the Middle Ages, and the characteristic locale of the section is the garden: the Eden in which dullness of root is a paradox, the polyglot Hofgarten, the Burggarten in which Tristan lies waiting for Isolde when the shepherd announces the emptiness of the sea, the hyacinth garden with its blindness, and the *hortus conclusus* in which one might, just conceivably, bury a corpse. Gardens are not unique to the Middle Ages, to be sure, but they assume a peculiar importance in the literature of the time, whether they symbolize the ideal or remind us of its absence:

the garden of love accommodated the classical traditions of the *locus amoenus*, still an active part of rhetorical teaching, to the nascent realities of the castle walled-garden and to the symbolic paradise of love, and established itself as the dominant motif in medieval landscape description.[15]

Given the possibilities, the period character of this section is less rich than might be hoped, but little of Pound's enthusiasm for things medieval seems to have rubbed off on his friend. In fact, the antiquarian quality of Pound's early poetry struck Eliot as "rather fancy old-fashioned romantic stuff, cloak and dagger kind of stuff."[16] His own conception of the Middle Ages emphasizes scholasticism and religious orthodoxy, rather than brawling troubadours and the robust metres that Pound delighted in imitating. Indeed, it was precisely Dante's stylistic inimitability that made him so attractive to Eliot.

"A Game of Chess," on the other hand, opens by mimicking Elizabethan blank verse, flourishing its derivativeness. The density of allusions to Renaissance drama is so striking in this section that its chronological focus can scarcely be doubted. Apart from a slight echo of *Paradise Lost*, Eliot's notes point to three plays from the period, and traces of at least another five may be detected within his "Shakespeherian Rag." In his critical writings Eliot returns frequently to the topic of blank verse, and here he seems intent on exploring the thematic implications of its Renaissance incarnation: the love of artifice and the linguistic trap. The mind is caught by the extended opening period which confuses past tense verbs with past participles to the point that syntactic analysis becomes almost impossible. The language is literally bewildering, as so often in the plays; it is an agent of metamorphosis. Both the draft title and the printed title of this section imply metamorphoses and both are immensely suggestive. Allusively, "In the Cage" recalls lines from *Cymbeline*:

> our cage
> We make a choir, as doth the prisoned bird,
> And sing our bondage freely
> (III.iii.42–45)

and Marcus Andronicus's reaction to his niece Lavinia's mutilation:

> O, that delightful engine of her thoughts,
> That blabbed them with such pleasing eloquence
> Is torn from forth that pretty hollow cage.
> (III.i.82–85)

Pleasing eloquence, artful rhetoric are dangerous, at least within the characteristic locus of this part of the poem, the hallucinatory, claustrophobic interior beloved of Jacobean dramatists, where lust luxuriates and loyalty decays. For encaging his sister-in-law, Tereus suffers an appropriate revenge: when he calls "*Ityn huc accersite*"

(6:652), bring in Itys, Philomela replies *"intus habes, quem poscis,"* you have within whom you seek, "where *intus* can mean both 'in the house' and 'inside'."[17] And the dead child in his belly anticipates Lil's aborted foetus.

"A Game of Chess" evokes, through Middleton's play, Renaissance diplomacy and religious controversy. An enduring icon, the chess board presents a bounded, binary configuration of social interaction, a violent but tightly controlled dance in a hierarchical arrangement attributing absolute importance to a king capable of doing almost nothing. There are always pawns like Lil, not tongueless but toothless, indentured, playing their parts according to a decorum that allows even rude mechanicals their moment in the sun.

Lil also recalls Belladonna, the lady of potions and poisons, whose cosmetics imply face-painting, "a distinctive recurring feature in Renaissance drama":[18]

In vials of ivory and coloured glass
Unstoppered, lurked her strange synthetic perfumes,
Unguent, powdered, or liquid—troubled, confused
And drowned the sense in odours....

This pharmacopoeia depends for its effect on interior, trapped air and artificial light. Significantly "the use of perfumes and cosmetics reached unprecedented heights in Britain during Elizabeth's reign," despite the fact that

not all the concoctions were safe, or beneficial. Prolonged use of some of these cosmetics produced blackened, decayed teeth, scaling and discoloured skin, or even worse conditions such as blindness.[19]

Thus in a tract of 1598 we are told that "simple women thinking to grow more beautifull, become disfigured, hastening olde age before the time, and giving occasion to their husbandes to seeke strangers insteede of their wiues."[20] Lil's problems are not new, whether dental or marital. Perhaps the chemist offered her a distillate of the savin tree mentioned by the Black Knight's Pawn of Middleton's play:

                          the savin tree
Too frequent in nuns' orchards, and there planted
By all conjecture to destroy fruit rather.
                    (I.i.217–19)

Lil finds another avatar in Fresca and the concoctions associated with her—purgative chocolate or tea, to help in her own particular labour, and perfumes confected by the cunning French. London and its river is the locus of Part III, the London that Johnson loved and that Eliot made so determinedly his own. Because Kenner has already discussed this section we shall allow the river to carry us supine out onto the high seas of Part IV.

As it is presently constructed, "Death by Water" lacks clearly demonstrable period character. Phlebas and his whirlpool echo the infernal vortex of Part I, and more loosely the gramophone of Part III. His metamorphosis relates him to *The Tempest*. Without the publication of *The Waste Land* manuscripts, one could only suppose that it ought to intimate nineteenth-century literature, and the whole sequential structure here proposed would be in doubt. Reassuringly, the manuscripts confirm what we would expect, though the avoidance of identifiable allusions (if we except the one to Eliot's own "Dans le Restaurant") makes period identification less secure than it might be. What can be said is that this account of a semi-mystical voyage with its unresolved ending participates in the nineteenth century's fascination with exploration, especially of polar regions, and with voyages. The Raleigh Club, "a dining club of which every member was an explorer," was founded in 1826, the Royal Geographical Society in 1830,[21] and the Hakluyt Society in 1846, at the very time that Sir John Franklin was sailing the Arctic Ocean "bound on other conquests" aboard the ill-omened *Erebus* and *Terror*. The mysterious disappearance of Franklin, who was Tennyson's great uncle, captured the popular imagination: in the ten years following his final voyage twenty-one expeditions were mounted to search for him.

Appropriately enough, nineteenth-century authors were, to chance another generalization, particularly pleased to exploit the literary symbolic potential of the sea voyage. From Coleridge through Melville to Conrad, the sea story explored the nature of the human quest. As Jerome Buckley remarks of Tennyson:

> in "The Voyage" he developed a characteristic metaphor to describe the tireless struggle of his aspiring age: life was a sea journey over troubled waters, a pilgrimage which demanded fortitude of spirit and steadfast defiance of the laws that seemed to condition man's ineluctable free will.[22]

In fact, apart from motifs reminiscent of *The Narrative of A. Gordon Pym* (to which Eliot refers rather fondly in "From Poe to Valery"), "Death by Water" in its original form recalls nothing so much as Tennyson, which may explain why Pound consigned almost all of it, as he might have said, "to Abraham's bosom, or some more fitting receptacle."

As I have mentioned, Eliot made no attempt to salvage this section, though some of it resurfaces in *The Four Quartets*. But if his later comments are to be trusted—and nothing but dire necessity would set us on so perilous a course—he was not quite sure how Part IV fit into the poem. In the interview already quoted, when asked about Pound's cuts, he replied: "There was a long section about a shipwreck. I don't know what that had to do with anything else, but it was rather inspired by the Ulysses Canto in *The Inferno*, I think."[23] And he elsewhere speaks of this Canto in terms oddly suitable to the original draft of "Death by Water": "the Ulysses episode may strike us at first as a kind of excursion, an irrelevance, a self-indulgence on the part of Dante taking a holiday from his Christian scheme."[24] The ur-"Death by Water" might also be described as a holiday, although contrarily from Eliot's non-Christian scheme, but that is a point to which we shall return shortly. For the moment, let us observe that Eliot seems always to have associated Tennyson's "Ulysses" with the Ulysses Canto. And while he refers to "Ulysses" in one breath as a "perfect poem," in another he comments: "Tennyson's poem is flat, it has only two dimensions; there is nothing more in it than what the average Englishman, with a feeling for verbal beauty, can see."[25] Stripped of allusions and irony as it is, the draft of Part IV has the merit of imitating Tennysonian blank verse, but no more successfully than Eliot had imitated Pope's metres. We cannot know whether Pound recognized its importance to the chronological survey, but it would have made no difference: he was never one to accept flat verse whose only redeeming function was to ensure symmetry of structure. Thus the pilgrimage to the Holy Land and the Chapel Perilous loses its sea journey and readers must find their way to Part V via Phlebas's drowning.

"What the Thunder Said" belongs to the chronological sequence only to the extent that it predicts the very modernist strategies that the poem as a whole chiefly introduced to Anglo-American literature. Allusions turn our attention to various epochs and poetic styles are less imitative. The landscape changes too quickly to be identified. One cannot blame the poet that history should have fulfilled his most apocalyptic and haunting visions:

What is that sound high in the air
Murmur of maternal lamentation
Who are those hooded hordes swarming
Over endless plains, stumbling in cracked earth
Ringed by the flat horizon only
What is the city over the mountains
Cracks and reforms and bursts in the violet air

Attempts to discover a formula which will confer on *The Waste Land* the kind of coherence that we feel entitled to demand of a significant work of literature have not been successful. Almost coeval with the man whose career we celebrate, the poem shows a similar vitality: consensus as to its thematic unity is no nearer now than it ever was. John Peter's proposal of a liaison between Eliot and Jean Verdenal, for example, though it accounts for the pervasive misogyny of the poem, has won relatively few converts.[26] My own argument, as I see it, has the advantage of subordinating thematic questions. It assumes only that Eliot was aware of the need for structure, for a matrix which would hold together his fragments, once he had rejected any narrative syntax and conventional poetic continuities. And his comments on Joyce's work demonstrate just such an awareness: "a new world must have a new structure" and "it is the structure which gives his later work its unique and solitary value."[27] This structure is the concern of Eliot's best-known discussion of *Ulysses*:

> in using the myth, in manipulating a continuous parallel between contemporaneity and antiquity, Mr Joyce is pursuing a method which others must pursue after him....It is simply a way of controlling, of ordering, of giving a shape and a significance to the immense panorama of futility and anarchy which is contemporary history.[28]

Critics have understood the myth that Eliot analogously used in *The Waste Land* to be that of the Fisher King, which is just what Eliot seems to want us to understand. But the perception of literary evolution as a series of identifiable stages is a simplifying explanatory fiction which also merits the designation *myth*. And it is a myth far more powerfully present in Eliot's mind than any he may have gleaned from Jessie Weston.

But if this was indeed the structural principle behind the poem, at least as originally conceived, why did Eliot so resist admitting it? The answer may have to be sought in his relationship with Joyce. Although Eliot is generous in his praise of *Ulysses*, he did not rejoice in confessing its possibly multiple influences on *The Waste Land*. He does not, despite our hopes, announce that he discovered the structural possibilities of the literary survey in the "Oxen of the Sun" episode of *Ulysses*, but it was a section that he knew early and well, and to which other important elements in the poem including even its title have been traced, though not to everybody's satisfaction.[29] Eliot was, it seems reasonable to suppose, in search precisely of "a way of controlling, of ordering, of giving a shape and a significance" to the heterogeneous visions that make up the poem, and he chose one which fitted very well with his own understanding of literary history, the idea of literary development expounded in "Tradition and the Individual Talent." But Pound felt that shaping weakened rather than strengthened significance, and his radical midwifery masked a family resemblance that might otherwise have fueled speculation as to the paternity of the poem.

The drastic cutting of Part IV has the effect of destroying another, less tangible pattern which also merits at least passing comment in the present celebratory context, the order of the liturgy. Placing a sermon at the centre of the poem provides the basic clue because it anticipates the similar location of the sermon in *Murder in the Cathedral*, a play in which Eliot appears to be testing the proposition announced in "A Dialogue on Dramatic Poetry" (1928): "the consummation of the drama, the perfect and ideal drama, is to be found in the ceremony of the Mass."[30] Thomas's martyrdom, like the sacrifice re-enacted in the communion rite, parallels Phlebas's transformative drowning. And the original "Death by Water" contains other eucharistic allusions as well, not only in the fishes but also more notably in the ship's biscuits which have undergone a sort of parodic transubstantiation:

> "Eat!" they said,
> "It aint the eating what there is to eat,
> For when you got through digging the weevils
> From every biscuit there's no time to eat."
> (32–35)

Whether or not this passage is prefigured in Tereus's eating of his son, the assembly of shipmates breaking bread anticipates the Gethsemane images of "What the Thunder Said." Thus, to pick up on an earlier point, Eliot reverses the procedure that he ascribes to Dante in the Ulysses Canto and provides a Christian moment, a *holiday* in the poem. In doing so he employs yet another of Joyce's structuring devices, for *Ulysses* too is riddled with liturgical phrases from its first *introibo* on.[31] Eliot's biscuits recall Joyce's blasphemous dog biscuits, the Easter cakes for the dead, and they suggest a Joycean doxology on which, but for a final grace note, we might close: "Namine. Jacobs Vobiscuits. Amen."

The phrase "Unreal city" recurs obsessively in *The Waste Land* and in the commentaries of those who have written about it, but no one, as far as I know, has taken up the crucial etymological substrate contained in the word *real*, namely, its derivation from *regal*. *The Waste Land* is the work of a royalist to be, and it contains directly or allusively a substantial number of kingly references, including Lil's Albert, who will not leave her alone, and the young George of whom she almost died. The sterility of the city derives, of course, from the wounding of the Fisher King, but it will be healed by Christ, who might redundantly be called the real king. Only through Christ, then, can the city become real, another Christianopolis.[32]

NOTES

1. *The Practical Vision: Essays in English Literature in Honour of Flora Roy*, ed. Jane Campbell and James Doyle (Waterloo: Wilfrid Laurier Univ. Press, 1978), 75. My attention was drawn to this essay by Tony Bures for whose research assistance and reflections acknowledgements are due.

2. Ruth Nevo, "*The Waste Land*: Ur-Text of Deconstruction," *New Literary History*, 13 (1982): 455.

3. "The Art of Poetry I: T.S. Eliot," interview with Donald Hall, *Paris Review* 6 (1959): 53–54.

4. Nevo, "*The Waste Land*," 457.

5. See "Tradition and the Individual Talent," *Selected Essays* (London: Faber and Faber, 1951), 23.

6. Barbara Everett, "Eliot In and Out of *The Waste Land*," *Critical Quarterly* 17 (1975): 14.

7. William V. Spanos, "Repetition in *The Waste Land*: A Phenomenological Destruction," *Boundary 2* 7 (1979): 244.

8. Donald Jay Grout, *A History of Western Music*, Shorter Edition (New York: Norton, 1964), 387.

9. See, for example, Alastair Fowler, "Periodization and Interart Analogies," *New Literary History* 3 (1972): 487–509; Walter F. Eggers, Jr., "The Idea of Literary Periods," *Comparative Literature Studies* 17 (1980): 1–15.

10. "Seneca in Elizabethan Translation," *Selected Essays*, 83.

11. "The Urban Apocalypse," *Eliot in His Time*, ed. A. Walton Litz (Princeton: Princeton Univ. Press, 1973), 34.

12. "The Urban Apocalypse," 35.

13. Grover Smith disagrees that "the Augustan literary modes predominate in 'The Fire Sermon'." And he maintains that its city "is basically modern London but melts into its past layers indiscriminately." *The Waste Land* (London: Allen & Unwin, 1983), 51.

14. "Chaucer's 'Troilus'," *Times Literary Supplement*, 19 August, 1926, 547.

15. Derek Pearsall and Elizabeth Salter, *Landscapes and Seasons of the Medieval World* (London: Paul Elek, 1973), 27.

16. Interview with Donald Hall, 52.

17. G. Karl Galinsky, *Ovid's* Metamorphoses (Oxford: Basil Blackwell, 1975), 196.

18. Annette Drew-Bear, "Face-Painting in Renaissance Tragedy," *Renaissance Drama*, n.s. 12 (1981): 71.

19. Frances Kennett, *History of Perfume* (London: Harrap, 1975), 123.

20. Quoted by Annette Drew-Bear, "Face Painting Scenes in Ben Jonson's Plays," *Studies in Philology* 77 (1980): 400.

21. Edward Lynam, "The Present and the Future," *Richard Hakluyt and His Successors* (London: The Hakluyt Society, 1946), 178.

22. *The Victorian Temper* (Cambridge, Mass.: Harvard Univ. Press, 1951), 88.

23. Interview with Donald Hall, 53.

24. "Dante," *Selected Essays*, 248.

25. Ibid., 248, 250.

26. "A New Interpretation of *The Waste Land* (1952)," *Essays in Criticism* 19 (1969): 140–175; James E. Miller Jr., *T.S. Eliot's Personal Waste Land* (University Park: Pennsylvania State Univ. Press, 1977).

27. "London Letter," *Dial* 71 (1921): 216.

28. "Ulysses, Order, and Myth," *Dial* 75 (1923): 483.

29. See Robert Adams Day, "Joyce's Waste Land and Eliot's Unknown God," *Literary Monographs*, 4, ed. Eric Rothstein (Madison: University of Wisconsin Press, 1971), especially 143, 182–85; Heinz Wetzel, "Spuren des 'Ulysses' in 'The Waste Land'," *Germanisch-romanische Monatsschrift*, Neue Folge 20 (1970): 452; Monroe K. Spears, *Dionysus in the City* (New York: Oxford Univ. Press, 1970), 78.

30. *Selected Essays*, 47.

31. Among the various studies of this question, see Michael J. O'Shea "Catholic Liturgy in Joyce's *Ulysses*," *James Joyce Quarterly*, 21 (1984): 123–35.

32. See Eliot's review of *Christianopolis: An Ideal State of the Seventeenth Century*—"a very out-of-the-way book and well worth reading"—*The New Statesman*, 1 September 1917, 523–24.

IN PARENTHESIS: THE DISPLACEMENT OF CHRONICLE

Thomas Dilworth

Aside from its merit as a work of literature, David Jones's *In Parenthesis* is of special generic interest as the only important epic written in English since *Paradise Lost*.[1] David Jones's poem is an epic partly because it concerns historical events of the First World War and partly because it involves literary, historical, scriptural and liturgical allusions by which it expands in subject to near-encyclopaedic proportions. It is a work which calls for subtle and far-reaching critical interpretation, but here I propose to restrict my attention to the basic issue which underlies the evaluation of all literature on public themes—its relation to history.

In Parenthesis derives from David Jones's experience on the western front during the eight months that culminate in the Battle of the Somme. He writes that

> Each person and every event are free reflections of people and things remembered, or projected from intimately known possibilities. I have only tried to make a shape in words, using as data the complex of sights, sounds, fears, hopes, apprehensions, smells, things exterior and interior, the landscape and paraphernalia of that singular time and of those particular men.[2]

This combination of projection and memory results in the hybrid form of fictionalized chronicle. It is a form involving a generic tension between imaginative fiction and a mixture of autobiography and history.

The narrative's relative accuracy in sequence and detail can be gauged by comparison with two books David Jones read while writing the poem. One is *A History of the 38th (Welsh) Division by the G.S.O.s I of the Division*, edited by Lt. Col. J.E.

Munby (London: H. Rees, 1920)—a brief history of Jones's division, which he read and annotated in July 1928.[3] The other is Llewelyn Wyn Griffith's *Up to Mametz* (London: Faber and Faber, 1931)—a memoir of the period covered in the poem by an officer in the poet's battalion.

On the first of December 1915, Jones's battalion, the 15th Royal Welch Fusiliers (London Welsh), marched from Winnal Down through Southampton, and then embarked for Le Havre. On the fifth they arrived at Warne and after a period of further training they marched down La Bassée road toward the trenches, resting on the way at Riez Bailleul. The dates and place-names are not given, but this is the exact sequence and setting to the end of Part 3. The battalion occupied the area in the Richebourg sector which is described in Part 4. Part 5 telescopes actual events of the spring and summer of 1916: the first, ominous issuing of metal shrapnel helmets; the "quite successful raid"; the general alert during an unsuccessful German offensive; the outdoor concert, at which someone really did sing *Thora*; the long march south to the Somme; an officer's reading of "the good news" of initial British success—this took place on July first and infantrymen actually were "permitted to cheer."[4] Also in Part 5 are the night march and reversal of direction which robbed the men of sleep and the subsequent marching which brought them weary into the field of bivouac on July ninth. "Part 5 has nothing in it," Jones writes, "that was not actually experienced."[5] In Part 6 is the subsequent confused marching around Mametz village which further robbed the battalion of sleep and brought it, exhausted, into battle. In Part 7 is the assault on Mametz Wood on July tenth commencing at 4.15 a.m. from an immense ditch called Queen's Nullah, and the digging of the trench that afternoon at map coordinates "V,Y,O & K." (The Nullah is still there today and so is the shallow trench in the wood, among other trenches, shell-craters and occasional, still-dangerous, unexploded artillery shells.)

To some extent, then, the poem is a chronicle with its scope determined by memory. Of the time leading up to the Somme offensive, Jones writes:

> While that first few months was for me patient of being, so to say, unrolled almost day by day, in 1928, the period from my return to France in Oct. 1916 (after being wounded in July 1916) was much more vague & simply repetitive, even apart from the more wholesale & impersonal, more 'mechanized' nature of the war. It may have been that the earlier bit remained more vivid just as memories of childhood remain vivid, I don't know. But I do know the thing became terribly tedious and repetitive.[6]

He remembered the early period more vividly also because he had already recorded part of it for himself in a diary which, he says, "chanced to be blown up in a dug-out along with much else when I was on some fatigue or other (rather luckily)." The recording and possibly the rereading of diary entries must have helped to etch events in his memory. After the diary was destroyed, he sometimes made brief entries in "a pocket-diary or calendar, only three pages of which survived." These too aided memory:

> one of them was pencilled, "Blankets taken in—rotten to find none when we came out of line." I cannot recall the whys and wherefores of this, but I do recall how damned annoyed we were and by the sheerest accident this surviving page of a pocket calendar gave of course the date and, though meagre & unimportant in itself, helped me to recall other matters relating to that period.[7]

He reconstructed parts of specific days which he was eventually able to join together in a fragmentary sequence (letter to René Hague, 9–15 July 1973). Part history, part autobiography, the remembered material gives the poem a documentary dimension which may partly account for Jones's original intention to print it "in long columns like a newspaper."[8]

In *David Jones, the man who was on the field: "In Parenthesis" as straight reporting* (Manchester: David Jones Society, 1979), Colin Hughes uses Griffith's book and divisional diaries to chart the events behind the poem. It is a historically valuable account, but has led one literary critic mistakenly to assume that *In Parenthesis* is a "marvellously exact, even literal record...of the 15th Battalion's experiences...down to the most insignificant details."[9] Jones's narrative is not strictly accurate. He says himself, "I have not hesitated to change the chronology when it appeared to serve my purpose."[10]

There are two important changes in chronology. Jones's battalion spent two weeks, not three (15), training in France, so that his battalion first entered trenches on the night of December nineteen. In the poem, this is moved to Christmas Eve, so that the first day in the trenches is Christmas. The change compresses the action to accommodate more effectively the poem's seasonal and liturgical imagery. The other change in chronology occurs at the end of Part 6 on the afternoon before the assault, when John Ball and some friends watch waves of infantry going forward to attack what must be Mametz Wood: they

> wondered for each long stretched line going so leisurely down the slope and up again, strained eyes to catch last glimpses where the creeping smoke-screen gathered each orderly deployment within itself. (150)

The terrain is right. To reach the wood the assault force had to cross over 500 yards of no-man's land which dropped steeply fifty feet into a valley and then rose for 400 yards to the edge of the wood. But the time is wrong. The wood was not under attack on the ninth. It had last been assaulted, unsuccessfully, on the seventh, when Jones was not in the vicinity to observe. But he did see what he describes.[11] And the only time he could have done so is the morning of the tenth, during the assault he took part in. From inside Queen's Nullah he could not have seen the first wave (the 16th Battalion R.W.F.) attack the wood, and he recalls that he "had little or no information of the previous assault."[12] He could only have seen the lines of walking men as he himself walked toward "the creeping smoke screen" which, in fact, had been laid down that morning. In the poem a description of the sight is placed in the previous afternoon where it becomes an objectively perceived, distant image of things to come and affords no alleviation of the next morning's emotional intensity. In the early drafts, which probably correspond more closely than the later ones to actual memory, there is no assault at the end of Part 6. The poet is certainly being over careful when he writes in his preface that "no sequence of events" in the poem is "historically accurate" (ix), but he is not primarily recording history. He does not intend to write "a description of the Battle for Mametz Wood, so the sequence of events was not meant to be accurate—but typic" (letter to Colin Hughes, 24 March 1971).

In other, more autobiographical respects too, the narrative is fictionalized. As the principal narrative reflector, John Ball is the poem's human centre and a focus for Jones's own remembered experiences. But Ball does not merely relive those experiences. On Christmas morning, for instance, Ball's section journeys away from the front line to a nonexistent fatigue duty and then back into the line again. Its historical basis is the whole of Jones's battalion marching out of the trenches that morning and proceeding two or three miles up La Bassée road to reserve billets for a few days' rest.[13] But fictional John Ball is not with his entire battalion, and he and his section do not move down the road, but only cross it with "a toward-home glancing, back down the broken avenue....To the reserves, to billets" (92), and they return to the front line that morning. The difference here between fact and fiction is greater than might be inferred from the poet saying that Part 4 is "virtually a pretty exact chronicle."[14]

Later on the eve of the assault, Ball visits two friends on a grassy knoll. Reggie "with the Lewis guns" (139) is Reggie Allen, R.A. in the poem's dedication. Olivier is Leslie Poulter. They were Jones's closest friends in the army. Like him they were middle class, not cockney. Although the poet describes their conversation in the poem as "straight reportage," John Ball takes an active part in it (142), whereas, as far as he can recall, Jones himself "said nothing" (letter to Harman Grisewood, Nov. 1970).

Even when it is accurate, disguised autobiography is subordinate to fictional intention. At the end of Part 2, for example, the shell explosion Ball experiences in vivid slow motion is a "Pandoran" epiphany of "all unmaking" (24). In conversation with William Blissett and me in August 1972, the poet said that he actually witnessed this explosion as Ball does in the poem. Like Ball, he had just given matches to a lieutenant whom he had failed to address properly as "sir." So the ironic contrast between a breach of etiquette and a breach in ontology is remembered, not invented. And after the explosion, he said, the blood-red sap of mangolds really did slobber "the spotless breech-block" of a nearby artillery piece. The image is remembered but included primarily for its contribution to the antithetical significance of artillery within the poem's fertility motif. The dramatic and symbolic impact of this explosion is partly owing to its being the first one in the poem. But in early drafts, and therefore probably in actual fact, the marching column comes under repeated artillery fire earlier. This historical shell-fire was deleted to emphasize the single archetypal shell-burst.

During the subsequent night march into trenches, Ball experiences dream-confusion of obstacles in the route of march with the obstacles of an art class:

> wooden donkeys for the shins of nervous newcomer to the crowded night-class, step over to get your place beside Mirita; it's a winding mile between hostile matter from the swing-door, in and out the easel forest in and out barging....Stepping over Miss Weston's thrown about belongings. (32–33)

As an ex-art student, Jones had such memories, of course: not from his years at Camberwell Art School but from an after-hours life-class he attended in 1914 (and again in 1919) in which "one just walked in, gave a chap a bob or something, signed the registry (I think), tried to get hold of an easel or at least a stool and started to paint after saying...'Good evening gentlemen, good evening miss' " (letter to Grisewood, 24 Aug. 1956). The memory of the chaotic prelude to the making of significant artistic order is recorded primarily to contrast with the current chaotic prelude to further and more inimical chaos.

Similarly, on Christmas morning Germans sing the carol "Es ist ein' Ros' entsprungen" and the British irreverently counter with "Casey Jones" (67–68). The singing is an ironic pastoral song-contest which heightens the morning's violation of the conventions of classical and Christian pastoralism. The poet told Blissett and me that on Christmas morning, 1915, the Germans really did sing that carol and the British really did try to drown it out with "Casey Jones." These songs are recorded, however, not merely because they are remembered but for the contrast they imply between the symbolic rose and the utilitarian, man-killing machine. They were not, of course, the only songs he heard that morning. In an early draft, the English sing "Tipperary." Its replacement by "Casey Jones" heightens symbolic tension.

During the assault at the end of the poem, Ball's experiences are generally those of the poet, but, even here, autobiography is, to a large degree, fictionalized. Jones remembered the "green-gilled" corporal restoring order (172), and he along with other men was withdrawn to an assigned position. In the poem an officer says, "I say Calthrop, have a bite of this perfectly good chocolate you can eat the stuff with your beaver up" (173). What the poet actually heard was, "I say, X, have a bit of this, old man, it's a perfectly good sandwich (or whatever he was offering)." The reference to chocolate comes from a 1918 memory (letter to Hague, 15 September 1973). The Shakespearean echo recalls another occasion, during a barrage, when Leslie Poulter answered Jones's question about the safety of a mutual friend named Harry Cook with the quotation, "I saw young Harry with his beaver up" (letter to Hague, 4 March 1974).

The poet does accurately record having heard on that morning someone with a very English public-school voice "shouting rhetorically about remembering your nationality" (180), but he decides not to record a Welshman's response, "*What nationality?*" (letter to Tom Burns, 2 July 1971). Like the poet, Ball is wounded in the leg early the next morning after over twenty hours of close combat. And like him, Ball crawls away, reluctantly abandoning his rifle. In the poem, Ball does not, however, share Jones's experience of being helped through the woods by someone until they met an officer named Jack Edwards, who "commanded, quite rightly,...'Put the bugger down, Corporal Davies,—there's a sod of a war on' " (letter to Hughes, 24 March 1971).

John Ball is not synonymous with David Jones, even though, in a physical and emotional sense at least, he is, most of the time, the poet's proxy. Next in importance to Ball are Lieutenant Jenkins and Lance-Corporal Aneirin Lewis. Together these two epitomize the battalion's dual Welsh-and-English character. More than John Ball, they are fictitious, yet they too have historical counterparts.

If there is a single figure in the poem whose sensibility corresponds to that informing *In Parenthesis*, it is Aneirin Lewis. He is an associative, rather than a narrative, reflector in that he perceives and meditates fully in the poem's allusive mode. If Ball is a focus for Jones's bodily sensations, Lewis reflects Jones's imaginative life. But Lewis is not modelled on the poet. When I asked him whether Aneirin Lewis, with his thorough knowledge of Welsh tradition, was a real person, he answered, "yes, as with other characters, a combination of people: he may have been Aneirin Evans and Cadwaladr Lewis." In his first appearance in the earliest draft of the poem, Lewis is Lance-Corporal Evans. Before reaching its final form, his name subsequently changes to Pryce, Evans Hughes, Owain Evans, John Merddyn Johns and Merddyn Prys-Jones. The last two of these names suggest that the poet was conscious of his affinity with this figure.

Like Lewis, Mr. Jenkins represents a combination of prototypes. Jones writes that one of these was "an attractive man, very absent-minded, and also fair-haired like the squire for the Rout of San Romano" to whom he is likened in the poem, but without "the 'elegance' intended to be implied by my choice of the names Piers, Dorian, Isambard."[15] The prototype of Jenkins is also the prototype of Talbot Rhys—Jenkins's friend in the poem who is killed in the raid in Part 5. (The raid corresponds to an actual raid in which the prototype of Rhys and of Jenkins actually was killed.) The other model for Jenkins is an officer who fell during the assault immediately in front of the poet soon after leaving Queen's Nullah and not, like Jenkins in the poem, close to the edge of the wood.[16]

In a draft of a letter to John H. Johnston, the poet writes:

I know it's a far cry from Brooke to Graves, but still *in the main* these men, including Sassoon, Blunden etc. are representative of an educated, variously sophisticated, certainly cultivated, more or less upper middle-class, *very* English group of chaps. My "Mr Jenkins" was *very* typic of all that: cultivated, considerate, liberal, humanistic, gallant. (27 April 1962)

The derivation of fictional characters from remembered people is characteristic of the poem and indicates that, while not a chronicle, it nevertheless remains commemorative. In this respect especially, it is conventionally bardic. And certain figures are based on single prototypes. These include Bomber Mulligan and Runner Meotti, Joe Donkin and Captain Elias.[17] Corporal Watcyn is based on Harry Cook ("with his beaver up"), who was repeatedly promoted for his enthusiasm and demoted for drunkenness.[18] Fr. Martin Larkin is based on Fr. Daniel Hughes S.J. M.C., whom Jones first met late in October 1916 after returning from recovery leave to the Boesinghe Sector north of Ypres. Colonel Dell represents Lt. Col. J.C. Bell, called Dell to preserve the incongruous rhyme, "well Bell" (cf. 154), which Jones actually heard as he lay face-down in the Nullah. (At the age of seventy-six, the poet remembered Bell as "a lovely old man of about fifty.") Sgt. Snell, he said, "really was my sergeant—he was terrified, poor thing." That explains the reference to Snell as "a windy tripehound" (42) and the snippet of conversation overhead in an *estaminet*: "it's the Minnies [*Minnerwerfer*, German trench-mortars] what gets you down—yes, Ducks Bill, same as where old Snell went sick from—" (103) from fright. "The little Jew" wounded in the Nullah and crying for Deborah his bride, offering bearers "walnut suites...from Grays Inn Road" (155) commemorates Lazarus Black who, Jones said, "attached himself to me." Before the war he had been an antique dealer in Grays Inn Road. He had a wife named Rebecca and four children. Later in the poem Lazarus Cohen also partly commemorates him. The "fussily efficient" Brigade Commander known to the men as "Aunty Bembridge" has his surname, Jones said, from a certain staff officer but his personality is based entirely on that of Brigadier L.A.E. Prise-Davies. In *Up to Mametz*, Griffith writes, "his mind was slow...but tenacious to the point of obstinacy. He spoke slowly, in a prim way—his fellow regular officers called him 'Jane' " (124).

There are two figures through whom the poet makes cameo appearances in the poem. In what resembles the depiction of quattrocento painters in their own works, we see for a moment "'79 Jones, in his far corner, rearrange and arrange again a pattern of match-ends" (108). David Jones once said, "there were three Joneses in my regiment; I was '79 Jones." The other figure is David Jones not in 1916 but at a later time. Temporarily attached to headquarters as a typist, Private W. Map (127) evokes Walter Map, the medieval Welsh politician attached for a while to Henry II's court, also a sort of headquarters.[19] But the name is also a cryptogram for that of the poet, whose first name was officially Walter and who was assigned to headquarters from September 1917 to March 1918 to draw maps for the battalion intelligence officer. According to the Welsh colloquial practice of calling a man by what he does professionally, Walter David Jones who draws maps would be called "Walter Map." The correspondence is clinched by the fictional figure (at headquarters in July 1916) being '79 Map and, like the real '79 Jones, of "6 Pla. 'B' Coy" (125). In both instances, the poet seems to be autographing parts of the poem to give them quasi-documentary authority.

Part of technique is knowing what not to include. Jones excludes anecdotes. He himself was an inveterate teller of war stories. In 1972, for example, he said that his Colonel, Bell, once caught him carrying on his back half a barn door which he had taken from a farmhouse:

> As I went, the door got heavier and I got more bent over. Suddenly I saw a pair of spotless boots. "What are you doing with that door?" "I'm going to make a fire with it, sir." "We pay rent to the French." It's true, we did pay rent, for the trenches. "I'm not saying your regiment isn't brave," he said, enjoying himself very much, "but you've got a bad reputation for *stealing*! Take it back where you got it." I did, and found some sticks somewhere instead. The next day the house was blown to buggery.

This farmhouse may be the one whose destruction is foretold at the end of Part 4, but the personal anecdote is not recorded. And there are other anecdotes, about J.C. Bell, Lazarus Black, General Prise-Davies, and about a night patrol Jones was part of, whose members suffered a dangerous attack of nervous giggling within a few feet of an occupied German trench.[20] Nothing like any of this gets into the poem. Such miniature dramas would distract from the larger pattern. You cannot plant little plots in a work that has no plot without the little plots dominating the whole. Anecdotes also round out character and, in order to give prominence to the poem's fields of allusion, Jones wants his characters flat.

Although aspects of commemoration permeate the narrative, the overriding criterion governing selection is tone, particularly the relationship of narrative consciousness to narrated event. Jones consistently ensures that this relationship is immediate, sometimes at the expense of broad historical perspective.

This is evident, for example, in the selective naming of places. Mametz Wood, which the 15th Battalion attacked, is unnamed and referred to merely as "the dark wood" (165). Acid Drop Copse, from which German machine guns sprayed the British flank, is called, simply, Acid Copse (168). This, says Jones, is "so as not to tie it [the battle] down to a particular action" (letter to Hague, 14 June 1970). The word Acid is retained more for symbolic than documentary reasons. The great summer battle is obviously the Somme offensive, and he indicates this in the Preface, but it is not named in the poem—partly, no doubt, because at the time common soldiers did not think of their action as "the Battle of the Somme" but also because the universality of battle-experience takes priority over a particular historical event.

A very important decision for immediacy over broad historical perspective involves the waves of men walking "so leisurely" (150) towards the anonymous wood. The usual and much safer tactic was (and still is) to assault in short rushes between cover. Old Sweat Mulligan refers to this standard procedure (117) and it is used once they are in the wood (168). But on July tenth, crossing no man's land towards the wood, the infantry walked slowly in "admirable formation / and at the high-port position" (162), four paces between each man, a hundred yards between each line of men. This carefully rehearsed slow walk was especially invented for the Battle of the Somme by General Henry Rawlinson, who believed the new recruits of his Fourth Army would not otherwise keep ranks in a frontal attack on strongly fortified enemy positions. And so line after long line of infantrymen walked slowly into the devastating fire of enemy machine guns. They were, in fact, forbidden to run until within twenty yards of enemy trenches. Seeing them coming so slowly, the Germans thought them mad. The number of British casualties was high, as Jones suggests: one-third of Ball's section reaches the wood, and of his platoon of sixty, only nineteen. But he does not inform us in the poem or in its notes that the lines of walking men are disciplined against their own safety on this occasion only, and by their own commanding officer. If he had told us this, he would have generated a bitter irony and gained historical perspective, but at the expense of immediacy and narrative consistency.

A final, all-pervading indication of the poem's relation to chronicle is the language of its dramatic mode. This is Jones's greatest technical achievement, for it is a language invented, not remembered. As he tells us, the speech of the army is cockney (xii). His infantrymen speak something like it but not the faithfully reproduced cockney of the poem's early drafts, which recalls the ludicrous colloquial speech of Kipling's verse. While reworking the drafts of the poem, Jones writes:

> The real thing I'm afraid of is this business of Cockney speech. It's the very devil to try & make a *real enduring shape that won't be embarrassing* with the stuff- dropped 'h's & 'yers' & 'bloody' & all that are *so* difficult. And yet you've got to get across that form of speech somehow because so much of the feeling of the sentences depends on all that. How to make it not *realistic* is the bugger. (Letter to Hague, 2 Dec. 1935)

An example of undesirable realism is Sgt. Snell complaining about Mr. Jenkins in an early draft of Part 2: "too damned heasy wiv the men—they take hadvantage." As the poet works through his hand-written draft foliation, he tones down the cockney by diminishing orthographical notation of cockney pronunciation while preserving cockney syntax, rhythms and vocabulary.

He also eliminates most of the coarse vocabulary, which pervades early drafts. As he told William Blissett, its impact in print is greater than in spoken language, especially language in which its use has become conventional.[21] What began, in an early draft, "fucking obliged" is now "signally obliged to yer, Jerry-boy" (138). So the most common of cockney expletives survives only, encoded, as "the efficacious word" (53, see 201 n.45).

The invention of a language which is only suggestive of Cockney sustains intimacy with the reader. For the sake of a close approximation of the effect of reality, the poet dispenses with strict imitation. As a result of his meticulous adjustments, furthermore, the poem's spoken language is closer than it would otherwise be to the broad middle range of its narrative language. This closeness allows for easy modulation between the coarse, lower-class eloquence of the dramatic mode and the more formally composed styles of the lyric and associative modes. The narrative mode consists, then, of a medial language like the unrealistic middle tone that unifies his paintings by serving as a basis for variation.

We have seen that, in various ways, *In Parenthesis* demonstrates both the validity and the limitations of the poet's favourite words of Picasso, that the artist "does not seek, he finds."²² The poem is faithful to remembered experience in a way that anticipates modern documentary fiction, which re-creates experience. Its dramatic speech has an authenticity reminiscent of Joyce in *Ulysses* and its descriptive vividness recalls that of Hopkins in his poety and journals. The physicality of Jones's poem bears out his commitment to an Aristotelian conception of reality. As one of his favourite Welsh proverbs expresses it, "truth is the best muse." But we have seen that the poem is more radically fictionalized than the conventions of documentary fiction allow.

NOTES

1. Despite the epic qualities of certain historical novels, they are not, strictly speaking, epics because they are not poems. Nor does length make a poem an epic. No one would be able to argue convincingly that either *The Prelude* or *Idylls of the King* is an epic. And, while Poundians habitually call it an epic, the *Cantos* cannot be an epic because it is not a narrative. John H. Johnston was the first to argue that *In Parenthesis* is an epic, in *The Poetry of the First World War* (Princeton: Princeton Univ. Press, 1964). In *The Shape of Meaning in the Poetry of David Jones* (Toronto: Univ. of Toronto Press, 1988), I demonstrate that *In Parenthesis* conforms to the various modern definitions of the genre—by Ezra Pound, C.M. Bowra, E.M.W. Tillyard, Northrop Frye and Paul Merchant.

2. *In Parenthesis* (London: Faber and Faber, 1978), ix–x. This edition of the poem contains the corrections Jones made for the 1963 edition and further corrections subsequently supplied by William Blissett. Other references to this text appear in parentheses. I am grateful to the trustees of the estate of David Jones for permission to quote, in this essay, from his unpublished letters and drafts. The drafts are in the National Library of Wales; the letters to Grisewood are in Yale University Library; the letters to Hague were purchased by William Blissett and donated to the University of Toronto Library.

3. See my article, "A Book to Remember by: David Jones's Glosses on a History of the Great War," *Papers of the Bibliographical Society of America* 74 (1980): 221–34.

4. *Dai Great coat, a self-portrait of David Jones in his letters*, ed. René Hague (London: Faber and Faber, 1980), 72.

5. René Hague, *David Jones* (Cardiff: Univ. of Wales, 1975),47.

6. Draft of a letter to Bergonzi.

7. Ibid.

8. Jones quoted by Hague, *David Jones*, 36. René Hague, the poem's type-setter, remembers having printed a few sheets: "it was just like columns out of a newspaper, and the idea was that you could fold the [book] in half [lengthwise]...and slip it into your pocket...it would have to have been in a paper cover....We must have been awfully young and optimistic because the idea of any publisher doing that is absolutely ridiculous...and de la Mare [at Faber and Faber] thought we were completely round the bend" (recorded conversation with William Blissett in 1975). Jones wanted his book "foolscap size with a limp greyish cover stiffened at back with red buckram" like the 1936 "Tablet Publishing Company's Memorandum & Articles of Association printed by 'Electric Law Press' " (letter to Hague, 23 March 1936).

9. Elizabeth Ward, *David Jones Mythmaker* (Manchester: Univ. of Manchester Press, 1983), 88. Neither Hughes nor Ward reduces the poem to mere chronicle, but the poet's treatment of chronology and factual detail is more creative and ahistorical than either of them allows.

10. Draft of the letter to Bergonzi.

11. Apropos of the assault on Mametz Wood, the authors of *A History of the 38th (Welsh) Division* record that "one of the most magnificent sights of the war" was "wave after wave of men...advancing without hesitation and without a break," and Jones notes in the margin of his copy of this book, "I saw something of this myself and it was an impressive sight."

12. *Dai Greatcoat*, 225.

13. Ibid., 47.

14. Hague, *David Jones*, 46.

15. Letter quoted by Colin Hughes, *David Jones*, 12.

16. Ibid., 20.

17. *Dai Greatcoat*, 249; William Blissett, *The Long Conversation, a Memoir of David Jones* (London: Oxford Univ. Press, 1981), 82 (Blissett's book, now distributed by Hugh Anson-Cartwright of Toronto, is, after *Dai Greatcoat*, the most important source of biographical information about David Jones); Colin Hughes, 6.

18. *The Long Conversation*, 133; *In Parenthesis*, 109.

19. See David Blamires, "The Medieval Inspiration of David Jones," *David Jones; Eight Essays on his Work*, ed. R. Mathias (Llandysul: Gower Press, 1976), 18.

20. These stories, which I heard Jones relate in some cases more than once, are recorded more or less as I heard them by Blissett in *The Long Conversation*.

21. See William Blissett, "The Efficacious Word," *David Jones: Eight Essays on his Work*, ed. R. Mathias (Llandysul: Gower Press, 1976), 26–27.

22. David Jones, *Epoch and Artist* (London: Faber and Faber, 1959), 99.

DAVID JONES AND LITERARY MODERNISM: THE USE OF THE DRAMATIC MONOLOGUE

Vincent Sherry

Most will agree that a major aim of literary modernism was to rescue poetry from a dated poetic language, to return it to the speaking voice, to revive it in the present tense of idiom. Yet the poets' interests tended to flow toward subjects far from the present: Pound's archaic Cathay and Provence, Eliot's medieval romances, Jones's imperial Rome and Roman Britain, and, for all three, the ancient rituals and myths compiled in Frazer's *Golden Bough*. Paradoxes can describe practical challenges for writers, not just theoretical conundrums for scholars, and in this one we find an incentive for some of the most significant technical innovations of the modernists: their attempt to restore a sense of the past in the consciousness of the present, in the language of the present. That ambition found its voice in the dramatic monologue. Through a dramatized "I" speaker, a poet could give speaking presence and intensity to historical materials. Thus Ezra Pound, in *The Spirit of Romance*, praised the main innovator of the dramatic monologue, Robert Browning, as the only poet after Ovid who "raises the dead and dissects their mental processes."[1] David Jones, along the same lines, told William Blissett that "Browning was the poet who showed the way to make the past part of the *Now*."[2]

It would be wrong to suggest that dramatic monologues manage to resurrect these historical personages wholly into the present. Witness, for example, Pound's monologues of troubadour poets: the steady cross-talking between modern slang and archaic diction shows the voice of the modern poet dubbed into the ancient character. As readers, too, we must project ourselves from our modern position to understand the poem. To preserve but reverse Jones's terms: we make the *Now* part of the *Then*, ourselves part of the past. This kind of dynamic response has been taken, moreover, as the rule of our reaction to all dramatic monologues. Thus Robert Langbaum maintains that we identify with the speakers of monologues, achieve a rapport with them, and understand the content of their poems through an act of empathy. And empathy comes into conflict with moral judgment, which is based on frames of reference external to the speaker. Ultimately, Langbaum asserts, we sympathize rather than judge. Thus many dramatic monologues give us characters who defy ethical norms—the duke in "My Last Duchess" is the best example—and as such measure the degree to which we must suspend moral judgment for the sake of experiencing their poems.[3] Judgment, in brief, seems the least interesting, the least useful response to these characters.

A sustained, intelligent counter to Langbaum's argument has come from Ralph Rader. We project and sympathize with speakers of dramatic monologues, Rader agrees, but not because they confound our moral judgment. Figures like Prufrock and Abt Vogler, after all, seem far from the villainy of the duke. Rader's model is cleanly mechanical: we understand all speakers, he suggests, by sympathetic projection, inferring from the outward gesture to the inward motive, a process to which moral judgment—or its absence—is simply irrelevant.[4]

We can reach a useful *rapprochement* between these strong but opposed theories, but we need to widen the scope of the two essential questions: the speaker's problematic character, and our judgment of it. As though by a rule of their nature, the speaking characters of dramatic monologues are unusual, idiosyncratic, eccentric. Norms may be a constantly fluctuating measurement. But it is safe to say that Prufrock and Gerontion remain marginal in relation to any social or psychological standards; the abnormality of Caliban and Childe Roland, who have their characters modelled (and their voices distorted) around the grotesque landscapes they describe, is even clearer. These speakers are as problematic in relation to human averages as, say, Browning's duke is to moral norms. To dismiss these strange personalities on the grounds of normality would match our judgment of them according to moral standards. And yet we do not dismiss them, we project sympathetically into them, as Rader too agrees. Thus we leave behind a judgment, based on a sense of the ordinary, to see the poem through the speaker's own extraordinary perspective. Perhaps in this way we can join the notions of Rader and Langbaum to describe the means and effects of the dramatic monologue. The act of sympathy we perform in understanding any speaker is reinforced by the problematic characters in these monologues, who force us to project over external norms in order to understand them, who thus allow us to participate in their extraordinary perspectives and experience their poems.

David Jones's work in verse has assimilated the modernist tradition, and absorbed with it the lessons and potentials of the dramatic monologue. His experiments with the long poem—the narrative of his experience in the Great War, *In Parenthesis* (1937), and his open-form sequence, *The Anathemata* (1952), as sprawling as the world history that provides its scope—match the ambitions of Pound or Williams in this mode. The historical imagination of both works is centred in monologue speakers. The mythic and historical richness of *In Parenthesis* converges in the vaunt of "Dai [David] Greatcoat": this dramatic monologue of a 1915 infantryman adapts the ancient heroic boast to relive the major conflicts in Western antiquity and legend. The monologue of a fourteenth-century London lavender-seller, "The Lady of the Pool," grounds the historical-religious vision of *The Anathemata*: as she turns bawdy tales of *medium aevum* into hymns of divine praise, a thing cursed (anathema) is made one of the holy things (anathemata); she realizes that etymological conceit—makes it real in her experience for us—as she injects a modern voice into a late medieval sensibility. The sequence of shorter poems published in *The Sleeping Lord* (1974), and the posthumous collection of poetic manuscripts in *The Roman Quarry* (1981), comprise an unfinished but unified work of great historical scope; the centre is in Roman Jerusalem at the time of Christ's death, but the viewpoints shift through a series of eccentric characters-in-voice, who quicken immeasurably the standard accounts of these events.

The dramatic monologue serves in all these works as an aid in Jones's primary task of contemporizing the past. An allied technique appears in his characterization, especially in the historical personages of his later poems. These speakers are placed outside the Christian religion—morally, historically, humorously, always problematically, for we are asked constantly to relate them to the Christian faith. In this way Jones refines the effects and expands the scope of the modern monologue. His outsiders invite a sympathetic response, and so intensify our experience of their poetic content; this is both historical material and, in a special sense we will find available to the monologue, religious content too.

The Lady of the Pool moves imaginatively and freely through history, as she refers to the various ship captains she has entertained on their arrival in London: her favours are like her flowers. In recounting her adventures, however, she presents us with moral riddles. As a woman of easy virtue, she makes claim on the sacred. Thus she pictures a sexual consummation in the imagery of Christ's passion and redemption, alluding to the drawing of water from Christ's right side (emphasizing the word *right* to stress that association):

> From the dripping impost the gusted drops moisted the ransom'd flesh of both
> of us—from the *right* side of the gate, cap-tin.[5]

The problem of moral judgment created by these contradictory signals is summed up in a reference to the "Sejunction Day," the Separation Day, when, as the Book of Revelation tells it, the saved will be separated from the damned; the point of her allusion is that humans cannot make such moral discriminations:

> And you never know, captain
> you never know, not with what you might call metaphysical
> certainty, captain: our phenomenology is but limited,
> captain.

> So of these let's say *requiescant*
> till the Sejunction Day!
> (*An*, 164)

An interesting addition to the moral ambiguity of the monologue in Jones's development of what we might call a rhetoric of non-judgment. As the last excerpt shows, the Lady speaks "lavenderese," a corrupted or cockneyfied version of learned idiom. This cant jumbles the terms and concepts of formal disciplines, undercuts the status of such external frames of reference:

> To prayers all is won
> no matter where his commas come they've nowt bar
> *concedo* to that one. You old God's arlot! well argued,
> that makes clear, that *re*-distributes their middle for
> 'em—now where's their premises? Ask of the strewed sea!
> (*An*, 147–48)

Jones mixes up the frameworks of formal logic and judgment, and makes necessary a sympathetic response to the speaker: we suspend for the nonce a stipulative consciousness of what is outside or inside morality. This latitude has as its most complex and important implication a pluralist view of religious truth: it is that inclusive vision of pancultural and transhistorical religion that Jones derived from the typology of Frazer's *Golden Bough* and shared with other high modernists like Eliot. The Lady mingles Christian, primitive, and classical rites and symbols, seeing, for example, the precessions of Mary the divine mother in local chthonic cultures, through this in-depth perspective on a London church:

> At the Lady-at-Hill
> Above Romeland's wharf-lanes
> at the Great Mother's newer *chapelle*
> at New Heva's Old Crepel.
>   (Chthonic *matres* under the croft:
> springan a Maye's *Aves* to clerestories
>   Delphi in sub-crypt:
> luce flowers to steeple.)
> (*An*, 127)

The dramatic monologue has served other modernists, too, in employing a primitive religious symbology. In *The Waste Land* and *Gerontion*, for example, Eliot's speakers use figures of pre-Christian, chthonic religions as counters for the Christian faith. It is because the monologue character tends to stand outside expected norms, we may surmise, that he produces the unorthodox form. Yet there is a combination of opposite motives and effects here. The pre-Christian figures are doctrinally neutral, and lay no claim on the belief or disbelief of the speaker, who can remain intellectually diffident toward them. At the same time these primitive configurations are a means of returning abstract concepts of faith to more intense, indeed visceral experience: spiritual salvation is physical rebirth. The monologue speaker seems to want to run the concepts of belief up and down the fibre of the sensual being. Thus the speaker's distance from orthodox faith builds paradoxically into a more intense experience of religion: as readers we likewise suspend judgment, based on moral norms, in favour of more immediate access to the character's experience, and it is a religious experience. I am not suggesting, of course, that David Jones confines his religious primitivism to dramatic monologues. But immediacy and intensity, aspects of our sympathetic response to the speaker of the monologue, are important aims in the modernist's use of these ancient types, and Jones may realize these aims best in his dramatic monologues.

He realizes these aims repeatedly in the Roman monologues of *The Sleeping Lord*. Here soldiers of the empire, stationed in Jerusalem near the time of Christ's death, reach back to the chthonic types of Roman and European myth to represent the nascent Christian faith. Their indifference to orthodox and historical Christianity helps them to approach anew the primary events of Christendom, to capture its significance as an original, felt experience. In "The Fatigue," for example, a Roman legionary detailed to assist at the crucifixion sees the victim in the figure of the Hanged Man, the scapegoat in the primitive fertility ritual. He conveys the meaning of this cult, the regeneration won through sacrifice, in vividly physical terms, while his own sensory presence at the event leads to the quality of felt intensity:

>   and it will come
>   your turn
> to stand alone under the meridian eye
>   between the Man Hanged
>   and the Joker....
> Beneath the implacable ray
>   that beats
>   where y'r scorching back-plates rivet
>   that beats
> where swarming flies
>   pattern black
>   the thirsting Yggdrasill
>   *In ara crucis torridum*
> he Frees the Waters.[6]

Correspondingly, in "The Dream of Private Clitus," this Roman soldier, in relating his dream, repeats the sayings of St. Paul on resurrection and spiritual transformation; but he establishes an intimate, companionable version of this idea, seeing himself gathered, with his mate, into the lap of Tellus Mater, the Roman earth goddess, who is his closely felt equivalent for the bosom of Abraham.[7] "The Tribune's Visitation" repeats and varies this pattern. Here the title character, paying a surprise visit to the men in his garrison, breaks martial routine and achieves a moment of intimacy with them: as he shares a meal with his men, he becomes a type of Christ; repeating the Roman formula of enlistment, "Idem in me," he recalls the words of Christ at the Last Supper, "do this in memory of me." Most important, he renews that prime event in Christian sacramental theology with the sombre gusto of this secular experience.

> See! I break this barrack bread, I drink with you, this issue cup, I salute, with you, these mutilated signa, I with you have cried with all of us the ratifying formula: *Idem in me*.
> (*SL*, 58)

As outsiders to Christianity for historical reasons, the Roman speakers find their complement in the outsider on moral grounds, a figure who appears intriguingly throughout the posthumous collection of poetic manuscripts, *The Roman Quarry and other sequences*. A brief survey of its contents reveals how extensively, indeed how compulsively the poet moves toward the outsider's viewpoint. Three poems on the Catholic mass, though distinct in matters of occasion and detail, all display parallel lines of movement toward the outsider figure. The first, "The Grail Mass," opens in the midst of a modern liturgy, but proceeds to a scene from Malory's *Le Morte d'Arthur*, where Lancelot, standing outside the Grail Chapel, is prevented by his sin from entering and achieving the Grail sacrament. In "Caillech" an Irish woman's musings take her from a sermon on chastity to the same figure of Lancelot, standing outside the chapel. And in "The Kensington Mass," the poet's associations move from a modern mass to Roman Jerusalem, where Peter is heard speaking in Pilate's courtyard, just after denying Christ, as much an alien as Lancelot shut out from the chapel. Correspondingly, in "The Old Quarry," a sequence of poems on events in Jerusalem surrounding Christ's death, the archetypal alien Judas Iscariot speaks a long, central monologue. Then an aging Roman administrator discourses at the hour of the crucifixion, and views this event from his perspective as an outsider.

Nearing the end of his monologue, the Roman Procurator refers anachronistically to Lancelot at the door of the Grail Chapel, and suggests important links between himself, Lancelot, and all the alien figures in Jones's work. He sees Lancelot outside as a man lost, and as such pictures him walking bewildered in a maze, the Celtic labyrinth at New Grange; he regards Lancelot's confusion, however, as a source of renewing mystery, like the magical cornucopia at the navel of that maze:

> No Lancelot no! you must be lost before you find the cornucopia, the lamb that bleeds beyond the double guard of Guenever within the vaginal traverses the Durotriges fence on their high places, at the navel of the spiral at New Grange, under the seal where the leaning stones deploy to loop the cist for Minoan or Menai Scylla. It's always from chamber to chamber—in and out the creep-way as you have done before....[Y]ou'll feel like a motherless child

before Rhea encloses you a second time, before you revive the maimed king
before you find your margarite. You must be lost, and the Roman way is to
be certain of one's bearings.[8]

The clearest things about this labyrinth are the poetic uses of being lost. Through the alien Jones can see religious themes with a quality of strangeness and wonder. He can renew the experience of religion at the subjective and elemental level of mystery, typified by the ancient magic cults and chthonic rites alluded to here. Estrangement is the first condition of the wonder, and it is a condition best fulfilled through the perspective of the outsider in the monologue.

Extending this principle in *The Roman Quarry*, Jones uses his aliens, the speakers of his dramatic monologues, to envision symbols, like themselves, outside the canon of received Christian tradition; in this way the monologues provide signs whose original, imaginative, and unusual nature conveys the wonder, aura, and numinous power of religion. Peter, standing as the outsider in Pilate's courtyard in "The Kensington Mass," uses the death of Absolam as a symbol for the imminent crucifixion of Christ. Although Absolam and Christ were both "sons of David," and were both pierced and hung in death, David's prodigal son is certainly an unusual, an arresting, an eccentric symbol for Christ. Another evocative and unorthodox type of Christ appears in the same passage. The fertility priest in the oak grove at Nemi, who was sacrificed to renew the life of the wood—represented here by the eternal "Golden Bough"—stands enigmatically for Christ's redemptive sacrifice. In this excerpt, as Jones depicts Christ in the double figure of Absolam and the Nemi priest, you can feel the fabric of foreign words (Latin and Greek as well as Old English) weaving the spell of strangeness and wonder which Jones sought to restore through symbols as unusual as these:

> That great lignum arbor una nobilis within the inmost *nemeton* of this wild
> Ephraim holt, had for Golden Bough the pierced & hanging son of the Lord
> of Salem (*RQ*, 96)

It seems paradoxical, finally, to speak of religious mystery as an effect created by a deliberate, mechanical technique. Jones's use of the outsider's perspective, indeed, discloses a source in his own experience, which provides the monologues of his outsiders with their depth and drive. The manuscripts of *The Roman Quarry* reveal that all three mass poems bore dedications to Fr. John O'Connor, the priest who received Jones into the Catholic Church; a scene in "Caillech," in fact, recalls specifically the church of St. Cuthbert in Bradford, where O'Connor baptized Jones in 1921.[9] The outsider figure in these mass poems seems to reflect, in a deeply imaginative way, Jones's own initial relation to the church as a type of outsider. Most compelling, the poet seems to be imaginatively re-enacting his conversion through this figure. In relation to Lancelot, specifically, he emphasizes themes integral to the convert's experience: initiation, reception into the church. Thus Lancelot at the chapel door is associated with a dog chained outside, as it were, "for a thousand *quarantines*" (*RQ*, 109), forty-day or Lenten periods, while the old Lenten motifs of the convert's preparation, initiation, and reception into the church (on Easter Eve) emerge dramatically in Lancelot's passion to be accepted within:

> Lake-wave Lawnslot
>   beats against that
> varnished pine
>   his quillon'd *cleddyf*-hilt
> fractures the notices for the week
> he would see
>   right through that chamber door....
>   (*RQ*, 110)

Clinching the personal connection between Jones and the outsider, particularly Lancelot, is an episode he relates from his service in the war. Once, in a rear area of the Flanders front, Jones came upon a shattered, apparently abandoned farm building; he discovered a Catholic mass going on inside. He stood for a long time at the wall, gazing in from outside, just like Lancelot at the door of the Grail chapel. In this account, most important, he emphasizes his place as an uninitiated outsider, and suggests that this experience was a turning point, the beginning of a conversion, an entry:

> I can't recall at what part of the Mass it was as I looked through that squint-hole and I didn't think I ought to stay long as it seemed rather like an uninitiated bloke prying on the Mysteries of a Cult. But it made a big impression on me....[F]or at that spying unintentionally on the Mass in Flanders in the Forward Zone I felt immediately that oneness between the Offerant and those toughs that clustered round him in the dim-lit byre—a thing I had never felt remotely as a Protestant at the Office of Holy Communion in spite of the insistence of Protestant theology on the "priesthood of the laity."[10]

That this outsider figure springs from Jones's personal experience may tell us, in conclusion, how profoundly ex-centric was his own perspective on religion, and so explain why he leaned inevitably toward the extraordinary viewpoint of the dramatic monologue. This personal connection provides, more simply, a final sign of the presence and intensity which he sought to give his poetic materials, an aim for which the dramatic monologue was again particularly effective. All in all, the dramatic monologue allowed Jones to combine the speaking presence of a character-in-voice with the unusual viewpoint of an extraordinary character, and so gave him a means of dislocating the familiar and traditional into fresh perspectives and striking configurations. To adapt a mildly appropriate phrase from Joyce, that other master of its speech: Jones would mystique us with the ineluctable magicality of the monologue.

NOTES

1. Ezra Pound, *The Spirit of Romance* (Norfolk, Connecticut: New Directions, n.d.), 16.

2. William Blissett, *The Long Conversation: A Memoir of David Jones* (London: Oxford Univ. Press, 1981), 100.

3. Robert Langbaum, *The Poetry of Experience: The Dramatic Monologue in Modern Literary Tradition* (1957; reprinted, New York: Norton, 1963), 75–108.

4. Ralph Rader, "The Dramatic Monologue and Related Lyric Forms," *Critical Inquiry*, 3 (1976): 135.

5. David Jones, *The Anathemata* (London: Faber and Faber, 1952), 130; hereafter cited parenthetically as *An*.

6. David Jones, "The Fatigue," *The Sleeping Lord and other fragments* (London: Faber and Faber, 1974), 34–35; hereafter cited parenthetically as *SL*.

7. See "The Dream of Private Clitus," *The Sleeping Lord*, 20: "it seemed that me and Lugo were caught up into that peace, whether in a marble body I cannot tell, if as Dioscuri of flesh and blood, I can't say—the genius of the dream knows—but such ones we seemed to be as merited her large embrace for keeping, so it seemed to my dream-thinking, the Middle Watch at the traverse of the wall. It seemed that now for ever me and my battle-mate would be for ever in the lap of Tellus, high on the wall,..."; cf. St. Paul, 2 Corinthians 12.2: "I knew a man in Christ above fourteen years ago, (whether in the body, I cannot tell; or whether out of the body, I cannot tell: God knoweth;) such a one caught up to the third heaven."

8. David Jones, *The Roman Quarry and other sequences*, ed. Harman Grisewood and René Hague (London: Agenda Editions, 1981), 182; hereafter cited parenthetically as *RQ*.

9. This observation is made in *The Roman Quarry and other sequences*, ed. Grisewood and Hague, xxi.

10. In *Dai Greatcoat: A self-portrait of David Jones in his letters*, ed. René Hague (London: Faber and Faber, 1980), 249.

"INTERMIXED LINGO": LISTENING TO DAVID JONES

W. J. Keith

Both *The Anathemata* and *The Kensington Mass*, the poem upon which David Jones was working when he died, open with an account—or, to use words more appropriate to Jones, a re-creation or even a re-calling—of a priest saying Mass. In both poems we are asked initially to listen: to accents, emphases, sounds, words, as well as to the meanings and implications that ultimately reveal the total significance implicit in the Latin liturgy. This would suggest that Jones's poetry is, above all, a poetry to be listened to, one in which sound, rhythm, and a verbal complexity are fundamental; yet, because of the difficulty inherent in his allusiveness, and also because the basic Christian vision upon which his work depends is no longer familiar to many readers, most of the critical commentary devoted to Jones has concerned itself with annotation, exegesis, or a much needed mapping of his poetic terrain. In the following pages I want to offer a few preliminary notes towards what I see as the next necessary step in Jones studies—emphasis on the poetic and linguistic as distinct from the intellectual and "theological" aspects of his work.

It is convenient to begin with a passage from *The Kensington Mass*:

clara voce dicit: OREMVS
       et ascendens ad altare
           dicit secreto: AVFER A NOBIS...
and in lowly accents
      he says the rest
should you be elbow-close him
      you may catch his
soft-breathed-out

> PER CHRISTVM DOMINVM
> NOSTRVM.
> Light as air
> > the Goidelic vowels of
> Maedb's own Munster
> > intermingle with
> that vocalic pulchritude
> he first had heard
> > long since
> in Alban hill-ways
> > in Latium
> loved at first hearing
> > and now
> as though innate in him
> indelibly marking him
> an unconscious part of him
> but far from unconscious
> the deliberate cultivation
> > in the years long fled.[1]

The priest in question was Father John O'Connor, who had received David Jones into the Catholic Church. It is characteristic that Jones should prove especially sensitive to the musical variety of O'Connor's Irish accent (Maedb's own Munster) and to the "vocalic pulchritude" of the Latin Mass, and even more appropriate that the distinction should be made within the sound and etymology of the words employed (Anglo-Saxon and Celtic words against ostentatiously Latin derivations). Moreover, here and throughout Jones's poetry, different kinds of language are "intermingled"—and that word, again characteristically, is taken up later in the poem when the disciple Peter refers to

> the intermixt lingo
> > and differing tongued-talings of
> half the peoples and nations & kin-gens
> > from under the bent arc of heaven.
> > > (*KM*, 13)

As René Hague notes in his textual commentary on the fragment, Jones is concerned here with "the multi-racial character of the country which lay between Damascus and the sea and Egypt" (*KM*, 18). Equally promising, of course, for Jones's poetry as a whole was the "intermixt lingo" available as a result of the blending of races over several millennia on the island of Britain.

Here, I suggest, we find a rich and intricate cluster of Jonesian interests, one in which Christian history, personal experience, and the possibilities of language all coalesce to form an elaborate poetic texture. To readers familiar with Jones's earlier work, this will hardly be surprising. One finds similar instances in *In Parenthesis*, where the words and symbols of the Mass shine through the slang and jargon of the World War I trenches; in *The Anathemata*, where the cockney accents of the Lady of the Pool are punctuated by extracts from Latin both ecclesiastical and classical; in *The Sleeping Lord*, where Jones deliberately introduced Welsh terms into his text, as he explains in a prefatory note, "in order to evoke the feel and ethos inherent in the 'materia' or subject matter."[2]

This "macaronic" quality in Jones's work is well-known, and has been the subject of controversy. Whether one finds it satisfying or irritating, however, it is not difficult to appreciate the poet's motives for the recurrent effect. These are most clearly manifest in the following passage from the "Angle-Land" section of *The Anathemata*:

Past where the ancra-man, deeping his holy rule
in the fiendish marsh
        at the *Geisterstunde*
        on *Calangaeaf* night
heard the bogle-*baragouinage.*
        Crowland-*diawliaidd*
Wealisc-man lingo speaking?
        or Britto-Romani gone *diaboli?*[3]

In these lines English, German, Welsh, French, and Latin rub shoulders, and give some indication within the sound of the verse of the ethnic mix that is the subject of the passage. The complicated racial movements and assimilations are embodied within the language itself.

At the opening of *The Anathemata*, we encounter once again the priest saying Mass and the intermixture of languages and other effects:

We already and first of all discern him making this thing other. His groping syntax, if we attend, already shapes:
    ADSCRIPTAM, RATAM, RATIONABILEM...and by pre-application and for *them*, under modes and patterns altogether theirs, the holy and venerable hands lift up an efficacious sign. (*An.*, 49)

What begins as dignified prose will soon blend into a form of verse. The emphasis falls immediately on syntax, albeit groping, but a syntax that also shapes. The consecration that makes "this thing" (the wafer) "other" (the body of Christ) is itself an image of transformation, of the mingling of substance and spirit. Latin is immediately juxtaposed with English; moreover, despite the fact that this paragraph is offered as prose, Jones even rhymes Latin and English ("ADSCRIPTAM, RATAM, RATIONALBILEM...and by pre-application and for *them*"), italics drawing attention not only to the emphasis but to the rhyme. Literary effects are mingled as well as languages and concepts.

This too is hardly surprising to the seasoned reader of Jones. *In Parenthesis* refuses to be categorized as prose or verse, since it includes both, and the same is true of *The Anathemata*. Jones, of course, developed as an artist in the age of modernism and free verse. If his mixture of languages parallels effects to be found in James Joyce, T.S. Eliot, and Ezra Pound, so does his poetic experimentation. What we find is not merely a mingling of prose and verse, but a juxtaposition of traditional and modern poetic effects. The opening of *The Anathemata* continues:

> These, at the sagging end and chapter's close, standing
> humbly before the tables spread, in the apsidal houses, who
> intend life:
>
>   between the sterile ornaments
> under the pasteboard baldachins
> as, in the young-time, in the sap-years:
>   between the living floriations
> under the leaping arches.
>
>   (*An.*, 49)

As we view the passage on the page, it looks as if prose gives way, formally and unequivocally, to verse at the fourth line; but if we listen, the effect is rather more complicated: "These, at the sagging end and chapter's close...." The paragraph opens with a ten-syllable phrase that would fit smoothly into a passage of regular iambic-pentameter blank verse. A coincidence? I think not. Jones does not belong with the stylists responsible for editorials in *The Times* where, the story persists, some thirty percent of the phrases can be roughly scanned. Jones was always deliberate in his rhythmic effects. Besides, this is not an isolated instance. On the following page, no less than three sections begin in the same way:

> These rear-guard details in their quaint attire...
> The utile infiltration nowhere held...
> The cult-man stands alone in Pellam's land...
>   (*An.*, 50)[4]

I suggest that, at this early stage in his difficult and challenging poem, Jones is leading the reader gently into his poetic method, providing some regular lines for reassurance, as it were, while at the same time developing his flexible and characteristic blend of rhythmical effects that we generally classify (and so falsely separate) into prose and verse.

But the extended passage just quoted deserves further consideration. The last five lines are set out as verse, each line containing between seven and nine syllables. What is important here, however, is the rhythmic patterning. We notice how "between" and "under" each repeat themselves at the beginning of lines, and how the grammatical units balance each other (disyllabic preposition + definite article + disyllabic adjective + noun). And the central line, seemingly an exception, establishes its own complementary balance ("in the young-time, in the sap-years"). Whatever we may say about this verse, we cannot call it "free."

Let us turn now to a shorter verse-paragraph a few lines later:

> The utile infiltration nowhere held
>   creeps vestibule
> is already at the closed lattices, is coming through each door. (*An.*, 50)

Hague, in his *Commentary on The Anathemata of David Jones*, is helpful here. Not only does he explain that "creeps" is used as a transitive verb (dictionaries recognize this as a poetic form meaning "creeps through"), but points out that the last quoted phrase "contains a memory of a little song, often sung by a painter whose friendship with D. reached back into the twenties: 'Close the door, they're coming through the window; close the window, they're coming through the door'."[5] This is all part of Jones's eclectic allusiveness, but what needs to be pointed out is the rhythmical variety involved. The verbal echoes make a contribution not only on the intellectual level but in terms of the sound and movement of the whole. This early effect of mingling song rhythms into the literary text prepares the reader for subsequent introductions of fragments of sea-shanties (in "Middle-Sea and Lear-Sea") and nursery-rhyme rhythms (at the opening of "Keel, Ram, Stauros").

Another effect is well illustrated in the following sequence:

> Within the railed tumulus
>   he sings high and he sings low.
>
>   In a low voice
>   as one who speaks
> where a few are, gathered in high-room
>   and one, gone out.
>   (*An.*, 51)

At first sight, the arrangement on the page seems arbitrary, but if we listen to the sound we note how the account of singing high and singing low (itself an echo from the song "O Mistress Mine" in *Twelfth Night*) is taken up in what might be called cross-stitch pattern with the later references first to "low voice" and then to "high-room." (This is developed on the next page with "the low porch" which is balanced by "the high nave," which in turn is echoed by "the high cave"— where, typically, Jones adds the delayed rhyme of "nave" and "cave" to the already complex effect.) The sequence of "one...a few...one" also augments the elaborate texture of this passage, as does the complementary contrast between "he sings" and "one who speaks."

Jones's effects of sound and rhythm are virtually inexhaustible, but I cannot close without commenting on the famous Venus of Willendorf sequence, which is a key passage not only in terms of his sacramental archaeology but also because of his exquisite control of language:

> Who were his *gens*-men or had he no *Hausname* yet
> no *nomen* for his *fecit*-mark
>   the Master of the Venus?
> whose man-hands god-handled the Willendorf stone
>   before they unbound the last glaciation
> for the Uhland Father to be-ribbon *die blaue Donau*
>   with his Vanabride blue.
> O long before they lateen'd her Ister
> or Romanitas manned her gender'd stream.
>   (*An.*, 59)

This passage is a veritable mosaic of word-play, involving mixtures of languages, hidden rhymes, assonantal repetitions, and serious puns. These are difficult to indicate adequately in print, but I must attempt to point out at least some of the verbal complexity. It begins with a concealed rhyme in "*gens*-men," which quickly develops into a trilingual pun ("men," "*Hausname*," "*nomen*"), while the three alliterating H's and the three "no"-sounds all add to the sound pattern. "Mark" and "Master" later connect through assonance, while "Master" combines both painterly and nautical associations. "Man-hands" and "god-handled" combine to produce a complex—and, *via* "man-handled," punning—statement about "making" (cf. "*fecit*"), and contains more concealed rhymes. Hidden beneath the German spelling is the Venus-Willendorf-Vanabride alliteration, and more rhymes, alliterations, and assonance too intricate and subtle to analyze here may be found by the diligent reader in the central lines.

But I have a further reason for focussing on this passage: the extraordinary, regular blank-verse lines that conclude it. David Jones clinches this important climax in the thematic context of this part of his poem with rhythms that fit smoothly into our metrical preconceptions. In addition, puns abound (lateen/Latin; "manned" in the double sense of "manning a ship" and "rendering masculine"). But the word-play goes even further: the repeated sound in "Romanitas manned" looks forward in meaning to "gender'd," which in turn recalls the "*gens*" of the opening line. The poetic texture here resembles the elaboration of Jones's paintings, where we pick up meanings and connections through forms, shape, colour, and positioning as well as through the representational mode.

For David Jones, then, the world of language is as ordered and full of meaning as other parts of the divine creation. The words, sounds, and rhythms out of which literature is "made" make possible a revelation of the sacred meaning of human life. God's "*fecit*-mark" is upon both. Moreover, just as, in the world of sense, the humble and lowly "creatures" are as essential to the divine scheme as the high and mighty, so in the world of language there is no effect that is not ultimately redeemable. Puns are traditionally considered a low, even vulgar form of literary effect, yet "good poets have a weakness for bad puns," as Auden has quipped,[6] and nowhere is this more evident than in Jones's work. Often such puns, like Joyce's in *Finnegans Wake* so admired by Jones, draw attention to the mingling of language as in "lateen/Latin" and "Romanitas manned" quoted in the previous paragraph, or in the following passage:

> But had they as yet morained
> > where holy *Deva*'s entry is?
> Or pebbled his mere, where
> > still the Parthenos
> she makes her *dev*ious exit?
> > > (*An.*, 67; my emphases)

Any Jones reader has his own favourite puns. Here is an almost random sample: "For anthropos is not always kind" (*An.*, 79); "for the men with the *groma*, even for the men of rule, whose *religio* is rule" (*An.*, 85); "Nudge Clio/she's apt to be musing" (*An.*, 88). "*Almost* random," because I have picked instances that pun across languages. According to Jones, the Greeks "back-cant on Parnassus" (*An.*, 170) because their sailors have taken back cockney slang to their homeland. The immediate context is packed full of puns, as well as a conscious allusion to Dryden explained in Jones's notes, while the very word "back-cant" contains a translingual pun on "Bacchant." Through all these puns, good or bad, comic or serious, the divine pattern of interrelation is made manifest.

Finally, "back-cant on Parnassus" is a classic instance of Jones's favourite effect with *levels* of language. Most poets, especially traditional poets, display an almost automatic respect for verbal decorum, but some, including Thomas Hardy, who appeared to believe in a kind of linguistic egalitarianism, habitually juxtapose words of varying levels of status and dignity. David Jones is one of the few who continually exploit the tension between "high style" and vernacular slang. This is conspicuous, of course, in *In Parenthesis*, where the earthy colloquialisms of the common soldiers contrast dramatically with the narrator's own poetic idiom. In *The Anathemata*, interestingly enough, the effect usually appears in connection with solemn or erudite allusion, and, once again, habitually crosses linguistic boundaries. Examples include: "Was their oral gloss from a Heidelberg gaffer...?" (*An.*, 61); "the syndicate's agent / pays-off the branch operatives / (his bit from the Urbs / waits in the car)" (*An.*, 89); "One thousand two hundred years / since the Dorian jarls / rolled up the map of Arcady" (*An.*, 90); "Half a mo Hector" (*An.*, 177). Intermixt lingo, indeed, but in David Jones the sacred and the profane, the remote past and the contemporary present, the mellifluousness of one language and the ruggedness of another, poetry and prose, the heights of formal speech and the depths of slang, are all united. In *The Anathemata*, and elsewhere, he made a heap of all that he could find, yet the heap is transformed into art through the metamorphosis created by words, sounds, and rhythms—if we will only listen.

NOTES

1. *The Kensington Mass* (London: Agenda Editions, 1975), 7–8. Subsequent quotations paginated in text (*KM*).

2. The Sleeping Lord (London: Faber and Faber, 1974), 70.

3. *The Anathemata* (London: Faber and Faber, 1952) 112. Subsequent quotations paginated in text (*An.*).

4. In the first line quoted, Jones would, of course, pronounce "details" in the English manner with stress on the first syllable.

5. René Hague, *A Commentary on The Anathemata of David Jones* (Toronto: Univ. of Toronto Press, 1977), 20. For much of the information presented in this article, I am indebted, as all writers on Jones must be, to Hague's book; for the most part, I am merely selecting and applying his gathered insights to my specific subject.

6. W.H. Auden, " 'The Truest Poetry is the most Feigning'," in his *Collected Poems*, (London: Faber and Faber, 1976), 470.

STANLEY SPENCER AND DAVID JONES

Guy Davenport

Roger Fry's insistence during the years when Bloomsbury was establishing its hegemony over British critical opinion that the subject of a work of art is always secondary to technique calcified into a dogma: the subject of a work of art is negligible. Further mischief followed, which Fry did not intend. A perverse logic developed his dogma into the more insidious one that subject-matter is merely a pretext for the artist to demonstrate a style of painting. The artist, we were to understand, is not primarily interested in the meadow, or nude, or bowl of apples before him. He is only interested in the aesthetics (Fry's great word) of their form. The British, notoriously suspicious of art, subverted Fry's noble attempts to redress an attention which he deemed too literal and too lacking in aesthetic appreciation into an excuse to ignore subject-matter altogether.

The barricades on which Fry stood were those of a necessary revolution. He was trying to wean the British away from painting which he felt had become a very glossy and accomplished set of illustrations to literature, and little more. In planning the post-impressionist exhibit of 1910 he was importing a sensibility. He wanted the British to see, and feel, and understand painting that had no text except nature, an art that was all "plastic significance," "significant form"—Picasso, Cézanne, Gauguin, Vincent van Gogh. He was thereby rendering two great schools of continental painting, impressionism and post-impressionism, iconographically sterile, a false step that is only now beginning to be corrected.

The greater loss caused by Fry's unfortunate teaching is that important British painters and poets, whose work was appearing toward the end of his life and in the generation after his death, could be easily dismissed. Although Walter Sickert could speak of Stanley Spencer's "fateful strangeness," Fry placed Spencer among the "pure illustrators" (that is, with Burne-Jones and Augustus Egg):

> Why is it that our *litterateurs* of the brush are so palpably inferior to their *confrères* of the pen? I may cite as an exception the case of Mr. Stanley Spencer, who is also a pure illustrator, indifferent to plastic significance, but whose psychological creations are at least original, curious, and vividly apprehended. They at least never sink to the deplorable level of stereotyped sentimentality which rules in the Royal Academy. [1]

These are strange words indeed to hear about Stanley Spencer, one of the century's greatest and most original painters. His perceived indifference to plastic significance was but half of the resistance the British put in his way. There was a dinner held at the Royal Academy in the late 1940s, when the Tate's acquisition of *The Resurrection in Cookham Churchyard* had made a scandal in the press. At this dinner Sir Alfred Munnings and his distinguished guest Winston Churchill (amateur painter in the impressionist manner Fry worked so hard to import, an irony to savour) noted that Spencer could not paint arms, that indeed he put them on backwards. Further, the fellow painted as badly as Picasso (pronounced with the short *a* Churchill also used for Nazi, *nazzy*). Sir Alfred agreed with Sir Winston. The painting was a farce and an outrage, Spencer an imposter. And the port and the walnuts went around the table again. We might note that Sir Winston's assessment of Spencer's draughts is precisely analogous to saying that Blake drew as maladroitly as Michelangelo.

More was implicit in Churchill's intended insult than Sir Winston could know; Spencer, like Picasso, was master of several styles, each with its own technique and iconography. Picasso's styles were a matter of periods in which he achieved, with Faustian éclat, another painter's work of a lifetime. A whimsically metaphysical writer (like Borges) could construct a science-fiction fantasy in which future critics might (after, say, a holocaust in which Picasso's paintings but no records about them survive) assign the Blue and Rose period to one painter, cubism to another, the neoclassical to yet another, and so on, ending up with ten or fifteen factitious painters.

Spencer used three styles. The first is academic, derived from seventeenth-century Dutch work modified by French realism (Courbet, for instance). This style lasted his lifetime. In 1917 there is the self-portrait now in the Tate, so wonderfully allusive in pose and rendering to Samuel Palmer's at the same age. (A parallel study of Spencer and Palmer would discover many similarities of religious temperament and iconography, flowering trees, symbolic roadways, humble truths suffused with ecstasy and vision). In 1958 Spencer did a portrait of Dame Mary Cartwright, Mistress of Girton College, Cambridge, in this academic style (and a final self-portrait the following year). In between, Spencer used this style for Cookham landscapes, still lifes, various portraits, and the erotic paintings which were intended for a cycle of religious subjects.

The second style is the first medievalized, that is to say, brought close to the styles of Giotto and Cimabue. Many British artists followed this trend: we can see it in Eric Gill (inspired by medieval page illuminations and stained glass), in David Jones, Clare Leighton, and others. This is Spencer's greatest style. In it he did the Burghclere murals, the series of resurrections, the village and domestic genre scenes, and the final, unfinished major work, *Christ Preaching at the Cookham Regatta*.

The third style was personal, sketchy, annotative, and unplanned. This is the style (always involving caricature and much humour) in which he painted The Beatitudes, The Temptations, and the autobiographical canvases, such as *Love Letters, The Dustbin, Cookham*," and all the strange paintings in which one needs to know how what Jacques Lacan calls an *hommelette* functions in Spencer's private psychology. An *hommelette* (egg broken and dispersed, treated as an object of desire: that is how the pun works) is what Freud named a fetish. In Lacan's schema it is anything that signals, or arouses, desire. Love, said Lacan, involves another, an Other, and this Other is a person. But human desire is sneaky, inventive, and highly talented. So Lacan recognizes another that is not a person but a dropped handkerchief, a snippet of hair from the beloved's head, or whatever "object-of-desire-with-a-little-o" (*"object-petit-a"*). The first scholar of fetishes was Krafft-Ebing, in whose *Psychopathia Sexualis* we can find an English gentleman who ate guardsmen's socks that had been worn for a month. Spencer is the first major artist to study the *object-petit-a*. His paintings of garbage, of dogs (his symbol for sexual energy), of barnyards of strong odour, are parallel to Joyce's reintroduction of the *inaccrochable* into art. We can see a similar claiming of tabooed subjects in David Jones, where there is an Augustinian insistence on the spirituality of matter however humble. The age-old tension between Gnostic, Manichaean rejection of (or indifference to) the world and Christian acceptance of creation as revelation and extension of God keeps cropping up in the oddest places. It is mildly entertaining to detect it in Roger Fry's Quakerish iconoclasm and in the artists whom Fry made it so difficult for the British to understand: David Jones's inclusion of the pagan in Catholic theology, Spencer's connoisseurship of the malodorous, the sexually eclectic, the total fusion of sacred and profane.

David Jones (1895–1974) and Stanley Spencer (1891–1959) are, for all their differences, spiritual twins, and together constitute a thoroughly British phenomenon: non-modernist modernists. The semantics of this can be made clear. Modernism kept penetrating England all of this century without including the British in the concerns of the great movement, as England had been wholly involved in the previous international style (Beardsley, Charles Rennie Mackintosh, Whistler, Wilde). English-speaking modernists tend not to be British: Joyce, Pound, Eliot, Yeats, Beckett, Wyndham Lewis, Gaudier-Brzeska, Jacob Epstein. Where modernism was imported into England, the influence was timidly imitative, as with Ben Nicholson's cubism, or the toe-in-the-water concessions to modernism of Paul Nash and John Piper.

Jones, poet, prose-writer, painter, engraver, calligrapher, was, like Spencer, a common infantryman in the worst gore of the Great War. The response of each to the war was a masterpiece of British art: Spencer's murals in the chapel at Burghclere, almost the exact equivalent of Jones's *In Parenthesis*, sharing a concern for the quotidian chores of military life, for the suffering of the enlisted man, for the ritualistic aspect of army routine. Neither knows anything of the heroic in official versions of the war, or of the romanticism of Lawrence's *Seven Pillars*, or even of the sentiment of Owen, Sassoon, or Brooke. Jones's favourite tone of the misery of the war is in an anecdote he treasured and frequently told. A mud-caked sergeant in a trench learns that Lord Kitchener had been drowned in the North Sea. " 'E 'as, 'as 'e?" replied the sergeant, "Well, roll on, fuckin' duration!"

What Jones was hearing was a *legionarius* in some Gaulish *castrum* hearing of Caesar's assassination, and genially damning all generals and emperors. He was hearing a trooper in Joshua's army whose feet hurt, who was weary of mule trains and camp grub and the hard desert ground at night. Both Jones and Spencer had their genius centred in an imaginative transparency of history and of ideas. They could collapse time where it suited their aesthetic ends to combine events and essences. Regard the opening of Jones's "The Roman Quarry":

There she blows, there she goes
the old tin tube rings clear
    Back to kip for section six
    The monkey's knackers for section seven.[2]

The diction of this reaches into the parlance of sailors and soldiers, and is grounded in Jones's perception that language encodes every nuance of culture. We are hearing reveille on a bugle, in 1917, in the first century B.C. (Roman soldier in Britain), cockcrow with all its symbolism (Peter's denial, Paul's "last trump"), Spartan trumpets, Roman trumpets at the Feast of the Cleansing of the Weapons on the Field of Mars in Rome (described by Plutarch), Joshua's trumpets, and on and on. We are also looking at a long tradition which flows in its own channel through European art. From the High Middle Ages through the Renaissance, antiquity was helplessly modernized. Shakespeare's Caesar wore trunk hose and doublet, felt hat with feather. There is no visual dimension to Gibbon; his readers would have been dependent on Poussin and the brothers Adam for imagery. With Scott the historical imagination begins to demand authenticities, a taste which reached its fulfilment in Kipling in England and Flaubert in France.

Spencer located the Gospels in Cookham-upon-Thames, and symmetrically clothed Old Testament angels in Edwardian and twentieth-century clothes. Before thinking that we can appreciate (or be offended) by this calculated anachronism, let us notice that the mythologizing of the Gospels began quite early and is by now undetected by most of us. No ox or ass stands in the stable at Christ's birth in the

Gospels; we put them there. The number of the Magi is not in Scripture; we made them three. And so on. Far from leaving tradition, Spencer is deep within many traditions of Christian iconography such as the Dutch tradition of localizing events of the Bible in finely detailed realism (the Annunciation in a Dutch room).

In Parenthesis fuses Malory and World War I battlefields, and discovers the sacramental in the ordinary. *The Anathemata*, a meditation throughout on the Mass, is concerned to find in all art and ritual, from the dawn of time, activities identical with those of the Catholic liturgy. "This thing other" is the phrase Jones uses for man's earliest (and continuing) recognition of the world beyond himself, whether a shard of flint or God. The "thing other" with which man is most involved is language itself, as words are as old as culture. Jones was alerted to his subject by his times. Archaeology (which Penguin Books kept track of) and anthropology made great leaps forward. The discovery and interpretation of prehistoric cave art was largely the work of French priests, and was thus, in a sense, an activity of the church. Psychoanalysis was Jewish and Protestant, but it came into being because of the kind of Angst and insecurity of which the Great War was a magnified example, but which was endemic to urban and unchurched life; it was no great step for David Jones to see two Jewish healers of wounded souls, Freud and Jesus, as in the same business. Art history had become vastly more sophisticated in Jones's time, aided by colour reproductions and slides. Jones's imagination, for these and many other reasons, was acquisitively inclusive, capable of appropriating almost anything.

Joyce inspired him, as did Braque. He admired Picasso, calling him "our Hercules." He liked medieval Latin and Welsh poetry as enthusiastically as he liked bawdy marching songs of the infantry. His ear was tuned to the cockney locution as accurately as it was to turns of phrase in the *Anglo-Saxon Chronicle*. The artist's eye notices, studies, retains. In the composition of a work, details are available that may have lain in waiting for years. In one of Jones's engravings for *The Ancient Mariner* there is a figure seen from the back who has his hand knuckles down on his hip, shoulder raised, elbow bent but in the plane of his body. Jones, talking about this print to Bill Blissett, said that it was a pose he had noticed in a soldier on the western front. Two decades later, he found a use for it in a composition. Clare Leighton once told me that Jones asked to do a watercolour of her humble student's bed-sitter in Kensington when they were both art students. The result was of "a room out of the *Arabian Nights*, or some vision in Revelation, so colourful, light, and airy he had painted it." Anyone who has walked along the Epte at Giverny begins to wonder how such dull, featureless countryside became the landscapes of Monet.

To see the Venus of Willendorf as a primitive fetish is one thing. To see her as one of man's first premonitions of the Virgin, as Jones does in *The Anathemata*, is wholly another. When Fry turned us away from subject matter, he bound off the lifeblood of art. Fry was correct in teaching that art encodes a new sensibility, age after age, and with accumulative effect (so that Poussin is "included in" Cézanne if one is coming to Cézanne ignorant of Poussin, Velazquez in Whistler), but he was wicked to suppose that this sensibility is not more in subject matter than in its treatment. Cézanne does indeed show us a new way of looking at the world, but he also decides what new world we are to see in his new way. "There were no apples before Cézanne."

Both Spencer and Jones give us a new world. Spencer, the more conservative of the two, rethought English art of the previous century. It has been said (by Max Beerbohm, I think) that the aesthetic movement made brick ugly. It is easy to believe that this is true. Spencer was doubtless aware of this shift in aesthetic judgment, and thus became the greatest poet of brick in all art. Brick. Tedious to paint convincingly, a brick wall is nevertheless a pattern captivating to the eye, having something of the primitive love of reticulated patterns (all of France is covered with diamond networks, their equivalent of the Greek key fret, or West African zigzag lines), something of the regularity modernism imposed on industrial design. And yet bricks are Biblical (especially when made without straw), Blakean, Joycean (the *Rosevean*, analog of Odysseus' homing ship, is loaded with English brick). Look at the brick structures in Spencer. They are always demarcations, boundaries. Usually they divide a utopian space in which a world freed from guilt and sin indulges itself in *objets-petits-a* (a woman is made love to by a sunflower while her husband, exempt from jealousy, watches with approval). There are brick enclosures with some mystical meaning, like the one in *The Resurrection in Cookham Churchyard*. A scholar can go a long way into whatever Spencer's passionate meaning may be by following the clue of bricks from painting to painting. A curving brick wall occupies a third of the background in the unfinished *Christ Preaching at the Cookham Regatta*.

And bricks are but one example of a reticulated pattern in Spencer. This pattern has something to do with sexuality in its highest spiritual state, as witness *The Angels of the Apocalypse* (plaids, polka dots, stripes). The dog a boy is kissing in *Sunflower and Dog Worship* is a Dalmatian.

Patterned language is to Jones what visual patterns are to Spencer. From Joyce and Eliot, Jones had come to see that a text can be woven with words and phrases from other languages. He may even have seen, with Joyce's guidance, that these words and phrases are not, ultimately, foreign; not, anyway, to English. At the beginning of *The Anathemata*, the words of the first sentence describe simultaneously man (humankind) learning to make tools, utensils, and figurines like the Willendorf Venus ("this thing other") and a priest preparing the altar for Mass, where "this thing other" refers to the transubstantiation of the host. Both prehistoric toolmaker and priest are making "an efficacious sign."

It was Joyce who returned fully the making of an efficacious sign to art. Art cannot, by its very nature, depart from making a sign. A still life by Chardin, *War and Peace*, a hat—all are signs rich in meaning. Meaning, however, inheres in the maker of the sign, which is why Tolstoy is a great writer, as we say, and Surtees a lesser one. (Jones would not agree, as Surtees is of his *gens*, his folk, and can speak to him with a music and familiar sign absent in Tolstoy.) The meaning of a work of art is efficacious only insofar as its charm (both senses) elicits a response. Thus a new kind of art, like Spencer's and Jones's, must educate an audience before it can communicate. It is significant that after *In Parenthesis*, in which Jones's art appeared mature and in full power (and baffled the readers of books), he turned to a work about the Mass, which historically was attended by Catechumens (learners by ear, being instructed in a mystery). One learns to read *In Parenthesis* by reading *The Anathemata*; there is a sense in which *Finnegans Wake* has taught us how to see the symbolic structure of *Ulysses*, the *Portrait*, and *Dubliners*. The Middle Ages read the Old Testament through the New.

How, then, can we learn to see Spencer? His religious meditation is as rigorous as Jones's. Is he a mystic descending from the heaven-on-earth designers (St.-Simon, Fourier, Mother Ann Lee) with a hope for political reformation? Clearly, his sexual paintings constitute a critique of society as we know it, comically different from D.H. Lawrence's, Ibsen's, or the yeastier psychoanalysts with bees in their bonnets about a society without repressions. Not even Fourier, that most imaginative of Utopians, considered orgies with sunflowers and dogs. A plausible answer might be that he is a disillusioned visionary. Apolitical, but a democrat in the philosophical sense, eccentrically religious, honest, a realist in matters of the flesh, Stanley Spencer was before all else a poet for whom the natural beauty of the world—meadows, gardens, trees in blossom, rivers—was the primary fact. That his gorgeous landscapes sold while his religious and domestic pictures did not must not tempt us into the cynicism of saying that he painted them for a quick pound. These handsome landscapes are as carefully and as lovingly wrought as anything he did.

The landscapes are the base of his statement about the world, for man is part of nature, God's creation. It is God as flesh that Spencer depicted with his most dramatic awe and reverence, Christ in the streets of Cookham, among children, animals, brick, flowers. These paintings are the ones most raked by brilliant light, designed in stunning symmetries.

The religious paintings are also the ones with freedom of movement, an orderly flow of running children or moving figures through a clarity of space. The domestic paintings, by contrast, are claustrophobic, full of people getting in each other's way. The military scenes are similarly congested, like the murals of men working, the resurrections. Even the baptism of Christ is in a crowded swimming pool. The domestic paintings are the most crowded of all, the most awkward. *Christ Preaching* was going to be a very crowded, Bosch-like tangle of people, picnicking, and punts. A great deal of eighteenth-century British humour comes from too many people in a space (Rowlandson, Hogarth, Smollett). This very British theme becomes for Spencer an *objet-petit-a*, an intimacy with gratuitous sensual content (*Domestic Scenes: At the Chest of Drawers, Christmas Stockings, The Dustman or the Lovers*). Carried into the inevitable absurdity of all obsessions, as in visionary paintings such as *Love among the Nations* and *Bridesmaids at Cana*, Spencer's compressing of space reveals its real identity: a cancellation of emotional distance.

Spencer's roadways have neither automobiles nor people on them. There is the occasional vehicle (army trucks, distant boats, punts), but they are shown as having reached a destination. They are arrivals, stationary. The foregrounds of the landscapes are occupied by large, interesting objects. Although his perspectives are deep (the horizon in *The Resurrection in Cookham Churchyard* is a good mile away), Spencer's statement of space is intimate, convivial, sacralized in his peculiar idiom, wherein a pack of dogs sniffing their own and human genitalia is as spiritually charged as St. Francis among Cookham poultry. In *The Resurrection: The Hill of Zion* a man is feeling his nose to see if it is still there, and an angel scratches her thigh. That is Spencer's art: an insistence that the world (not a world created ideally by a choice of attentions) is there.

David Jones in *The Anathemata* creates something like a Spencerian unfolding and conflating of time. The Mass reiterates an event, the Crucifixion, which itself was a repetition (with a new and final victim) of an age-old sacrifice. Jones tells us that his instigation for the poem was in realizing that a British soldier whom he saw on duty in Palestine in the 1930s was in some sense identical to a Roman soldier in the same place in the time of Christ. This kind of historical rhyme is characteristic of modernist art. Pound and Eliot (and Kipling and Doughty before them) saw the two great empires, Roman and British, as a historical recurrence. The idea is throughout Spengler, whom Jones read with interest; and in his friend Christopher Dawson. Joyce's is the most eloquent shaping of this idea.

Space, however, remains a geographical reality in David Jones. If anything, he magnifies its slow distances, as the majestic pace of *The Anathemata* must move Christianity and its enveloping cultures, Greek, Roman, and Syrian, along certain routes, by land, and most lyrically, by sea, to Britain. This poetic act is a redoing of Charles Doughty's *The Dawn in Britain*, for which *The Anathemata* serves as a critique and as a successful rendering of a previous work whose density and solemnity limited it to a small audience. The history of art is rich in such repetitions.

Jones intended to be as British as Doughty, who intended to be as British as Jonson, Chaucer, and Spenser. Traditions keep to their family trees. Jones, for instance, knows that he does not descend through Tennyson, Browning, Shakespeare. He is "matter of Britain" all the way: Welsh, cockney, Catholic, English farmer and shipwright, a northern European who came into a heritage from the Mediterranean (a heritage with religion for its life's-blood). His culture was old when William the Bastard landed at Hastings in 1066. The dialect of Latin that William spoke would overlay English, and English ways, thereafter. A fruitful reading of David Jones is to enter into his exploration of British ways, beliefs, thoughts, manners which eluded the

Normans. In scholarly parlance, David Jones spent his career stripping away the Renaissance, the Age of Reason, and the romantic period to lay bare the England whose invader was not William but Caesar and Claudius, Danes and Norwegians, and the sweetest raptor of them all, the Christians with Greek gospels in their possession.

The distance traversed by Christianity to arrive in Britain was immense. That some Norman lords won a battle against a weary Harold becomes a trivial local event. *The Anathemata* is the great poem it is because of the historical configuration it invents. The past is both nightmare (as Joyce said) and a deposit of meaninglessly spent energies. Historian and artist give it its shape. When Jones was writing *In Parenthesis*, with *The Anathemata* in his head, H.G. Wells was presenting neolithic man as a monster of unrestrained primal passions (and accounting for war by man's inability to civilize those passions). The Hearst Press in the USA was inventing the caveman, grunting brute. Known to a few only, knowledge of Neolithic times was carefully being sorted out by French, British, and German archaeologists. Jones was the first to take up what they had to teach. His neolithic man has now displaced Wells's: the carver of Solutrian flint arrowheads, the painter of Lascaux and some four hundred other caves, a builder of villages, weaver, potter, and theologian.

Jones displaced Pound's periodic history (bursts of energy, "springtimes" in Provence, China, Egypt, Italy, Greece) with a slow, patient, vegetating history, one whose lines of force are all but invisible.

Jones's contemporary Fernand Braudel had the same understanding of history. The time for grass to become wheat eludes the imagination in its awesome length. History is "long durations" and where it seems to introduce a novelty, such as Christianity, or arithmetic in tens, or farming, or the Indo-Iranian languages, we have learned to look again and to recompose our ideas.

The genius of Jones's imagination is that he was willing to believe that Christianity is religion, seamlessly continuous from its beginning we know not when or where. It is a dialect of the one religion; the Catholicism of a Welshman is Catholic but it is also Welsh, very Welsh, and cannot be otherwise, and before it was either Catholic or Welsh it was Roman, Greek, Syrian, on back to the artist-poet-priest who shinnied up the chimney piercing a rock in Southern France from an underground river to a cave overhead, and painted a dancing man wearing an elk hide, with elk horns, and with the genitalia of a panther. The painting (of what? tutelary spirit? god? shaman?) finished, the painter descended the rock chimney, and a band of children went up and danced in a circle in the clay of the cave floor on their heels. This sacred place was then sealed. It was next entered, some twenty thousand years later, when David Jones was on the western front. He knew about it, later, shell-shocked, surviving one depression after another, struggling to be one of these who depict the spirit in its search for form, order, truth, God. (He always said that the bear he drew as a child was his best drawing. The skill of that bear would have qualified him, 20,000 years before, as the elect painter of Elk Man with Lion Sex deep inside caves.)

Modernism has been owned and operated by various groups with their own interests to look after. It is scarcely surprising that two religious artists of the first order have taken far too long to assume their proper place in modern art history. Their seeming eccentricities and radical innovations soon turn out to be solidly within the deepest traditions of British and European poetry and painting. Their work constitutes an occasion for religious art to communicate with the world at large, in its ancient manner; and an occasion for religion to consider the visionary donations of Spencer and Jones. Christianity began as a renewal of the prophetic tradition of God working through man, each godly man closing the distance between God and man (as in Amos's vision), and can only proceed by constant renewal of this awareness and responsibility. That is what Spencer was doing. There is an unfocussed confusion, except to a talented few, in trying to imagine the crucifixion on a hill in Judaea. To imagine it, in all its ugly cruelty, as happening in the familiarity of an English village, is both to renew one of the oldest strategies of European art and to effect what that strategy can accomplish: the vivid and periodically necessary reshaping of the narrative through which Christianity has its life.

David Jones refinds Christianity in history. With inevitable regularity history liquifies and needs rechannelling, while religions petrify, paralysing their spirit in pedantry. The guardians of both must constantly keep history from meaninglessness and religion from the death of its symbols. David Jones's guardianship of both is great and beautiful.

NOTES

1. Roger Fry, "Some Questions in Esthetics," in *Transformations: Critical and Speculative Essays on Art* (London: Chatto and Windus, 1926), 27.

2. David Jones, *The Roman Quarry and Other Sequences*, ed. Harman Grisewood and René Hague (London: Agenda Editions, 1981), 3.

H.D.'S *TRILOGY* AND THE POETICS OF PASSAGE

Thomas R. Whitaker

When Wallace Stevens placed a jar in Tennessee,

> The wilderness rose up to it,
> And sprawled around, no longer wild.

So every figure tames its ground. And so, as "Anecdote of a Jar" also reminds us, the figure now stands out with a fresh clarity of form:

> The jar was round upon the ground
> The tall and of a port in air.[1]

If we place H.D.'s *Trilogy*, her "tale of a jar or jars,"[2] in the wilderness or wildness of its transgeneric context, we may observe similar effects, even though figure and ground are here not starkly opposed but richly in converse. And this placing may also show us how H.D.'s artifact, like many that have been imagined by Stevens and other modern poets, celebrates through its form an immanent and world-ordering power that it can never adequately name, "the Genius in the jar" (*CP*, 515).

The wildness with which we must cope is evident enough as soon as we ask: On what ground should we place these three books of forty-three poems each? Hoping perhaps to acknowledge the work's serial composition, improvisatory movement, and mixed style, we may call it a "modern long poem" or "modern poetic sequence." But what genre are we invoking? If the modern long poem or poetic sequence is as open and self-revising, as genuinely wild, as its major writers have suggested, we can hardly expect to snare it in our usual descriptions. We may seek it with thimbles, seek it with care, and pursue it with forks and hope; but, as in Lewis Carroll's allegory of methodological failure, we will find that our Snark has the dissolvent power of a Boojum.

We have been warned. According to William Carlos Williams, all poetry is "a supersession...not surpassing rules but disintegrating them." *Paterson* is therefore, among other things, "a plan for action to supplant a plan for action;...a dispersal and a metamorphosis." According to Hart Crane, every poem is a "new word" or a voyage toward "New Thresholds, new anatomies!" *The Bridge*—"a symbol of all such poetry as I am interested in writing"—is therefore a "teeming span" or "passage to the Chan" that seems repeatedly to dissolve in mid-leap. According to Wallace Stevens, poetry names "something that never could be named," engages "the difficulty of what it is to be," and leads through "ghostlier demarcations" toward "fragant portals." Ezra Pound's voyage into the unknown required in the *Cantos* a descent into hell, a continuing project of translation, and a breaking on unpredictable rocks. David Jones, who celebrated an infinite mystery of transformation, began *The Anathemata* with this sentence: "We already and first of all discern him making this thing other." T.S. Eliot declared in *Little Gidding*: "Every phrase and every sentence is an end and a beginning."[3] And the poet who had once let Pound sign her manuscript of "Hermes of the Ways" with the name "H.D. Imagiste" was able to confess, three decades later, that her poems had often expressed an

> invasion of the over-soul into a cup
> too brittle, a jar too circumscribed,
>
> a little too porous to contain the out-flowing
> of water-about-to-be-changed-to-wine
>
> at the wedding...
>
> (*CP*, 534)

In those phrases H.D. takes W.B. Yeats's critique of Pound's *vers libre*—"one gets an impression...that he has not got all the wine into the bowl"[4]—toward an ontology of continual metamorphosis.

The Walls Do Not Fall, the wartime book that offers this confession, was composed during the same year in which Eliot's *Little Gidding* was completed and published in the *New England Weekly*.[5] And it just as firmly commits itself to the inherence of a beginning in every end, an end in every beginning. In doing so, it resolutely moves beyond all inadequate cups and jars. It starts, indeed, by evoking a London ruin that

leaves the sealed room
open to the air,

(*CP*, 509)

a destruction that portends inspiration. And it proceeds to enact a meandering exodus from many images of closure. If it repeatedly attempts to celebrate the Word or the "Christos-image" (*CP*, 525), it does so with no firm bearings. And it arrives at a final assertion of exploratory ignorance—

we know no rule
of procedure,
we are voyagers, discovers
of the not-known,

the unrecorded;
we have no map;

—that can allude to the securities of Hopkins's nun in "Heaven-Haven" only by denying their certainty:

possibly we will reach haven,
heaven.

(*CP*, 543)

That end soon became another beginning, the epigraph for *Tribute to the Angels*, a book that is in part a re-vision of the making of all things new that had been envisioned in *The Revelation of St. John the Divine*. And the more confident but still open ending of the second book—

...pause to give
thanks that we rise again from death and live
(*CP*, 577)

—in turn became the epigraph for *The Flowering of the Rod*. In these two books the probing of images and names gathers coherence, the "jar" returns as an image of containment, and the writing finally commits itself to didactic narrative. Nevertheless, the "jar" remains as fragrantly open as it is hermetically closed, the narrative leads to images of circularity or riddling reciprocity, and the teaching remains free of conceptual finalities. Although *The Flowering of the Rod* can say that "in resurrection, there is simple affirmation" (*CP*, 579), its affirmations are mythopoeic encounters with signs that must always remain open to further interpretation. That is why this book must also say: "resurrection is a sense of direction" (*CP*, 583).

Such a commitment to hermeneutic openness will turn any long poem or poetic sequence into a hieroglyph of life in transit. Perhaps at some level writing is always such a hieroglyph, inviting us to imagine further translations of its own metamorphosis. But when this process controls a work's major form, it acts to dissolve our definitions of genre, of literature, and even of ourselves and our world. "The goal," as Williams has said, "is to keep a beleaguered line of understanding which has movement from breaking down and becoming a hole into which we sink decoratively to rest."[6] Though we try to domesticate such writing, we can hardly cope with its most evident signs of diversity. *The Bridge* seems closed and chiastic in form, while the *Cantos* are open and incomplete, and *Paterson* breaks out of its four-book cycle into a new openness. *Notes Toward a Supreme Fiction* constructs, deconstructs, and reconstructs itself repeatedly within a numerically plotted series; *The Anathemata* shapes its inventory of historical deposits through something like classical ring-composition; and *Four Quartets* develops a complex and echoing symmetry. Whatever generic definition we propose, we risk depriving these loose and baggy but often strangely symmetrical creatures of their organs of motion or perception in order to fit them into our box.

Even the account offered by M.L. Rosenthal and Sally Gall of the "modern poetic sequence," which they regard as the "genius of modern poetry," sets before us too brittle, circumscribed, and porous a container. For Rosenthal and Gall, "poetic sequences" are essentially sequences of "affects" that move toward "the chief end of lyric poetry," an "equilibrium" among their "volatile possibilities."[7] But this is to favour the lyric over the narrative, mythopoeic, and didactic modes, even in works that invoke the tradition of visionary epic that runs from Dante, Spenser, and Milton on through Blake, Wordsworth, and Whitman to our own time. And it is to favour "feeling" over Williams's "beleaguered line of understanding" or H.D.'s "sense of direction"—the affective over the cognitive or hermeneutic. Such a theory, in harmony with Poe's animadversions against the long poem and with the early Pound's anti-Victorianism, can support brilliant readings of certain aspects of *The Waste Land*, the *Cantos*, or *Paterson*. But it often requires us to carve out from a "series" its "organic sequences," and it cannot illuminate the forms of *The Anathemata* and *Notes Toward a Supreme Fiction* or show *Trilogy* to be more than the self-indulgent mixture of modes that some admirers of H.D., Imagiste, have imagined it to be.[8]

All of these works, though informed with feeling, are essentially projects of interpretation. And, in their self-reflexive shaping, they become expressive and imitative signs of just such an undertaking. They ask us to participate in exploratory, mediating, and constitutive acts that may render any notion of "poetry" suspect, "a way of putting it—not very satisfactory."[9] David Jones therefore called himself a "sign-maker" and *The Anathemata* "fragments of an attempted writing." Williams saw in the early *Cantos* "poetry as I understand it"—"daring thought toward a constructive understanding of human destiny." Eliot came to imagine poetry "so transparent that we should not see the poetry, but that which we are meant to see through" it, a writing that gets "*beyond poetry*" as the later Beethoven "strove to get *beyond music*." And

Stevens could suggest that his "endlessly elaborating poem" points toward the possibility of yet

> Subtler, more urgent proof that the theory
> Of poetry is the theory of life,
>
> As it is, in the intricate evasions of as....[10]

H.D. therefore risks in *Trilogy* a style of expository plainness:

> This search for historical parallels,
> research into psychic affinities,
>
> has been done to death before,
> will be done again;
>
> no comment can alter spiritual realities
> (you say) or again,
>
> what new light can you possibly
> throw upon them?

And in her response to that question she can risk banality:

> ... my mind (yours)
> has its peculiar ego-centric
>
> personal approach
> to the eternal realities...
>
> (*CP*, 539–540)

Such language, however, might not surprise or dismay the nineteenth-century ancestor of all these poets-beyond-poetry, who said in *A Backward Glance O'er Travel'd Roads*: "No one will get at my verses who insists on viewing them as a literary performance, or attempt at such performance, or as aiming mainly towards art or aestheticism." Indeed, these modern long poems or poetic sequences are quite evidently instances of the transgeneric enterprise that Whitman called an experimental "sortie" in a "field of aim and escape and construction."[11] As such, they are analogous and even complementary. Each begins "searchingly, with what's to hand," as David Jones has put it,[12] in a situation of adversity. Their hermeneutic quests engage our loss of accepted definitions of self and world, our perplexity in the face of knowledge too great for any system, and our understanding of language as a problematic act of mediation. They must therefore become trajectories of interpretation that make heuristic use of many tropes, myths, and modes of discourse as they call in question our assumptions about literary genres, separate selves, external objects, or the ground of experience. Despite many reasons for doubt, each work remains convinced that it speaks with or among us toward some undisclosed verity. Indeed, each enacts a primary allegiance to what even the sceptical Stevens could call "the bread of faithful speech."[13] Their forms are consequently intensified versions of the dialogical process that shapes our life. ("That would be a writing," said Williams, "in which the conversation was actual to the extent that it would be pure design."[14]) Admitting that all knowledge is mediated by interpretation, and understanding interpretation to be a potentially endless process carried out by a community whose members are themselves functions of that process, these works must remake their speech from moment to moment and shape designs that enable us to share in that remaking. In doing so, each develops its own version of a poetics of passage.

As some titles strongly suggest—Conrad Aiken's *The Divine Pilgrim*, for example, or Robert Duncan's *Passages*—these works are quite personal passages to more than India. They are approaches to the universal field of conversation or the global city that both Crane and H.D. could call Atlantis. Each is engaged in a continual probing of its own enabling conditions and a continual attempt to discover and articulate its immanent end. For each, as Duncan put it in "Towards an Open Universe," both "consciousness" and "the poem" come to us in "a dancing organization between personal and cosmic identity."[15] They must therefore chart circuitous paths from the object-world of common sense toward the adumbration in every poetic act of what, according to their preferred tropes, they must imagine as the absolute Word, Act, Light, Music, or Self in which we participate. Each is therefore also poetry as Gary Snyder has defined it in *Myths and Texts*: "a riprap on the slick rock of metaphysics."[16] Through what Jones calls "hidden grammar" and Crane a "pervasive Paradigm" they celebrate the ground of their own language.[17]

As each work must recognize, however, such riprap is never enough to enable a scaling of the ontological mountain. Finite speech can never adequately focus or name either its immediate speaking subject or its ultimate source. Whenever these works point to their immanent but finally untranslatable source, they must offer some version of Whitman's closing challenge: "You will hardly know who I am or what I mean.... / Missing me one place search another, / I stop somewhere waiting for you."[18] That is why these hermeneutic trajectories, these dances toward and around the hidden principle of a necessarily figurative world, must be broken shapes. And that is why we can discern in them three major traits. In its temporal movement, each work renders the trace of an unfinished interpretive quest. But that quest repeatedly discovers tropes that point beyond any temporal sequence toward an immanent source and end. And, when completed and viewed in its completion, the work emerges as a quasi-spatial or synchronic form oriented toward these tropes and seeking harmony with their implications—in effect a labyrinthine icon of an imperfectly apprehended *telos*. *The Bridge* forges a chain of tropes for its Vision-of-the-Voyage, the metaphorical and cosmic principle of "bridging." It must break off with a question and "whispers antiphonal."

But its chiastic form emerges as an icon of "one arc synoptic of all tides below," the "pervasive Paradigm" of "Love." The *Cantos* compose a thesaurus of tropes for their goal, the city or principle of intellectual "light." They must admit that "Le Paradis" exists only in fragments, and must therefore define themselves at last, "a little light, like a rushlight / to lead back to splendour." But they also become a "palimpsest" shot through with distinctions in "*claritas*" and finally "*caritas*," pointing toward the Neoplatonic "crystal jet" or "rain" of light that images their end. *Notes Toward a Supreme Fiction* must engage ever fresh tropes for its informing agency, the principle of naming. It avoids closure at last with a proleptic naming of a revolving and crystalline "mundo" that is always a "change not quite completed." But despite its discontinuities, the work emerges as a symmetrical icon that points toward the nameless—from its opening apostrophe ("And for what, except for you, do I feel love?") through its wry fictions of an absolute ("Logos and logic, crystal hypothesis") to its almost sacramental "bread of faithful speech."[19]

In analogous ways, *Four Quartets* moves through its continually redefined moments toward a fuller understanding of "one end, which is always present." It must close with a proleptic gesture toward ultimate knowledge. But through its emergent symmetries, it becomes itself a "Chinese jar" that "moves perpetually in its stillness." *Paterson* moves through its various blockages toward a principle that hides in all its central tropes: beauty, radiance, love, play, flowering, and dance. It must end with the assertion that "we know nothing and can know nothing. / but / the dance." But its synchronic form, answering the world of experience with that of art, finally celebrates that principle by enacting against "a millefleurs background" its own version of the "secret world, / a sphere, a snake with its tail in / its mouth." And *The Anathemata*, moving through the prehistory and history of making and naming, finds everywhere tropes that expand the implications of the Roman Mass. It ends with a gesture toward infinite transmutation, a historical action that is a revolving upon the Axile Tree. But its labyrinthine trace finally declares itself an instance of the sacred dance, a chiastic image of the cave or temple that houses a principle beyond all making and naming, "HE-WITH-US," who said, "I am your Bread."[20]

In *Trilogy*, too, we may discern these three traits, these ways in which a shimmering display of signs declares itself in the service of what must remain beyond all signs. The work moves searchingly from war-blasted London through hermetic redefinitions of its names and images toward a figuring of its Atlantis as a Lady whose "book is our book," and whose gift—both given and received—is a fragrance "as of all flowering things together" (*CP*, 571, 612). Like Whitman's "I," Jones's "he," or Williams's Paterson, the "she" of H.D.'s "unwritten volume of the new" (*CP*, 570) has no single form or simple location. She is a trope that helps to convey an endlessly reflexive vision of the nameless power on which the act of poetry must found itself—"the Genius in the jar" (*CP*, 515). But as an emergent synchronic form, *Trilogy* reads its own "palimpsests" or "hieroglyphs" as a "mariner's map," opens up its words like "little boxes," and retrospectively discloses behind its quest the fragrant and rainbow principle of Love (*CP*, 512, 533, 607, 540, 612). A somewhat closer look at this figure that we have now placed in the wilderness or wildness of its transgeneric context may enable its distinctive form to stand out with fresh clarity.

In the "maplessness" of *The Walls Do Not Fall*, where ruin "leaves the sealed room / open to the air," we already find that "shivering overtakes us, / as of old, Samuel" (*CP*, 509, 510). A bit later H.D. can say:

...gods have been smashed before

and idols and their secret is stored
in man's very speech...
(*CP*, 517)

That secret opens onto the universe. The strange etymologizing and punning, the repeated probing of images, the understanding of the Holy Ghost as "the Dream" or the "go-between, interpreter," who "follows the Mage / in the desert," and the readiness to invoke the stars ("little jars of that indisputable / and absolute Healer") as presences that

will reveal their individual fragrance,
personal magnetic influence,

become, as they once were,
personified messengers

—these all follow not just from H.D.'s hermetic definitions but from the many-sided hermeneutic endeavour that she shares with other major poets of the century (*CP*, 526, 528–29).

Tribute to the Angels proceeds to converse with these and other hints. It draws those stars nearer by something like the Kabbalistic process that enables the soul to ascend through the spheres of planet-angels to its divine home in the fullness of God's light. But that meditation on names, that verbal alchemy, correlated here with a revisionary conversation with *Revelation*, approaches a "fragrance" or "quality / for which there is no name." And it is also interrupted by utterance from other realms: a meeting with "a charred tree" that is "stricken to the heart" and that discloses itself to be "a half-burnt-out apple tree / blossoming," and a lunar dream of a Lady who also resists the traditional process of naming by conventional attributes and whose book may contain "the blank pages / of the unwritten volume of the new" (*CP*, 554, 555, 558, 561, 566–67, 570). These too must be addressed and reinterpreted. Gradually the journey toward that "point in the spectrum / where all lights become one" (*CP*, 573) is acquiring its own provisional maps; and as it does so, its narrative coherence increases.

In *The Flowering of the Rod*, after a preliminary evocation of the wild-goose flight toward "what men say is-not," the entire work discloses itself to be a multi-perspectived anecdote not of a jar but of "the Genius in the jar / which the Fisherman finds" (*CP*, 579–82, 515). Already evoked in *The Walls Do Not Fall* (with its references to "jars," "shells," "little boxes," "sealed room," and "shrine," and to the "shell" or "urn" of the "heart" that contains a seed or savour of fragrance) and in *Tribute to the Angels* (where jars become planetary messengers and the book of Our Lady or Psyche contains written or unwritten pages that will reveal "a tale of a jar or jars") this motif is now explored again in a narrative about the "Mage, / bringing myrrh," who had earlier been named the "new Master" of Love (*CP*, 515, 528, 512–13, 521, 524, 509, 540, 531, 571, 515, 514). We begin to see that resurrection must indeed be a "sense of direction" precisely because every act of interpretation is tacitly oriented toward a hidden goal in which it already participates—whether that goal be evoked as "food, shelter, fragrance / of myrrh and balm," or "the lost centre-island, Atlantis" (*CP*, 583, 601). The journey of interpretation must therefore unfold, by an unpredictable and conversational route, the secret meanings of its very first images. As it does so, the spiralling progress tends to become an icon of infinitely reflecting circularity.

The temporal end of such a trajectory of interpretation, however, must always be something like Crane's "whispers antiphonal," Stevens's speech to a "fluent mundo," Eliot's memory of a hidden waterfall and children in an apple tree "heard, half-heard, in the stillness," Williams's "dance to a measure," or Pound's "rushlight / to lead back to splendour." It must be a prophetic and conversational image of a finality never attainable within "conversation as design." So it is in *Trilogy*, according to its "peculiar egocentric / approach / to the eternal realities." *The Flowering of the Rod* shifts into the mode of a glossed apocryphal narrative, which presents the story of how Mary of Magdala (here speculatively identified with Mary of Bethany and already associated with the Mary who bore a Son and wept bitterly) came to request from a merchant a jar of myrrh (or perhaps spikenard, for the contents remain uncertain) which she would use to anoint the head of Jesus. During this encounter with Mary, the merchant, identified as Kaspar the Mage, has within two half-seconds some experiences that take him through spiralling primordial echoes and circles of apocalyptic vision to what seems the very heart of the cosmos. The narrative continues however, by giving us three signs that we confront a hermeneutic "not yet"—a threshold or portal that must lead toward some interpretation that lies beyond the finitude of our quest.

The first sign consists of a crucial gap in the narrative, over which the discourse repeatedly leaps. We can never see the precise manner in which Kaspar responded to Mary's request by giving her the second of his two jars:

...all we know is,
the myrrh or the *spikenard, very costly*, was Kaspar's,

all we know is that it was all so very soon over,
the feasting, the laughter.
(CP, 604)

The fragrance requested by the Magdalene and given in tribute to the Incarnate Word remains mysterious in its provenance and, though ever-appearing, transient in each appearance.

The second sign of the hermeneutic "not yet" amplifies Kaspar's experience of that truth after Mary closes the door behind her. It consists of his swift return to our ordinary state of baffled but pregnant vision:

and the door shut, and there was the flat door

at which he stared and stared,
as if the line of wood, the rough edge

or the polished surface or plain,
were each significant, as if each scratch and mark

were hieroglyph, a parchment of incredible worth or a mariner's map.
(CP, 607)

And the third sign, with which *Trilogy* ends, is Kaspar's memory of an earlier "fragrant portal" or gesture toward the leaves of grass under our boot-soles, which now brings together our ignorance and our tacit knowledge, our "maplessness" and our immersion in a signifying world that always draws us toward a prolific secret that we somehow already contain and inhabit. This sign gives us Kaspar's interpretation, necessarily partial and conjectural, of the response of the earlier Mary who in Bethlehem had accepted for her son the first of Kaspar's two jars. In this memory Kaspar meets again, now in her most innocent manifestation, the Lady whom *Trilogy* has invoked as the bitterness of *marah* and *mar*, the passion of the Magdalene, the power of the Great Mother of pagan lore, and also that Psyche who is both she-who-must-be-interpreted and, in effect, the muse of interpretation. Now as the Mary of youthful grace, she seems to detect a fragrance emanating from Kaspar's sealed jar:

she said, Sir, it is a most beautiful fragrance,
as of all flowering things together;

but Kaspar knew the seal of the jar was unbroken.
he did not know whether she knew

the fragrance came from the bundle of myrrh
she held in her arms.

(*CP*, 612)

Whether her interpretation is a human mistake, a supernatural intuition, or a spontaneous poetic act, it points—by way of Kaspar's own interpretation—toward the hidden androgynous centre of a fragrant and echoing world. For Kaspar, the new-born son she holds in her arms is itself the "myrrh" that the etymological punning of *Trilogy* has disclosed as the female source of all fragrance that draws us toward a One that we can never name.

This hermeneutic threshold unveils and at once reveils the generative and directive power of the Genius in the jar. It recalls many previous instances of such fragrance, including that emanating from that "quality / for which there is no name" *(CP*, 555). As a flowering of the fragrant "ultimate grain" dropped into the urn of the heart by the *bennu* bird (*CP*, 529–530), a flowering of the Caduceus and the Rood (*CP*, 512, 561), it joins the two Marys, the two jars, the beginning and the end. For the woman born in Bethlehem, Pennsylvania, and writing these lines in London, England, this moment of reflective figuration names the ever-present end and beginning of a passage that is not merely "lyric" or "literary." But if the "Genius of modern poetry" is at work in her "tale of a jar or jars," we must surely find it in the poetics of passage that brings us with her to this threshold.

NOTES

1. Wallace Stevens, "Anecdote of the Jar," *Collected Poems* (New York: Knopf, 1967), 76.

2. H.D., *Collected Poems, 1912–1944*, ed. Louis L. Martz (New York: New Directions, 1983), 571. This work is hereafter cited in the text as *CP*.

3. William Carlos Williams, *Selected Letters* (New York: McDowell, Obolensky, 1957), 133; Williams, *Paterson* (New York: New Directions, 1963), 2; Hart Crane, *The Complete Poems and Selected Letters and Prose*, ed. Brom Weber (Garden City, N.Y.: Doubleday, 1966), 221, 24, 232, 51; Stevens, *Collected Poems*, 381, 130; David Jones, *The Anathemata* (London: Faber and Faber, 1952), 49; T.S. Eliot, *Collected Poems and Plays* (London: Faber and Faber, 1969) 197.

4. W.B. Yeats, "Introduction," *The Oxford Book of Modern Verse* (New York: Oxford Univ. Press, 1937), xxvi.

5. See Peter Ackroyd, *T.S. Eliot* (New York: Simon and Schuster, 1984), 266. *Little Gidding* appeared in October. Sections from *The Walls Do Not Fall* (then called *The Coming One*) appeared in *Life and Letters Today*, 33 (April 1942): 42–45, and also in 35 (October 1942): 17–18, and in 35 (November 1942): 87–88.

6. Williams, *Selected Essays* (New York: Random House, 1954), 118.

7. See M.L. Rosenthal and Sally M. Gall, *The Modern Poetic Sequence: The Genius of Modern Poetry* (New York: Oxford Univ. Press, 1983), 6–18.

8. Rosenthal and Gall's dismissive treatments of Jones, Stevens, and H.D. (298–99, 361, 478) and their strictures concerning *The Bridge* and *Four Quartets* (315–323, 183) demonstrate the limitations of their criteria.

9. Eliot, *Collected Poems and Plays*, 179.

10. Jones, *The Anathemata*, 23, 3; Williams, *Selected Essays*, 167; Eliot as quoted by F.O. Matthiessen, *The Achievement of T.S. Eliot* (New York: Oxford Univ. Press, 1958), 90; Stevens, *Collected Poems*, 486.

11. Walt Whitman, *Leaves of Grass and Selected Prose*, ed. Sculley Bradley (New York: Holt, Rinehart, Winston, 1949), 486–87, 474.

12. Jones, *The Sleeping Lord* (London: Faber and Faber, 1974), 60.

13. Stevens, *Collected Poems*, 408.

14. Williams, *Imaginations* (New York: New Directions, 1970), 286.

15. Robert Duncan, *Fictive Certainties* (New York: New Directions, 1985), 78.

16. Gary Snyder, *Myths and Texts* (New York: Totem Press, 1960), 43.

17. Jones, *The Sleeping Lord*, 16; Crane, *The Complete Poems and Selected Letters and Prose*, 115.

18. Whitman, *Leaves of Grass and Selected Prose*, 77.

19. Crane, *The Complete Poems and Selected Letters and Prose*, 117, 114, 115; Pound, *The Cantos*, 797, 449, 501, 620, 795; Stevens, *Collected Poems*, 406–7, 380, 387, 408.

20. Eliot, *Collected Poems and Plays*, 171, 175; Williams, *Paterson*, 239, 231, 214; Jones, *The Anathemata*, 244, 75, 82. For the capitalization of "HE-WITH-US" see Jones's letter of 29 December 1952 to Desmond Chute, in *Inner Necessities*, ed. Thomas Dilworth (Toronto: Anson-Cartwright, 1984), 29.

THE HIGH MODERNISM OF F.T. PRINCE

Michael Kirkham

Academic criticism for the most part deals with works or authors of established reputation. With modern or contemporary literature, however, a critic has the opportunity—I would rather say the privilege—of opposing the vagaries of literary fashion and contributing, however slightly, to the reformation of current taste. One of the more obviously useful services a critic may perform, both for the writer and for the qualified readers most likely to appreciate him, is the promotion of unrecognized or sparsely recognized literary excellence.

Prince had published two volumes of poetry, *Poems* (1938) and *Soldiers Bathing* (1954), when in 1956 Donald Davie, quoting extensively from one of the poems, "Epistle to a Patron," spoke of him as a "most unjustly neglected contemporary."[1] The continuing neglect and the injustice of it are more glaringly evident now that we have the *Collected Poems* (1979), and since then another volume, *Later On* (1983), with the proof they contain that indeed much of his best work was written in the thirty years that have elapsed since Davie made his protest.

Michael Roberts, reviewing his first book in 1938, was perceptive: "the poems of Mr. Prince...represent the direction in which poetry seemed to be moving before the incursion of W.H. Auden and Stephen Spender."[2] For Prince was then and has remained a poet of what David Perkins has called "the high Modernist mode."[3] This means that among twentieth-century poets in English, Pound, Eliot and the later Yeats are his exemplars; there are also French influences. It may suggest a partial explanation for Prince's literary loneliness then and since. If he was untouched by what might be called the "low" modernism of Auden and MacNeice (Spender seems now beside the point), he has been equally immune to the persuasions of succeeding collective poetic fashions. Eliot's definition of tradition, his notion of a European mind, the doctrine of impersonality, and his version of a literary formalism first propounded by the English aesthetes in the 1880s and 1890s would seem to be the chief theoretical influences upon Prince's conception of his poetic aims. The poet, he might say, labours not to express himself, but to continue and add to a literary and cultural tradition. The "classical" view of form and convention is central; only by putting his individuality at the service of literary form can the poet hope to exceed himself and achieve impersonal, or transpersonal, expression. Prince's verse invariably keeps a formal distance between words and experience, poet and reader. Very occasionally his early poems have indeed an air of *fin de siècle* dandyism and a certain preciosity of phrasing.

Although he shares the alienation and aloofness of Pound and Eliot from the modern world, Prince has, unlike them, almost entirely avoided direct treatment of twentieth-century history and of personal or everyday experience. Michael Roberts doubted Prince's "ability to deal directly with actual and important experience,"[4] by which he seems to mean the personal and the topical (Prince's *Poems* appeared in the same year as MacNeice's *Autumn Journal*). But do these categories comprise all that we mean by the actual and the important? It is dangerous to lay down rules for what poetry must be. All that is certain is that the exclusion of the directly personal and the circumstances of contemporary life has been in Prince's case a necessary condition of some fine and ambitious poems. In his recourse to the past for models of style, manners, feeling and conduct, Pound has evidently been his guide, notably in Prince's longer dramatic monologues and portraits. Together these poems cover a wide range of experience. In the first person monologues we have the meditations, among others, of Edmund Burke, Henry James, Michelangelo, Gregory Nazianzen (a fourth-century bishop), and Campanella (a Christian Platonist of the sixteenth century). The third person portraits, more elaborate constructions and mainly of a later date, include "Strafford...," "Drypoints of the Hasidim...," a composite picture of a cultural milieu, "Afterword on Rupert Brooke," "A Last Attachment" (between Laurence Sterne and Eliza Draper). Even in the portraits, in which description and exposition play a part, the method is essentially dramatic: as the monologues take us into the inner conflicts of their speakers, so in the portraits we share the tension between viewpoints in the mind of the poet-historian interweaving fact and comment. Yet it is also true to say that these characters—complex, three-dimensional creations—are offered as images of nobility, sometimes tragic nobility, chosen to display in Jamesian fashion the workings of exceptional moral sensibility. It is hardly necessary to insist that, far from diminishing the actuality and importance of what they think, feel, suffer and perform, it is their exceptional self-knowledge, honesty, insight and dedication, their capacity to register the depths and nuances of their experience, that give it a wider human representativeness.

Many of the shorter poems, though less complex in attitude and organization, have a similar purpose. Prince has, for example, drawn on medieval French poetry for models of spiritual tone. "Les Congés du Lépreux," indebted for the general situation and a few details to a much longer poem of the early thirteenth century by Jean Bodel, is the poet's valediction on contracting leprosy; it may be regarded, however, as a demonstration of what is meant by "courtesy," a quality of tone and behaviour in which manners are the social reflection of a spiritual state. To those friends who have forgotten him he speaks with simple dignity and sweetness, blending sorrow with gratitude, pain with acceptance; though he distinguishes them from those who have tended him in his sickness, he remembers that

> They relieved my body once,
> And gave it pleasure in their hour,
> And the body I renounce,
> But I would not be rude or sour.

Poems such as this exemplify two kinds of distancing procedure. Not only does the poet take on the sensibility of another age but also the period styles and voices he has chosen to imitate themselves generalize, or depersonalize, personal feeling. He addresses "One who taught me how to write":

> What he taught me, now I find
> Serviceable to my pain,
> So beyond my scabby rind
> I touch his friendship yet again.
> Now there's nothing sweet or sound
> Left about me, but my heart,
> Sorrow, as you go your round,
> Give him that, and so depart.

This has an equitable tone that keeps moral proportion, tempering poignant feeling with a sort of practical reasonableness (the restraint of self-pity in "serviceable" is, indeed, shocking in its reasonableness). The distinction of such style is that it can express extreme emotion with almost vulnerable directness but without losing robust and judicious self-control. It is partly the effect of a rich traditional vocabulary: "nothing sweet or sound," juggling physical and moral meanings, poised between physical revulsion and a nostalgia for virtue, is personal confession purged of self-absorption.

Hints for other styles are taken from the sixteenth and seventeenth centuries. In his superb study, *The Italian Element in Milton's Verse* (1954), Prince analyzes with precision and sensitivity the prosody and diction of those Italian poets who in the sixteenth century created a tradition of heroic poetry and an epic "magnificence" of style, and traces their influence upon Milton. A deliberate cultivation of surface complexity by these poets, an intricate word-order delaying and obscuring the sense, was intended to produce "an impression of rigour and tension, even where the thought is not in itself difficult." While not sounding like either Milton or his mentors, in some of his poems Prince has by complication of syntax and verbal puzzles similarly contrived "a language of sublimated emotion and intellectual excitement." These are the opening lines of "To a Friend on his Marriage":

> A beautiful girl said something in your praise.
> And either because in a hundred ways
> I had heard of her great worth and had no doubt
> To find her lovelier than I thought
> And found her also cleverer, or because
> Although she had known you well it was
> For her too as it had once been for me
> Thinking of her: I thought that she
> Had spoken of you as rare and legendary.

By the suspension of the sense through the long second sentence and the riddling convolution of the thought, the sequence of anticipation, frustration, consummation, and release into the serenity of the main clause builds up in the reader a feeling of breathless, marvelling admiration equivalent to that expressed with playful extravagance in the concluding statement. The method derives from the Renaissance school of "magnificence," but the calculated awkwardness of syntax and movement is contemporary; the plain courtliness of speech suggests less the seventeenth century than a collaboration between Henry James and, in the stylized diction ("beautiful girl," "great worth"), Yeats. Other poems adapt the rhetoric—extended conceits and intellectual play—of the "wit" writers, Elizabethan and metaphysical. Donne presides over the best of them: "The Book" explores with Donne's mixture of impudent hyperbole and solemnity, lucidity and surprise, the part played by the visible book of the body in bringing us to the soul's truth; "The Question," with a hauntingly subtle music and grave punning, wonderingly questions the relationship of the ideal of love ("The thing we know of but we do not know") to the fact and of human love and mortality to the love of God.

These personae, voices and stylizations of speech are, as I have said, embodied ideals of moral sensibility; but also of course they mediate the poet's own sensibility, supplying analogues for his mental life. The situations in Prince's poetry are varied in period and details, in tone and style, but, as in any serious literary artist, we find recurrent patterns of experience. An obsessive theme throughout his work is the tension between soul and body, sometimes explicit, often latent in the pervasive imagery of light and dark. Theme and imagery disclose a unifying personal presence and charge of feeling in poems which in subject-matter are far removed from the circumstances of the twentieth-century public world and the poet's private life. "Soldiers Bathing," his best-known poem, a meditation on this theme arising out of his experiences as an officer in the war, is the one exception, betraying in places an uncharacteristic uncertainty of tone. "The Old Age of Michelangelo" explores the conflict of flesh and spirit in the artist's life and its consequence for his work.

"Campanella" exposes a Christian Platonist's view of the same division, but is centrally concerned with the related issue of unworldliness and otherworldliness in the motivations of a political idealist and activist. "Gregory Nazianzen," reflections of a natural recluse reluctantly embroiled in the violent doctrinal and ecclesiastical disputes of the early Greek church, dramatizes the conflict between the need for contemplative withdrawal and the world's demands for action. "Strafford" examines—in a very different situation, the struggle between Charles I and his Parliament that led to Strafford's execution and the Civil War—the internecine relations of mind and body and the question of worldly and unworldly motivations in the actions and statements of this wilful, proud, dedicated servant of an unworthy, indecisive king. The list could be extended. The principle informing the composition of all of them is that identified by Pound when he said that his "Homage to Sextus Propertius" "presents certain emotions as vital to me in 1917...as they were to Propertius some centuries earlier."[5] (I have omitted Pound's extension of the comparison to include the poet's respective historical situations, since such parallels do not enter directly into Prince's poetry). Yet the personal engagement that directs and concentrates these poems is entirely submerged in the historical facts. "Strafford" and "Drypoints of the Hasidim," vignettes and impressions of the East European Hasidic Jews and their beliefs—to take two of Prince's finest poems based on extensive reading—are, though imaginative studies of their subjects, faithful reconstructions and plausible interpretations, which any scholar or historian might consult. A distinction should be drawn. The characters are not alternative selves, the dramatic meditations are not means of vicarious self-expression: each portrait or impersonation constitutes an opportunity to explore for its own sake a situation into which temperament and experience have given the poet sympathetic insight but which in externals is far from his own situaton. The relation between poet and the past is reciprocal: if the individual brings feeling and insight to history, history in return enlarges the individual's humanity.

Prince writes from within a Christian tradition; it is a Christian intuition that senses a religious dimension in all experience, frequently imaged as a quality of light. Many of his love poems are tinged with a "glimmering" (his word) awareness of the divine in human love. More striking perhaps is his ability to infuse worldly themes with religious feeling; one finds it where one would least expect to find it, in "Epistle to a Patron." This is an artist's appeal for noble patronage, with lavish promises to "my lord" of absolute personal devotion and copious performance, but through the barrage of flattery that urbanely mocks its own inordinacy, sounds a note of urgent need exceeding the occasion; as when, seeking a social role for his art, his terms are those of abject supplication and Christian paradox: "Save me, noble sir, from the agony / Of starved and privy explorations.../ I wish for liberty, let me then be tied."

Memoirs in Oxford, a long autobiographical meditation published in 1970 and revised for the *Collected Poems*, contains some clues to the personal motivation of his poetry. Born and raised in South Africa, be began his life in England as an undergraduate at Oxford in the early 1930s. His arrival coincided with "the year / Of 'crisis,' nineteen thirty-one," and he found himself to be both socially and spiritually a "displaced" person: he suffered, it seems, a prolonged religious "crisis," self-hatred dividing him from himself and therefore God; culturally he felt himself a stranger both in his homeland and, doubly, in the country of his adoption. I say "doubly" since he came to Oxford with *fin de siècle* notions of English literary culture, seeking the fellow spirits he lacked at home, only, as he says, "to find / The whole scenario was dated." The culture he expected no longer existed, European civilization was under siege: the young man was afflicted with "the sense of everything acutely / Set going in reverse." We may infer, therefore, that his poetry is impelled by a need to fill this cultural and religious vacuum: culturally, as we have seen, by the Eliotic incorporation of European tradition; religiously, by saturation in the religious tones of the same past, whether fourth-century Greece, thirteenth-century France, Renaissance Italy or seventeenth-century England.

Pound's and Eliot's stress on objectivity and impersonality, which has been a major influence on Prince's work, was in reaction against Victorian poetry and taste, and Eliot came to see this as a "classical" attack upon the romantic view of poetry. That was only one element, however, in the poetry of high modernism. Another, romantic element, which also left its mark on Prince's verse, was contributed by the later Yeats. Like his romantic predecessors Yeats regarded poetry as *personal* utterance, "thoughts which [a man] had in some definite situation in life,"[6] except that the man and the thoughts and the life were to be given the bold outlines and emphasis of drama. The style like speech sought by the new realists in the second decade was also cultivated by Yeats, but since for him, as for the Romantics, poetry was essentially the expression of *intense* emotion—"the actual thoughts of a man at a *passionate* moment of life" (my italics),[7] he constructed a poetic dialect that was, in a phrase of his father's, "an idealization of speech." The "modernized" poetry of his middle years, though tougher, barer and wide awake, did not cease to be a poetry of the emotions; it required a *stylized* realism to incorporate the inflections and cadences of desire. What Prince admired in Yeats was reinforced by what he found in the sixteenth-century Italian poets and Milton: the "conveyance of deep feeling by finished poetic artifice," and rhetoric used to gain "the effect of emphatic, excited, or passionate modes of speech."[8]

Prince's literary manners tend, more markedly in his early work, towards courtliness, grandeur, and occasional flamboyance; his allegiance is to "luminous" intelligence, spiritual grace, and aesthetic splendours. His imagination is drawn to the extraordinary or, in the words of James's Isabel Archer, "the finer essence [of life] that appeals to the consciousness." It is appropriate that the voice we hear in one of his early dramatic monologues, a virtuoso piece, should be that of James's notebooks and prefaces and that its title, "The Tears of a Muse in America," should suggest the isolation of the civilized intelligence. The romantic ingredient in the composition of Prince's sensibility is, in a word, an "insatiable sense of *glory*." It is more prominent in his first collection, and this phrase appears in the youthful "To a Friend on his Marriage" in the lines immediately following those already quoted:

> Now again, hearing that you marry,
> My insatiable sense of glory and
> My passion for the gay and grand
> Deliver you up to fiction.

"Fiction" like "insatiable" discloses the poet's amused consciousness of his own extravagance before he proceeds to indulge it. Whereas Yeats controls his romanticism by a pose of robust manliness enacted in his rhythms and a selectively colloquial idiom, Prince reins in his sense of glory with either a light urbanity such as this or a distancing formality and elegance. The balance is more easily illustrated in a slight but attractive early poem, "To a Man on His Horse":

> Only the Arab stallion will I
> Envy you. Along the water
> You dance him with the morning on his flanks.
> In the frosty morning that his motions flatter
> He kindles, and where the winter's in the wood,
> I watch you dance him out on delicate shanks.

The poet's ardent response produces the expansive gesture of "the morning on his flanks" and gives us the glory of the horse; the parallelism of the two following sentences, distantly echoing the pattern of Hebrew verse, makes a ceremony of it. Set these lines, however, against the poem's conclusion:

> And to do honour to his whiteness
> In remembrance of his ancient blood,
> I have wished to become his groom
> And so his smouldering body comb
> In a simple and indecorous sweetness.

The faintly archaic decorum here acts as a constraint upon the "indecorous" license of the idealizing imagination. It contains extravagance, decorum playing the part more commonly played by irony in twentieth-century English poetry. That this way of writing has its dangers is shown by the mincing affectation of the last two words. Such lapses, I would say, are rare and occur only in his first volume, *Poems*. The most ambitious poem in that volume, "Epistle to a Patron," is triumphantly successful in achieving a more complex balance of forces. It is in the style of Leonardo's letter to the Duke of Milan, teeming with projects and promises, with a sumptuous language to match the prodigality of the artist's imagination and both, addressed to the "intelligent glory" of his prospective patron, engendered by a sense of his nobility and magnificence of state. As he enumerates his architectural splendours and attests his engineering skills, certain double meanings and the virtuosity of the poem itself hint at the skills of the poet:

> ...I have acquired a knowledge
> Of the habits of numbers and of various tempers, and skill in setting
> Firm sets of pure bare members which will rise, hanging together
> Like an argument, with beams, ties and sistering pilasters...

Here, in the poetry as in the speaker's vision of mathematics, engineering and imagination working together, profusion is *tied* by knowledge, skill and argument and the marriage is enacted in the verse. We have, then, the "opulence" of the princely patron and, in response, the impetuous feeling and abundant invention of the artist; but there is also an acknowledgement of limits:

> I wish for liberty, let me then be tied: and seeing too much
> I aspire to be constrained by your emblems of birth and triumph,
> And between the obligations of your future and the checks of actual state
> To flourish...

Aspiration and constraint, liberty and service: the "checks" and "obligations" of power must also be the artist's, the soil of fact in which alone his talent can "flourish"; without them abundance is "too much" ("Abundance" not "Too Much" was precisely the measure commended by Marianne Moore in the subtitles of "The Jerboa").

Prince has not been a prolific poet. Being so infrequently in the public eye has certainly contributed to his neglect. But there is nothing in *Collected Poems* that is not distinctive and finely wrought. His best work is indisputably among the longer poems, dramatic monologues and dramatic portraits and meditations: deeply pondered and put together with a natural elegance that conceals laborious care and intricacy of design. The point to stress about them is that they are indeed *dramatizations* of thought: this is the source of their poetic vitality and interest. In each the verse-movement and the larger organization respond to the movements of either (in the monologues) the character's mind or (in the portraits) the poet-historian's, sifting evidence and reflecting upon the significance of character and events.

To illustrate the suppleness of the writing and the way tensions of thought and feeling are realized in these dramatic poems, we need an extract of some length which can be detached without too much damage to the whole. A passage in "Campanella" will serve. The speaker—Christian Platonist, campaigner for political reform, author of a socialistic Utopia *The Kingdom of the Sun*—has been incarcerated in a rock dungeon for conspiracy and heresy. In the first section he recalls how, to escape the death sentence, he had feigned madness, setting fire to his bed and, in the character of Prometheus tied to a rock on Mt. Caucasus for stealing from the gods, "calling this dull cell my Caucasus / Where I lie chained." By "rock" and "fire" Campanella is initially linked to the champion of humanity and antagonist of Zeus; at the same time he is no atheist—unlike Shelley's Prometheus, he is, and thinks like, a Christian:

> Sighs are my sustenance, my meat is groans,
> Because I preached the Kingdom of the Sun.
> And now I may remember what I saw
> Out of this ditch of death, that I am here
> For thinking otherwise than bats and owls
> And blinding their old dens with too much light.
> And now, my body lying on a bed,
> Worn, meagre, bruised and broken, and my mind
>   Filled with a wound-like sorrow,
> I concentrate and meditate and find
> All my old reasons as they were, their fire
>   Lighting the golden world
> Where I had argued things to my desire:
>   It was a world
> Of a luminous sea- richness where I saw
> No more of yours and mine, or you and me
> But all things were in common; ancient law
> Made new morality shine light as air...

The thought, as in a Shakespearean soliloquy, veers and grows with the speaker's feelings. Language and rhythm reflect the changes: the declamatory self-dramatizing elegance of the opening, giving way to impatient contempt, sinking suddenly into the broken tones of pathos, quickening finally with visionary fervour. The central conflict in the character's mind is between humanist and transcendental aspects of his thinking: is the Kingdom of the Sun also the Kingdom of the Son, the return of which, in the language of Revelation, "to triumph here on earth" is fervently anticipated in the immediate sequel to this passage? Campanella's "broken" body and "wound-like sorrow" seek comparison with the suffering Christ; the light is certainly the Light of the World and the new covenant replacing the old: yet "ancient law," aligned subversively with the "old dens" of ecclesiastical authority and both associated with the "ditch of death," his dungeon, suggests not so much a superseded covenant as the dark prison of religious obscurantism, in which case the blinding light of revelation also radiates the scornful light of philosophic reason. Most disturbing of all, because the speaker is unconscious of it, is the possibility of a moral equivalence existing between *his* "old reasons" and the "old dens" of benighted orthodoxy or the invalidated "ancient laws"; "old reasons" could then only be, by analogy, the arguments of Platonist philosophy, and a world fired by such "reasons" would not be a world reborn in Christ but a humanistic renaissance. We see a man, and through him an age, deeply divided in their motivations, either aspiring to a "golden world" that would reconcile contradictory properties or not noticing their contradiction.

The doubt expressed by Campanella in the poem's conclusion, whether in believing Platonism and the new humanism to be reconcilable with Christianity he had in truth been mad, is a doubt informing everything he has said and a question in the reader's mind that makes him at once participant and judge—straddled as he is between the sixteenth and the twentieth centuries. How far are we experiencing-witnessing the heroism of faith and how far the delusions of a crazed desire? The poem does not attempt an answer: more fruitfully it enables us to *live* the question. The poem holds in unresolved tension the conflicting impulses, judgments and interpretations of speaker and reader alike. Furthermore, we experience directly, by occupying the mind of a representative—exceptional and therefore deeply representative—figure, the religious and political issues of the time. And this exercise of the historical imagination has a two-way effect. As we sympathetically and critically re-enact the past, so the past enters into us and modifies the present. For in gaining inner access to a fanaticism and otherworldliness foreign to a modern sensibility, we at the same time distance ourselves from utopian generosities of political idealism that would normally command our immediate retroactive sympathy.

It is not possible in a short space to demonstrate the dramatic organization of a *whole* poem. A compromise, however, suggests itself in the case of *Strafford*. This portrait exhibits a conception of character centred on the conflicting demands of body and soul, and one may convey at least a partial impression of the subtlety in its dramatic evolution by tracing the development of the imagery of light and dark which, as so often in Prince, interprets that conflict. Frequently employing Strafford's own words, the poem meditates on his character as it revealed itself in letters, speeches, and the momentous events of 1641 that culminated in his execution by the Commons. We see him first as his contemporaries saw him, as the portrait painters painted him:

> Dark steel, the muffled flash
> On iron sleeve and cuff; black storm of armour,
> Half-moons and wedges, scaly wings and hinges,
> Ovals and quadrilaterals and cylinders
> Moulded in nightshade metal.
>   So he stands
> With rod and sword of office, living fingers
> Poised lightly on the sword-hilt, pale and still,
>
> Wentworth, the black-browed Yorkshire magnate, with a rent-roll
> Of Norman-English quarters and alliances...

We feel the weight of armour as the panoply of power; "dark steel," "black storm," dragonish scales and deadly "nightshade," linked to "the rod and sword of office," give us not just a dangerous, ruthless man but the Prince of Darkness himself. Only "pale" half hints at something else, the body's frailty, and ("pale and *still*" standing in antithesis to "*living* fingers") that the armour of power may also be the crushing burden of responsibility. The five lines that follow, not quoted here, listing his pedigree, are ponderous with the weight of a tyranny both exercised and suffered. We have now a less simple picture:

> And still the dark eyes gloom beneath the bent brows
> As if impatient of himself, his greatness
> Rooted in limitation, strength and weakness
> Of fiery piercing mind, that wears the waning body...

The "dark eyes" betray division, arrogance undermined by discontent, a restiveness provoked by the limiting conditions of mortality itself. He is, in a later phrase for the condition imaged here, a "fettered angel," a title of ambiguous implications: the rebel angel aimed too high and was fettered for his presumption, but the phrase also defines the tragedy of all spiritual aspiration. The pun on "wears" concentrates the ambiguity and confounds judgment. We all *wear* and are confined by our bodies; only the man of will, who feels most strongly the disparity between conception and performance, *wears out* the body. Pride or heroism? It is a fine line between a "fiery" pride and a "fiery" spirit, self-deification and self-sacrifice, a vicious and a virtuous excess. Strafford confesses to being a victim of his "thirst" for power and the momentum of inherited power, in both senses "the power that drives us onward"; but he also claims that it is a "chaste ambition," seeking "power to do more good." "Haunted by thirst and shadow...Lurking within," nevertheless in "climbing higher" he seeks the sun. In the event he finds a "greater darkness" than his own, the "black clouds" of envy, malice, a "taste for blood and lies," and as he moves towards his martyrdom (teaching Charles the way to go), the inner shadow fades from view and the outer darkness thickens. At the same time "his burning winged intelligence" ("fiery piercing mind" here new-minted into shining praise) is the light that at the last burns away the darkness and breaks open the prison of self and adverse circumstance (which also includes the "sad *shut* face" of Charles, who would or could not save him, and "the *closing* circle of his rule").

This imagistic method of organizing a long poem is worth examining in more detail. It resembles Eliot's practice in *The Waste Land*, in which, as Perkins says, he "created symbols by the incremental return to the same or closely similar images."[9] If *The Waste Land* suggested a congenial way of structuring a longer poem—and the combination of dramatic impersonation and impersonal meditation must have appealed to Prince—the network of image patterns discovered by Wilson Knight in Shakespeare's plays is likely to have reinforced the authority of that suggestion. It is notably a device, too, of the modern poetic novel: in the words of Henry Green, a practitioner in that genre, "a gathering web of insinuations."[10] The quiet, ruminative manner of *Memoirs in Oxford*, though written in rhyming stanzas, in fact invites comparison with the art of the prose writer. Part III, for example, acts out the hesitant coming together of clues to the religious significance of certain scattered fragments of experience. Words of similar import strike up seemingly chance relationships: "dull," "faded," "faint," "glimmering," "distant," "shadows" adumbrate a sense of separation, while such words as "fire," "light" and "pure" point forward to a coming revelation; after five pages the cumulative suggestion concentrates itself into one unassuming, understated stanza ("insinuation" not proclamation is the method):

> There were some voices in the distance,
>   Children at play. It was a dull
> Day, but one felt the spring for sure,
> The faint warm breath; and then that pure
>   Insight that nothing could annul.

The same method is used to tie together, in the open form of Pound's *Cantos*, the miscellaneous materials—description, commentary, anecdote and quoted doctrine—that compose "Drypoints of the Hasidim." Take the first episode, a sharply etched picture of the Hasidic milieu and general image of the Jewish situation. Several motifs are interwoven, the most conspicuous being the "dark" fate of the Jews (the word occurs three times in twenty-two lines), with the glint of something else, its antithesis: "*dark* hollow faces" but "*eternal* names" among them. The various strands are pulled a little tighter in the closing lines, which imagine the travelling tradesmen:

>   Riding and plodding on bad roads
> By valleys in the dark Carpathians
>   threaded with tawny crystal
>   Past battered cottages and farms
> With yellow middens and a dog in chains
>   And osiers by a stream

In the factually informative and at the same time symbolic landscape we glimpse captivity, poverty, suffering and endurance; the "tawny crystal" of rivers blend dark and light, history and a thread of hope, and the osiers stand as though in melancholy waiting. A sense of waiting, though it is not yet an explicit theme, is immanent in the conclusion of the next episode:

>   And moonlight silvering wooden walls
> And greasy alleys and the market square
>   Left empty but for litter

There is a poignancy in "left empty," which cannot be explained by the facts of the scene. The emptiness is waiting to be filled—and not with "litter," and not even with people. With what, then? An answer is implicit in the juxtaposition of this closing stanza with the opening of the next episode, in which the opinion of Dov Baer is cited "that true thoughts and purposes / And meanings / Can shine out only in ends." "Shine out" gives meaning to the moonlight's transfiguration of urban shabbiness and squalor, for God is in that shining: Dov Baer continues, "thus when men saw God manifest his glory / In Egypt," and "when he gave the Law on Sinai / They could see it was that Israel / Might wear it as a crown," and finally, "the people of Israel...They are the purpose of the world." The emptiness is waiting to be filled with meaning. Several pages later this is given explicitly metaphysical amplification. The world is not actually, it seems, a shell to be filled with God:

> Everything is in exile
>   everything will return
> Because everything desires to be redeemed—
> Everything in the world and worldliness—
>
> Not to be emptied of itself or worldliness
> But to be hallowed in the *kawannoth*

(the intention directed towards God while performing a religious deed). Enough has been quoted, with the addition of sufficient commentary, to indicate the delicacy with which poetic meaning is established—fact, symbol and abstract thought integrated in a living, changing unity.

F.T. Prince began writing in the 1930s, in complete independence from his contemporaries. High modernism influenced his technique, but no more perhaps than the poetry of the Renaissance. The singularity of his preoccupations and his single-minded pursuit of them, which made his work at first seem strange, have set him apart among twentieth-century poets in English. He has not been, in any sense that Michael Roberts, spokesman for modernity in the 1930s, would have recognized, an interpreter of the times. But his interest in the past, I have suggested, is that of a modern, civilized, catholic intelligence maintaining continuity with its European heritage, illuminating and illuminated by intellectual history.

NOTES

1. Donald Davie, *Articulate Energy* (London: Routledge and Kegan Paul, 1955), 92.

2. Michael Roberts, "Distinction in Poetry," *The Spectator*, 7 (1938): 576.

3. David Perkins, *A History of Modern Poetry: From the 1890s to the High Modernist Mode* (Cambridge, Mass.: Harvard Univ. Press, 1976).

4. Roberts, "Distinction in Poetry," 574–76.

5. Quoted Perkins, *A History of Modern Poetry*, 470.

6. *The Egoist*, 2 February 1914; report of a speech given by Yeats on the occasion of a presentation to W.S. Blunt.

7. Quoted Perkins, *A History of Modern Poetry*, 578.

8. *The Italian Element in Milton's Verse* (London: Oxford Univ. Press, 1954), 28, 122.

9. Perkins, *A History of Modern Poetry*, 505.

10. Henry Green, *Pack My Bag* (London: Hogarth Press, 1940), 88.

THE LANGUAGES OF CONTEMPORARY WEST INDIAN POETRY

J.E. Chamberlin

In the slogans marked on the walls of Kingston and Port of Spain and the other towns and cities of the Caribbean, a language has taken shape. It displays both the dignity and the despair that characterize life in those sometimes troubled places; and its economies of form are matched by its extravagances, as the international rhetoric of standard English is set alongside local expressions in dialect, merging in the political determination painted on a wall in Grenada: "We freedom is ours"; or in the Rastafarian testimony on the side of a house in Surinam: "The love of Jah is like a bucket of fire."

The writings on the wall bear witness not only to the significance of the experiences and events they chronicle, but also to the importance of words in the intermittent violence and tranquillity of contemporary life in the Caribbean, and in the shaping of people's attitude to life and to each other. In these circumstances, poetry has emerged as unusually important, with its richer and more complex potential to speak of social and political realities and of collective ideals. It has also become the meeting place of the different traditions that inform life in the Caribbean, establishing a kind of commerce between African forms of imaginative expression and Anglo-Saxon or Mediterranean imaginative inheritances. It is not an easy commerce, to be sure; but poetry at the very least provides the currency, and proposes some transactions between what Rex Nettleford of Jamaica calls the rhythm of Africa and the melody of Europe, and between the territorial piety and the imperial power that the Northern Irish poet Seamus Heaney describes as competing allegiances in all countries that inherit the colonizing authority of the English language.

The poets of the West Indies bring together familiar counterparts, the ideals of a new sense of national identity and of a renewed language, cultural renaissance confirming political independence. To use terms that have some currency, the poetry brings the language home, countering the colonialism that alienates people from their own past, and from their own dreamings. In itself, this does not put the poets of the Caribbean in a special category, for in some sense these are the obligations and opportunities that all poets inherit. What makes this poetry unique is the combination of extraordinary obligations, as chroniclers of nothing less than the making of nations, and extraordinary opportunities, the coincidence of a refreshing release from the autocracy of international modernist poetry in standard English and a renewed realization of local languages and oral traditions. This has produced some distinctive poetic styles, which like all styles combine the authenticity of natural expression with the idiosyncracy of creative artifice. But in the West Indies, the urge to re-create what Wordsworth called "the real language of men in a state of vivid sensation," has been especially strong, and this has led to a lively mixture of common speech and consciously heightened style. "All styles yearn to be plain as life," says the St. Lucian writer Derek Walcott in a poem called "The Gulf";[1] and the considerable achievement of much contemporary poetry expresses that yearning. But it is a yearning for style nevertheless, for a craft that appears as candour. "A line will take us hours maybe," said Yeats, "yet if it does not seem a moment's thought, / our stitching and unstitching has been nought." [2] The making is masked, but making plain and making sense are makings nonetheless; and plain speaking is still a kind of style, as contrived as any other.

The use of dialect provides an obvious access to a spoken language, a "real language" of men and women; but within the spectrum of speech in the West Indies, there is a wide range, and a complex set of relationships with written language. The richly textured voice of a Barbadian woman in a poem by Bruce St. John is apparently very close to speech, though even then the poet draws attention to its written character by calling the poem a "Letter to England":

Girl chile darlin' yuh ol' muddah hay
Praisin' de Lord fuh 'E blessin' and 'E mercies
You is many blessin's an'all o'me mercies
Glory to God!
Uh get de 5 pound note an' de Christmas card
God bless yuh!
But de carpenter ain' come to put on de shed-roof
So uh spen' it an uh sen' Rosy pretty to de
Exhibition gal, you should see she!
Nex' mont' when yuh sen' me allowance again,
We will see wuh kin happen in de name o' de Lord...[3]

Another poet whose work depends on patterns of speech is Paul Keens-Douglas, who draws attention to the distinctiveness of Trinidadian and Grenadian speech as against the style and the sound of standard English by telling of listening for years to the line from the King James version of the Twenty-Third Psalm, "surely goodness and mercy shall follow me all the days of my life," and finding out late in the day that Shirley was no woman.[4] English is full of ostentatious adverbs; but then, every language has its own genial affectations. Keens-Douglas illustrates some of them with affectionate delight in a poem called "When Moon Shine":

> Tim, Tim?...papa welcome!
> Ah send an' call de doctor
> An' de doctor reach before me?
> Don't tell me, ah know-coconut!
> Is Nanci story time on de step,
> Is full moon an' everything bright
> All little children teafin' ah 'stay up,'
> Playing' rounders an' catchers,
> Nobody mind, not when de moon full,
> Is like everybody find excuse
> To leave de house.
> Tanti on de porch lookin' out,
> "Cover yu head, gal, yu want dew kill yu?"
> But Tanti mind elsewhere like she eye.
> Long time now she watchin' dem two shadow—
> Two dat look like one-under de mango tree.
> Other tings goin' on besides catchers tonite.
> Tanti like de moon—she silent, but she see.[5]

One of the appeals, perhaps the first appeal, of this to foreign ears is its novelty, not only of sound and rhythm, but also of figuration, with picturesque phrases like "teafin' ah 'stay up,' " (thieving a "stay-up") and the amusing identification of Tanti with the moon—"she silent, but she see." But the elements which delight a reader not from the islands with their freshness and unfamiliarity will delight listeners from the Caribbean with their comforting closeness, no less refreshing perhaps but much more familiar.

As a final, and more obviously literary, example of the use of a local idiom within a structure that is unmistakeably appealing to a wider audience, there is the poem "Uncle Time," by the Jamaican Dennis Scott:

> Uncle Time is a ole, ole man...
> All year long 'im wash 'im foot in de sea,
> long, lazy years on de wet san'
> an' shake de coconut tree dem
> quiet-like wid 'im sea-win' laughter,
> scraping away de lan'...

> Uncle time is a spider-man, cunnin' an' cool,
> him tell yu: watch de hill an' yu se mi.
> Huhn! Fe yu yi no quick enough fe si
> how'im move like mongoose; man, yu tink'im fool?
>
> Me Uncle Time smile black as sorrow;
> 'im voice is sof'as bamboo leaf
> but Lawd, me Uncle cruel.
> When 'im play in de street
> wid yu woman—watch 'im! By tomorrow
> she dry as cane-fire, bitter as cassava;
> an' when 'im teach yu son, long after
> yu walk wid stranger, an'yu bread is grief.
> Watch how'im spin web round' yu house, an'creep
> inside; an' when 'im touch yu, weep....[6]

Here we have a familiar literary trope, the personification of time, given both a Jamaican figuration and a Jamaican voice. The poem draws on a familiar West Indian (and West African) folktale about Anancy the spider—the "Nanci story" of Keens-Douglas's poem—and transforms the image into an ambiguous and menacing representation of Time, in a distinctly and delightfully refreshing Jamaican idiom.

My use of the words "delightfully refreshing" raises a critical issue about literary language that is of considerable importance. It was focussed some years ago by the English critic Owen Barfield in a book called *Poetic Diction* (1928). Barfield argued that it is the quality of "strangeness" in poetic language that constitutes its central imaginative appeal. He began his discussion of poetic diction with the example of a line of pidgin English, from the south Pacific islands, for a three-masted steamboat with two funnels: "Thlee-piecee bamboo, two-piecee puff-puff, walk-along inside, no-can-see." His discussion then focussed on the quality of strangeness inherent in this text:

> When I try to describe in more detail than by the phrase "aesthetic imagination" what experience it is to which at some time or other I have been led, and at any time may be led again, I find myself obligated to define it as a "felt change of consciousness," where "consciousness" embraces all my awareness of my surroundings at any given moment, and "surroundings" includes my own feelings. By "felt" I mean to signify that the change itself is noticed, or attended to. To take the simplest example: when I, as a European adult, actually observe or visualize a three-masted screw steamer with two funnels, the manner in which I immediately experience my surroundings, the meaning which they have for me, is determined by the various concepts which I have learnt, since my childhood, to unite with the percept, or complex of percepts, underlying the phenomenon in question. By "percept," I mean that element

in my experience, which in no way depends on my own mental activity, present or past—the pure sense-datum. The concepts likely to be operative in this case are reflected in such English words as "mast," "mechanical propulsion," "steam," "coal," "smoke," "chimney for smoke to escape by," etc., all of which are summed up and, as it were, fused in my own peculiar and habitual idea of "steamer." It is this idea which determines for me the quality, or meaning, of my immediate experience in observation.

Now when I read the words "thlee-piecee bamboo, two-piecee puff-puff, walk-along-inside, no-can-see," I am for a moment transported into a totally different kind of consciousness. I see the steamer, not through my own eyes, but through the eyes of a primitive South-Sea Islander. His experience, his meaning, is quite different from mine, for it is the product of quite different concepts. This he reveals by his choice of words; and the result is that, for a moment, I shed Western civilization like an old garment and behold my steamer in a new and strange light.[7]

Barfield provides a number of other examples of texts that are more conventionally poetic, and his idea of strangeness includes complex questions of rhythm and tone; but it still begins with a question of unfamiliarity, whether it is the unfamiliarity of a strange dialect as against conventional speech, or the unfamiliarity of the heavily charged rhythm or heightened language of poetry as against the more casual and relaxed patterns of everyday conversation.

The sense of difference between the relaxed immediacy of dialect speech and the disciplined universality of literary traditions is particularly apparent (as Walt Whitman demonstrated) when poets return to one of the venerable sources of poetic power, the power of naming, wherein by a kind of radical naiveté the poet recovers the characteristic authority of language that is both conventional and magical, both representational and abstract. This naming is both an act of symbolic expression and an act of routine description; and more than anything else, it can create a sense that the word is both everyday and unique. One of poetry's traditional forms, the catalogue, takes its authority from this; but the authority never comes easily, requiring both a self-consciously insistent selection, and a surrender to local realities, to things as they are. The balance between the imaginative authority of the words and the power of the reality to which they refer is always a fragile one; and catalogues can easily degenerate into shopping lists. Poets are typically uneasy about this hazard, and this unease is a special affliction for poets whose local language has no tradition of symbolic power within the conventions into which the naming is being introduced. Derek Walcott describes how in his early years "what I wrote had nothing to do with what I saw. While I honoured and loved them in my mind, I could not bring myself to write down the names of villages, of fruits, or the way those people spoke because it seemed too raw....And I found no lines that mentioned breadfruit, guava, plaintain, cassava in 'literature'."[8]

Later, he found a voice to celebrate his native St. Lucia, with its French and English creole and distinctive names:

> Laborie, Choiseul, Veuxfort, Dennery...
> Pomme arac,
> otaheite apple,
> pomme cythere,
> pomme grante,
> moubain,
> z'anananas
> the pine apple's
> Aztec helmet,
> pomme,
> I have forgotten
> what pomme for
> the Irish potato,
> cerise,
> the cherry,
> z'aman
> sea-almonds
> by the crisp
> sea-bursts,
> au bord de la'ouvière.
> Come back to me
> my language.
> Come back,
> cacao,
> grigri,
> solitaire,
> ciseau
> the scissor-bird...
>
> O so you is Walcott?
> you is Roddy brother?
> Teacher Alix son?
> and the small rivers
> with important names...
>
> generations going,
> generations gone,
> moi c'est gens Ste. Lucie.
> C'est la moi sorti;
> is there that I born.[9]

Establishing the realistic authenticity of local speech has long been part of the achievement of prose writers and playwrights as well as of cartoonists, and of poets using such speech as local colour. But establishing the imaginative authority of local speech is a different matter altogether, especially when the credibility of language itself is at stake, as it always is with poetry. It is not the mirroring of a given reality that is at issue here, but the making of a new one. Some of the finest West Indian poetry now hovers between these alternative allegiances, as in a couple of lines in a poem called "Jah Music" by the Jamaican writer Lorna Goodison. Speaking of "this red and yellow and dark green sound"—the colours are of Rastafarian significance, linked to the imagery of an Ethiopian homeland—Goodison describes how it "has the healing and it pulses without a symphony conductor / all it need is a dub organizer."[10] ("Dub" refers here to the practice [by many disc jockeys, especially during the 1960s and 1970s in Jamaica] of adding [or dubbing] words to accompany an instrumental rendering of a popular song, which was sold as the flip side of a hit record. "Dub" poets took their name from this, as they performed their work to the accompaniment of music.) The parallelism of these lines from Goodison's poem highlights the similarity and the difference, both between the concert hall and the popular radio station, and between the languages of each; and it highlights the fact that the language of poetry is not exactly at home in either place; or perhaps can be located comfortably in both.

It is in the last twenty-five years that this awareness of language has come to the foreground in the West Indies, and has informed the poetry. During the 1950s, there was an increasing recognition of the variety of cultural expression that was specifically Caribbean in character, and of its distinctive languages. The National Dance Theatre Company in Jamaica, and the Little Carib Theatre in Trinidad, were two institutional examples of a widespread interest in indigenous artistic traditions. Calypso and the steelband flourished, and local forms of religious expression received more attention, and more acknowledgement as important in the lives of the people. Political writings of the 1930s and 1940s, including C.L.R. James's *Black Jacobins* (1938) and Eric Williams's *Capitalism and Slavery* (1944) were reinforced by a new generation's revision of colonial history, in books such as Elsa Goveia's *A Study of the Historiography of the West Indies* (1956).

These interests were fused in some literary innovations, beginning with novels such as Vic Reid's *New Day* (1949), telling of the time in Jamaica between the Morant Bay Rebellion in 1865, when the local constitution was abolished, and the return of constitutional government with a full franchise in 1944. More important than its subject, however, was the way in which it was written, entirely in local dialect. This established an important precedent, suggesting the literary credibility of dialect, and providing a challenge to other writers to unite forms of written art with the nature of the spoken tongue.

Within a few years Samuel Selvon's *Lonely Londoners* (1956) and other novels of a similar sort recognized more of the rich literary possibilities of dialect, in Selvon's case Trinidadian and Jamaican speech transported to England, where many West Indians were migrating during the 1950s. Selvon translated West Indian dialect into a language not quite like any other, a language of lyric authority within a narrative structure, sustaining an illusion of dialect all along the spectrum from creole speech to standard English. In Roger Mais's novel *Brother Man*, published in 1954, there was also a combination of a complex array of languages with a subject that focussed contemporary issues, specifically the contrast between Rastafarian visionary ideals and the squalid realities of life for the Kingston urban poor, the sufferers in the yard.

Leading up to the mid-1950s, there was a succession of poets who had emerged out of the social and economic troubles of the 1930s and the political developments of the 1940s. Their work was informed by an awareness of the Caribbean life, and a particularly powerful rendering of its landscapes. The language tended to be bound by English conventions, and the use of dialect was often very self-conscious. Occasionally, as in the beginning of Philip Sherlock's "Pocomania"—about the Jamaican religious cult combining the dynamics of Christian revivalism with possession by ancestral spirits—the rhythm and the language flow effectively together:

Long Mountain, rise
Lift you' shoulder, blot the moon,
Black the stars, hide the skies,
Long Mountain, rise, lift you' shoulder high.[11]

But for a while the poets of this period seemed to be giving place to the writers of prose. Some writers, such as the Barbadian George Lamming, began publishing poetry during the late 1940s, and then turned to fiction; though as a writer of prose, Lamming's concern was still very much with language. The Guyanese writer Wilson Harris published a notable volume of poetry, *Eternity to Season*, in 1954, which he substantially revised twenty-five years later. His first novel, *Palace of the Peacock*, appeared in 1960, followed by over a dozen novels and a number of short stories and essays; but it is apparent that his poetry is continuous with his prose in ways that illuminate something of the rich texture and subtle tones of Guyanese speech.

Much of the writing of this period was bounded by local circumstances; but the local character of the work was itself a formidable strength, especially in generating a consciousness of and a respect for local languages. Louise Bennett's contribution to the annual pantomime in Kingston from the 1940s was one popular manifestation of this, as was the publication in 1966 of her book of dialect poems, *Jamaican Labrish*, edited by Rex Nettleford. To this enthusiasm for writing in dialect Frederic Cassidy provided formidable scholarly grounding, both in *Jamaica Talk* (1961), subtitled "Three Hundred Years of the English Language in Jamaica," and in the *Dictionary of Jamaican English*, published in 1967. This had reference only to a particular region, of course; but Cassidy's work had an authority that helped to create a new respect for local languages throughout the Caribbean.

Derek Walcott and the Barbadian poet and historian Edward Kamau Brathwaite produced their first major work during the 1960s, and along with them came younger writers such as Dennis Scott, Anthony McNeill, Wayne Brown, Mervyn Morris and Edward Baugh. The establishment of the University of the West Indies in 1949, and its expansion during the 1950s, provided both energy and focus to much artistic activity, both on the first campus at Mona in Kingston, and later in Cave Hill, Barbados and St. Augustine, Trinidad. The extramural programmes of the university were equally important, establishing lively exchange within and between the islands. Periodicals such as *Bim* in Barbados, *Kyk-over-al* in Guyana, and the anthology *Focus* in Jamaica provided important forums for writers, complemented by radio broadcasts such as the Caribbean Voices programme, which originated in London. Poetry, never a simple affair, was part of a range of enterprises, from the lively language of calypso songs, with their intensely topical character, to the lyrics of reggae, the musical form (first called, variously, "blue beat," "ska" and "rock-steady") which combined Rastafarian religious ideologies with the frustrations of the so-called rude-boys, the disaffected youth whose "rudie ridims" challenged conventional (and largely imported) musical forms, and raised the profile of Rastafarianism, which emerged as a major social and political force during the 1950s and 1960s, first of all in Jamaica.

Rastafarianism combined a legacy of black rage and frustration in the New World with dreams of an African homeland, expressed first as truths revealed to a few chosen leaders. Scriptural texts identified the arrival of the living God in the person of Ras Tafari, who became Haile Selassie on his coronation as Emperor of Ethiopia in 1930; and they indicated the need to return to Africa as the true source of spiritual strength. Rastafarian beliefs extended from this basis in a variety of directions, including on the one hand extremes of political activism such as those advocated by the Nyabungi brethren, with their doctrine of death to white oppressors. On the other hand, many Rastafarians embraced a co-operative collectivism that committed them to a complete retreat from the materialistic society of the contemporary West Indies. The use of ganja (marijuana) and the growing of long matted and plaited hair—"locks" or "dreadlocks"—were two of the most familiar traits associated with many, though not all, Rastafarians, and were never exclusively associated with a particular ideology. The popular identification of some Rastafarian groups with violence is more complex, in large part because it is caught up with the rhetoric of the movement. In the words of a report prepared by Rex Nettleford, Roy Augier and M.G. Smith for the University of the West Indies and submitted to the Prime Minister of Jamaica in 1960,

> the language of the movement is violent...because it is the language of the Bible, and especially of the Old Testament. It is apocalyptic language, in which sinners are consumed with fire, sheep are separated from goats, oppressors are smitten and kings and empires are overthrown. All Christians use this violent language, in their religious services and elsewhere. The use of such language does not mean that they are ready to fight in the streets. It

does, on the other hand, mean that the concepts of revolution are neither frightening nor unfamiliar. [12]

The language of the Rastafarians has considerable importance for contemporary West Indian poetry. In the first place, its distinctiveness arises from a commitment to the liberating energies of language, which is to free the mind and heart from bondage and corruption, and so nourish the spirit. Related to this is a widely shared perception of the language of Rastafari as a heightened discourse that still is rooted in common speech, what one Rastafarian called a language of the poor "stepped up" to reflect the philosophical ideas of Rasta. It is very much the product of Biblical traditions of rhetoric, and to that extent an inherited mode, and part of a distinct tradition. But it is also a deliberately constructed language, developed to reinforce an ideology of black liberation that is both religious and political, and has a determined exclusiveness about it, being as it were the language of choice of a chosen people. At the same time as the language of Rastafarianism concentrates attention on its arbitrariness, however, it lays claim to growing out of the natural speech of those whose specialness it celebrates, of specialness which for many takes the temporary form of marginality. One of the reasons it makes this claim is because of its unusually strong, indeed its ostentatious, commitment to the authority of sound over sense in language, and its dependence on the compulsions of rhythm. This is evident in many ways, such as the use of the I-sound, which includes a punning reference to "eye" (and a corresponding acknowledgement of the necessary far-sightedness of the Rastafarian) and then extends beyond this to an acceptance of this I-sound as generally representing a positive force, so that words are reformed to begin with "I," as in "Ital" (for vital, and thereby for pure and natural Rasta food), "Iration" for creation, and "Inity" for unity. Other changes that depend on sound include changing "oppression" (which of course sounds like "up-pression") to "downpression." There are as well more straightforward shifts and neologisms, less dependent on sound but also common in Rastafarian language, such as when "overstand" replaces "understand," and "outformer" is used instead of "informer." Some transformations are intensely metaphorical, as in the use of "heights" to mean "have knowledge of, comprehend"; which in turn is shifted to "ites," which becomes a greeting of comparable significance to the salutation "roots."

Such changes make Rastafarian language unusually congruous with the language of poetry, with its corresponding concentration on the intersection of sound and meaning. But they do not prove that such language is any more natural than any other. On the contrary, they concentrate its artificiality, both by drawing attention to its made-up character and by insisting that this language embodies a new tradition of speech in English, and thereby a new tradition of imaginative discourse.

The creation of this special language is part of a process of distinguishing the community from others, and reinforces the broader determination in the West Indies to acknowledge the authority of local languages. Increasingly through the 1950s and 1960s, as we have seen, such languages were celebrated in poems and novels, and also in plays. In 1976, Derek Walcott's play *O Babylon!* was produced in Trinidad. It is set in a Rastafarian community near Kingston in 1966, during Emperor Haile Selassie's visit to Jamaica, with "Babylon" referring to the places and peoples representing European civilization, corrupt and corrupting. Contemporary Jamaica, for the Rastafarians, is inevitably such a place. In a note to the play, Walcott describes how

> in trying to seek a combination of the authentic and the universally comprehensible, I found myself at the center of a language poised between defiance and translation, for pure Jamaican is comprehensible only to Jamaicans. But the promulgation of a national language is as much a part of education now as it is of politics. When I considered that, within the language itself, the Rastafari have created still another for their own nation, I faced another conflict: if the language of the play remained true to the sect, it would have to use the sect's methods of self-protection and total withdrawal. This would require of the playwright not merely a linguistic but a spiritual conversion, a kind of talking in tongues that is, by its hermeticism and its self-possession, defiantly evasive of Babylonian reason.
>
> The Rastafari have invented a grammar and a syntax which immure them from the seductions of Babylon, an oral poetry which requires translation into the language of the oppressor. To translate is to betray. My theatre language is, in effect, an adaptation and, for clarity's sake, filtered.[13]

In 1971, in this period of emerging political independence and artistic vitality, two important anthologies of contemporary Caribbean poetry appeared. One was edited by the Jamaican writer Andrew Salkey, with the title *Breaklight*. It was divided up into sections, the titles of which give a sense of the progress that was chronicled: The Concealed Spark, The Heat of Identity, The Fire of Involvement, The Blaze of the Struggle, Breaklight. The other anthology, which included some prose and several poems also in *Breaklight*, took the form of an issue of the magazine *Savacou*. It was a product of the consciousness-raising energies of the London-based Caribbean Artists' Movement, begun by John LaRose from Trinidad, Salkey, and Edward Brathwaite, who edited the anthology. Both anthologies were mixed bags, as anthologies often are, but *Savacou* 3/4 caught considerable attention, and provoked considerable criticism. Its "Forward," written by Brathwaite, described the "revolutionary questioning" that was implicit in the texts as a concern that "remains with the bone of awareness, with word, rhythm, style, truth"; and he praised the "dream of wholeness" that "has so far dominated over the fragments, the pebbles, the divided island of ourselves." "Art-revolution-society" in Brathwaite's view, were becoming "a continuum of imagination, a seamless garment of expression."[14]

The *Savacou* anthology included poetry that took West Indian languages seriously, in a way that was cumulatively significant because the languages were often quite different from one poem or poet to the next, and covered the continuum from local dialects to standard English, itself very much a local language. Much of the poetry incorporated rhetorical conventions in a way that emphasized their connection to local traditions of spoken discourse, and this contributed to the distinctive hovering between oral and written forms that characterized many of the individual poems. In addition, differences of one kind—between black and white, say, or between oral and written performance— were used to shape and to intensify differences in language. Bongo Jerry's poem "Mabrak" (a Rastafarian word meaning "black lightning," insisting upon associations of illumination and revelation with blackness as well as with whiteness) provides a useful example, vulnerable in its distinctively Caribbean outrageousness, but focussing, among other things, the way in which the natural rhythms of speech may push against the artifice of the text with explosive energy.

MABRAK,
Enlightening is BLACK
hands writing the words of
black message
for black hearts to feel.

MARRAK is righting the wrongs and brain whitening—HOW?
Not just by washing out the straightening and wearing dashiki t'ing:
MOSTOFTHESTRAIGHTENINGISINTHETONGUE [15]

Other contributors to this issue spoke with voices that were less easily confused with the poet's own predicament, but no less engaged with the realities of West Indian experience. A fine poem called "Valley Prince" by the Jamaican Mervyn Morris about the jazz trombonist Don Drummond was included (as it was also in the *Breaklight* anthology). Drummond hovered on the edge of musical brilliance and of mental breakdown, until in 1969 he killed his girl-friend and then committed suicide. Morris's poem brings Drummond's language into the centre by using it, paradoxically, to illuminate his eccentric genius, a gift of grace in a society that seemed unredeemably false. The phrasings in the poem combine the popular ("I love a melancholy baby") with the more obviously contrived, and move from the poetic simplicities of "I blow the sounds, the pain" to the more complex ambiguities of "I blow me mind." The poem is very highly organized, and subtle in its juxtapositions between "me one" and "the crowd," inside and outside, truth and lies. Its language is both common and uncommon: made up specially for the occasion, and just in off the street, as the naturalness of the speaking voice intensifies our sense of the poem's artifice, and of Drummond's unnatural individuality.

Me one, way out in the crowd
I blow the sounds, the pain
but not a soul
would come inside my world
tell me how it true.

> I love a melancholy baby,
> sweet, with fire in her belly;
> and like a spite
> the woman turn a whore.
> Cool and smooth around the beat
> she wake the note inside me
> and I blow me mind.
>
> Inside here, me one
> in the crowd again,
> and plenty people
> want me blow it straight.
> But straight is not the way; my world
> don' go so; that is lie.
> Oonu gimme back me trombone, man:
> is time to blow me mind.[16]

Some critics, such as Gerald Moore, praised the anthology for drawing attention to the fact "that the West Indies has languages of its own, not curiosities [but] essential to the full revelation of West Indian life and literature."[17] Other critics were not enthusiastic. The challenge was taken up first in a review by the Trinidad poet Eric Roach. He insisted that "to thresh about wildly [like Bongo Jerry] in the murky waters of race, oppression and dispossession [is] to bury one's head in the stinking dunghills of slavery." But what if these murky waters or stinking dunghills are where the poet's reality, and thereby his imagination, is centred? Roach had another metaphor ready at hand. "One must erect one's bungalow by the sea out of the full knowledge of the architecture of English places and cottages."[18]

The issues raised by Roach are significant, and had been disputed with intermittent urgency during the period leading up to the 1960s. Various critics had prefigured Roach's argument by castigating writers for choosing what were deemed to be the limitations of local languages and local subjects. Others more explicitly shared Roach's conviction that English architecture provided the only worthy model. Reviewing Walcott's *In a Green Night* (1962), A.N. Forde (who was at the time co-editor with Frank Collymore of *Bim*) argued that "it is only by working in this (English) tradition that there is any future for our writing."[19] It was clearly an issue that was both unsettling and unsettled. Gordon Rohlehr picked up the argument in an article titled "A Carrion Time," which appeared in *Bim* in 1975, directly in response to Roach's review and the surrounding controversy. He took Roach to task for not recognizing the craftsmanship of much of the work in the anthology; and he defended Bongo Jerry, "bawling for a bloodbath" in Rohlehr's words, as "needing to be judged in the context of the vocabulary, sermons, music and symbolism of the Rastafari brethren."[20] In Rohlehr's terms, the issue of the appropriate critical criteria for judging literature is continuous with the issue of the appropriate language for literary expression. Whitman's "barbaric yawp," after all, was not easily read by those schooled in classical critical conventions; and this was to be expected, "barbarian" originally meaning "one who does not speak Greek."

The issue is an urgent one in the Caribbean because this critical machinery is part of the mechanism of colonial determination, and is an instrument of language. In 1970, in an article in *Bim* on West Indian writing,[21] John Wickham juxtaposed two poetry reviews. One was from 1833, and praised the author of a book entitled *Barbados and other Poems* for "writing the English language like a Gentleman." The other review was by Robert Graves, who applauded Derek Walcott for "handl[ing] English with a closer understanding of its inner magic than most (if not any) of his English-born contemporaries" in his 1962 volume of poems *In a Green Night*. High praise, from an Anglican pulpit. The criteria are relentless, and in large measure foreign. For poets trying to find their own voice, it is little comfort to be praised precisely for having failed to do so.

It begins and ends, of course, with words, just words. Words of common speech, made uncommon; with a primitive power, in a civil tongue. And above all, with a sense of style. Sometimes these words reach towards their subject; sometimes they rise out of it, what Martin Carter called "these poet words, nuggets out of corruption / or jewels dug from dung or speech from flesh / still bloody red."[22] Realism, as Seamus Heaney suggests, may be simply "visible speech." But whatever the case, these poet words, these words of a certain style, are hard to find, and hard to hold. What contemporary West Indian poetry has demonstrated is that it is not a matter of making a silk purse out of a sow's ear, or turning water into wine, but of making a sow's ear as precious as a silk purse, and water as precious as wine. Silk and wine are not immutable standards, any more that is some Gentleman's English. In every generation, and for every audience, it is the responsibility and the achievement of poetry to prove just this.

NOTES

1. Derek Walcott, *The Gulf* (New York: Farrar, Straus and Giroux, 1969), 27–30.

2. W.B. Yeats, "Adam's Curse," *Collected Poems* (London: Macmillan, 1950), 88.

3. Bruce St. John, *Bumbatuk 1* (Bridgetown, Barbados: Cedar Press, 1982), 44.

4. Paul Keens-Douglas, "Paul Keens-Douglas on Communication and the Art," *Caribbean Contact* (October 1984): 11,15.

5. Paul Keens-Douglas, *When Moon Shine* (Port of Spain, Trinidad: College Press, 1975), 9–10.

6. Dennis Scott, *Uncle Time* (Pittsburgh: Univ. of Pittsburgh Press, 1973), 32.

7. Owen Barfield, *Poetic Diction* (London: Faber and Faber, 1952), 48–49.

8. This selection is from the manuscript first draft (in prose) of what became Walcott's autobiographical poem *Another Life*. Dated (in Notebook 1) 12 October 1965 (West Indies Collection, Library of the University of the West Indies, Mona, Jamaica).

9. Owen Barfield, "Sainte Lucie": Section 2, *Sea Grapes* (New York: Farrar, Straus and Giroux, 1976), 35–39.

10. Lorna Goodison, *I Am Becoming My Mother* (London: New Beacon, 1986), 36.

11. *Focus*, ed. Edna Manley (Kingston, 1943), 80.

12. "Report on the Rastafari Movement in Kingston, Jamaica" (Kingston: Institute of Social and Economic Research, 1960), 27. For a discussion of the language of Rastafari, see Velma Pollard, "The Language of Rastafari in Barbados and St. Lucia," *Jamaica Journal*, 17 (1984): 57–62; and Jah Bones, "Language and Rastafari," *The Language of the Black Experience*, ed. David Sutcliffe and Ansel Wong (Oxford: Basil Blackwell, 1986), 37–51.

13. Derek Walcott, *The Joker of Seville and O Babylon!* (New York: Farrar, Straus and Giroux, 1978), 155–56.

14. *Savacou: A Journal of the Caribbean Artist's Movement*, ed. Edward Brathwaite, 3/4 (1970–71), 5–9.

15. Ibid., 13–16.

16. Ibid., 38. Also published in *The Pond* (London: New Beacon, 1973), 7.

17. Gerald Moore, "Use Men Language," *Bim*, 15, (1974).

18. Quoted in a two-part article by Gordon Rohlehr, "West Indian Poetry: Some Problems of Assessment," (1972), 82, 141.

19. A.N. Forde, *Bim*, 9 (1963), 288–90.

20. Gordon Rohlehr, *Bim*, 15 (1975): 92–109.

21. John Wickham, *Bim*, 13 (1970): 68–80.

22. Martin Carter, "Words," *Poems of Succession* (London: New Beacon, 1977), 79.

THE SOUND OF VERSE

Kenneth Quinn

How do we go about reading a poem—aloud, or to ourselves with our inner ear attuned to the sound of the verse?[1] Suppose we take a simple case, the opening stanzas of a poem by A.R.D. Fairburn:

> hitched up my bundle
> went down the street
> long way to go
> walking on my feet
>
> went past Charley's
> didn't turn in
> broke to the wide
> had a good spin
>
> toting my gunny
> hit the south road
> long way to go
> got a heavy load
>
> tired already
> walking on my feet
> dust in my mouth
> and damn this heat.[2]

A strong stress at the beginning of each line (nearly always on the first syllable), a second strong stress at the end of the line (usually on the last syllable; sometimes the last but one). The poem works because the strong stresses give shape to the sense. An illusion of inevitability builds up; as though only *those* words could bear the stress— when, in different contexts, other words in almost every line might equally well take the stress these words bear here. The way the lines follow one another, each with its small bundle of sense, each inviting the same (or nearly the same) rhythmical structure, aids and abets the process of selecting the stress. The unstressed syllables separating initial stress from concluding stress, the occasional third weaker stress working within the dominant trochaic-iambic pattern, suggest the shambling, slurring gait of the tramp with a long road ahead of him, in no great hurry, following his thoughts as he walks, the rhythm of his thoughts adjusting itself to the rhythm of his steps. The poem works because it suggests a rhythm of thinking and a persona as much as it suggests a rhythm of walking.

2

"Walking on my feet" is, if you like, written in lines consisting of a trochee followed by an iamb—occasionally an anapaest instead of an iamb; sometimes a hypermetric unstressed final syllable. The description, though accurate, does not explain why the variations occur. Even if we invoke the Hopkins doctrine of "sprung rhythm" (the essence of which is that a line retains its identity through a fixed number of stresses, despite wide variations in the number of syllables—a doctrine that in modified form has had much influence on twentieth-century practice), we are still purporting to explain variation in terms within which no real explanation is possible.[3]

Nor is our description much help as a guide to how the line should sound when read. Factors other than stress enter into play: variation in tempo (speeding up, slowing down, breaking the tempo at key points); the level of the voice (volume); attitudes suggested by the tone of voice to what is being said. All these enter into what is usually called "interpretation."[4]

The complex of factors which determine the reader's decisions about the interpretation of a poem, leading him beyond mechanical observance of the metrical beat (the actual pattern of stresses in the poem, not the nominal metre), the "overriding pattern" (the pattern of meaning which overrides the metrical pattern) I shall call the "movement of the thought" in the poem: the stresses and tempi imposed or suggested by the actual words of the poem; the rhythmical blocks these build up by their syntactical groupings—the relative length of those blocks as well as their internal structure, their internal density or simplicity, their compactness or diffuseness; the relation of these blocks to one another and to the run of the narrative or argument. These variations in stress, tempo and the tone of voice elicited in responsive reading act as a *representation* (in the Aristotelian sense) of the thinking mind behind (and within) the text; what they represent is the complex sequence of psychic events which builds up in and around the text as we read it.

3

My argument invites acceptance, in other words, of two related awarenesses. An awareness, first, of a basic metrical pattern (the nominal metre) and a consciousness of a departure built into the text from that pattern which, in a successful reading, must be reconciled with (felt as compatible with) the basic pattern (or else the poem loses metrical coherence and becomes a kind—an unsatisfactory kind—of prose). An awareness, then, of a movement of thought (and feeling) which overrides the metrical pattern so modified (the pattern we might accept if we neglected totally the meaning of the lines) and a simultaneous consciousness of the need to reconcile the movement of the thought with the metrical pattern (failure here resulting, as before, in something that feels like some kind of unsatisfactory prose). A twofold awareness and a twofold reconciliation. The first determined by the poet (who has built that departure into the text); the second felt as called for by the text, but determined by the reader, as part of the act of interpretation.[5]

Every reader is an interpreter of what he reads. The text he has before him is both the finishing point in a process of creation on the part of the writer and a starting point for a process of creation on the part of the reader.

What disconcerts all who care about poetry is the extent to which poets we respect seem unready to face the matter of interpretation. Leonard Woolf's story of how he and Virginia were invited by Eliot to listen to a draft of "Ash Wednesday" is an ironical simplification (not wholly devoid of malice, perhaps), but it has the ring of truth:

> one summer evening we went round to his house after dinner....We all sat solemnly on chairs...and Tom began...by reading the poem aloud in that curious monotonous sing-song in which all poets from Homer onwards have recited their poetry.[6]

No doubt, a poem can speak for itself to the poet who made it; reading it aloud will bring his understanding of it alive for him even if that understanding finds no expression in the way he reads it; in a way that is hard for the rest of us to understand poets seem to feel the sense of what they write subordinated to the metrical structure of their creation. Letting the poem speak for itself is not much help, however, to us, the poet's audience. True, Eliot's familiar recorded performance of "Four Quartets" has a certain authority: it shows how Eliot grouped the words in his mind; where in cases of doubt he wanted the stress to fall. One listens with respect, if with an odd sense of disappointment. Robert Graves comes, perhaps, closer to what we can accept:

Good poets, I think, write poems that correspond with how they themselves talk...If a poet called upon to read his poems, chants or croons or declaims, something is wrong. A true poem is best spoken in a level, natural voice: slowly or solemnly, and with suppressed emotion, but in a natural voice. The voice addressed to intimate friends: not the one in which we try to curry favour with children at a party, or with an election crowd, or with a traffic cop, or with a suspicious Alsatian bitch growling over her litter.[7]

We can understand that poets find it distasteful to play the part of actors, feigning a state of mind that has now passed. "In my poems," said Dylan Thomas in an introduction to a reading at MIT in 1952, "I've had my say, and now I can only repeat it."[8] Some actors pursue meaning to the exclusion of everything else. What goes wrong is usually the opposite, however. The actor has his text in front of him: he knows what is coming; his interpretation tends to be over-confident, over-emphatic. He sees it as his object—not to pursue meaning to the exclusion of everything else, but rather, in Dylan Thomas's phrase, "to give the poem the works."[9] The changing impulse of living thought now freshly formulated is lost.

Not all poems of course "represent" the changing impulse of thought, but many do: the movement of the thought is like a child building with blocks—each block tentatively added, as if the poet were unsure the structure will bear the load of sense now added, alert, like a tightrope walker, to make no false step. Reading such poems calls for considerable sensitivity. It should be possible none the less, if not quite to "reduce the principle of distortion to a working technique" (because the structure of words in a poem is ultimately subtler than a structure of musical notes), at any rate to set out some guiding principles descriptive of the complex reality with which "reading a poem" is the reader's attempt to cope.

4

Let us take a poem closer to how most poems work. Blake's "A Poison Tree" will make my point for me as well as any modern poem:

I was angry with my friend:
I told my wrath, my wrath did end.
I was angry with my foe:
I told it not, my wrath did grow.

And I waterd it in fears,
Night & morning with my tears:
And I sunned it with smiles
And with soft deceitful wiles.

> And it grew both day and night,
> Till it bore an apple bright
> And my foe beheld it shine,
> And he knew that it was mine.
>
> And into my garden stole,
> When the night had veild the pole;
> In the morning glad I see,
> My foe outstretchd beneath the tree.[10]

Stanza 1 consists of four statements, all beginning with "I," forming an elaborate grammatical structure within the metrical structure. In stanza 2, the movement of the thought accelerates: line 5 strides over into line 6. The movement of the thought then slows down again as the alternation of stresses and unstressed syllables falters:

> And I waterd it in fears,
> Night & morning with my tears

("with my tears" really requires a stress on each syllable). The variation in pace continues (the simple statements sweeping impatiently forward, then a heavy rhythm working against the sweep forward) until the first line of stanza 3. Then three lines (lines 10–12) in which the stresses fall heaviest on the last word in the line:

> Till it bore an apple bright.
> And my foe beheld it shine,
> And he knew that it was mine.

Stanza 4 begins with two lines in which the pace is fairly even; then a sudden deceleration at "glad" (line 15), no pause at the end of the line, and even more marked slowing down at "outstretched" in the last line; the solid bulk of "outstretched," the rhythm it imposes (two strong stresses), the unexpected sense, combine to hurl the word at us. Try substituting "curled" and the sinister magic of the climax disappears; even "stretched out," by inviting a light stress on "stretched" and a strong stress on "out" would destroy the drama of the surprise ending.

In any competent modern reading aloud of "A Poison Tree" there can be no question of a regular, mechanical beat. The movement of the thought must take precedence; the metrical beat is still respected, still felt, but it is subordinated to the movement of the thought. To read "A Poison Tree" in this way is not to reduce Blake's text to prose. The metrical pattern is still heard and keeps reasserting itself. But it is now only one element. It is customary to borrow the term "counterpoint" to describe this phenomenon. The term suggests two independent systems rivalling for our attention. But what happens, it seems to me, is that each system (the pattern of the stresses and the movement of the thought) entails a modification of the other, so that the stresses are not absolutely even, the movement of the thought not absolutely that of prose.

5

The twentieth century has seen the completion of the takeover of lyric by a new kind of poetry, freed from the strict observance of the beat which song, or the illusion of song necessitates.

I must content myself with two features of this takeover. We can regard them as successive steps towards increased realism in the representation of living speech.

The first is a quality which needs to be brought out in good reading—and often is not. The rhythms now are not those imposed by the melody of sung lyric but by what Edward Thomas called the "patterns of stress and pause which reflect a mind actually engaged in the act of thinking, rather than offering concluded thoughts."[11] Actors tend to be overawed by what seems to them the settled finality of a poetic text. They read Lawrence's poem "Moonrise," for example, as though it were mere embellishment of the obvious (all worked out beforehand, static) when it should be read as a poem in which the thought appears to stride forward in excited pursuit of an idea, seizing upon the words which come to hand:

> And who has seen the moon, who has not seen
> Her rise from out the chamber of the deep,
> Flushed and grand and naked, as from the chamber
> Of finished bridegroom, seen her rise and throw
> Confession of delight upon the wave,
> Littering the waves with her own superscription
> Of bliss...[12]

Imagine the intonation rising (in a continuing crescendo) on each of the stressed words (the rise representing the poet's excitement at hitting upon that word) instead of following the normal stress pattern of a periodic sentence. It is the difference between an actor reading (say) a letter by Yeats or Fairburn, externalising the rhythmic structure (making it statically "rhetorical") instead of getting inside it. However dramatic the "rhetorical" reading, the text remains dead; however accomplished the performance, it is clear that the speaker has not put those words together himself.

In a decent reading what we hear is a structured representation of a more or less inchoate psychic reality. The voice hesitates while the speaker looks for the right word (or gropes for the least wrong word); hesitates before key words, calculating their impact before launching them upon us; settles with triumph upon the word or phrase which has just suggested itself.

One thinks perhaps first of Hopkins's tortured sonnets; but Hopkins (as I have said) was more concerned with reconciling his practice with traditional metrics than with identifying the nature of its originality. The leading theoretician and practitioner of planned conflict between metrical beat and the rhythm of the thinking mind is Edward Thomas's friend Robert Frost.

In a letter written in 1913 (shortly before he first met Thomas), he insists that a poet must learn to "get cadences by skillfully breaking the sounds of sense with all their irregularity of accent across the regular beat of the metre."[13] Take Frost's "Spring Pools" (published in *West-running Brook*, 1928). The poem consists of two six-line stanzas.

The first is irreproachably regular—if we read "flowers" (lines 3 and 4) as a single syllable, only "dark" in the concluding line resists reduction to the status of unstressed initial syllable of an iambic foot:

These pools that, though in forests, still reflect
The total sky almost without defect,
And like the flowers beside them, chill and shiver,
Will like the flowers beside them soon be gone,
And yet not out by any brook or river,
But up by roots to bring dark foliage on.[14]

But to read "Spring Pools" as a sequence of iambic pentameters is to ignore the sense. Innocent as it sounds (from the point of view of sense), "though in forests" by "breaking across" the division into feet sets up the conflict from the beginning (if "conflict" is not too dramatic a word to denote the hesitant, patiently logical rhythm of Frost's poem): "though" provides the stressed syllable of the second iamb; "forests," the unstressed syllable of the fifth, but the sense requires a distinct pause before "though" and after "forests." Line 2 offers no open conflict, though to read the line as a simple sequence of iambs is to neglect the rallentando in "The total sky" and the rising emphasis on the stressed syllables (so that "sky" becomes the most prominent word in the line). Line 3, despite the innocent-sounding "And" which introduces it, describes a different scene from line 1 (not an additional detail of the same scene): on a first reading we probably took the "still" of line 1 as adverbial (to be paired off with "though"); it now assumes an adjectival force (where in line 1 all is stillness, in line 3 all is movement; "chill" is intransitive and inceptive—like "shiver" it denotes an action, not a state); on a second reading we will read "still" with a different emphasis, therefore. In line 4, the repetition of "like the flowers beside them" (with a different emphasis) both makes the scene clear and, by delaying "gone," throws "gone" into prominence. In line 5, "yet" adds itself to "though" in line 1 to help suggest a speaker with a logically thought-out argument to represent, if in no hurry; the careful reader lingers on the word. But, if in no hurry, the speaker warms to his subject in the concluding line of the stanza. The tempo is hesitant no longer. The strong stress falls (we discover) on "out" in line 5, which pairs up with "up" (the opposition underlined by the repetition of the unstressed "by"). The monosyllables "out," "up" and "dark" form the three points of a triangle—these are the words that bear the strongest emphasis in the stanza-close; "brook," "river," "roots" form a second triangle. Because the visual impact of "brook," "river," "roots" is greater, the reader is perhaps tempted to give this second triangle greater emphasis. But that is to neglect the logic of the poem: "out" and "up" lay out the ground for the rhythmically unexpected "dark."

Stanza 2 explains that emphasis on "dark." In stanza 2 a regular iambic reading becomes increasingly impossible. The opening line

The trees that have it in their pent-up buds

gives a first hint of a new rhythmical independence: "in" can sustain no more than a token stress, the two syllables of "pent-up" require almost equal stress. In line 8,

To darken nature and be summer woods

the stress on "and" (again the third foot of the line) is purely nominal. In the first half of line 9,

Let them think twice...

the sense asserts itself irresistibly: the four syllables ring out like so many blows on some resounding surface, each stronger than the blow before. What with a less forceful rhythm might have sounded like precociousness or animistic whimsy and left us feeling uncomfortable, sweeps us along by its rhythmical strength. The second half of line 9 is immaculately regular (reading "powers" like "flowers" as a monosyllable), and then in line 10 the rain of blows begins again:

To blot out and drink up and sweep away

The stress falls six times (on "blot," "out," "drink," "up," "sweep," and the second syllable of "away"). Syntactically the line takes the form of a tricolon crescendo (three syntactically parallel cola, the last the longest): "and drink up" repeats the rhythm of "To blot out"; we expect a third sequence of unstressed syllables followed by two strong stresses, but in the third colon an additional unstressed syllable transforms the rhythm (consider how much "and sweep off," or the like, would have coarsened the rhetoric). Line 11

These flowery waters and these watery flowers

by its rhythmical flourish and the wit of its strained sense slows the rhetoric down. Line 12

From snow that melted only yesterday

rounds the poem off in limpid, simple statement and impeccable iambics.

6

If the object of poets was to represent the rhythms of actual twentieth-century speech, it would seem only natural that their verse should represent also the syntactical structures, the patterns of thought adopted for the expression of their ideas by those who attempt to set out their ideas in sustained speech or in contemporary prose. There are plenty of poets who are content with the naive, loosely structured, strung-together style of archaic lyric and the beginnings of literary prose—or the rambling, casually strung-together style of casual speech. In this section I shall leave these aside, in order to concentrate on what I shall call "the highly-structured" style—the kind of poem which "represents" the rhythm of thinking which contemporary prose has accustomed us to in advancing an argument.

The effect, when the conflict is isolated or occasional, is to set up an ironical distancing from the sense where normal prose rhythm would imply full commitment, as in Graves's picture of the aging laureate:

Arrogant, lean, unvenerable, he
Still turns for comfort to the western flames
That glitter a cold span above the sea.[15]

A normal prose reading would link "he still turns" in a single phrase—no stress on "he"; a weak stress on "still"; the strong stress on "turns." The verse form requires a pause and some kind of stress at "he"; a strong, even stress (probably) on "still" and "turns." Often in such verse the sense flows on from line to line in a single complex stanza, the individual clauses sometimes coinciding with the line-end, sometimes appearing to overrule the anticipated pause:

An aged man is but a paltry thing,
A tattered coat upon a stick, unless
Soul clap its hands and sing, and louder sing
For every tatter in its mortal dress,
Nor is there singing school but studying
Monuments of its own magnificence;
And therefore I have sailed the seas and come
To the holy city of Byzantium.[16]

The conflict is not confined to the highly-structured style (nor is it found only in twentieth-century verse.[17] What makes conflict at the line-end in the highly-structured style in twentieth-century verse especially interesting, however, is not just what

Harding calls the "launching" of the sense from the line-end (and the consequent throwing into prominence of the initial syllable of the following line), but the extended interplay between metre and syntax. Instead of sense paid out line by line, there is a less predictable movement—at times more flowing, at other times stopping unexpectedly in mid-line—and yet offering mind and ear something more satisfying, more complexly "right" than prose arbitrarily cut up into lines that simply cut across the sense (or verse misread as prose, the signal of the line-end simply disregarded). There are interesting parallels in Roman verse of the Augustan Age, especially Horace and Virgil, whose practice probably did more to guide Auden (the great practitioner of this style) than its obvious English antecedent, the blank verse of Milton, or even the early discursive manner of Wordsworth (as in "Tintern Abbey").[18]

"In Memory of Sigmund Freud" is one of a group of poems for which Auden constructed a kind of alcaic stanza in which the sense hesitates or slows in a shortish third line, then crashes down, or rings out, in a strongly rhythmical fourth line; as in Horace's "Roman Odes," the syntactical structure sometimes rolls on stanza after stanza (sometimes without a pause at the stanza-end), the strong pauses in the sense falling, as often as not, in mid-line:

> If some traces of the autocratic pose,
> the paternal strictness he distrusted, still
>   clung to his utterance and features,
>   it was a protective coloration
>
> for one who'd lived among enemies so long:
> if often he was wrong and, at times, absurd,
>   to us he is no more a person
>   now but a whole climate of opinion
>
> under whom we conduct our different lives...[19]

Our first reaction, perhaps (as often with Auden), is one of despair—despair of reconciling the conversational rhythms with any concept acceptable to us of how verse should move or sound. But that is to miss what Auden's verse gains from conflict between syntactical informality and metrical formality.[20] We are happier with poems whose metrical structure is more familiar. With "Voltaire at Ferney," for example: the rhymes are as strict as in a Shakespearean sonnet;[21] the syntax less elaborate and formal than in "Sigmund Freud."

7

In most verse since Auden, the possibilities offered mind and ear by the conflict between two sources of rhythm (the line-end contradicting the conversational phrasing and thus revising—not just the rhythm of utterance, but the rhythm of thought) have been less than fully exploited. The Auden manner has been imitated, one feels, by poets who have not grasped its basis.

Often the line-end seems little more than a gesture intended for visual effect—at most a guide to the reader to aim at a reading different from ordinary prose, rather than an active, audible component of the verse. A guide not always observed by the poets themselves when reading. A way of writing in which rhyme has gone, in which the lines vary in length and seem to acknowledge no metrical responsibility other than a general readability, can still work. But where so much has been abandoned, what remains lacks subtlety, and will not perhaps work for long. Its appeal seems to be to the democratic mind. In an age where Auden himself lost all faith in his role in society—one thinks of those terrible, blandly immaculate lines:

> After all, it's rather a privilege
>   amid the affluent traffic
> to serve this unpopular art which cannot be turned into
>   background noise for study
> or hung as a status trophy by rising executives,
>   cannot be 'done' like Venice
> or abridged like Tolstoy, but stubbornly still insists upon
>   being read or ignored...[22]

we should not perhaps expect more than democratic modesty. It is not simply that one misses the formal complexity of Yeats, Graves, or Auden. What one really misses is that, with that complexity gone, the ironic stance within the conversational rhythms has to be either too evident, or too unfocussed. The reader is not forced to hear the line modified, corrected, stood back from, by the constant contradiction of the everyday rhythms which the words upon the page seem to invite by the rhythm which asserts itself when we read the lines aloud.

NOTES

1. My own interest in the subject was first aroused by the University College Monday afternoon poetry readings organized in the late 1970s by Michael Kirkham and Hans de Groot, with the collaboration of colleagues, including Bill Blissett. Our object was to rescue the experience of listening to poetry from the formal structures of the classroom; in particular, the tradition which, if it did not originate with F.R. Leavis, was familiar to all who had heard him lecture as part of the Leavis ritual: reading a poem before you talked about it was reduced to the status of a perfunctory refreshing of the memory, to be got through quickly before the critical talk began, as though it were indecent to suggest your audience might not have heard the poem before; the reading was commonly preceded or followed by a word of apology, as though in different circumstances (which never seemed to arise) one might go about things differently. It was Michael Kirkham who

introduced me to D. W. Harding's modest, sensitive, illuminating *Words into Rhythm* (Cambridge: Cambridge Univ. Press, 1976), originally delivered as the Clark Lectures for 1971–72; see Kirkham's review, *Univ. of Toronto Quarterly*, 47 (1977–78): 182–88.

2. A.R.D. Fairburn, "Walking on my feet," *Collected Poems* (Christchurch, N.Z.: Pegasus Press, 1966), 121.

3. For Hopkins's explanation of "sprung rhythm" see his introduction to *Poems 1876–89* and his letter to R.W. Dixon, 5 October 1878 (in which Hopkins uses the nursery rhyme "Ding, dong, bell" as an example of sprung rhythm). G.M. Hopkins, *Poems*, 3d edition, ed. Robert Bridges, rev. W.H. Gardner (London: Oxford Univ. Press, 1948 [1956]), 7–10; *The Correspondence of Gerard Manley Hopkins and Richard Watson Dixon*, ed. C.C. Abbott (London: Oxford Univ. Press, 1935), 12–16.

4. "Interpretation," though used more often in criticism of the deconstructive act of commentary, is used also of the constructive, or reconstitutive, act of putting our deconstructions together in a reading or performance. It is in this second sense that I use the term here.

5. The act of reconciliation is fundamental to all "representation" in art: a representation both is not, and yet is, that which it represents.

6. Leonard Woolf, *Downhill All the Way* (London: The Hogarth Press, 1967), 109.

7. Robert Graves, "The Making and Marketing of Poetry," *Food for Centaurs: Stories, Talks, Critical Studies* (Garden City, N.Y.: Doubleday, 1960), 130.

8. "Some Words of a Kind," recorded on Phillips B 94016 L.

9. Ibid., "The printed page is the place to examine the working of a poem; the platform, the place to give a poem the works."

10. William Blake, "A Poison Tree" in *Songs of Innocence and of Experience*, ed. Geoffrey Keynes (New York: Orion Press, 1967), plate 49.

11. Quoted by Andrew Motion, *The Poetry of Edward Thomas* (London: Routledge and Kegan Paul, 1980), 82.

12. D.H. Lawrence, "Moonrise," *The Complete Poems*, ed. Vivien de Sola Pinto and Warren Roberts (New York: Viking Press, 1964), vol. 1, 193.

13. Letter to John Bartlett, 4 July 1913, quoted by W.H. Pritchard, *Frost: A Literary Life Reconsidered* (New York: Oxford Univ. Press, 1984), 77; the famous phase "the sound of sense" occurs for the first time in the same letter.

14. *The Poetry of Robert Frost*, ed. Edward Connery Latham (New York: Holt, Rinehart and Winston, 1969), 245.

15. Robert Graves, "The Laureate," *Collected Poems 1975* (London: Cassell, 1975), 92.

16. W.B. Yeats, "Sailing to Byzantium," *Collected Poems* (London: Macmillan, 1955), 217.

17. See Harding, *Words into Rhythm*, 110–15, where the phenomenon is described as "pivoting."

18. See P. Toohey, *Syntax and Meter in the Odes of Horace*, unpublished dissertation (University of Toronto, 1978).

19. W.H. Auden, "In Memory of Sigmund Freud," *Collected Poems*, ed. Edward Mendelson (London: Faber and Faber, 1976), 217.

20. I remember the readings Auden gave in Toronto, about 1971, towards the end of his life and the miraculous ease with which he managed to make what seemed on the page mere lifeless words flow smoothly through a complicated pattern of sense.

21. The arrangement of the rhymes in the six-line stanzas varies, however: stanza 1—a,b,b,c,c,a; stanzas 2,4 and 5—a,b,c,c,b,a; stanza 3—a,b,c,b,c,a. See Auden, *Collected Poems*, 199.

22. Auden, "The Cave of Making," *Collected Poems*, 522.

A CHECKLIST OF THE PRINCIPAL WRITINGS OF WILLIAM BLISSETT

Douglas Freake and H.B. de Groot

The Long Conversation: A Memoir of David Jones (London: Oxford Univ. Press, 1981).

Contributions To Books

"Spenser's Mutabilitie," in Millar MacLure and F.W. Watt, ed., *Studies in English Literature from the Renaissance to the Victorian Age Presented to A.S.P Woodhouse* (Toronto: Univ. of Toronto Press, 1964), 26–42. Reprinted in Hugh MacLean, ed., *Edmund Spenser's Poetry* (New York: Norton, 1968), 615–23, and in A.C. Hamilton, ed., *Essential Articles for the Study of Spenser* (Hamden, Conn.: Archon Books, 1972), 255–66.

"James Joyce in the Smithy of his Soul," in Thomas Staley, ed., *James Joyce Today* (Bloomington: Indiana Univ. Press, 1966), 96–134.

"Your Majesty is Welcome to a Fair," in George Hibbard, ed., *The Elizabethan Theatre* 4 (Toronto: Macmillan, 1974), 80–105.

"The Efficacious Word in David Jones's *In Parenthesis*," in Roland Mathias, ed., *David Jones: Eight Essays* (Llandysul, Wales: Gomer Press, 1976), 50–72.

"Wagner in *The Waste Land*," in Jane Campbell and James Doyle, ed., *The Practical Vision: Essays in English Literature in Honour of Flora Roy* (Waterloo, Ontario: Wilfrid Laurier Univ. Press, 1978), 71–86.

"Coriolanus and the Helms of the State," in Patricia Bruckmann, ed., *Familiar Colloquy: Essays Presented to Arthur Barker* (Ottawa: Oberon Press, 1978), 144–62.

"The Oddity of Ben Jonson's *Every Man Out of his Humour*," in *The Elizabethan Theatre*, forthcoming.

"G.K. Chesterton and Max Beerbohm," in Michael H. Macdonald and Andrew A. Tadie, ed. *G.K. Chesterton and C.S. Lewis: The Riddle of Joy* (Grand Rapids, MI.: Eerdmans, 1989), 100–124.

"Caves and Labyrinths in *The Faerie Queene*," in George M. Logan and Gordon Teskey, ed., *Unfolded Tales: Essays on Renaissance Romancea* [A.C. Hamilton Festschrift] (Ithaca: Cornell Univ. Press, 1989), 281–311.

"The Wagnerian Cycle," to be published in forthcoming Proceedings of conference on literature and music in nineteenth-century Germany (McMaster University), ed. Hans Schulte.

Articles In Encyclopedias

with John Arthur Tucker, "Charles M. Doughty," *Dictionary of Literary Biography* 19 (1983): 137–48.

"Elizabeth Jennings," *Dictionary of Literary Biography* 27 (1984): 163–70.

"Max Beerbohm," *Dictionary of Literary Biography*, forthcoming.

Articles in the *Spenser Encyclopedia* on "Caves," "Labyrinths," "Calepine," "The Spenserian Stanza," and (with Barker Fairley) "C.M. Doughty." forthcoming.

Works Edited

Reid MacCallum, *Imitation and Design* (Toronto: Univ. of Toronto Press, 1953).

The University of Toronto Quarterly, 1965–76.

with Julian Patrick and R.W. Van Fossen, *A Celebration of Ben Jonson* (Toronto: Univ. of Toronto Press, 1974).

Editing Illustrated Books (New York: Garland Press, 1980).

Articles

"I.A. Richards," *Univ. of Toronto Quarterly* 14 (1944): 58–66.

"The Argument of T.S. Eliot's *Four Quartets*," *Univ. of Toronto Quarterly* 15 (1946): 115–26.

"T.S. Eliot," *Canadian Forum* 28 (1948): 86–87.

"Franz Kafka," *Hillel Scribe* (Hillel Club, University College, Univ. of Toronto) 4 (1950): 11–15.

"Synge's *Playboy*," *Adam* (1953), included in *Colonnade* 2 (1954): 17–20.

"Pater and Eliot," *Univ. of Toronto Quarterly* 22 (1953): 261–68.

"Poetic Wave and Poetic Particle," *Univ. of Toronto Quarterly* 24, (1954): 1–7.

"Robert Graves," *Canadian Forum* 34 (1954): 59–61.

"Dylan Thomas: A Reader in Search of a Poet," *Queen's Quarterly* 63 (1956): 45–58.

"Lucan's Caesar and the Elizabethan Villain," *Studies in Philology* 53 (1956): 553–75.

"Caesar and Satan," *Journal of the History of Ideas* 18 (1957): 221–32.

"Samuel Daniel's Sense of the Past," *English Studies* 38 (1957): 49–63.

"Strange without Heresy, *Love's Labour's Lost*, 5.1.1–6," *English Studies* 38 (1957): 209–11.

"Explorations," *Canadian Forum* 38 (1958): 106–107. Reprinted in Gerald E. Stearn, ed., *McLuhan Hot and Cold* (New York: Dial Press, 1967), 116–21.

"Bernard Shaw: Imperfect Wagnerite," *Univ. of Toronto Quarterly* 27 (1958): 185–99.

"Ernest Newman and English Wagnerism," *Music and Letters* 40 (1959): 311–23.

"The Despots of the Rings," *South Atlantic Quarterly* 58 (1959): 448–56.

" 'The Secret'st Man of Blood': A Study of Dramatic Irony in *Macbeth*," *Shakespeare Quarterly* 10 (1959): 397–408.

"Thomas Mann: the Last Wagnerite," *Germanic Review* 35 (1960): 50–76.

"George Moore and Literary Wagnerism," *Comparative Literature* 13 (1961): 52–71. Reprinted in Graham Owens, ed., *George Moore's Mind and Art* (Edinburgh: Oliver and Boyd, 1968), 53–76, and in Douglas Hughes, ed., *The Man of Wax* (New York: New York Univ. Press, 1971), 185–215.

"Wagnerian Fiction in English," *Criticism* 5 (1963) 239–60.

"From Wagner to Jung," *Queen's Quarterly* 70 (1963–64): 598–606.

"Florimell and Marinell," *Studies in English Literature 1500–1900* 5 (1965): 87–104.

"D.H. Lawrence, D'Annunzio, Wagner," *Wisconsin Studies in Contemporary Literature* 7 (1966): 21–46.

"Recognition in *King Lear*," *English Exchange* 9 (1967): 5–16. Reprinted, in revised form, in Rosalie L. Colie and F.T. Flahiff, ed., *Some Facets of* King Lear: *Essays in Prismatic Criticism* (Toronto: Univ. of Toronto Press, 1974), 103–116.

"The Language of the Collects," *Anglican Dialogue* 5 (1967): 5–6.

"Dramatic Irony in *Antony and Cleopatra*," *Shakespeare Quarterly* 8 (1967): 151–66.

"David Jones: Himself at the Cave-Mouth," *Univ. of Toronto Quarterly* 36 (1967): 259–73.

"The Venter Tripartite in *The Alchemist*," *Studies in English Literature* 8 (1968): 323–34. Reprinted in Harold Bloom, ed., *Ben Jonson: Modern Critical Views* (New York: Chelsea House, 1987), 79–88.

"Composer and Audience," *Contemporary Music and Audiences* (Montreal: Canadian Music Council, 1970), 7–17.

"This Wide Gap of Time: *The Winter's Tale*," *English Literary Renaissance* 1 (1971): 52–70.

"*In Parenthesis* among the War Books," *Univ. of Toronto Quarterly* 42 (1973): 258–88.

"Paradox and Ambiguity in *Troilus and Cressida*," *Wascana Review* 9 (1974): 5–28.

"The Liturgy of *Parsifal*," *Univ. of Toronto Quarterly* 49 (1979–80): 117–38.

"*The Ball and the Cross* (1910)," *Chesterton Review* 8 (1982): 30–34.

"To Make a Shape in Words," [on David Jones, *In Parenthesis*,] *Renascence* 38 (1986): 67–81.

"George Johnston: Three Conversations," *Malahat Review* no. 78 (March 1987): 37–51.

"Barker Fairley 1887–1986," *Transactions of the Royal Society of Canada*, Series V, Volume 2 (1987): 217–221.

"A Letter on Annotation," *Chesterton Review* 14 (1988): 346–50.

Reviews

"Auden as Editor," a review of W.H. Auden and Norman Holmes Pearson, ed., *Poets of the English Language*. *Univ. of Toronto Quarterly* 21 (1952): 200–202.

"History and Providence," a review of Ernest Lee Tuveson, *Millennium and Utopia*. *Univ. of Toronto Quarterly* 21 (1952): 320–23.

George Whalley, *Poetic Process: An Essay in Poetics*. *Queen's Quarterly* 60 (1953): 578–80.

R.S. Crane, *The Language of Criticism*. *Canadian Forum* 33 (1954): 283–84.

Stephen Spender, *The Creative Element*. *Canadian Forum* 34 (1954): 44.

Ezra Pound, *The Classic Anthology Defined by Confucius*. *Canadian Forum* 34 (1954): 166–67.

"In Medias Res," a review of David Jones, *The Anathemata*. *Univ. of Toronto Quarterly* 24 (1955): 212–15.

e.e. cummings, *i six non-lectures*. *Queen's Quarterly* 62 (1955): 142–43.

"Natural Theology," a review of Jean Seznec, *The Survival of the Pagan Gods*, and Erich Neumann, *The Origins and History of Consciousness*. *Queen's Quarterly* 62 (1955): 283–84.

"Turning New Leaves," a review of Malcolm Mackenzie Ross, *Poetry and Dogma*. *Canadian Forum* 34 (1955): 281–83.

Robert Graves, *Homer's Daughter*. *Canadian Forum* 35 (1955): 95.

"Kenner's Lewis," a review of Hugh Kenner, *Wyndham Lewis*. *Queen's Quarterly*, 62 (1955): 460–61.

D.R.G. Owen, *Body and Soul: A Study of the Christian View of Man*. *Canadian Forum* 37 (1957): 47.

"Turning New Leaves," a review of St. John Ervine, *Bernard Shaw*. *Canadian Forum* 37 (1957): 85–87.

T.S. Eliot, *On Poetry and Poets*. *Queen's Quarterly*, 65 (1958–59): 711–12.

"Portrait of the Artist—Full Length," a review of Richard Ellmann, *James Joyce*. *Queen's Quarterly* 67 (1960): 111–16.

Theories of History, ed. Patrick Gardiner. *Canadian Forum* 40 (1960): 24.

"Turning New Leaves," a review of Pierre Teilhard de Chardin, *The Phenomenon of Man*. *Canadian Forum* 40 (1960): 189–90.

"Renaissance Studies," a review of Jonas A. Barish, *Ben Jonson and the Language of Prose Comedy*; *Elizabethan and Jacobean Studies presented to F.P. Wilson*; Alvin Kernan, *The Canker'd Muse*; Robert Ornstein, *The Moral Vision of Jacobean Tragedy*; F.P. Wilson, *Seventeenth Century Prose*. *Univ. of Toronto Quarterly* 30 (1961): 251–54.

Pierre Teilhard de Chardin, *Le Milieu Divin*. *Canadian Forum* 41 (1961): 187.

"Santayana," a review of M.M. Kirkwood, *Santayana: Saint of the Imagination*. *Alphabet* 1 (3 December 1961): 79.

"Art and Sacrament," a review of David Jones, *Epoch and Artist*. *Queen's Quarterly* 68 (1961): 185–86.

J.M. Cohen, *Robert Graves*; G.S. Fraser, *Ezra Pound*; D.W. Jefferson, *Henry James*; Frank Kermode, *Wallace Stevens*. *Queen's Quarterly* 68 (1962): 695–96.

A.C. Hamilton, *The Structure of Allegory in* The Faerie Queene. *Queen's Quarterly* 69 (1962): 314.

C.S. Lewis, *An Experiment in Criticism*. *Canadian Forum* 42 (1962): 93.

Paul E. McLane, *Spenser's* Shepheardes Calender: *A Study in Elizabethan Allegory*. *Renaissance News* 15 (1962): 238–39.

"Preface to the Gods," a review of Jay Macpherson, *Four Ages of Man*. *Canadian Forum* 43 (1963): 167.

G.K. Hunter, *John Lyly: The Humanist as Courtier*. *Queen's Quarterly* 70 (1963): 457–58.

E.L. Mascall, *Theology and Images*. *Anglican Dialogue* 2 (1963): 79–80.

"Spenser," a review of Graham Hough, *A Preface to* The Fairie Queene. *Queen's Quarterly* 70 (1964): 615.

Samuel Daniel, *The Civil Wars*, ed. Laurence Michel. *English Studies* 45 (1964): 61–63.

Claes Schaar, *Elizabethan Sonnet Themes and the Dating of Shakespeare's Sonnets*. *English Studies* 46 (1965): 262–63.

"Reasonable Fun," a review of F.E. Sparshott, *The Structure of Aesthetics*. *Canadian Forum* 43 (1964): 239.

Northrop Frye, *Fables of Identity*; *Romanticism Reconsidered*; *T.S. Eliot*; *The Educated Imagination*; *The Well-Tempered Critic*; *Learning in Language and Literature*. *Univ. of Toronto Quarterly* 33 (1964): 401–408.

"Spenser's Heartland," a review of Thomas P. Roche, Jr., *The Kindly Flame*. *Canadian Forum* 44 (1964): 93–94.

A.L. Rowse, *Christopher Marlowe*; J.B. Steane, *Marlowe: A Critical Study*. *Canadian Forum* 45 (1965): 71.

Raymond Klibansky, Erwin Panofsky and Fritz Saxl, *Saturn and Melancholy*. *Humanities Association Bulletin* 16 (1965): 102–103.

Elizabethan Minor Epics, ed. Elizabeth Storey Donno. *English Studies* 50 (1969): supplement, xcvi.

Joan Rees, *Samuel Daniel; A Critical and Biographical Study*. *English Studies* 51 (1970): 558–59.

A.S.P. Woodhouse, *The Poet and his Faith*. *Anglican Dialogue* 4 (1966): 29.

"Five Monarchies at Bayreuth," a review of Geoffrey Skelton, *Wagner at Bayreuth*. *Queen's Quarterly* 74 (1967): 182–85.

The Poems of Gerald Manley Hopkins, ed., N.H. Mackenzie and W.H. Gardiner. *Univ. of Toronto Quarterly* 37 (1968): 421–22.

B. Rajan, ed., *Paradise Lost: A Tercentenary Tribute*. *Univ. of Toronto Quarterly* 39 (1970): 365–68.

"Couplets," a review of John A. Jones, *Pope's Couplet Art*, and William Bowman Piper, *The Heroic Couplet*. *Univ. of Toronto Quarterly* 40 (1971): 183–84.

"David Jones," a review of David Blamires, *David Jones; Artist and Writer*. *Univ. of Toronto Quarterly* 41 (1972): 275–76.

John F. Lynen, *The Design of the Present*. *Univ. of Toronto Quarterly* 41 (1972): 374–76.

George Moore, *Confessions of a Young Man*, ed. Susan Dick. *Univ. of Toronto Quarterly* 42 (1973): 422–23.

"Miltonists in Mosaic," a review of *A Variorum Commentary on Milton's Minor Poems*. *Univ. of Toronto Quarterly* 43 (1973): 90–91.

"Shakespeare Present and Future," a review of Clifford Leech and John Margeson, ed., *Shakespeare 1971*. *Univ. of Toronto Quarterly* 43 (1974): 191–92.

Anthony Adamson and John Willard, *The Gaiety of Gables*; Alan Jarvis, ed., *Douglas Duncan*; J. Russell Harper, *A People's Art*; Harold Town, *Albert Franck*. *Univ. of Toronto Quarterly* 44 (1975): 419–21.

Ian Boyd, *The Novels of G.K. Chesterton*. *Univ. of Toronto Quarterly* 45 (1976): 417–19.

Paul Fussell, *The Great War and Modern Memory*. *Univ. of Toronto Quarterly* 45 (1976): 268–74.

George Parfitt, *Ben Jonson: Public Poet and Private Man*. *Renaissance Quarterly* 31 (1978): 256–57.

"The Longest Study of Spenser," a review of James Nohrnberg, *The Analogy of* The Faerie Queene. *Univ. of Toronto Quarterly* 48 (1978): 76–80.

Thomas H. Cain, *Praise in* The Faerie Queene. *Univ. of Toronto Quarterly* 48 (1979): 406–408.

Ronald Arthur Horton, *The Unity of* The Faerie Queene. *Renaissance Quarterly* 32 (1979): 420–23.

Douglas Duncan, *Ben Jonson and the Lucianic Tradition. Univ. of Toronto Quarterly* 49 (1980): 416–18.

John Matthias, ed., *Introducing David Jones. Western Humanities Review* 35 (1981): 79–81.

"Threads for Three Labyrinths," a review of Philip and Averil Gardner, *The God Approached: A Commentary on the Poems of William Empson*; Henry Summerfield, *An Introductory Guide to* The Anathemata *and the "Sleeping Lord" Sequence of David Jones*; Christopher Wiseman, *Beyond the Labyrinth: A Study of Edwin Muir's Poetry. English Studies in Canada* 78 (1981): 370–77.

Darryl J. Gless, Measure for Measure, *the Law, and the Convent. Renaissance and Reformation*, n.s., 6 (1982): 154–55.

Barker Fairley Portraits, ed. Gary Michael Dault. *Univ. of Toronto Quarterly* 51 (1982): 497–99.

Charles O. Hartman, *Free Verse: An Essay on Prosody*; John Hollander, *Rhyme's Reason. Queen's Quarterly*, 90 (1983): 237–39.

"'There's a Welsh Poet named Jones,'" a review of Neil Corcoran, *The Song of Deeds*; Thomas Dilworth, ed., *Inner Necessities: The Letters of David Jones to Desmond Chute*; Philip Pacey, *David Jones and other Wonder Voyagers*; Elizabeth Ward, *David Jones, Mythmaker. Univ. of Toronto Quarterly* 55 (1985–86): 212–15.

John D. Coates, *Chesterton and the Edwardian Cultural Crisis. Chesterton Review* 11 (1985): 492–96.

Radio Talks

"Poems of Cummings and Stevens," *Critically Speaking*, CBC, Spring 1955.

"The Lord of the Rings," *Anthology*, CBC, 1956.

"Berlioz Centennial," CBC, 1969.

"David Jones: William Blissett interviewed by Peter Haworth," CBC, 1979.

"The Wanderer Redeemed," [on Wagner's *The Flying Dutchman*], CBC, 1 September 1984.

Talks At University College Symposia

"Aubrey Beardsley, Wagnerite," January 1979.

"Ben Jonson: The Rediscovery of Comedy," January 1982.

"Richard Wagner, Romantic Revolutionary," January 1983.

"Roman Ben Jonson," January 1984.

" 'A Good Kind of Peace'," [on David Jones], January 1985.

"Richard Wagner in Bismarck's Reich," January 1986.

"The Scapegoat in Art: Pre-modern, Modern, Post-modern," January 1987.

"Ibsen's War with Trolls," January 1988.

"Dawn as Liberation: C.M. Doughty and Ezra Pound," January 1989.

"Ben Jonson's *Volpone, or The Fox*," January 1990.

Other Papers Delivered

"Matthew Arnold and Celtic Literature," University College, Matthew Arnold Symposium, November 1988.

"Shadow of Turning: The Myth of the Earthly Paradise in William Morris," William Morris Society, Toronto, April 1989.

"Wagner and Proust," Toronto Wagner Society, April 1989.

"Spenser and the Poets of the Mid-20th Century," Friends of the Fisher Library, November 1989; revised form, Dept. of English, Univ. of Toronto, February 1990.